Coffeehouse Culture in the Atlantic World, 1650–1789

Coffeehouse Culture in the Atlantic World, 1650–1789

E. Wesley Reynolds, III

BLOOMSBURY ACADEMIC
LONDON • NEW YORK • OXFORD • NEW DELHI • SYDNEY

BLOOMSBURY ACADEMIC
Bloomsbury Publishing Plc
50 Bedford Square, London, WC1B 3DP, UK
1385 Broadway, New York, NY 10018, USA
29 Earlsfort Terrace, Dublin 2, Ireland

BLOOMSBURY, BLOOMSBURY ACADEMIC and the Diana logo are trademarks of Bloomsbury Publishing Plc

First published in Great Britain 2022
This paperback edition published 2023

Copyright © E. Wesley Reynolds, III, 2022

E. Wesley Reynolds, III has asserted his right under the Copyright, Designs and Patents Act, 1988, to be identified as Author of this work.

Cover image: Scene in a London coffee house during the reign of Queen Anne, from *Cassell's History of England* King's Edition Part 29. Timewatch Images / Alamy Stock Photo

All rights reserved. No part of this publication may be reproduced or transmitted in any form or by any means, electronic or mechanical, including photocopying, recording, or any information storage or retrieval system, without prior permission in writing from the publishers.

Bloomsbury Publishing Plc does not have any control over, or responsibility for, any third-party websites referred to or in this book. All internet addresses given in this book were correct at the time of going to press. The author and publisher regret any inconvenience caused if addresses have changed or sites have ceased to exist, but can accept no responsibility for any such changes.

A catalogue record for this book is available from the British Library.

Library of Congress Cataloging-in-Publication Data
Names: Reynolds, E. Wesley, author.
Title: Coffeehouse culture in the Atlantic world, 1650–1789 / E. Wesley Reynolds, III.
Description: 1 Edition. | New York, NY : Bloomsbury Academic, 2022. | Includes bibliographical references and index. |
Identifiers: LCCN 2021042332 (print) | LCCN 2021042333 (ebook) | ISBN 9781350247222 (hardback) | ISBN 9781350247239 (pdf) | ISBN 9781350247246 (ebook)
Subjects: LCSH: Coffee industry–Great Britain–History–18th century. | Great Britain–Intellectual life–18th century. | Coffeehouses–Social aspects–Great Britain. | Coffee industry–United States–History–18th century. | United States–Intellectual life–Intellectual life. | Coffeehouses–Social aspects–United States. Classification: LCC HD9199.G72 R39 2022 (print) | LCC HD9199.G72 (ebook) | DDC 338.1/73730941–dc23/eng/20211110
LC record available at https://lccn.loc.gov/2021042332
LC ebook record available at https://lccn.loc.gov/2021042333

ISBN: HB: 978-1-3502-4722-2
PB: 978-1-3502-4725-3
ePDF: 978-1-3502-4723-9
eBook: 978-1-3502-4724-6

Typeset by Newgen KnowledgeWorks Pvt. Ltd., Chennai, India

To find out more about our authors and books visit www.bloomsbury.com and sign up for our newsletters.

Contents

List of illustrations	vi
Introduction	1

Part I Coffee's transatlantic society

1	'Trifling', an urban experience	15
2	'Trifling' in the colonies	31
3	Murders, officers and naval headquarters	51

Part II Polishing communities and negotiating empire

4	Coffee-women, licensure and a polite public sphere	73
5	Coffee-men, lobbyists and conmen of empire	99
6	Transatlantic news feeds and imagined coffeehouse publics	129

Part III Empire and revolution

7	Empire, free association and slavery	149
8	Bringing down the empire	167

Conclusion	189
Notes	195
Bibliography	235
Index	251

Illustrations

1	Gentlemen busy 'trifling' in a coffeehouse, with seemingly no concern about their states of undress	27
2	Hogarth's depictions of the disorderly conversations which were usually had inside coffeehouses	28
3	Gaming and brawls were regular parts of coffeehouse conversations	28
4	These coffeehouse gentlemen meticulously study *The London Gazette* for news and social commentary	29
5	Gentlemen reading the news in their coffeehouse overlooking the New York harbour	96
6	The General Post Office in London was conveniently situated adjacent to Lloyd's Coffeehouse	97
7	The beginnings of the Wall Street Stock Exchange in the New York Tontine Coffeehouse	97
8	Thomas Taylor, proprietor of perhaps the most successful coffeehouse of his time, Lloyd's of London	98
9	Bostonian patriots accosting a customs officer	164
10	Revolutionaries gathering at a coffeehouse in Paris	165
11	Washington chose coffeehouses and taverns as places for public ceremonies and Republican pageantry	165
12	The restored R. Charlton coffeehouse in Colonial Williamsburg is the only functioning historic British coffeehouse of its kind in existence	166

Introduction

In September 1765, John Hughes took up his office in Philadelphia as stamp distributor in accord with the new and unpopular Stamp Act. Parliament wanted revenue from its North American colonies, and it was willing to tax the very paper with which Americans expressed their discontent. Throngs of furious patriots roamed the streets at night. Hughes sat alone with his pistols at the ready, 'determin'd to stand a Siege' as he put it.[1] Patriots in New York City were even angrier. When one popular publisher was suddenly arrested, the patriots seized the postal service and dispensed the mail personally through their own coffeehouses, not, of course, insisting that anyone need pay a tax on the paper for the privilege. In disbelief, James Parker, a newly appointed customs officer in New York, told Benjamin Franklin, 'The Moment a Vessel comes in, the Letters are seized by Force, and carried to the Coffee-House, where they are carried out, and delivered even before Mr. Colden's or my Face, and the Collector durst not, or will not refuse to enter any … The Spirit of Independance [sic] is too prevalent.'[2] Try as he might, Parker said he could not stop these Sons of Liberty from compelling 'Captains of Vessels [to] deliver their Letters at the Coffee-House after their old accustomed Manner'.[3] These patriots understood what Hughes and Parker did not; that the postal service and the coffeehouse had long been intertwined and that the intrusion of a new stamp method would require a violent overhaul of the pre-existing arrangement. 'The Lives of Some were lost on both sides,' admitted Parker in dismay.[4] Merchants of the eighteenth century had a choice between many public venues to post their letters and announcements. While tradition holds that taverns were hotbeds of revolutionary activity, the coffeehouse was an institution over which there was considerably more at stake than the tavern. Because of its connections to maritime trade, the coffeehouse played a key role in conveying the post between Great Britain and her colonies. It came to represent the struggle for free speech.

This is a book about coffeehouses and the social networks they forged across the northern British Atlantic, not about coffee production or even the origins of coffee in British society.[5] Further, it is about a particular kind of coffeehouse social life, one dominated by the values of London's journalizing Enlightenment. It reveals the power of an idea which created new coffeehouse communities and empowered these communities with the principles of free association, political news and civil liberty. Coffeehouses and the coffee trade fostered international finance and commerce, spread transatlantic news and correspondence, built military might, determined political fortunes and promoted status and consumption. The coffeehouse became a place where American patriots drank in ideas of revolution. The East India Company's decline and the American protests against taxation were brewed in coffeehouses. Coffeehouses became channels of communication for British economic control of the Atlantic world, but they developed a political culture all their own, which became increasingly hostile to British control. Coffeehouse publics extended the empire by launching transatlantic newsfeeds, encouraging conspicuous consumption and celebrating free association. They also organized revolutionary activities against the government to rid the public sphere of corrupt regulations and to free the press.

Coffeehouses have been hailed by historians as 'penny universities', polite alternatives to taverns, places for sober conversation and civil society, informal office buildings and, most significantly, places for political discussion.[6] But they were even more than that. Coffeehouse patrons invented their own private and public postal system which forged new communities across Atlantic cities. The coffeehouse news ring allowed readers to construct their own local neighbourhoods remotely while travelling abroad. These communities institutionalized a vital communications network for marine insurance, naval protection and customs officers bringing the goods of empire to cities around the world. Transatlantic travellers transformed coffeehouse publics into cosmopolitan communities, which helped to structure the civil service, and ran the shipping interests of the British Atlantic.

The world of the long eighteenth century was one of change, and nowhere was this more reflected than in the history of coffeehouses. London coffeehouses helped supervise the Royal Exchange, marine insurance for all British shipping and much of Britain's first naval correspondence. Coffeehouse proprietors worked with marine insurers and merchants on the Exchange to stabilize British trade. At the Admiralty Coffeehouse, the Sword Blade, Jerusalem and Will's, naval officers supplied bases and issued orders. The coffeehouse connections that naval officers formed with agents in the West Indies and Quebec enabled the Royal Navy to manage transatlantic resources with relative ease. Yet, the pivotal role of the coffeehouse in the rise of British naval power and the struggle against the corruption of the East India Company has largely passed unnoticed. During the 1720s, coffeehouse investors and proprietors linked hands to protest the East India Company's noncompliance with warehouse inspections.[7] Years later, Americans imitated coffeehouse protests when they were suddenly met with the new power of the East India Company and tea.[8] The South Sea Bubble, East India Company scandals and the taxation of tea, sugar and coffee were all first exposed and discussed in coffeehouses, perhaps making them among the most important global institutions in the eighteenth century. The news culture and financial interests which linked colonial American cities with London lobbyists were transported through coffeehouse social networks.

Unlike our multicultural globalized social media, for the eighteenth-century imagination, cosmopolitan life depended upon a highly cultivated mind and new sociological categories of human behaviour. Coffeehouse goers coupled the classical ideals of decorum and taste with a more empirical form of sociability, which emphasized dexterity in conversations. The coffeehouse became the symbolic embodiment of urban wit and leisure, where 'triflers', 'tattlers', 'idlers', 'ramblers' and the like practised their right to associate and observe.⁹ Gradually, coffeehouse audiences articulated these behaviours as aspects of *humanitas*, or the civic and intellectual pursuit of culture. The right to association and the civilizing process of coffeehouse culture spurred a more deliberate critique of society at large. Indeed, the modern critic was born in the coffeehouse social environment of London and later became a potent force in literature, drama and politics. The cultural success of the eighteenth-century coffeehouse was in connecting the language of *critique* with new urban lifestyles, such that its 'Connoisseurs', 'Guardians' and 'Spectators' became social commentators of not just politics but also humanity (both as individuals and in their social columns in journals). The coffeehouse gradually became a symbol of cosmopolitan culture, recognized on both sides of the Atlantic.

Books on coffee and clubs are revealing new insights about the interconnected lives of travellers and readers. Take, for example, Leo Damrosch's *The Club* (2019), Brian Cowan's *The Social Life of Coffee* (2005) or Abigail Williams's *The Social Life of Books* (2017). We recognize how important social networks are to our everyday lives and we are finding out that social networks existed inside coffeehouses long before the internet. Thanks to the work of an older generation of scholars on consumer culture including John Brewer, Roy Porter, Peter J. Albert, T. H. Breen, Cary Carson, Brendan McConville and David Shields, historians are now ready to map the social worlds of the eighteenth century. Also, histories like Sidney Mintz's *Sweetness and Power* (1986) and Mark Kurlansky's *Salt: A World History* (2003) have demonstrated the transformative power of commodities to early modern lifestyles. Since T. H. Breen's argument for an 'empire of goods' in *The Marketplace of Revolution* (2005), the stage is set to connect coffee to Atlantic trade and power networks and the American Revolution. This book will fill that gap. It will demonstrate that coffee culture was an Atlantic project. Eric Hinderaker in *Boston's Massacre* (2017) states that during the Stamp Act Crisis a battle emerged between British officials and Americans over 'imperial spaces', such as public buildings, where local business was conducted.¹⁰ This book expands the horizons of such a claim.

My approach will merge older public sphere theory, evident in Lawrence Klein, Stephen Pincus and John Barrell's work on coffeehouses, into the new social history of gender and class. What Helen Berry has accomplished with eighteenth-century shopping, Williams with books, Gillian Russell with Georgian theatres, Tim Reinke-Williams with domestic spheres and Dena Goodman with female epistolary culture, this book will demonstrate with Atlantic coffee culture. My research reveals the social and political unrest which birthed the gendered coffeehouse public sphere (relegated to men because it was public). Coffee culture grew into the middling tastes of cosmopolitan peoples traversing the Atlantic, which although still masculine blurred the lines between the consumer worlds of ladies and gentlemen. Coffee culture is also illustrative of the Atlantic world systems theory articulated by David Armitage, Amy Turner Bushnell, Jack P. Greene and Eliga H. Gould. Atlantic administrative networks depended upon coffeehouse social networks. Like Breen's notion of a tobacco culture across the American tidewater and Lorena S. Walsh's discussion of how Chesapeake planters combined pleasure and profit with honour and gentility, coffee became the drink of the transatlantic merchants and their cultural sphere of influence.

As British naval power increased during the eighteenth century, maritime traders drove the demand for intellectual stimulation, entertaining public accommodations, polite amusements aligned with new sociability and, most importantly, news. In London, coffeehouse proprietors served a merchant clientele in close contact with pleasure gardens, theatres and card clubs.[11] Pleasure and politeness were two necessary elements of eighteenth-century urban life. Lawrence Klein states that politeness was an idiom, widely used 'as a medium facilitating interaction and access to shared experience'.[12] Rules of order were brought into the public forum in a number of venues. Lord Burlington and his London following propagated among landed elites a new Palladian style of architecture.[13] Beau Nash instituted these ideals in Bath's social innovations during the 1710s, creating a template of relaxed elite sociability for the subsequent rise of spa towns. Leisure towns depended on a number of new urban spaces such as summer houses, assembly and club houses, concert halls, pleasure gardens, coffeehouses, theatres and masquerade balls. Klein asserts that because interior domestic spaces were still often cramped in the eighteenth century, the urban world outside the household was more important than domestic areas to display politeness: what John Wood has called the 'theatre of the polite world'.[14]

As coffeehouses began taking in more and more printed news in the eighteenth century, politics increasingly became another vital element of coffeehouse life. Whether in London or in America, the ideal coffeehouse always provided customers with a free subscription to the running newspapers and gazettes. Reading and discussing the newspapers remained a persistent reason in the historical record for visiting the coffeehouse throughout the Anglophone world. That the pursuit of pleasure and the development of free association were vitally connected in the eighteenth century is the subject of much debate and discussion since Jürgen Habermas published *The Structural Transformation of the Public Sphere* in 1962. He argued that during the late seventeenth and early eighteenth centuries, a new urban public sphere emerged out of the early modern commercial revolution. Public discourse served as a social tool for normative judgement in which public opinion vested itself with authority. A literate and well-informed public, mostly comprised of merchants, gentry visiting the metropolis and Enlightened nobility, fostered a political alliance in social circles and pushed for reform.[15]

Habermas sparked an interest in the rise of early modern sociability and politeness which Robert Darnton, Dena Goodman and Lawrence Klein have come to articulate as 'the republic of letters'. The public sphere depended on new social spaces outside of the conventional court, including salons, coffeehouses and clubs. In these spaces, the public defined itself through consumption and writing. Amateurs submitted writing to peer-reviewed academies or journals on various topics related to science or knowledge. These publications circulated a newfound interest in classical education and liberal learning. The gazettes established a colloquial style of conversational etiquette and politeness. Through these outlets, the Whigs in England and the *philosophes* in France created a new political sociability of public freedom and civil liberty. The influence of new public spaces continued to advance reforming political ideals until the revolutionary era of the late eighteenth century, when new political outlets altered the dynamics of the public sphere.[16]

The coffeehouses became centres of an enlightened culture of civic morality, manners, taste and political debate. Paul Langford and Lawrence Klein have connected the rise of eighteenth-century etiquette in England with merchant coffeehouse clubs and Whig pamphleteering. This 'Spectatorial Whiggery' school, or new Whig consensus theory of coffeehouse development, sees Richard Steele and Joseph Addison's *Spectator* (published in 1711) as the ultimate statement of polite coffeehouse culture.[17] Klein claims that the urge of coffeehouse owners to attract the attention of an emerging political press which extolled the virtues of civility and sobriety encouraged a common cultural sphere of polite conversation. Drawing on the social morality of the earl of Shaftesbury, Klein claims that the Whigs gravitated towards Protestant values of liberty and taste disassociated from the corruption of the Court.[18] Even scholars more critical of the male emphasis on Whig values, such as Gillian Russell and Clara Tuite, admit that Joseph Addison and Richard Steele's daily society journal *The Spectator* laid the foundations for Whig sociability. Russell and Tim Reinke-Williams bring women to the forefront of emerging conceptions of taste, arguing that middling patrons of theatres and shopkeepers strengthened the notion that civility depended upon polite sociability in public company. Reinke-Williams stated, 'Participants in civil society were expected to conform to forms of behavior such as good manners and honest conversation as well as demonstrate wit and ingenuity.'[19] Wit and good manners were the instruments Whig social commentators believed would lead to a more just civil society.

The 'republican' tradition of coffee culture holds that coffeehouses were the true voice of the people by virtue of their intrinsic affordability and non-intoxicating substances. Often citing seventeenth-century slogans like 'Penny Universities' and a 'Wakeful and civill Drink', these authors see the coffeehouse as the origin of English clubs, both political and mercantile. Lord Macaulay, William Ukers and A. H. Arkle laid the foundation for this school, but Stephen Pobranski and John and Linda Pelzer have applied it to the Commonwealth era and the Georgian period, respectively.[20] Stephen Pincus argues that coffeehouse discussion was inherently political but not always Whiggish or middle class. He cites the scholastic and mercantile audiences of provincial coffeehouses in cities like York, Cambridge and Exeter as examples of political dissent not directly linked with Whig politicians in London.[21] Similarly, Rudi Matthee claims that coffeehouses were always available to people of all classes, and that its popularity in Europe may be traced to the individualization of society in the Renaissance and Reformation and the proliferation of imported substances through exploration and wars. Nicholas Rogers and Gary de Krey argue that coffeehouses opened up political prints to the common man.[22]

However, there remain some doubts as to the public nature of coffeehouse life and its connections to polite middling values. Peter Albrecht argues that coffee was first patronized by European elites rather than plebeians, and Jonathan Harris calls into question the optimistic view of the proliferation of coffee. Harris claims that historians have not evaluated actual coffeehouse conversation from the inside. He argues that scientific and Whig societies like the Commonwealthmen at the Grecian Coffeehouse held a secret and uncritical club which favoured ancient Greek and Roman orthodoxy over empiricism. Harris's dissection of just one coffeehouse club actually demonstrates that coffeehouse conversation was not as open to the public as has previously been assumed.[23] Similarly, Larry Stewart believes that scientific experiments conducted in coffeehouses were not the public displays that historians have made them out to be. He calls the scientific coffeehouses 'centres of calculation', rather than centres for scientific debate. While Stewart admits that merchant coffeehouses played host to public scientific lectures, these lectures focused on the applied sciences of particular interest only to shipmasters and the like. Stewart claims that coffeehouse politeness was linked with a political 'ideology of productivity'.[24] Stephen Copley elaborates that this politeness was reflective of Hume's understanding that the sociopolitical 'conversible world' belonged to the domain of leisure and that the public academies were masculine endeavours of industry.[25]

Some specialists are desperately attempting to find another theoretical structure for coffeehouse sociability. Markman Ellis claims that the polite coffeehouse never actually existed, and that Addison and Steele merely imagined the coffeehouse as a metaphor for urbane and gentlemanly fellowship. They created rather than discovered a mode of coffeehouse life, one which was highly selective and too elitist to be real. Ellis claims that much of the nineteenth century looked back to the club culture of Queen Anne's time as a mythical golden age of coffeehouse public life which overstated coffee's role in defining a polite public sphere. Still, the *Spectator* was a tremendous success, selling 3,000 copies per issue and forged an experience which coffee-goers wanted to see in coffeehouses.[26] Might we not expect coffee-goers and proprietors to be affected by this culture in some way? Curiously, most coffeehouse studies focus on the era of coffeehouse broadsides (1660s–1690s) and give relatively little attention to coffee club culture after Queen Anne's time, or the period which might most obviously be modelled after Addisonian values. It is an anachronism to expect coffee to conform to the *Spectator* before 1711.

Brian Cowan disassociates modernity from coffee, arguing that the old regime controlled coffeehouse licensure in a way which harmonized the old political culture with the new commodification of coffee. Furthermore, Cowan adds that the clientele in coffeehouses included far more than simply a Whig oligarchy, stating, 'Both highbrow connoisseurship and low-brow popular print culture flourished in the early coffeehouse milieu.'[27] By focusing on the relationship between centralized ecclesiastical and royal power and coffeehouses, Cowan argues that the Whigs were not the first to socially police coffee. Cowan also adds that the Whig attempt to reform manners reflected a profound anxiety about masculinity and a reinforcement of gendered social space.[28] He claims that coffeehouse 'civility' was a particular blend of urban rational discourse which did not wait for the *Tatler* and *Spectator* to arrive. It originated in the scholastic societies of England's first coffeehouses in Oxford and developed in James Harrington's Rota Club, controversial as that sort of republican discourse was to most respectable coffeehouse patrons. Yet, Cowan still distinguishes coffeehouse civility from the court civility which Norbert Elias first delineated as a defensive strategy of calculated status. Coffeehouse sociability was associated with the air of a 'gentleman'.[29]

Helen Berry offers criticism from the other direction: that coffeehouse sociability was not always all that polite. Coffeehouses were a vital part of social life for both the middling and even lower classes. Politeness was an ideal constructed through, as she describes, 'rituals ... [which] could thus in themselves become a pleasurable pursuit, associated with sociability, display and the exercise of discerning taste'.[30] The ideals had quantifiable parameters, one of which was a fascination for *impolite* behaviour in print, functioning as a counterpoint to outward social conformity. Whereas previous scholars of coffeehouses tended to follow the Whigs and literary wits in St. James's and Will's coffeehouses, Berry cites one noteworthy example of a coffeehouse with a nightlife, Moll King's Coffee House, run by the infamous prostitute Sally Salisbury. The patroness promoted 'flash talk', a form of urban slang which was used as a fashionable display of streetwise low-lifers.[31] This impolite behaviour stood in stark contrast to the politically constructed polite coffeehouse behaviour. There was then a pull between impoliteness and the coffeehouse rhetoric of social reform which infused many of the Whig clubs with civility. Coffeehouses cannot be simply summed up in the Whiggish polite rhetoric of Shaftesbury or Addison.

Historians of European sociability agree that the ideal for Whig social consensus for sociability fell apart during the 1790s. Terry Eagleton and Jon Klancher have claimed that a radical counter public sphere emerged. Gillian Russell and Clara Tuite have since revised the thesis, jettisoning the counter sphere in favour of a broader influence of Romantic egalitarianism in political discussion. They still maintain a process of radicalization. Revolution widened rather than contracted the public sphere as political discussion moved from civil liberties to natural rights. Yet, as James Epstein and Anne Janowitz demonstrate, revolution also made coffeehouses more dangerous. William Pitt's government prosecuted seditious speech in coffeehouses and the Whig clubs of Regency London moved into private apartments, where they would not be persecuted.[32] Yet, European historiography has entirely neglected to account for American revolutionary ideas. Surely, if radicalization is a viable lens for European coffeehouse sociability, then American coffeehouses radicalized in the 1770s, when Americans first pioneered the language of natural rights. If such was the case, then revolution and not Romanticism was primarily responsible for challenging the older classical consensus of the Whig coffeehouse essayists.

Coffeehouse history can benefit from a transatlantic perspective, one that considers coffeehouse sociability in the long eighteenth century as an aspect of economic expansion and free association in the British Atlantic world. This approach evaluates the changes in the structures of empire as the Board of Trade, the Royal Navy, civil servants and colonial governors argued a fuller transatlantic system of trade and consumer culture. Coffeehouse patrons pioneered a new form of communication, developing an eighteenth-century analogue to the modern newsfeed. Three distinct eras are discernible in this development: the growth of competitive group consumption from the 1650s to the 1750s, which I label 'conspicuous society'; the extension of the news gazette to transatlantic coffeehouse audiences from the 1750s to the 1760s, which constructed 'remote neighborhoods' of readers; and the era of revolution from the 1760s to the 1790s, which ironically severed the transatlantic 'news feeds' that coffeehouse patrons had worked so hard to create.

Chapters 1 and 2 demonstrate that coffeehouses were specialized to accommodate the growing social fashions of an interconnected British Atlantic world. Commercial orientation to British urban development can be seen in London's unique proclivity to display status and consumer activity in its coffeehouses. London coffeehouses provided a centre to public discourse which was connected to every social activity in the city. Similarly, the coffeehouse served both as a resort and as a workplace for emerging colonial elites emulating London fashion. Its patrons enrolled themselves into a 'conspicuous society' which involved living out the new sociology of leisure. They did this by organizing coffeehouse societies of arts and leisure; going to balls, concerts and plays; and returning to their respective coffeehouses to review them over cards.[33] Because coffeehouses came later to America and because licensure was different there than in England, coffeehouses in America often went by the designation of tavern rather than coffeehouse, but they were equivalent to the London coffeehouse in two respects: they sold coffee and they distributed news. The American coffeehouse tavern was just that: a tavern which also sold coffee. Although these coffeehouses were often volatile institutions, subject to crime and poor credit, they served to create an ideal in the public mind of transatlantic travel and an economic empire of polite goods and fashions.[34]

Growth of coffee culture and its transatlantic commercial interests in London increased social disorder, crime and even murder.[35] Chapter 3 introduces the first of three groups who independently took on the problems of crime and corruption in coffeehouses and tried to make them safer for Atlantic trade. These include naval officers, coffeehouse proprietors and coffeehouse lobbyists. The Royal Navy saw the uses of the coffeehouse as an informal officers' club and also headquarters for issuing orders and supplying naval bases in prominent Atlantic port cities. From their coffeehouses, British officers and spies rooted out the enemies of the state and enforced law and order.[36] But they could not stop frequent duels, brawls and murders which continued to plague coffeehouse life.

Chapters 4 and 5 explore how coffeehouse proprietors and lobbyists joined hands and completed a civilizing project which by mid-century unified coffeehouse culture across the Atlantic world. Women coffeehouse proprietors appealed to a more middling audience of readers, shoppers and transatlantic merchants. Coffeehouses became places where middling gentlemen and occasionally their ladies could imagine they were aristocrats.[37] Coffeehouse proprietors chose to buy newspapers which attracted private clubs, middling readers and civil servants who in their turn transformed the coffeehouse into a stronghold for rational sociality and commercial empire. Coffeehouse lobbyists launched a petitioning campaign against the East India Company, provided stability to customs procedures through the Atlantic world and formed a political culture of peaceful protest. This last movement (protest) was keenly observed by colonial Americans fearing imperial corruption in their economic affairs. The gazettes were their vital newsfeeds.[38] Thus, coffee-men and coffee-women, middling readers and civil servants suddenly found themselves bound together in a new coffeehouse community based on transatlantic news and free association.

Chapter 6 reveals how newsreaders created a unique community dedicated to consuming, selling and governing the economic empire of the British Atlantic world. The coffeehouse postal service, customs offices and subscription syndicates encouraged a new phenomenon: the remote neighbourhood. Distinct remote neighbourhoods of readers emerged, mostly civil servants and colonial aristocrats, who followed their own colonial news and reunited with their fellow colonists while in London.[39] Transatlantic travellers, civil servants and colonial governors used the coffeehouses to connect the business of the empire. The coffeehouse news circuit brought royal officers and governors serving the colonies closer to London news, their patrons and the Crown, allowing them a greater stake in the empire. They looked to their colonial coffeehouses for a communicative focal point in commercial empire.[40]

Chapter 7 highlights the irony of an institution dedicated to both free association and economic empire. It is meant to pause and reflect on the cultural dilemma of the coffeehouse as an imperial institution. Here was an establishment designed to encourage free association, where the ideas of rule by consent, free trade and limited power were openly discussed; yet coffeehouses paradoxically supported human slavery. Coffee could only be harvested in sufficient quantities with the labour of slaves. The bitter coffee drink had grown in popularity alongside sugar plantations, which again only produced sugar with the labour of slaves. Slaves themselves were bought and sold in coffeehouses. Although slaves featured prominently in the production of coffee, and the retail culture of coffeehouses, they were not the subjects of much critical discussion in coffeehouse clubs promoting Enlightenment, liberty, free association and rule by consent. Instead coffeehouse patrons celebrated the conquests of entire peoples and cultures as the outworking of a free system of trade.[41]

Chapter 8 shows how the pressures of imperial exploitation of goods and social venues brought the eventual downfall of the political consensus in transatlantic news. These pressures and the ensuing tax crisis of the 1760s finally unravelled the coffeehouse community of polite gazettes and dispassionate discourse. Revolution undid the public sphere with the same sort of political rhetoric which had been used to justify it and link coffeehouse publics across the Atlantic. As coffeehouse proprietors had once fought to end East India Company control over the supply of coffee and tea, dissatisfied colonials now planned the destruction of English tea from their coffeehouses and attempted to dominate the coffeehouse news circuit.[42] The ideas of Jefferson and Paine replaced the moralizing language of Steele and Addison in the news culture of coffeehouses in England and America. While founders undertook the task of preserving anew the civil social order of legislatively independent colonies and states under Continental Congress and the Articles of Confederation, the larger public sphere which had united the American order with Britain through the coffeehouse succumbed to revolution. The literate coffeehouse public fractured all across the Atlantic because of revolution. By the end of the American War for Independence, most of America's coffeehouses had radicalized, some even changing their names, and associating themselves with the revolution from below. The tax crisis (1764–75) sparked a revolutionary counterculture in American coffeehouses, where the postal system was summarily bypassed. The Sons of liberty hijacked the mail service and systematically turned coffeehouses in major American cities into distribution centres for private letters and patriot propaganda. Coffeehouse audiences polarized. George Washington's army made coffeehouses elaborate stages for military pageantry. The Declaration of Independence was read from American coffeehouse balconies as ecstatic crowds lit bonfires nearby. London was no longer the centre of an imperial culture of coffeehouse discussion. Many London clubs retreated into private quarters, never to return to the coffeehouses.

Other clubs radicalized with the French Revolution, and the coffeehouse public sphere was forever fractured.[43]

The emphasis on leisure and news throughout this work assumes two functions of coffee culture. Approaching coffeehouses as both consumer spaces and discursive spaces has proved essential when considering public consumption of coffee in the transatlantic context. Coffeehouses were places of public consumption, not just of coffee but of tobacco and other imported items. Coffee very often corresponded to other venues of urban entertainments, like concerts, dances and gambling. A night on the town never fully ended without hearing a verdict of the evening's play by the coffeehouse critics and perhaps a card game or two. Coffeehouses also encouraged discourse on the empire's new and exciting adventures. Verbal discourse was either the spontaneous result of thousands of the shopping and working public or the more planned discourse of prearranged merchant and society meetings. In either case, coffeehouse proprietors took great interest in encouraging polite modes of discourse in order to avoid conflict. This was a task which brought a pattern to the construction of coffeehouses; the standard design included an open room and side booths, with upstairs rooms reserved for prearranged meetings, although many merchant coffeehouses placed the common room upstairs.[44]

The interests of coffeehouse proprietors will become vitally important in this work, more important than in previous narratives of London coffeehouses. As Berry illustrates with Moll King, the proprietors often set the tone and social character of their coffeehouses. Ellis demonstrates that the coffee-man was a new sort of tradesman, dealing in news, exotic drinks, smoke and public controversies.[45] If print culture did begin to influence coffeehouse publics, it was the proprietors who decided which newsprints and what sort of literary culture to sponsor in their coffeehouses. They might often select literature which appealed to specific associations, clubs, politicians and critics who frequented their establishments in an effort to secure a dependable set of customers and advance the social standing of their coffeehouses among Britain's increasingly competitive social world. And as Berry intimates, coffee-women were just as important to the development of coffeehouse social life and literary culture as coffee-men.

A deficiency of source material has always plagued coffeehouse research. The chief difficulty is that far more stylized versions of fictitious coffeehouse life are available to historians than actual accounts of coffeehouse encounters. Notable exceptions are the diaries of Samuel Pepys, Robert Hooke and James Boswell, which have been mined by coffeehouse historians, but these have generally served to buttress an overly political or gentrified interpretation of coffeehouse discussion.[46] Indeed, most of the interpretive work only modifies our understanding of pre-existing material. The lack of investigation into coffeehouse violence demonstrates the problem. Although the issue of prostitution has been debated, no history of coffeehouse murder has ever been written. It has been entirely passed over for the far more alluring but less truthful caricatures of coffeehouses in the pamphlets of the latter seventeenth century.[47] To rectify these problems, I have brought to bear several coffeehouse murder cases from court records or cases published in the press. I have also combed the naval correspondence posted from coffeehouses and stored at the British Library and British National Archives, which have never before been used by coffeehouse historians. These provided me with countless examples of male honour and personal conflict from coffeehouses. My findings indicate that in coffeehouses like Will's and the Jamaican, a military sociability emerged where politeness was often a prerequisite to promotion.[48] Will's has always been claimed as the origins of Whig politeness, but its naval connections have hardly been noticed before.

Five major source categories appear in this work. Firstly, archival material from the British Library and National Archives has opened new dimensions of naval and transatlantic trade networks in London coffeehouses. These include letters, journals, and importation and exportation data from coffeehouse proprietors and customers in London. Secondly, published gazettes, gentleman's magazines and news journals in London, Scotland and key colonial cities provide insight into everyday coffeehouse life across the British Atlantic world. Thirdly, published letters and journals of colonial merchants and authorities in contact with colonial coffeehouses yield a more personal side to transatlantic coffeehouse exchange. Since little actual colonial American coffeehouse conversation has been left behind, I have relied heavily on family papers and the printed press including hundreds of coffeehouse mentions in the *Virginia Gazette* (digitally archived through Williamsburg's Historical Society) and other colonial gazettes. Records of these coffeehouses are stored at their respective state historical archives rather than at the conventional libraries in American eighteenth-century studies, although they yield very little in the way of actual recorded conversations. Some records of colonial governors with connections to American coffeehouses remain in the UK, like the Eden papers (chronicling the career of Sir Robert Eden, 1st Baronet of Maryland and colonial governor who patronized the Annapolis coffeehouse during the 1770s) which are stored at Durham University Library. However, these make no mention of the coffeehouse. The correspondence of Governor Sharpe in the Archives of Maryland returned only one important coffeehouse conversation. The archives at London and Kew yielded more results of coffeehouse correspondence. Fourthly, the recent archaeological research of Richard Charlton's coffeehouse at the Colonial Williamsburg Foundation provided some unique aspects of coffeehouse material culture and has largely inspired the approach of this entire book. Fifthly, social commentary from notable eighteenth-century thinkers, including the Johnson Papers, serves as the basis for much of my treatment of coffeehouse intellectual culture.

Part I

Coffee's transatlantic society

1

'Trifling', an urban experience

A writer in 'The Trifler' column of the *Aberdeen Magazine* with the provocative pseudonym 'Nich. Nonentity' complained that his stay in Aberdeen during the winter of 1788–9 was not nearly leisurely enough. The city musicians only stayed a few weeks at a time, concerts ran only once a week during the cold months and socials ended before the season was usually expected to begin. Golf, the local sport, was only played during the day, and the card tables were scarce of players three out of every four nights. The people themselves were the 'methodical and stupid' types; those who engrossed themselves in the 'vulgar cares' of their shops kept to their own families and were judicious in their use of liquor. The writer lamented that his prospects for city refinements may be forever dried up:

> Alas! when I reflect on the happy six months I once spent in London! Ah! London is the place for triflers, Sir – In a morning I rode on my nag for a few hours – came home at 3 o'clock to dress, which employed me very seriously till 5, when I went to the coffee-house to dine, where I was sure to meet with my fellow-creatures – about 8 I went to the play, where I remained until ten – then to the coffeehouse or tavern, or perhaps a dance, masquerade, or other entertainment … Next day, and every day the same, with the agreeable variations of auctions – morning concerts – learned pigs – fencing matches – sales of horses – reviews – card parties., &c. &c. &c. Why I left this land of delights, I cannot now inform you; my father obliged me to it, and added some motives which I have now quite forgotten.[1]

Whether the young man's alias was the description of a genuine third party or the product of the satiric imagination of the editor, the gentleman's plight embodies the social aspirations of an entire age. He was describing an urban attitude, a social atmosphere which found its centre in London. It was above all a British experience, where consumption and public life ran into one, with an English language of sociability to accompany it. Yet, the focal point of his exercise in 'trifling' was deceptive. Without colonial materials found across the Atlantic world, London's urban atmosphere would have been deprived of its most novel social engagements. The new delights available to eighteenth-century urbanites were the products of a colonial system. Shopkeepers, coffeehouse owners and opera houses imported the smells, tastes and textures of the British Atlantic trade network and assembled them into a material culture of pleasure. But the coffeehouse was one important feature that made eighteenth-century public life uniquely sociable, pleasurable and frequent. Here, the middling sorts of the Anglo world standardized their public urban experience by consuming colonial products and then venturing forth to the theatres or pleasure gardens. The night on the town most often began with coffee. If Mr 'Nonentity' had not been so obsessed with finding the absence of society embodied in his own name, he would have noticed that Aberdeen too was changing, as wealthy visitors like himself throughout the British Atlantic world expected the same sorts of entertainments.

At the heart of every chronicle like Mr 'Nonentity's' were three recurring consumer items transmitted across the British Atlantic and usually accompanying fine wine: coffee, sugar and tobacco. The early modern consumer experiences of these products were all intertwined, since coffee and sugar were often consumed simultaneously, if not always together, and the mass interest in coffee only arose after sugar plantations in the Caribbean made it possible for the Anglo world to eventually cancel coffee's naturally bitter taste.[2] Also, coffee was almost exclusively reserved, unlike tea, for public rather than private consumption, and therefore lends itself to a study of urban sociability in eighteenth-century British cities.[3] Coffeehouses possessed both social mores unique to their urban environment and broader standards for consumer behaviour which reached beyond their immediate social circles. Consumer patterns of the British Atlantic world and coffeehouses are subjects with long trains of scholarly literature behind them, but no comparative analysis has been attempted to bring the two together.[4] Scholars of British Atlantic consumption have almost entirely neglected the vital importance of coffee consumption as a means of public sociability, while literature of early modern coffee culture is almost entirely Eurocentric. On either side of the Atlantic, sources remain a problem. Endless inventories exist of the Atlantic consumer trade, but accounts of *how* these items were used in urban environments remain the subject of intense speculation. Nonetheless, the history of coffee should begin to move in a transatlantic direction and include the evolving complexities of broader Anglo-American modes of public consumption.

Coffeehouse culture depended upon a new consumer society of middling elites across the Atlantic world interested in London fashion and sociability. Not only were coffeehouses places of leisure, they were also resorts where investors in the business of sugar and coffee negotiated the process of urbanization in Atlantic cities. As the middling sorts in the Anglo world began to standardize their consumer habits around material culture from the colonies, they often celebrated etiquette and politeness, pleasure and excess, friendship and animosity, excitement and leisure, and all of the diversions which came with new sources of wealth and spending. The newfound wealth of the consumer revolution encouraged a new lifestyle where elites displayed their right to govern and freely socialize. They displayed their status in public venues dedicated to their use and entertainment. The draw of fashion, as emulated by colonial American consumers, was a powerful force in transforming colonial American associations into British publics.

London's renaissance and the experience of coffee

The city of London experienced a cultural revolution from 1550 to 1750, in which merchants, clubs with a vocal press and proto-modern institutions all contributed to the loosening of London's civic hierarchy (the Lord Mayor, the Common Council, wards and parishes). Robert O. Bucholz and Joseph R. Ward claim that 'with the possible exception of Amsterdam, no other city on the planet did more to catalyze modernity'.[5] The London expansion began when the Tudor dissolution of Catholic family lands in London made way for new aristocratic housing tracts at Convent Garden. Notable families and rich merchants built lavish town houses and patronized entire social districts around their new fashionable addresses, like Russell, Bedford, Clare, Salisbury, Grosvenor, Cavendish and most notably Drury Lane. Although the Whitehall–Westminster office complex was the administrative junction of the government, no London central authority presided over Westminster until the Common Council began regulating lighting, maintenance and urban markets in 1747. Joint-stock merchants challenged the chartered Livery guilds which had previously limited skilled labour to a chain of apprentices, journeymen and masters. New merchant ventures promoted a new financial elite preoccupied with luxury trade overseas. These merchants adopted a new ethos of urban sociability. Suburban families freely organized a new political and social order in their neighbourhoods by leasing their town houses to fashionable renters during London's social 'season' when courts were in session. Middling sorts viewed operas in the Vauxhall Gardens and paraded horses and carriages at Hyde Park. From these stations of eminence, reformers launched new reform projects like the Foundling Hospital founded around 1741 and the Bow Street Runners organized in 1749 to lower crime. Watchmen were organized ward by ward, totalling an increase from 543 watchmen in 1642 to 672 in 1737.[6]

It was upon this exciting new backdrop that coffee made its first entrance on the London scene. Coffee's proximity to London's shops, theatres and pleasure gardens meant that coffeehouses were places filled with noise, games and expectant visitors. Coffeehouse men usually wished to find some form of genteel amusement, whether it took on high-life or low-life manifestations. The art of 'trifling' was simply the dexterous ability to combine several urban events together, to begin with a meal, to see a play and to return to the coffeehouse for discussion, games or news. Some coffeehouses were gambling dens, like the Greyhound Coffee House in London, which was outfitted with a billiards table. Others like Mary-le-Bone Gardens Coffee House were furnished with a lavish ballroom which, as one observer described, 'was illuminated in an elegant manner with colored lamps: at one end of it women attended selling orgeat, lemonade, and other cooling liquors. This was intended as a representation of the English Coffeehouse at Paris'.[7] Gambling could be an activity in its own right, with regular customers on scheduled nights or merely a space filler until the beginning of a play. Although gentlemen frequently gambled in some of the more notable coffeehouses, gambling was a sort of low-life language across the hundreds of coffeehouses throughout London, many of which never grew in size or clientele beyond the working classes. On the other end of the social spectrum, the West End coffeehouses like Mary le-Bone Gardens

Coffee House would have hosted London's high social life and, as such, would have been displays of grandeur, in their own right, with lavish balls, a variety of drinks and possibly comic operas on their premises. It was very easy to overspend in these venues. When one needed to economize, one never went to London. One 'trifled' in cheaper towns. As Jane Austen explained in *Persuasion* (1818), '"What! Every comfort of life knocked off! Journeys, London, servants, horses, table ..." but Mr. Shepherd felt that he could not be trusted in London, and had been skillful enough to ... make Bath preferred.'[8] London was dangerous because it was very often too expensive even for the rich!

The most socially diverse coffeehouses in eighteenth-century London were located in Exchange Alley, where a permanent transatlantic community of merchants ran the shipping interests, or in Covent Garden, which had the literary and political coffeehouses. Here 'triflers' abounded. Jonathan's Coffeehouse and Garraway's hosted the nation's stock exchanges: the great games of chance which made and broke the fortunes of those who manipulated the goods of empire. As early as 1671, Garraway's Coffeehouse auctioned off a large assortments of beaver coats and later slaves, indicating a substantial market connection to colonial America. Tea and claret were also available. That same year, the Hudson Bay Company sold stocks for an expedition of adventurers to the Hudson Bay. Jonathan Miles established Jonathan's around 1680. Stockbrokers began moving into Jonathan's during the 1690s, but its boom was not until 1720, when the South Sea Company unloaded many of its bonds there. Meanwhile, South Sea investment schemes at Garraway's included up to £1,200,000 speculation in ship building, £2,000,000 in snuff manufacturing and £2,000,000 in Virginia walnuts. No less than 190 new companies organized. The ensuing uproar when the bubble burst first sounded from its coffeehouse investors, who angrily stormed out with whatever they could salvage and determined to erect a more restricted and responsible system of exchange. Stockbrokers at Jonathan's eventually moved to Threadneedle Street in 1773 and established the Stock Exchange Coffee House, or simply 'New Jonathan's'. The coffee room there was exclusively reserved for brokers and merchants who paid a subscription. Dissatisfied brokers at Lloyd's did the same thing, splitting off in 1769 and moving into the upper floor of the Royal Exchange in Cornhill in 1773.[9]

The South Sea Bubble was no small affair. It set in motion a challenge to Robert Walpole's Whig 'Court' regime. Although the earl of Stanhope, Sunderland, and Charles Stanhope, secretary of the Treasury, only narrowly escaped being implicated in the scandal, the impeachment votes were very narrow indeed. Further, *The London Journal* and the *Freedholder's Journal* upbraided Walpole's government for running a corrupt fiscal state of stock-jobbers and monopolists who ruined fair trade. They called for a coalition opposition and the electoral results of the most contested election of the period, that of 1722, returned thirty-five more seats to the Hanoverian Tories.[10]

After the South Sea Bubble burst in 1720, colonial merchant coffeehouses in London began maturing and diversifying overseas investments. The Virginia Coffeehouse and the Baltic were major shipping exchanges that also brought in North American interests. In 1744, these interests united into the Virginia and Baltick Coffeehouse near the Royal Exchange in connection with a post office to receive foreign news. Up to that point, many Virginia coffeehouses existed. From 1702 to the 1720s, the Virginia Coffeehouse of Birchin Lane housed investment schemes worth thousands of pounds in wool, flannel, iron, copper, brass and trade with Germany. Pennsylvania shares were sold at the Virginia Coffee House of St Michael's Alley in 1720. The owners of ships to Virginia and tidewater region of America moved again in 1798 to the Virginia and Maryland Coffeehouse in Newman's Court, Cornhill. The Jerusalem Coffeehouse served as a maritime newsroom and captain's headquarters, while the Jamaican was home to West Indian investors and also dealers in slaves. Directories of the mid- to late eighteenth century list a variety of traders lodged in the Jamaica Coffeehouse, including rum and brandy merchants and shipowners.[11] Yet, the colonial shipping industry relied on the vast forests of Canada and New England more than the South, and The New England, New York and Quebec coffeehouses of Threadneedle and Lombard streets hosted the great ship brokers. The Pennsylvanian interest eventually consolidated into the Pennsylvania Carolina and Georgia Coffeehouse of Birchin Lane in 1748. Until then, it had operated independently on Birchin Lane, dealing in furs and manufacturing experiments.[12] These coffeehouses kept London and American merchants connected.

As the vast variety of material wealth of the colonies poured into London, coffeehouse proprietors arranged an array of news around the coffee-table. At first, this coffeehouse news culture was neither primarily political nor was it exclusively dominated by Whiggish thought. Instead, it was cosmopolitan, financial and sociable. It reflected new civic interests in the business and leisure of the city's public life. London was especially successful at marrying its new civic attitudes with its coffeehouses. Lloyd's Coffeehouse of Lombard Street towered over them all. Its proprietor Edward Lloyd launched a newspaper *Lloyd's News* the same year the Bank of England was founded. By the 1730s, all the great investors of London turned to *Lloyd's List* for shipping news and investment prospects. J. McCusker estimates that *Lloyd's List* alone cost merchants at Lloyd's the modern equivalent of £12,000 per year at the Post Office for the exclusive right to consolidate shipping news. This bulk postage arrangement forever brought the postal networks of the Atlantic in close connection with the coffeehouses in Cornhill and Change Alley. Thirty-two correspondents in twenty-eight British port cities collected information for *Lloyd's List*. It functioned as Britain's first consumer report, indexing commodity price currents and exchange rate currents. The editor Richard Baker was also the master of Lloyd's marine insurers, who had flocked to the coffeehouse in the early days of the publication. Lloyd's insurance brokers supervised exchange rates and nearly monopolized shipping news for decades to come, and the coffeehouse was moved to Pope's Head Alley in 1769 and on to the Royal Exchange in 1774.[13] Before the advent of the Colonial Office, coffeehouse proprietors did more than just serve coffee. They indexed exchange rates, consumer reports and stock in colonial projects across the world so that investment would be less of a gamble and more of a science.

London was unique for birthing modern literary criticism in the cosmopolitan context of the coffeehouse. The chief literary coffeehouses were Tom's, Miles's, White's, St James's, Will's and Button's. Miles's, or 'The Turke's Head', hosted nightly meetings of James Harrington's Coffee Club of the Rota from 1659 to 1660. After its Rota usage, Miles's vanishes from public record. It was to Will's Coffeehouse of Covent Garden that Court poet John Dryden and his following of literary wits, including Samuel Pepys, resorted from 1663 to 1700. The next generation of literary wits at Will's included

William Wycherley and Alexander Pope. One French critic even declared that it was the intellectual equivalent of the Académie Française in Paris. It carried the name 'Wit's' Coffeehouse until Joseph Addison established a new social commentary syndicate at Button's Coffeehouse. References of Will's appear in the *Tatler* and *Spectator*, but already its reputation was dimmed by the intrusion of card playing in the common room. Tom's Coffeehouse of Russell Street Covent Garden acted as an alternative home for writers, including Addison himself. One commentator in 1724 explained that play-goers would retire to Tom's and Will's and engage in conversation until midnight. However, Tom's real literary debut was from 1727 to 1738, when the anti-court publication *The Craftsman* was published at Tom's. By the 1760s, it hosted Samuel Johnson, James Boswell, Oliver Goldsmith, Sir Joshua Reynolds, Sir Philip Francis, the Duke of Northumberland, the Marquise of Granby and many Shakespearean commentators. So universal was the literary interest at Tom's that in 1768 it closed to the public and was open only to a subscription club. Tom's Coffeehouse of Cornhill was also linked with England's writers, issuing a subscription list in 1727 for the relief of John Milton's daughter. The invitation posted in the *London Journal* drew from three main literary areas: White's Chocolate House, St James's Street and Tom's. The writer boasted that the liberal education of Tom's customers and their knowledge of the classics was equal to the Court or college.[14] In every other European capital, such a boast would have been laughed down as preposterous. The 'Enlightened despots' of the Continent guarded too closely classical learning in the official universities, salons and academies but not in London.

And London did have its salons, but they were public chocolate houses rather than the closed parlours of Paris. One did not need an invitation. Italian chocolate entrepreneur Francis White founded White's Chocolate House in St James's Street in 1693. Swift identified it as a resort of half of the English nobility in London. Tickets could be had for operas at Queen's Theater or balls at King's Theater in the Haymarket. The sporty White's Club consumed White's delicious spiced chocolate while they bet on the games of chess played there and talked of West End plays and concerts. When George Frederick Handel donated an organ to the Hospital in 1750, tickets for his *Messiah* were had at White's. No less than sixty articles in the *Tatler* were listed under White's, where stories of 'gallantry, pleasure, and entertainment' abounded.[15] French moralist Jean de La Bruyère commented in the *London Journal*, 'we see nothing but what wears the mask of gaiety and pleasure; powder and embroidery … that intolerable stink of perfumes … Conversation is not known here; the enquiries after news turn chiefly upon what happened last night at the Groom Porters. The business of the place is to promote some musical subscription'.[16] White's claim on the literary men of London was perhaps more social than practical. Yet, this stage for conspicuous display among London society also served as a standard for taste. It was this spirit of gaiety which is perhaps most aptly celebrated in the old Mother Goose rhyme:

> Hey diddle dinketty poppety pet,
> The merchants of London they wear scarlet.
> Silk at the collar, and gold in the hem,
> Very fine are the merchant men.[17]

White's Chocolate House was not alone for hosting such refinement. St James's Coffeehouse and Button's Coffeehouse stand out for hosting the polite Whig literary commentaries which so defined eighteenth-century discourse. St James's served as the personal address for Steele, Swift and Addison during the early years of the eighteenth century. When Steele took up his pen from St James's to write *The Tatler* in 1709, it was one of the newest houses in St James's Street, founded by John Elliott in 1705. Addison and Steele rendezvoused there weekly on Sunday nights while writing *The Spectator*, and formed a small committee for political discussion. There, Addison cemented the term 'coffee-house politicians' into the literary psychology of his day with this very famous passage in *The Spectator*: 'I first of all called in at St. James's, where I found the whole outward room in a buzz of politics ... by the knot of theorists, who sat in the inner room, within the steams of the coffee-pot.'[18] In Whig parlance, coffee intensified not only political discourse but also the rationality by which to understand it. Other notable intellectuals kept up coffeehouse political discussion throughout the eighteenth century. St James's coffee-tables hosted Joseph Warton, Edmund Burke, David Garrick, Reynolds and Goldsmith. It was perhaps the most notable coffeehouse for literary distinction in history.

Button's was not far behind. Founded sometime around 1712 by Daniel Button who had been a servant to Addison's future bride the Countess of Warwick, Button's was a collaborative effort between Button and Addison and was perhaps the first coffeehouse in London with a literary manager. Addison bore the title 'master of the Coffeehouse' and migrated his literary following from Tom's and St James's to Button's. Button's coffeehouse became the final endpoint to Whig political and social commentary, housing Joseph Addison's and Richard Steel's satirical columns in *The Guardian* (1713). The success of *The Spectator* had proved that the editorial process of giving and receiving social commentary in the form of published letters was a literary genera in its own right. Button's Coffeehouse was founded to prove the point, establishing a permanent home for this new genre which rightly belonged to London's sociable writers. Since Button's was intended to house an editorial project, satirical printmaker William Hogarth designed a great lion's head on the western side of the house to receive letters to the editor to Addison's and Steel's columns. Button's instantly gained entrance into the very centre of coffee and tea consumer culture, as indicated by Thomas Twining's frequent references to it in his ledgers recording sales in the Strand. At that time, Twining was supplying Button and other coffeehouse owners with coffee, tea, chocolate, snuff and sugar.[19] Thus, the London coffeehouse made editorial participation an urban reality by anchoring it into the sociable context of news-writing. London was unique for giving the coffeehouse a civic place in organizing transatlantic trade, news and fashion.

Building an Atlantic coffeehouse culture

By the end of the seventeenth century, coffeehouses sprang up throughout British cityscapes and signalled a rise in caffeinated sociability at the heart of urban experience. Yet, London remained unparalleled in the number of coffeehouses registered in any

British city. Four coffeehouses were registered in Oxford as early as 1650. Brian Cowan estimates that Birmingham, Bristol, Ipswich, Newcastle, Northampton and Norwich possessed two to six coffeehouses during the Georgian period. Three coffeehouses were to be found in York in the mid-1660s and possibly grew to thirty during the long eighteenth century. Edinburgh, Glasgow and Dublin all possessed similar numbers of coffeehouses. Philadelphia had about six coffeehouses throughout the eighteenth century. At least four coffeehouses were to be found in New York, with a number of smaller converted taverns, and about three converted taverns in Boston served coffee during the eighteenth century. London, by contrast, possessed eighty-two coffeehouses in 1663 and at least 551 coffeehouses by 1734. Cowan argues that this divergence made London socially unique, but perhaps an equally plausible explanation is that coffeehouse clientele across the British Empire was heavily dependent upon London social life. Coffeehouse franchises were imitations of a unique British social phenomenon best found in London.[20]

Provincial coffeehouses and club culture expanded during the mid-eighteenth century, when print and associational life had taken root in London. These were enhanced by the political clubs originating in Queen Anne's time, which in provincial towns tended to favour oppositional politics. In towns like Alnwick, Bath, Bristol, Birmingham, Chester, Newcastle, Norwich, York and Salisbury, coffeehouses and clubs pushed for wider participation in the public and political arenas for the literate traders and middling sorts of the town. They contributed to a sense of the 'nation', a subject which will be returned to later. Oppositional politics in the towns and cities of England did not fully mobilize until the 1770s and 1780s when Wilkite clubs began arguing for electoral reforms. Still, oppositional feeling informed the social life of clubs in the inns, taverns and coffeehouses of provincial towns. While provincial news outlets in England often criticized London politics for being corrupt, colonial American towns were busy embedding their interests into the fiscal system of London itself. All, however, fully participated in London's urban renaissance and associational way of life.[21]

Provincial towns like Newcastle-Upon-Tyne and Norwich serve as examples. Although the Newcastle Corporation dominated political and economic life with its exclusive rights to coal, new-coming investors began challenging the Merchant Adventures' cartels during the early eighteenth century and by the end of the Seven Years' War had managed to level prices and expand private interests. Monopolists and 'newcomers' alike however shared in the exciting free world sociability and discourse. In the Moot Hall of Castle Garth, in the Turk's Head Long Room and finally in the theatre of Bigg Market, built in 1748, plays were enjoyed by the middling 'triflers' of the town. Balls and concerts were performed for the magistrates during guild weeks at the Assembly Room, constructed in 1736. Bowling greens, ballrooms and sporting venues pervaded the more public areas of the city by the 1760s. The original Newcastle Theatre Royal was finished soon thereafter. Freemasons, tradesmen's clubs, the Sons of the Clergy and the Society of Florists held frequent social dinners and events. Similarly, of the 450 taverns and 176 inns inside the town of Norwich, the White Swan, Rampant Horse and King's Head hosted plays and concerts. In 1752, Norwich's Theatre Royal opened. Six dozen artisanal and middling clubs flourished. The town had the oldest provincial 'city' library, dating since 1630. Two newspapers and many booksellers and printers brought the populous up to date with London news. Admiral Vernon's naval victories in the West Indies during the 1730s and 1740s were celebrated with fireworks and bonfires in the taverns and coffeehouses across the country: Southwark, Ipswich, Norwich, Hackney, Lymington, Durham, Newcastle and Sunderland. Still, Cowan's assessment holds true for provincial towns. In older towns where inns and taverns abounded and where port merchants were not continually establishing a coffeehouse postal network of maritime trade, 'trifling' took place outside of the coffeehouse. Newcastle only possessed two coffeehouses throughout the century that are known. The situation was very different for American civil servants and merchants in port towns like Liverpool and Aberdeen, who required the coffeehouse as an institution of financial and economic survival, as well as just another great place to spend the evening in good talk.[22]

Coffeehouses spread across the Atlantic where merchant outlets were strongest and united entire colonial urban regions with London's life. Not only did London and British North American coffeehouses share a clientele, they shared place names. Thus, we find the Pennsylvania Coffeehouses in London and the London Coffeehouse in Philadelphia. The assumption was that rich colonial merchants would associate in their respective London coffeehouses while visiting the capital and that London connections might be maintained in colonial cities. Britain alone managed to transplant its peculiar arrangement of leisurely institutions from the capitol to America in a permanent web of transatlantic society. Colonial urbanites in New York, Philadelphia, Annapolis and Williamsburg constructed public spaces like ballrooms, coffeehouses and theatres to display their social status and fondness for London tastes. 'Triflers' and 'wits' were found bustling from coffeehouse to coffeehouse between these cities.[23]

Coffee's customers not only bought and displayed items of status in cities but also consumed goods and enjoyed artistic entertainments in public according to certain standardized rhythms of urban life. The pleasure garden mixed public dancing with tea, coffee and outdoor spas. The theatre was a place to view not only costumed actors but also costumed audiences, who were communicating by how they dressed not only what they *bought* but also what they *did* in the city. The coffeehouse brought theatrical reviews of both players and audiences to the public, and a new class of artist, the critic, was born. The urban British public instinctively understood that this web of leisurely experiences, or 'trifling', was an amalgamated category for human behaviour. 'Conspicuous society', or the display of polite amusement within which 'conspicuous consumption' was enjoyed, encapsulates the new sociology of entertainment, which was dependent on cosmopolitan tastes, transatlantic travel and eventually colonial emulation of London lifestyles.[24]

James Boswell was a trifler. His London journal (kept from 1762 to 1763) chronicles his many adventures in London coffeehouses. His enduring *Life of Johnson* (1791) describes his friendship with Dr Samuel Johnson, which developed in the coffeehouses and taverns of London. Although Boswell began his experience with the troublesome feeling that London would be no better than Edinburgh, he enjoyed himself in good style and in the end concluded that London was the best place to observe men and manners. He breakfasted and discussed the news at Child's Coffeehouse, Bedford's and Somerset Coffeehouse; regularly watched plays at the Drury Lane and Covent Garden theatres; dined at Dolly's steak-house; visited Northumberland House; heard countless sermons at St Paul's, Whitehall Chapel and many other churches; discussed Dryden and Pope with Goldsmith and Dodsley; saw in passing the royal family; and fraternized with many important men and women of the town. Boswell purchased a violet frock suit and even a dress sword (on credit). At every turn, Boswell compared himself to Steele passing judgement on a play or Addison making observations as to the various tastes of the people on the town. Mr Digges he pronounced to be the finest example of a man of fashion.[25] 'Mr. Sheridan said that this age was (as Henry Fielding styled it) a trifling age,' wrote Steele, but he added that Sheridan thought that its glitter had somewhat faded since Addison's time. 'He said trifling was the greatest joy in life, provided that the mind was properly prepared to relish it, by hard study.'[26] That one qualification, or the cultivated balance between virtuous taste and gaiety, was what made Addison great. Boswell knew his weakness was to engage in the delights of city life but not always to reflect on their merits or be wary of their dangers.

Johnson too was a trifler. In *Rambler* No. 89, he wrote, 'There must be a time in which every man trifles.'[27] Yet, whereas Boswell seems to have been all excitement, Johnson was more introspective and doubtful as to the merit of the public life of London. His Literary Club occupied itself with establishing a classical grammar for civil discourse rather than celebrating eating and drinking. The Club possessed what Leo Damrosch has described as an 'atmosphere of relaxed thoughtfulness'. After all, its members became some of the most distinguished minds of the eighteenth century, such as Sir Joshua Reynolds of the Royal Academy, the statesman Edmund Burke, the novelist Oliver Goldsmith and others.[28] Johnson's public life in London as interpreted by Boswell's pen earned him a reputation even greater than that of Addison in the century which followed him. The irony was that Johnson had lifelong doubts as to whether pleasure was instructive. 'It is necessary that we weaken the temptations of the world, by retiring at certain seasons from it.'[29] Johnson dedicated several issues in the *Rambler* to the problematic nature of pleasure-seeking, defending a rational and virtuous form of trifling over an epicurean sense of enjoyment.[30] Very often though, both Boswell and Johnson knew that the opposite was true, that coffee-goers were customers serving only their own desires. They were not always the polite men in velvet suits which Addison made them out to be.

Far from being polite and reserved places of social intercourse, most London coffeehouses were filled with a bustling clientele and chaotic combinations of gamers, businessmen, shoppers and opera-goers. Only a few coffeehouses eventually housed the clubs for which the characteristic coffeehouse was primarily represented in the society journals of the eighteenth century. Plate engravings of the period show us a sample of what life must have been like. Men gesticulating wildly over the table pamphlets and news, scuffles between men and coffee-women (servers and proprietors), broken crockery and brawls between men were not infrequent scenes in a coffeehouse. The depiction of men in all states of dress and frequently without wigs is enough to suggest that coffeehouses did not always display the starchy image which 'politeness' naturally suggests to us. Coffee was an exciting and novel drink in a new atmosphere of urban entertainment, newsprints and expanding business ventures.

Coffee's very wakeful quality made it perfectly suited to London's social life. Consumed hot, it was a drink which paced conversation by imposing new dangers and forcing intervals of speech between sips, all within a period before the drink cooled. Unlike alcohol, it could not be imbibed in long draughts or taken for granted in conversation. One always had to keep an eye on one's coffee while conversing, and the risks of spilling naturally caused a certain level of alertness independent of the stimulant. Coffee's bitter taste became less appealing to drinkers as it cooled. Indeed, most early accounts of coffee's social advent in London from the 1660s to 1690s portray the disgusting taste and novelty of conversation under such conditions. One critic remarked, 'If any Pragmatick, to shew himself witty or eloquent, begin to talk high … They listen to him a while with their mouths, and let their Pipes go out, and Coffee grow cold, for pure zeal of attention, but o'th' sudden fall all a yelping at once with more noise.'[31] Coffee was a liquor from the 'Stygian Lake', being 'blacker far within, then ever was the Negars outward skin'. Satirical characterizations of coffeehouse customers included names like 'Mr. Suck-foul the Usurer', 'Mr. Black-burnt the Coffee-man' and 'Mr. Antidote the Mountebank'.[32] One characteristic poem ran:

> They load their guns and fall a smoking,
> Whilst he who coughs sits by a choaking,
> Till he no longer can abide,
> And so removes from th' fier side.
> Now all this while none calls to drink,
> Which makes the Coffee boy to think
> Much they his pots should so enclose,
> He cannot pass but tread on toes.
> With that as he the Nectar fills
> From pot to pot, some on't he spills
> Upon the songster, Oh cries he,
> Pox what dost dot thou'st burnt my knee;
> No says the boy, (to make a bald
> And blind excuse,) Sir twill not scald.
>
> With that the man lends him a cuff
> O'th' ear, and whips way in snuff.[33]

Servers of coffee, or coffee boys walked over customers' feet answering orders for coffee. They often took the heat for giving heat and interrupting conversation by spilling coffee on their customers. Tobacco also determined the distance at which conversants felt comfortable sitting beside each other, but the room itself was crowded beyond the spatial dimensions of comfort.

And the coffee tasted terrible. It sat in large caldrons over the fire to be ladled out into pots and poured into dishes. Coffee roasting was uneven and varied because most proprietors hand-stirred their coffee roasts in frying pans over an open fire. This often left a smoky flavour. Seething methods did not improve until a cloth bag was introduced around 1710 for fresher infusion. Still, simply boiling coffee grounds was the common method. Although most average coffee-goers probably drank it black, some certainly did use a little sugar when their budgets allowed. These drinkers were oblivious to the addictive nature of caffeine, a molecule not officially isolated until 1821 by Pierre Jean Robiquet and Joseph Pelletier, and later by Adolf Strecker in 1861, who proposed its molecular structure. The idea that the drink was itself creating an urge for more and more was probably beyond the ken of most coffee drinkers of the seventeenth and eighteenth centuries. What brought them to coffee was conversation and the news.[34] Whether or not coffee was a 'wakeful and civil drink' remained in dispute for the rest of the seventeenth century.[35]

What is plain is that coffee drinkers believed themselves partaking in a whole new urban experience. One broadside defended coffee on the grounds of modern expediency, or for 'those many conveniences Coffee-houses afford us both for business and conversation'.[36] Convenience, business and conversation accounted for three novel ingredients in London's cosmopolitan development. For these businessmen, running to a tavern was inconvenient and alcohol dulled the senses in a corporate world of business and hurried leisure. They were 'perswaded to play the Good-fellows in this wholesome wakeful Innocent drink'.[37] At its root, the urban experience was an exercise in knowing man. 'To read Men Is acknowledged more useful then Books,' and somehow, coffee's patrons throughout the Anglophone world believed they were articulating man's nature and his social and political rights in new ways.[38]

The long eighteenth century saw a consolidation throughout the Anglo world of notions of pleasure and taste in which coffeehouses and gazettes played a central role. Travellers and clubs pollinated Anglo ideas across the Atlantic and brought a public and civil pattern for enjoying amusements in an English way. Not all establishments lived up to middling and aristocratic expectations and there was a definite hierarchy of reputation among social outlets. Johnson once observed, 'When I had sold my racers, and put the orders of architecture out of my head, my next resolution was to be a "fine gentleman". I frequented the polite coffee-houses, grew acquainted with all the men of humour, and gained the right of bowing familiarly to half the nobility.'[39] Some institutions and social activities were more advantageous for moulding 'fine gentlemen' than others. *Tatler* No. 232 refers to 'the top coffee-houses', inferring a polite standard of rank among London's coffeehouses.[40] This polite ideal was something which many coffeehouse proprietors aspired to and helped develop, ever searching for more respectable patrons.

Conclusion

By the mid-eighteenth century, consumers across the Anglophone world recognized a dominant pattern of leisurely institutions which defined what it meant to be an urbanite. These institutions included ballrooms, leisure gardens, theatres (all independent from the court or old hierarchy, although possibly frequented by notable families), private club rooms and public spaces devoted to eating. The coffeehouse dominated the social scene of pleasurable activity, by virtue of its wakeful drink and discursive atmosphere. Adventurers on the town often began their evening from a coffeehouse, went forth to a play or concert and returned there to discuss the play and find a game to wind down. It was this very habit which the Londoner in the *Aberdeen Magazine* identified as the defining English experience. Although he believed the rest of the Anglo world limped behind London (and indeed London's sheer expanse of urban activity seemed to validate his point), cities throughout the British Empire emulated this arrangement of urban pleasure. The coffeehouse became branded as a British institution and followed English merchant communities along trade routes.[41] Trifling required a socially acceptable air of urbanity, an adaptable costume and, most importantly of all, a sociable demeanour which revelled in light talk. Although the *Tatler* would have us believe that a clear line delineated polite and impolite company, the coffeehouse was an institution plagued with uncomfortable aspects and crowds of loud, gaming types who constantly offended the ears of the polite frequenters who came to discuss a play. Adding to the discomfort were clouds of smoke from tobacco, frequent coffee accidents, sudden uproars over the card table and unpredictable quality in coffee and tea. The 'man of pleasure' was someone well acquainted with all of these difficulties. He possessed the tact and savvy to manoeuvre seamlessly through these obstacles and enjoy the cities' pleasures with poise. Many an eighteenth-century urbanite of London, Scotland and America shared Johnson's resolve to be a 'fine gentleman' in this way.

Figure 1 Gentlemen busy 'trifling' in a coffeehouse, with seemingly no concern about their states of undress.

Photo credit: Look and Learn/Peter Jackson Collection/Bridgeman Images.

Figure 2 Hogarth's depictions of the disorderly conversations which were usually had inside coffeehouses.
Photo by Heritage Art/Heritage Images via Getty Images.

Figure 3 Gaming and brawls were regular parts of coffeehouse conversations.
Contributor: Chronicle/Alamy Stock Photo.

Figure 4 These coffeehouse gentlemen meticulously study *The London Gazette* for news and social commentary.

Photo by Guildhall Library & Art Gallery/Heritage Images/Getty Images.

2

'Trifling' in the colonies

An American writing for the *New York Journal* on 19 October 1775 made this startling observation: 'In all cities; therefore, and all large towns that I have seen in the British dominions, sufficient encouragement has been given to support one or more coffee houses in a genteel manner.'[1] Such a statement was proof of the success of an idea, a new experiment in urban leisure imported from Britain. By the 1680s, the term 'men of pleasure' was in vogue in London social life. It described those who went to plays, balls and coffeehouses. Consumption and pleasure were linked in the minds of many eighteenth-century urbanites, but here, British North America had some decided disadvantages. Firstly, American cities were much smaller than their European counterparts, and European consumer items took longer to reach colonial destinations. Secondly, colonial elites were largely self-made government officials, merchants or landed proprietors who struggled to make ends meet. Thirdly, European consumer goods in British North America required a sophisticated and protected shipping interest, which did not arise until the eighteenth century. Thus, historians have termed colonial American consumption, 'emulation', in which Americans mimicked pre-existing consumer habits from Europe well after polite society had subsumed these items into their everyday culture. It was not until the mid-eighteenth century that urban elites in Philadelphia and tidewater planters in Maryland and Virginia could generally afford large brick mansions, with servants, dining rooms, carved doorways and mantelpieces, carpets, drapes and mahogany and walnut furniture.[2]

This habit of emulation served to develop a healthy competition among consumers in European spheres of influence.[3] First-generation tidewater planters put most of the money into capital for tobacco, but as the market grew and slave gang labour boosted profits, planters became the first American elites to craft a lifestyle off of the English gentry. Beginning in the 1670s among the richest planters and then accelerating after 1725, planters bought common comforts and fashionable items like feather beds, imported chairs, looking glasses, chests of drawers, wine glasses and fine silver. These items became imbedded into ritualistic social activities which set off sociable pleasures from the mundane and raised fashionable gentry above the level of the common man. Polite hosts used the serving of wine, the toasting of healths and even the elaborate methods of storing and ageing wine as genteel ways of setting fine dining apart from its common use. And yet, as demand increased, wine, tea and coffee all became elements of everyday nourishment. By the 1740s, government officials, merchant clubs and middling households drank Madeira wine at almost every conceivable venue. As David Hancock has expressed it, wine became the drink of 'sudden friendship'. It kindled hearts towards the pleasure of discourse and embodied the new cosmopolitan experience of British sociable elites.[4]

Although polite consumer society took longer to establish itself in colonial America than in England, some of the apparent disadvantages in the American economy actually served to speed the rate of consumer fashion and dependence on British goods. Since 90 per cent of all Americans lived in the countryside and the only proper American industry was shipbuilding, Americans specialized in exporting produce and bought British manufactured goods on British credit. The reciprocal nature of colonial consumption then rested entirely on the assumed amicable relationship of trust in which colonial elites indebted themselves to British firms. Americans bought British goods because the British gave them credit. Philadelphia's entire dry goods market demonstrates the reciprocal nature of colonial American consumption. Most Philadelphian merchants depended upon credit firms in dry goods houses in London, Bristol and Manchester. A merchant required a recommendation or bill of exchange proving financial soundness before he could purchase an order of merchandise. Invoices were to be paid after twelve months. Merchants needed a reputation of sound credit policy with England and had every incentive to gain a sociable reputation for good credit among other merchants in the city. Here, the coffeehouse was invaluable. Much of the talk in the William Bradford's London Coffee House in Philadelphia concerned merchants who possessed good backing from English suppliers, the value of their goods and the price index.[5] America's first coffeehouses were imitations of the merchant coffeehouses in London. Their primary customers were merchants with transatlantic assets.

Americans were especially dependent upon English suppliers for consumer items and manufactured goods. The Navigation Acts and their lists of enumerated goods confirmed pre-existing trends in American markets. Timber, fish, grain and oil, or most of the northern economy was already firmly in English hands when the Acts made it only legal to pass goods through British ports. Still, these Acts closed competition, especially from Dutch rivals, and led to British naval supremacy. As a result, transatlantic shipping tripled throughout the eighteenth century. It seemed a matter of destiny that Britain's merchant navies were built from American timber and that these fleets carried back the riches of a colonial empire. If it benefited the colonies, it benefited Britain far more. Arguably the entire colonial experiment in British North America was an exercise in mercantilist economics, where Britain sought to gain more hard currency through duties on imports and exports than her rivals on the continent of Europe. During the eighteenth century, Britain reoriented its trade to include non-European routes and tap into new colonial sources of wealth.[6] T. H. Breen states that colonial newspapers attest to an explosive rise in 'goods of all sorts', as the conventional phrase went. They served as 'an index of consumer choice', which reinforced British national feeling in an 'empire of goods'.[7]

Tea from the East India Company, madeira, oranges, cotton frocks and even wallpaper freely traversed the Atlantic and fed a burgeoning consumer culture as never before. British exports to the colonies totalled £461,000 in 1700 (10% of total exports) and grew to £3,875,000 in 1772 (38%). Imports from the North American mainland totalled 68 per cent of Britain's total imports, much of which was later reshipped to European markets. The rise of this shipping industry across the British Atlantic world necessitated insurance offices on both sides of the Atlantic and with that need came the advent of news into American life. The *Boston Gazette* and the *Philadelphia American Weekly Mercury*, founded in 1719, set out to publish price currents in Boston, Philadelphia and New York and the publisher's partner of the first paper in Philadelphia also opened a marine insurance office.[8] Beginning in 1737, the *New York Gazette* became the first American newspaper to publish prices for the London market.[9] Of course, most of the marine lists in London were handled in the city coffeehouses. Through marine insurance and consumer price indexes, London's coffeehouse merchants and colonial American consumers were connected. Americans depended upon English consumer news in coffeehouses across the empire for their very livelihoods.

Bringing coffeehouses to America

By mid-century Americans had fully adopted coffeehouses after the London model to bring transatlantic merchants together and also to serve as hubs for social activity in their cities. Coffee prices had dropped and several major colonial cities had at least one coffeehouse which existed alongside the city tavern as a place of conversation. In the colonies, little real difference existed between city taverns and coffeehouses, since many of the taverns in colonial port cities also served coffee imported from the West Indies. Sometime between 1700 and 1702, Samuel Carpenter, owner of the Globe Inn, erected the first Philadelphia coffeehouse, called simply 'Ye coffee house' on east French Street. It was of brick construction, perfectly suited to take a civic role. It housed both the merchants' exchange and the postmaster of the province, Henry Flower. In 1734, Benjamin Franklin lauded the great ease with which Flower posted letters throughout the colony from his coffeehouse circuit.[10]

Philadelphia emulated London in linking colonial trade interests with London investors through its coffeehouse post. Just as there was a coffeehouse dedicated to Pennsylvania investors of London, William Rodney opened the London Coffeehouse in Philadelphia in 1702. It became a fashionable resort for the 'genteel' Philadelphia clubs and brought London news and letters from the harbour directly into the public parlour of respectable elites. The inventory for the London Coffeehouse included silver tankards, canisters, a porringer, a pepper pot, a teapot and spoons: an array of finery which would have equalled the finer coffeehouses of London. By the 1730s, it had cemented a respectable reputation among the Penn family. John Penn dined there with the General Assembly and the Philadelphia City Corporation in 1733. William Bradford, publisher of the *Pennsylvania Journal*, opened the second London Coffeehouse in 1754, soliciting the support of merchants directly by organizing as a joint-stock corporation. Bradford did more than any other colonial coffeehouse proprietor to inculcate literature into colonial coffee life. His paper had over 200 subscribers and his coffeehouse printing press published widely on contemporary geography, commerce and politics, even reprinting books and price currents from London. Most importantly, Bradford opened a postal collection service, which received letters until recipients could collect them. Not only news, but the mail ran from Bradford's coffeehouse. Bradford applied for a city licence to sell coffee alongside spirits, and served lemonade and wine, demonstrating a general openness to an array of new, colonial products. Even the location connected Bradford with British culture. Situated on the waterfront near the city wharfs, Bradford's London Coffeehouse served as an exchange for carriages, food and horses and as a public auction block. The wood structure stood three-storeys high on the corner of Second and Market streets. When the first tea captain arrived up the Delaware, he solicited the London Coffeehouse.[11] Thus, Philadelphia's coffeehouses linked material culture, news and visitors from London with Philadelphia's social life.

In Philadelphia, however, visiting merchants from London were not allowed to carouse in the way they had grown accustomed in London, where dissipation was more easily hidden by a crowd. Justice was more intimate in Philadelphia because of a smaller population and less diverse metropolitan area. In 1720, Philadelphia's population totalled about 4,883 and by 1777, it had reached about 32,073, over twenty times smaller than London.[12] Even though Bradford's London Coffeehouse solicited a diverse clientele among transatlantic merchants, his house maintained the pietistic civic order of the city.[13] In his transfer of property to John Pemberton in 1780, the sublease prohibited gambling, swearing and taking the Lord's name in vain: a mode of holiness far beyond London coffeehouse life. Dice, cards, back-gammon and other games prohibited by the City had a penalty of £100 placed upon them.[14] In short, carousing was not allowed in taverns or coffeehouses in Philadelphia. These establishments were to serve the civic needs of the city. In 1773, Daniel Smith founded the City tavern, which quickly overtook the London Coffeehouse as the city civic centre. It was considered the largest inn in British North America, with its three-storey brick exterior and its fifty-foot-long dining room and adjoining club rooms. Modelled after the London Coffeehouse, it served coffee and took the name of Merchants Coffeehouse around the turn of the nineteenth century. It had a fabulous reputation among the city traders. In addition to the City Tavern, Philadelphia was home to some lesser coffeehouses, such as Robert's Coffeehouse and the James Coffeehouse, which became home to the governor's social circle and served as recruiting stations for the British army bound for Jamaica in 1744.[15] Philadelphia integrated British military and commercial culture into its coffeehouse social life, without compromising its Quaker holiness.

Indeed, the North American colonies were unique for their holiness laws, which often transformed public houses into orderly meeting houses.[16] These laws nuanced the new atmosphere of 'trifling' but did not hinder its transatlantic growth. Under Penn's Great Law, adultery got a public whipping and a year in prison and fornications got the death penalty. Drunkards received a five shilling fine for each offence. Scolding was punishable by three day's imprisonment, and after 1693 included a five shilling fine and an hour of public gagging. Swearing by God's name or by Jesus Christ got a five shilling fine or five days in jail. The Newcastle Code of 1700, later ratified by the Privy Council in 1705, strengthened these laws for the remainder of the century. From 1700 to 1810, third-time offenders of adultery received twenty-one lashes, branding and seven year's imprisonment. Scolding involved a choice of gagging or five days hard labour. From 1700 to 1779, duelling got twenty pounds and three months' prison time. Yet unlike Puritanism in New England, Penn provided for liberty of conscience within Protestant parameters which encouraged not just Quakers but also other Protestant groups to fully participate in the civic pallet of Philadelphia.[17]

Because of its Dutch origins, New York City serves as an example of a more cosmopolitan colonial coffeehouse society where merchant life, both for business and for pleasure, drove the beating heart of the city. Yet many coffeehouses in New York seem to have been quick and unsuccessful affairs. There arose an elaborate labyrinth of modest merchant houses. New York's connection with Dutch markets makes it likely that coffee was available at market as early as 1640, but it was not until 1668 that the city burgers actively patronized it. Still, the coffeehouse as an institution did not come until well after the advent of British rule. John Hutchins built the first New York coffeehouse in 1696 on Broadway and called it the King's Arms. Later its name became the Atlantic Garden House, since most of its clientele looked across the Atlantic for wealth and status. This coffeehouse imitated English design with a common room on the second floor and balconies overlooking the beauty of the river and harbour. Merchants peered out of the windows to spot approaching ships. It was constructed of imported Dutch yellow brick and had a common room with booths to the side and green curtains which harmoniously integrated public and private space. Colonial records bear witness to its use by colonial statesmen, the Common Council and travelling merchants. Here, Governors Benjamin Fletcher and Richard Coote, earl of Bellomont, supported a network of English merchants and statesmen who sought to replace the old Dutch Calvinist settlers. Armed with a coffeehouse and a new newspaper by a Philadelphian bookseller, Fletcher fought to establish an 'English party'. Sometimes, the group of English merchants could be critical of their own government, as when Hutchins clashed with authorities in 1702 over his collecting petitions form his patrons calling for reform. The New Coffeehouse was constructed sometime thereafter and was formally used by the General Assembly in 1709. The Exchange Coffeehouse opened around 1729 next to the Exchange on Broad Street and Water Street and was also used by the Assembly in 1732. It may have even had a ballroom in 1750. Yet for some unknown reason merchants changed the name of the Exchange Coffeehouse to the Gentlemen's Exchange and moved their headquarters to Hunter's Quay in 1753. Soon the Exchange disappeared from public record altogether. A more permanent financial coffeehouse establishment came sometime around 1737, when the Merchants Coffeehouse was built at the corner of Wall Street and Queen Street. It changed hands between mariners quite frequently before it was taken up by the coffee woman Mrs Ferrari. Its proprietor during the Revolutionary War, Cornelius Bradford, decided to make it a headquarters of war intelligence, but such efforts were abruptly ended with British occupation. Arguably, the Merchants Coffeehouse came into its own when the Royal navy patrolled the New York harbour. Here, ships were sold and the Chamber of Commerce met in 1779. During the Federal era, the Merchants Coffeehouse became the home of many of New York City's civic societies, like the Society of Arts, Agriculture and Economy, the New York Committee of Correspondence, the Society of the Cincinnati and, most notably, the Society for Promoting the Manumission of Slaves. In the 1780s, the city bankers founded the Bank of New York at the Merchants Coffeehouse in 1784. It was the 'Lloyd's' of the city and housed America's first Wall Street bankers. In 1793, they moved to the imposing Tontine Coffeehouse building on Wall Street and formed the New York Insurance Company, a predecessor to the New York Stock Exchange.[18]

Lesser coffeehouses in New York City included the Burns Coffeehouse, the predecessor of the King's Arms, and Whitehall Coffeehouse, which opened in 1762 to erect a chain of news and correspondence between London, Bristol and New York. Such establishments either had very short lives or were little more than taverns and little real merchant business was conducted there.[19] It is, therefore, highly unlikely that any permanent coffeehouse public sphere emerged in New York before the mid-eighteenth century. Yet, the citizens of New York were not ignorant of the sociable reforms of coffeehouse life in London which made public life more pleasurable and useful. Many longed for a London-style coffeehouse and the politeness that it brought. New York saw itself as one of the grandest cities in the British Empire and emulated English tastes even though its coffeehouses were not always very successful. In 1775, a certain 'friend to the city' voiced in the *New York Journal* a complaint which must have been felt by many a polite citizen:

> It gives me concern, in this time of public difficulty and danger, to find we have in this city no place of daily general meeting, where we might hear and communicate intelligence from every quarter and freely confer with one another on every matter that concerns us. Such a place of general meeting is of very great advantage in many respects, especially at such a time as this, besides the satisfaction it affords and the sociable disposition it has a tendency to keep up among us, which was never more wanted than at this time. To answer all these and many other good and useful purposes, coffee houses have been universally deemed the most convenient places of resort, because, at a small expense of time or money, persons wanted may be found and spoke with, appointments may be made, current news heard, and whatever it most concerns us to know. In all cities; therefore, and all large towns that I have seen in the British dominions, sufficient encouragement has been given to support one or more coffee houses in a genteel manner. How comes it then that New York, the most central, and one of the largest and most prosperous cities in British America, cannot support one coffee house? It is a scandal to the city and its inhabitants to be destitute of such a convenience for want of due encouragement. A coffee house, indeed, there is, a very good and comfortable one, extremely well tended and accommodated, but it is frequented but by an inconsiderable number of people; and I have observed with surprise, that but a small part of those who do frequent it, contribute anything at all to the expense of it, but come in and go out without calling for or paying anything to the house. In all the coffee houses in London, it is customary for every one that comes in to call for at least a dish of coffee, or leave the value of one, which is but reasonable, because when the keepers of these houses have been at the expense of setting them up and providing all necessaries for the accommodation of company, every one that comes to receive the benefit of these conveniences ought to contribute something towards the expense of them.[20]

This passage is telling in three main respects. Firstly, it attests to a certain American desire for a settled British way of public life, even as the American Revolution was just underway (although the writer probably hoped for reconciliation with parliament). It identifies the London coffeehouse as a social model. Coffee was the social arbiter of British values, a role which later became relegated to tea. The author genuinely believed what many historians of coffeehouses have since called into question: that what made British coffeehouses unique was their democratic social order. Coffeehouse customers entered for a penny, openly resolved matters of public interest and shared civic responsibility, more or less equally. Coffeehouse politeness was taken for granted in the Anglo public mind and functioned as a British trope on both sides of the Atlantic. Furthermore, the writer considered the coffeehouse a necessary facet of civic life in British dominions. In insisting on the public consumption of coffee, the writer was insisting on his right of association under the English constitution. Colonial Americans like this New Yorker not only took civic pride in their English 'things' but also their British institutions and way of life. Consumption of coffee was clearly a subset of a humane sociability which embodied the Enlightenment values of right to assembly, speech and press.

Secondly, the writer in the *New York Journal* considered coffeehouses cultivated aspects of a free society. Proprietors must take pains to make them 'comfortable', 'well-tended' and accommodating for public discourse. Customers should pay for this sociable atmosphere by taking at least one dish of coffee, thus paying the proprietor for the use of the public room and engaging with the coffee company for as long as it takes to drink a dish. The writer reinforced classical ideas of public order and decency and, in this case, private property. The proprietor and not the customer held exclusive rights to the coffeehouse, and as such, visitors should pay for the privilege of use. This writer at once noticed and respected the proprietary care which coffeehouse owners offered in sponsoring news and hosting conversation. Perhaps the proprietor's importance explains the frustration the writer felt in its being taken for granted by so many customers. The historical record has hardly been kinder, emphasizing coffeehouse writers and clubs over the proprietors.

Thirdly, the writer asserts that 'coffee houses have been universally deemed the most convenient places of resort', a view not inconsistent with idealized views of coffeehouses and Britain in the society journals of the eighteenth century. Indeed, it is most likely that the writer actually acquired his perspective from the *Tatler* and *Spectator*. His was an 'Addisonian' view, firmly rooted in the new ethos of convenience and politeness. Convenience spoke of emerging British middling values, where trade and genial association were inseparable. This broader British public imagination of coffee in the eighteenth century viewed coffeehouse life as sociable and polite, an assertion which increasingly carries less and less weight among historians. In our haste to diversify the coffeehouse experience, we ought not to forget what middling customers of coffee writing in the gazettes and journals saw in their coffeehouses. They believed that they had birthed a unique institution which crossed oceans and united colonial experiences with an ethos of public convenience, refinement and free association.

What the writer in 1775 failed to notice was that New York succeeded in establishing an outdoor resort for British sociable experience in its pleasure gardens. New York tavern owners began experimenting with tea garden additions to their establishments. By the mid-eighteenth century, two greater gardens opened, named Vauxhall and Ranelagh, after London's gardens. Tea and coffee were on demand all day long, concerts were given twice a week, fireworks were demonstrated on special occasions and the dance halls and breakfast tables were regularly opened for ladies and gentlemen of the city.[21] This development is startling when viewed in comparative perspective. No less than a second London society was aimed at here and not just a generic British sociability. From Thomas Bowles's 1754 print, Ranelaph Gardens, London, was fitted with a large Rotunda to house lavish concerts and a floating 'Chinese House', which served tea to its ladies and gentlemen. Vauxhall was London's most successful public pleasure garden throughout the eighteenth century. It had an open balcony for concerts and was laid out in broad avenues which ran in straight lines through the gardens, bordered on either side by trees. The piazza was a circular promenade for dancing, boarded by an elegant wall with many spires. In New York, both Ranelagh and Vauxhall gardens were divided into linear walks with trees into which were nestled box seats for music and fireworks displays. Although visitors knew their gardens were only little imitations of their London counterparts, the New York gardens featured a grand garden house with a fifty-eight-foot-long reception hall, several adjoining rooms and twelve fireplaces.[22] The New York high society mirrored London's social experience in which might be 'conspicuous society', or the display of polite amusement within which 'conspicuous consumption' was enjoyed. Coffee played as much a roll in this outdoor form of leisure as it had in other indoor establishments across the empire. New York's diverse population and scattered public organization made it difficult for indoor coffeehouse establishments to take the dominant role in organizing a pleasurable experience among its middling citizens, but the British ethos of pleasure was still very much alive in New York. American historians have devised no other word for this other than emulation. If so, it was a simultaneous emulation in which British citizens on both sides of the Atlantic shared in the same cultural revolution. It was also cosmopolitan. Place names like Ranelagh and Vauxhall transcended geography as they became part of a synthetic urban experience of riverside delights.

The gentrifying American South was late in coming to the British coffeehouse. It was not until the mid- to late eighteenth century when coffeehouse clubs were at their height in London that high society across the southern plantations of Virginia and Maryland eventually settled into coffeehouses in cities like Annapolis and Williamsburg. Perhaps that is why what little attention has been paid to American coffeehouses among historians has left southern coffeehouses completely out of the story.[23] Yet, southern entrepreneurs played perhaps the greatest role in instituting English gentility inside the American coffeehouses. During the 1760s, the General Assembly of Maryland legally recognized the coffeehouse as a new institution, exempting coffeehouses from stabling and bedding requirements and thereby setting them apart for formal business meetings and fine dining. These licences were expressly granted 'for the Entertainment of Company' in the larger cities of Annapolis, Chester Town, Baltimore and Frederick Town.[24] It can only be assumed that this legal delineation was based on the Addisonian assumption that the coffeehouse was the most convenient resort for the 'clubbable' gentlemen of the city. In this respect, the South furthered a peculiarly English urban assumption which was steeped in the popular Enlightenment of London's coffeehouse thinkers and journalists. The assumption was that free association in coffeehouse clubs gave rise to a rational public sphere. Maryland politicized this Enlightened culture. In the 1770s, the General Assembly met in the Annapolis Coffeehouse. Its lavish ballroom held the Royal Governor's public galas.[25] The political class made the coffeehouse their home in Maryland.

Coffeehouse life in Williamsburg was more associated with the theatre than with the political class, but it was no less 'polite' in the Addisonian sense of the word. Richard Charlton took out the following advertisement on 25 June 1767 in the *Virginia Gazette*:

> The Coffee-House in this city being now opened by the subscriber as a TAVERN, he hereby acquaints all Gentlemen travellers, and others, who may please to favour him with their company, that they will meet with the best entertainment and other accommodations, such as he hopes will merit a continuance of their custom.[26]

Here, Charlton combined two technically different dining classifications to solicit a specific polite clientele. By informing his readers that he opened a tavern, Charlton spoke to a modest range of housing accommodations, going beyond the minimum coffeehouse requirement. Yet by identifying it as a coffeehouse, Charlton specifically catered to 'gentlemen travelers'. Similarly, the coffeehouse tavern at Norfolk advertised, 'Genteel LODGINGS, with good Stabling for Horse', and even drew industrious customers by housing a candle-making tradesman within its walls.[27] Mrs Julian of Fredericksburg promised that 'Gentlemen may be genteely accommodated with Lodging &c. for themselves, Servants, and Horses.'[28] Genteel lodgings signified a new British-Southern hospitality.

The very success of hot liquid in balmy cities of the American South attests to the power of a British ideal. Coffee was conspicuous for the very reason that it was not as comfortable to drink in the heat of the Southern sun where relaxation and cool air were necessary prerequisites for gentlemen visiting Southern cities. If anywhere, it would be expected that pleasure gardens and lemonade would be the preferred social arrangement of the middling sorts in the South, but instead, the coffeehouses of Annapolis and Williamsburg brought polite sociability indoors around the coffee table as no other part of the British colonial world. The South seamlessly blended good lodging and coffeehouse company into one. This synthesis offered more comfort than most London coffeehouses, which rarely offered servants, stables, horses or private sleeping quarters. Although late in the colonizing process of coffee, Southern coffeehouses housed many of the planters and governing colonial elites. In many ways the unique Southern coffeehouse tavern was the epoch of the Anglo experiment in urban sociability.

New England primarily embraced coffeehouse politeness as a functional conduit for print culture. From the beginning, coffeehouses in New England were linked with printing houses and merchant news. When the Selectmen of the council allowed Mrs Dorothy Jones and Mrs Jane Barnard to keep a coffeehouse in 1670, neither Paris, Vienna, nor Venice had yet opened a coffeehouse. Ellis claims that Boston possessed perhaps one of the first coffeehouses in America. The next coffeehouse to open was by Captain James Johnson and Abell Porter in 1671. John Sparry opened a coffeehouse for 'severall Merchants & Gentlemen' in 1676. It was located right next to the Exchange and near several bookshops. But these interests did not solidify into one until printers began opening their own coffeehouses. In 1689, an enterprising Boston merchant and puritan bookseller Benjamin Harris who had lived in London among the coffeehouses on the Exchange decided to merge his Boston bookshop into a coffeehouse, the London Coffeehouse, which he situated on King Street near the Town House. His monthly newspaper *Public Occurrences* was the first newspaper in the colonies, but it was quickly closed down by the governor for not having a proper licence. Harris eventually returned to England in 1695, but two other coffeehouses soon opened: the British Coffeehouse, which housed the merchants, and the Gutteridge Coffeehouse, which took out an inn licence in 1691 and moved into Nicholas Buttolph's bookshop which published Cotton Mather's theological works. By 1700, Buttolph employed two printers, B. Green and J. Allen, at the corner of the Gutteridge Coffeehouse, but the establishment was destroyed by fire in 1711. Next, J. Mein opened the London Bookstore in the 1760s, just two doors from the British Coffeehouse on North Kingstreet. Popular theology was a regular subject for these Boston coffeehouse printers.[29] By mid-century, coffeehouse culture had encouraged a colonial network of printers. New England booksellers relied on coffeehouse printers in New York. Publication details on books served a secondary purpose of referring readers to city coffeehouses. One such work, *A Conductor generalis*, which described New Jersey's judiciary in 1764, contained the following publication details, 'Woodbridge, in New-Jersey: Printed for and sold by Garrat Noel, near the merchant's coffee House, in New-York.'[30] It is unclear whether the work was actually published in Woodbridge, New Jersey, or in New York, but it was surely distributed within the precinct of the Merchant's Coffeehouse. This book tells a story of cooperation between coffeehouse merchants and booksellers.

New Englanders emphasized literacy and local diversity in their coffeehouse culture. Coffee was more equally dispersed throughout Boston than in other colonial cities. Most of the taverns and inns of the city served coffee. The two most popular city inns, the Green Dragon Inn and the Bunch of Grapes, served coffee and were home to prominent transatlantic merchants and free masons. The Ship Tavern on the corner of North Street and Clark hosted the Crown commissioners of King Charles II in 1663 to settle the terms of the Massachusetts charter. The King's Head and the Indian Queen were also places of resort for Crown officials and well-established colonial citizens. The Blue Anchor in Cornhill was home to Boston's jurists, clergy and even the General Court. Most of these shared clientele with other minor coffeehouses like the Crown Coffeehouse, a small hostelry and the Royal Exchange Coffeehouse, mentioned as early as 1711 and where the first-stage coaches in Boston began. Perhaps the tallest coffeehouse was the North-End coffeehouse, built of brick around 1740 and reaching three storeys, but this was dwarfed in 1809, when Asher Benjamin constructed the Exchange Coffeehouse with two hundred rooms and a domed exchange hall which stood ninety-five feet high. It contained Palladian windows, a fan-topped panel, neoclassical tracery, a balustrade and Corinthian plinths. European visitors said it was equal to anything in Europe. Jack Quinan argues that it was the prototype of the

American hotel. Ukers compared it to Lloyd's coffeehouse in London, with its maritime insurance agencies.³¹

It is probably more likely that such a coffeehouse was a departure from coffeehouse design altogether and was instead a grand statement of American Federal principles. Like so many state capitals and judicial halls, it embodied an austere neoclassical design. It was certainly unprecedented in Boston, and there is little evidence to claim that Boston coffeehouses before the Federal period were particularly preferred over taverns and inns. For most of the seventeenth and eighteenth centuries, Bostonians sprinkled their public life across a wide range of diminutive taverns which sold coffee, not unlike the small towns and family farms which dotted the countryside. The only coffeehouses with any measure of long-standing distinction in Boston were connected to publishing houses. Transatlantic travellers filtered through these houses and brought with them new standards for colonial culture and political connections to Britain.

The coffeehouse transatlantic political discourse of middling merchants altered the British commercial system. Alison Olson observes, 'By 1706 English coffee house leaders were in informal correspondence with merchant groups in Charleston, Philadelphia, New York City, and Boston. The cumulative growth of Anglo-American interests is suggested by the fact that the Board [of Trade] received fifty-one petitions from such groups before 1709.'³² The Board of Trade established in 1696 acknowledged transatlantic lobby groups to better accommodate American interests in London politics. This was all the more necessary when the Crown transitioned many of its North American colonies into Royal colonies. Between 1685 and 1696, colonial officials forwarded their laws to England for review through the Board. Because the Board of Trade supervised the terms of the Navigation acts, colonial merchants networked with London merchants who passed pamphlets to specific MPs recommending reform. Olson asserts that Virginia merchants were particularly active until 1715, New York merchants lobbied during 1710–30, and South Carolina and Massachusetts lobbying increased during the mid-eighteenth century. So responsive was the Board to these merchant petitions that George Grenville once claimed that Rockingham's administration was effectively ruled by a club of merchants. The Board was generally responsive to colonial interest groups until 1764, when it suddenly ceased listening to all Anglo-American lobbyists in the wake of the Sugar Act and soon thereafter the Stamp Act.³³ Transatlantic political negotiation took two forms. Coffeehouses were informal means of moulding imperial power, just as the Board of Trade represented the formal process for lobby power. When Grenville's government ceased to listen to America's petitions, it suddenly became deaf to its coffeehouses, both in London and throughout the empire.

In pursuit of leisure and manners

Although less expensive than in London, cityscapes changed dramatically in colonial America to accommodate the growing importance of refinement and leisure in British North America. Many of the larger cities (still small by European standards) became miniature versions of London. Refinement and capitalism made precarious allies, as

Richard Bushman has argued. Books on politeness and gentility evoked scenes of lavish balls, graceful dancing, refined card-playing or fanciful garden parties officiated in decorative tea services or Venetian wine glasses. Everything done in a refined manner seemed without calculation or effort. Grace rather than work was the subject of polite society, but its energy was capitalism, or rather the modern economy which literally kept refined goods afloat on the high seas and brought them to rest on the tables of aspiring Americans.[34]

American cities like Philadelphia, Annapolis and Williamsburg could more easily adapt to modern gridlines and definite public sectors than European cities precisely because they did not contain medieval elements. Public life, business and leisure thus became the guiding ethos in many American cities during the eighteenth century. Leading citizens banded together to construct assembly rooms for concerts, balls and dinners. The great hall in the assembly house in Salem, Massachusetts (constructed 1766), measured forty feet long, and the building was also fitted with drawing rooms and a music gallery. George Washington boasted that the assembly house in Portsmouth, New Hampshire (built 1750), rated among the best. Francis Nicholson, who served as lieutenant governor of Virginia and royal governor of Maryland, helped design two new colonial capital cities, Williamsburg and Annapolis. Nicholson incorporated two London features into his cities. Like London, Nicholson constructed a ceremonial square for church and state buildings and a widely assessable port or dock area for merchants. His residential square adjoining the government buildings in Annapolis even carried the name Bloomsbury, as in London. For these elite families serving in the government, dancing and card rooms lined the Duke of Gloucester Street in Annapolis. Lacking a major river, Williamsburg tended even more to favour the ceremonial sector. The Capital building, the Governor's Palace and Bruton Parish Church dominated public life. Although small in size, eighteenth-century fashion and leisure had transformed these cities into resorts for the gentry.[35] American cities were as distinct from their seventeenth-century antecedents as Dr Johnson's London was from Shakespeare's 'London Towne'.

As theatres did not appear until the latter half of the eighteenth century, taverns and coffeehouses served both as theatres and as places for critical debate of the performing arts. These were often no mere taverns, as in London. Perhaps the most extravagant of these was the City Tavern of Philadelphia, measuring about fifty feet long and thirty feet wide. The Merchant's Coffeehouse claimed to be an exclusive 'Tavern and Hotel', with fashionable sociability. The Frary Tavern in Deerfield, Massachusetts, was fitted with a musician's gallery and a second-storey ballroom. The City Tavern served as the dance hall for Alexandria, Virginia. In New York, Edward Willet's Province Arms and Samuel Fraunces's Tavern hosted the city's dancing assemblies. New York's Tontine Coffeehouse also made a respectable showing, but found it difficult to contend with the fashionable City Hotel of Broadway.[36] Taverns and coffeehouses brought together pleasure-seekers and critics who publicly reviewed plays according to the standards of gentility expressed in London's society journals. Nevertheless few American communities were large enough for playhouse managers to turn a profit during the first half of the eighteenth century. Because laws frequently barred theatrical establishments throughout Protestant America, itinerant troupes were by far the most viable form of drama available. They frequently performed wherever possible, most often at county fairs. Music was largely a local affair. Williamsburg seems the earliest city to successfully sponsor some form of theatrical entertainment in 1716. Charleston and New York followed during the 1730s, and by the 1740s, Boston had patronized the stage. Boston also established a dancing school and amateur ensemble of musicians. Small theatres like Southwark Theatre, Philadelphia, or similar versions in Charleston and New York were built by patrons during the 1760s and the 1770s. Philadelphians even converted an old warehouse into a theatre in 1749. By the 1760s, public musical venues were within the reach of subscribing connoisseurs in almost every major town, including Philadelphia, New York, Boston and Charleston. Their memberships included private clubs which met in taverns and coffeehouses throughout the city, at once linking performances with critical review and pleasurable discourse. Also, by the mid-1760s, many of the high-steepled Anglican and Congregational churches were fitted with music galleries and included violin, flute and clarinet accompanists. Larger, more decorative theatres arrived in Philadelphia, New York and Boston in the last decade of the eighteenth century, such as the Chestnut Street Theatre of Philadelphia in 1794.[37] Pleasure-seekers in tavern and coffeehouse clubs and assemblies ushered in a transformation of public life which finally brought lasting performing arts establishments to American cities.

The eighteenth-century transatlantic economy transformed American public spaces as well as private lives in the city in accord with the new spirit of consumption and refinement. Good town houses reckoned at £4,000 with all the fashionable trimmings sprang up during the mid-eighteenth century. While only twenty-six houses in Philadelphia were worth over £2,000, a number of lesser townhouses dotted the city landscape, like the Stamper-Blackwell House (valued at £1,600) and Bishop White House (valued at £1,500). Philadelphia's richest families, including the Allens, Dickinsons, Hamiltons, Logans, Norrises and Tilghmans, could afford a liberal education and sent their young men on the Grand Tour of Europe. Although these men went primarily for the intellectual climate of the courts of Europe, most were drawn into the pleasurable experience of travel for its own sake and considered it the greatest asset in their education. Samuel Power said on his tour, 'Your two friends have been lolling in the lap of ease. Italia, nurse of the softer arts, has detained them from mixing with the turbulent throng. The pleasures and entertainments she affords have rendered our time most pleasing.'[38] From the vantage point of these elites, 'trifling' with the public pleasures of life was the primary reason for emulating consumer habits.

Colonial Americans attempted to moderate both public leisure and private consumption in accord with English taste. As Americans bought British consumer goods and followed British news outlets, American economic growth soon overtook even that of the mother country.[39] British booksellers dominated the market in the colonies with novels, *belles-lettres* and courtesy manuals. The annual average shipment of British books in the colonies rose from 345 hundred weights between 1739 and 1748 to 1,137 hundred weights between 1764 and 1774. P. J. Marshall comments, 'Culturally the British Atlantic was also becoming one world ... The Colonial American taste for British luxury goods had become discerning and demanding.'[40] Much of the discernment rested in the Enlightenment philosophy of consumer refinement espoused in British books. By pursuing a cosmopolitan approach to pleasure, Americans became consciously English in manners and tastes. British workshops evolved to meet the transatlantic nature of consumer demand and colonial elites fashioned for themselves a lifestyle of imported goods; sugar from the West Indies, tea from Asia, English furniture, silver knives and fine silks. Since the only real distinctions between genteel and common in America were absence of manual labour, a liberal education and wealthy professions, ladies and gentlemen carefully cultivated a genteel style in manners, politeness in speech and taste in acquiring possessions. Although gentility only amounted to 20 per cent of the American population at large, America was more socially mobile than Europe and gentility was an attitude rather than a hereditary custom. Ladies and gentlemen achieved respectability only when they mastered the fine art of displaying genteel learning in their possessions and public manners.[41]

Thus, by the time public and private pleasures were available in America during the mid-eighteenth century, urbanites with means had refined the discourse of consumer goods and sought a mode of politeness which moderated and civilized new pleasures. Since liberal education was not native to the aristocracy in America, they often gained it through a study of contemporary English journalistic commentary. Episcopalian minister William Smith explained that the English school of the new college of Philadelphia required an extensive reading of 'Spectators, Ramblers, &c. for the improvement of style and knowledge of life'.[42] This, of course, was shorthand for the great editorial projects of London's coffeehouse 'wits': Swift, Addison, Steele, Fielding, Goldsmith and so on. These public letters were considered the contemporary equivalent of Ovid and Pliny, because in the coffeehouse, men studied the public manners of man as they once had in the Roman forum. Marshal argues that although colonial Americans followed the parliamentary debates between Court and Country, most often Americans interpreted the British constitution through the lens of Whig commentators, such as William Blackstone's *Commentaries on the Laws of England*. Because Whig commentators like Steele and Addison hosted their editorial projects in London coffeehouses, they left an enduring impression of moderated discussion on the minds of colonial American readers, who could only visit London coffeehouses through the imaginations of London's essayists. Colonial elites like Nicholas Ridgely of Dover, Delaware, read *The Spectator* essays alongside *The Young Man's Companion*. Both were moral commentaries of the manners of men. Until Lord Chesterfield's *Letters* were publicly available in the colonies in 1774, *Tatler* and *Spectator* were London's definitive statements on contemporary English manners. They were widely read alongside Francis Hawkins's English translation of the French work *Youth's Behavior, or Decency in Conversation among Men* and America's own *The School of Good Manners* (1715) by Eleazar Moody, a Boston schoolmaster.[43]

It was this social atmosphere of polite learning which the colonial gazettes and American coffeehouse readers attempted to emulate. As Breen has argued, colonial newspapers realized a Lockean vision of contractual society, where enterprising citizens of any rank possessed the natural rights to improve their public station through individual choice. The Scottish Enlightenment had previously embraced the consumer revolution as a 'revolution in manners' and an exercise in civility. While

Americans possessed a proclivity to emphasize the egalitarian aspects of political identity in their consumer choices, colonial elites still clung to the importance of civility in public association.[44] American burgeoning society was perhaps more Addisonian than Lockean. Public consumption of hot liquids marked the beginnings of a social age in the minds of most Americans. An article in the *New York Gazette* in 1736 titled 'A Speculation of the late wonderful Discoveries, and Improvements, of Arts and Sciences' proclaimed that before the age of trade, 'Coffee and Tea (those modern Blessings of Mankind) had then never been heard of.'[45] Coffeehouses and their news culture were one of many venues which by the mid-eighteenth century assumed the validity of certain sociological categories of urban behaviour set forth in the London society journals and gentlemen's magazines. With a view then for London's public pleasures and not merely a private consumer sphere did colonial Americans emulate Anglicized tastes.

However, in London and America, 'trifling' was a two-edged sword and reckless pleasure-seeking was often the downfall of gazetting literature. We hear of 'the Huzzaers, where to Huzzah; the Plotters, where to Consult; the Men of Pleasure, where to Treat their debonnair Misses'.[46] Coffeehouse authors required a polite environment within which to act as an impartial observer of human behaviour, and the reality of all too many coffeehouses was enough to sour the reputation of even the most revered critics. Thus, in *Rambler No. 10*, Samuel Johnson desperately attempted to defend his social column from the popular objection that his commentary was nothing more than a frivolous narrative of gaiety and amusement. Johnson pointed to the rise of English manners as a justification and contrasted the 'impertinences of a trifling age ... the weakness of minds softened by perpetual amusements' with 'the manners of the age ... even the genius of an Addison'. Johnson, like many American writers, was sceptical of the supposed success of Addison's efforts to reform manners according to taste and good judgement.[47] The tension which existed between the 'trifling ... amusements' and Addisonian manners ran through the transatlantic discourse of Anglo coffeehouses. It is one of the surest proofs that Americans were connected to a larger British Atlantic culture.

Colonial gazettes were universally worried about pleasure. Readers knew all too well that theirs was a world of public pleasures, and any attempt to civilize them was reactionary rather than pre-emptive. The polite remedy may not prove a realistic goal. 'Varsety is the Life of Man', stated one moralist in the *Virginia Gazette* in 1739 with the pseudonym *Socrates*, 'they have more Pleasure by the Return of Business and Leisure, than by constant and perpetual Leisure. Those who have no Employ, but are forc'd to saunter from Coffee-House to Coffee-House, and trudge from one Amusement to another, that they may get rid of their troublesome selves.'[48] Idle pleasure was always painful. *Socrates* continued, 'They carry about aching Hearts under clean Linnen, a well Powder'd Wig, and a seeming easy, carless Genteel Look: 'tis unnatural, and therefore will be always Painful. Thus have we laid before you the Necessity of Business in order Health, Virtue and Pleasure.'[49] Colonial gazettes feared, just as London journalists had, that the apparent gaiety of the age was so often a cover-up for existential despair and boredom. Enjoying the city in a whimsical manner lay at the heart of this new sociability and came with a host of difficulties.

Steele and Addison's essays had attempted to rationalize amusement, to articulate an English cultural solution to the problem of pleasure. The city's refinements transformed men into new refined beings, they argued. Urban leisure invented the 'man of pleasure' as a sociological category. Such is evident from the twelfth issue of the *Tatler*, where Steele wrote, 'I hope I shall soon have little more to do in this Work, than to Publish what is sent me from such as have Leisure and Capacity for giving Delight, and being pleas'd in an elegant Manner.'[50] Scholars agree that Steele and Addison initiated a periodical education programme to reform society but differ as to its rationale. Michael G. Ketchan and Jon Klancher reinforce the narrative of politeness, considering the *Tatler* a 'colonizing mission'. G. J. Barker-Benfield sees a gender divide in the journal, taking note of the running discussion of women and sensibility in Steele and Addison's rhetoric. Stephen Copley argues that the central focus of their journals was to exercise control in a new age of trade with less fixed social hierarchy, what he calls 'consumer sovereignty'.[51] In particular, Copley brings to bear one powerful issue from *Spectator*: No. 93, which argued that empty time will inevitably be filled with amusement. Steele and Addison wrote, 'If we divide the Life of most Men into twenty Parts, we shall find that at least nineteen of them are mere Gaps and Chasms, which are neither filled with pleasure nor Business.'[52] Men of action should either fill up their time by cultivating 'Social Virtues' in 'Intercourse and Conversation' and, retiring from public company, converse 'with the great Author of his Being', or find 'Conversation of a well chosen Friend ... useful Amusements ... a Taste of Music, Painting, or Architecture.'[53] As these diversions could only be found in the public life of the city, amusement and social life featured as the two ingredients in reforming manners. Copley argues that the end result of the *Spectator* was to construct a linguistic framework for masculine, free and polite conversation in public and domestic settings, which he describes as a 'semi-public clubbable conversation in the coffee house ... deployed to offer women limited and vicarious participation as observers of the circle of male conversants'.[54]

Yet most of the implications of pleasure in Steele and Addison have remained unexplored by scholarship primarily concerned with conversation and trade. It is easy to miss that pleasure and conversation took place in new urban environments and this was not lost on the eighteenth-century imagination. *Tatler* No. 15 speaks of a play preformed at Will's Coffeehouse where 'pleasure is less understood in this age, which so much pretends to it, than in any since the creation'.[55] To uneasy society journalists like Steele, pleasure had corrupted rational conversation, even as it opened up new opportunities for discussion. Washington Irving would later write, 'There is more of dissipation and less of enjoyment. Pleasure has expanded into a broader and shallower stream, and has forsaken many of those deep and quite channels where it flowed sweetly through the calm bosom of domestic life.'[56] With much of the same sort of nostalgia for pre-modern times, Steele reflected in No. 15, 'In old times, we used to sit upon a play here after it was acted; but now the entertainment is turned another way.'[57] Men of pleasure often dissipated themselves with an inundation of activity rather than moderate themselves. Steele continued, 'The happiness of him who is called a Man of Pleasure ... I found myself not a little disappointed in my notion of the pleasures which attend a voluptuary, who has shaken off the restraints of reason ... That perfect inaction of the higher powers prevented appetite in prompting him to sensual gratification.'[58] Thus, the *Tatler* speaks of a snuff merchant and seller of fashionable canes and eyeglasses with a useless 'genius for bawbles'.[59] Everywhere were artificial people who 'crowd the streets, coffee-houses, feasts, and public tables' who imitate rather than converse and street musicians fit with only 'modern inventions of the bladder and string, tongs and key, marrow-bone and clever'.[60] The city was an orchestra of sham delights. Perhaps this is why Steele recommends a more experiential form of preaching in the Church of England to counter gratification with spiritual affections, or 'a decisive air ... without hesitation ... Thus, the force of action is such, that it is more prevalent, even when improper, than all the reason and argument in the world without it.'[61] The main alteration in sociability was the force of action, or a change in the pace of life which should be reflected in the pace of conversation. Wit and ingenuity had to be sharper in this new age of action.

For Addison and Steele, the city itself provided solutions to excess. It moulded humanity. Steele redefined the 'man of pleasure' as a man of wit, and it was this central proposition which eventually set the eighteenth-century imagination apart. Steele was very familiar with the fact that urban experience had birthed new sociological categories, such as 'a Gentleman, a Pretty Fellow, a Toast, a Coquet, a Critic, a Wit, and all other appellations of those now in the gayer world'.[62] These sociological categories were attributes which men on the town acquired through experience, but Steele was not satisfied to take urban characteristics at face value. Instead, he used them as frameworks within which to communicate politeness and good breading. Steele wrote,

> The most necessary talent therefore in a man of conversation, which is what we ordinarily intend by a fine gentleman, is a good judgement ... he acts with great ease and freedom among the men of pleasure, and acquits himself with skill and despatch among the men of business ... with so cheerful a spirit, that his conversation is a continual feast, at which he helps some, and is helped by others.[63]

Steele redefined the gentlemen as a man of conversation: an urbanite, with innocent deftness in argument. The gentlemen was to be at ease with both pleasure and business, help his fellow men and know their essential characters. In the *Tatler*, good judgement was altruistic and sociable. It involved a peculiar flavour of 'town politeness' which experientially assessed, rather than passively watched, the sociable aspects of town life.[64] Accordingly, the sorts of advertisements that appear in *Tatler* were intended to encourage good taste and sociability, including tickets to plays sold at White's Chocolate-house, St James's Coffeehouse and Young Man's Coffeehouse and a dancing school at Nando's Coffeehouse, both considered polite amusements.[65] These activities were meant to mould the social character of the men of the town. As Addison said, 'Our Modern celebrated Clubs are founded upon Eating and Drinking, which are Points wherein most Men agree, and in which the Learned and Illiterate, the Dull and the Airy, the philosopher and the Buffoon, can all of them bear a Part.'[66]

Steele and Addison served transatlantic frequenters of coffeehouses in the mid- to late eighteenth century with a guidebook to the pleasures of urban life. American cities intentionally patterned their social clubs after Addisonian values. Among the colonial elites in Annapolis, the coffeehouse served as a ballroom for the governor's social circle and clubhouses for the Homony Club.[67] Much like its London counterpart the Kit-Cat Club, the Homony Club celebrated both pleasure and good judgement. A contemporary description of the club ran, 'meeting to promote the ends of Society, and to furnish a rational amusement for the length of one Winter evening in a week, There did meet at the Coffee house in the said City'.[68] David Shields argues that the Homony Club furthered a cultivated epicurean view that 'appetite governed human action' and relates it to the Beefsteak Society and the Cheshire Cheese Club in England. If so, then it was still governed by the Addisonian rules of reason. Dr Alexander Hamilton, secretary of the highest social circle in Annapolis, the Tuesday Club, laughed away the charge that his club might be overly epicurean, assuming that gentlemen knew how to cultivate civility among themselves. The Society for Promoting Virtue and Knowledge, by a Free Conversation in Newport, Rhode Island, parallels the Tuesday Club.[69] Among coffee's transatlantic customers, two examples stand above the rest for their desire to acquire cultivated pleasures, William Byrd of Virginia and Benjamin Franklin of Philadelphia. Byrd often supped at London's famous coffeehouses and brought back a vision for the Tidewater elites. Accordingly, Williamsburg arose in the 1730s as a gentrified city, with dancing masters, wigmakers and theatres.[70] Franklin was inundated with London life as early as 1724 when he wrote, 'I was pretty diligent; but spent with Ralph a good deal of my Earnings in going to Plays and other Places of Amusement.'[71] Learning the hard way, Franklin would write an Addisonian tract of his own *A Dissertation on Liberty and Necessity, Pleasure and Pain* and would set up a regular address in various London coffeehouses from the 1750s to the 1770s from which he orchestrated a news circuit in Philadelphia and other colonial cities.

American news mimicked Addison and Steele's moralizing style and were primarily focused on reforming public manners. Above all, these prints reinforced the idea that sincerity in conversation was the chief virtue in society. It was the chief moderating influence of pleasurable pursuits. Always, the gazettes were on their guards for incivility in public life. One moralist in the *Maryland Gazette* argued, 'The Foolish Vain Man will be apt to fancy that his Deity takes Pleasure in what he finds himself to be most delighted with. He is ravished with flattery and fawning addresses.'[72] This author featured a regular column which addressed subjects like discerning truth from doubt, the evils of superstitions, atheism, enthusiasm, the proper development of painting and poetry, and instructions for keeping the 'fair sex' from 'useless triflers'.[73] Nowhere was this moral anxiety more keenly felt than in New England, where a disestablished Protestantism warned against the evils of materialism. A long-standing Puritan morality which feared excess extended well into the eighteenth century. The Puritan was always on his guard against sin in his enjoyments and wished to free pleasure from excess. John Cotton had stated, 'Life is not life, if it be overwhelmed with discouragements ... wine it [is] to be drunken with a cheerful heart.' He attacked 'gluttony and drunkenness ... swaggering and debauched ruffians' for spoiling the true enjoyment of Christian liberty.[74] Increasingly Mather proposed a moderating and rational influence over pleasure, stating, 'The Scriptures commend unto Christians, gravity and sobriety in their carriage at all times; and condemn all levity.' This he said in reference to the 'regular madness' of mixed dancing, which he considered entirely forbidden in the Bible.[75]

Bruce Daniels argues that this ambivalence for pleasure continued into the eighteenth century with the publication of the only book in colonial New England devoted entirely to the subject, *The Government and Improvement of Mirth, According to the Laws of Christianity, in three Sermons* (1707). Its author, Benjamin Coleman, proposed the notion of 'sober mirth' to avoid the sin of excess. In 1726, twenty-two ministers from the larger Boston area published a tract entitled *A Serious Address to Those Who Unnecessarily Frequent the Tavern*, which argued for a rational and Godly alertness when drinking publicly. Gambling, cards and billiards were banned across New England and a social predisposition to oust such from the public sphere lasted well beyond the loosening of sumptuary laws in the eighteenth century.[76] Public amusement was difficult to justify for the very reason that it was a collective rather than individual experience. In curtailing such activities and assigning limits to pleasurable experiences, New England encouraged a rational approach to public leisure which preceded Addison and Steele's compromise with leisurely institutions.

Nor did this fervour for a well-mannered public sphere end with the advent of the Revolutionary War. If anything, colonial authorities and the press desired to elevate the manners of popular support for the revolution. A writer named 'Cathegrus' in the *Virginia Gazette* considered that the oppressive taxes of Great Britain were encouraged by the deep-seated American passion of luxuries and warned that there was 'little ground of hope for any present redress, unless from our own prudence and virtue'.[77] Connecticut army chaplain Samuel Wales made much the same argument in 1785 when he declared that Americans in embracing luxury would inevitably threaten their civic virtue. Said Wales of the empire of Rome, 'By adopting the luxuries of Asia where her arms proved victorious, she soon enfeebled her true republican spirit and prepared the way for her own ruin.'[78] In Wales's criticism of luxury loomed the menace of Oriental lifestyles, exemplified in the early modern world by tea and coffee, which would eventually bring the cultivated industry of the American republic to its knees. The General Court of Massachusetts was determined not to let that happen. It issued a proclamation in the *Boston Gazette* in February 1776 stating, 'It is the duty of all ranks, to promote the means of education, for the rising generation, as well as sure religion, purity of manners, and integrity of life, among all orders and degrees ... That piety and virtue, which alone can secure the freedom of any people.'[79] Even as Americans nationalized their public sphere, gazette moralists, ministers and colonial authorities continued to insist on an Addisonian view of public conversation and leisure.

Conclusion

In British North America, urbanites of colonial cities constructed a parallel form of London entertainment to further the social context for civic development and transatlantic discourse. Coffeehouse proprietors desired to participate in a new urban way of life which emulated London society. It was more than emulation; it was an experiment in transatlantic exchange and economic empire. Coffeehouse proprietors and American merchants mirrored London's social spaces in the hopes of participating in an emerging public sphere centred on London. In such a project, London finances and politics would become colonial issues and colonial investments would become London interests. Behind this endeavour, colonial American consumers believed they were transforming their world into the image of London's middling and freer community; they were in essence declaring what it meant to be British. The Exchange coffeehouses, which connected colonial cities with London finances, ships and private correspondence, became the basis for a new commercial British society in Atlantic cities. Both Boston and Philadelphia had a 'London Coffeehouse', Philadelphia and New York had a 'Merchants Coffeehouse', Boston and New York had an 'Exchange Coffeehouse', New York had a Vauxhall Gardens and Boston had a 'British Coffeehouse'. Southern cities like Annapolis, Williamsburg, Fredericksburg, Norfolk and others went out of their way to establish coffee as a conversational culture. These cities usually had one dominant coffeehouse resort which catered to a polite elite and offered special lodgings and rooms for the 'entertainment' of company.

The consumer ethos of the Anglo Atlantic world was never confined to private expressions of taste but rather embraced a public dimension with conversation at its centre. Thus, coffee functioned as a discursive grammar to the rules of public life and economic empire and was negotiated in various localities after a form of conversational sociability found in London. Boston and Philadelphia brought literacy and Protestant theology into its coffeehouse culture. New York constructed an outdoor culture of business recreation to its consumption of coffee in leisure gardens. The South encouraged companionship in incorporating good lodgings and personal entertainment into its coffeehouses. Throughout British cities, the culture of coffee officiated the terms of 'conspicuous society', just as tea represented 'conspicuous consumption'.

Not all succeeded in navigating the chaotic gaming world of the coffeehouse. Coffee's disorder and violence is the subject of the next chapter. It will go back in time to coffee's beginnings in English society. Coffee was a dangerous drink. It bred crime underworlds. It dismantled pre-existing hierarchies in English urban life and replaced them with often unstable social relationships which were forged around risky business deals. It encouraged a masculine culture of quarrelling, duelling and gambling, which both shut women out and hemmed them in as servers and officiators of public hospitality. Coffeehouse murders became so common that well after the dawn of the eighteenth century, they circulated in both the London and colonial American gazettes. These issues were not only debated in pamphlets, they were confronted by three distinct interest groups in coffeehouse life: naval officers who used the coffeehouse postal network to negotiate rank and issue orders across the Atlantic; many women proprietors who felt personally at risk in a violent male coffeehouse world; and the lobbyists who worked with proprietors to establish sound credit and customs procedures for the coffee and tea trades. These three groups worked independently during the first half of the eighteenth century to establish a polite middling public of merchants and civil servants invested in the emerging economic empire of the Atlantic world.

3

Murders, officers and naval headquarters

Sometime between eight and nine o'clock at night, Mrs James Joyce was startled by a terrific clamour proceeding from below in the common room of her coffeehouse, the Garter, Suffolk Street, London. It sounded like angry shouting and one voice was obviously Scottish. Running downstairs with her maid, she discovered a broken and bloody sword tip. One gentleman stumbled out of the doorway to pursue a group of fleeing men in the street who had just thrust him through with a sword. Mrs Joyce's maid ran after the wounded man and brought him safely upstairs, where she tended his wounds and heard his story. His name was Mr Chauviau and he told the legal Examiners on 29 March 1685 that he would follow up his testimony in person to Lord Dumbarton, a prominent general soon to become commander of the Scottish armed forces.[1] Mrs Joyce had retired upstairs for the evening and had left a company of five men downstairs, or in the words of her inquest, 'a Gentleman of my Lord Thosauror of Scotland railed Mr. Harralt & 3. other persons with him and two strangers, who of one was in a red Coat & the other in a Crown'.[2] To Mrs Joyce, the affair involved men, or more specifically soldiers, and a heated coffeehouse discussion. She actually remembered how much hot liquid they consumed that evening: 'There were some wroth persons … having drank foure dishes of Tea'.[3] At this early period in London coffeehouse life, drinking hot liquid of any kind in public, whether tea or coffee, always carried with it the possible danger of inciting men to violent and uncongenial behaviour. It was not at all a given that boiling liquid was the safest drink for dispassionate conversation, and Mrs Joyce must have wondered what kind of concoction drove these gentlemen to sporadic, excessive male aggression. Was keeping a coffeehouse safe?

The whole affair represented the interests of one specific set of coffeehouse customers: the officers and their soldiers, at a time when the Royal Navy was gaining strength in the Atlantic. From the Admiralty Coffeehouse, the Sword Blade, Jerusalem and Will's, officers of the army and the navy came to utilize the coffeehouse post, sending letters to junior officers, contract agents and ship captains and managing an emerging Atlantic empire. Unquestioning respect for authority and a sociability of deference were foundations to this system of command, but officers of the Crown were very often met with violence and crime in the coffeehouses. Lord Dunbarton instinctively recognized the disgrace that this quarrel, involving a gentlemen of the Lord Treasurer of Scotland and an unnamed redcoat, posed to his own military class. Those who took the king's shilling were to give unquestioned deference to higher ranking officers and to all peers of the realm. Doing so was a matter of duty and honour. Furthermore, if a soldier got out of line, his senior officer was responsible for him. Officers were gentlemen of a very definite sort: having a social hierarchy and modes of polite address all their own. This chain of command and the drama of failing to meet its obligations played out in the coffeehouses.

The chief difficulty in the situation lay in the increasing mobility of the army and navy and what to do with soldiers when they were on leave. Officers were entrusted with their men in a manner similar to that of a lord of a manor over a serf. Lords had once had boundaries of the manner to confine their serfs, but armies were always on the march. Inns, taverns and coffeehouses served a vital need to the military in quartering and victualling troops.

> It was upon an afternoon,
> Sir Johnie march'd to Preston town;
> He says, 'my lads come lean you down,
> And we'll fight the boys in the morning.'[4]

Thus, officers regularly mixed with local riff-raff in the inns and reserved public places for their own uses, setting up private posts at coffeehouses, organizing officer's clubs and hosting public social events for their regiments. But did proprietors have any rights when it came to quartering troops? Did they have a legitimate say in how these soldiers behaved? Certainly they did, as Mrs Joyce's inquest proved. Most often though, affairs of honour were settled between persons and without the interference of law. The proprietors learned that trusting politeness to the gentry's notion of honour often protracted the very outbursts of violence that it claimed to restrain.

This side of coffee was of particular interest in colonial America, where a distrust of the army and a concern for the rights of middling proprietors reigned. Americans read with a peculiar mix of horror and excitement stories of London coffeehouse murders reprinted for them in their gazettes.[5] These stories kept them up to date with the more unpleasant aspects of emulating British metropolitan society. As they saw it, such violence threatened the free association upon which 'conspicuous society' depended. What transatlantic travellers wanted to see in the coffeehouse was a place of business leisure with an emerging systemization of commercial interests, marine insurers and shipowners. However, coffeehouses freely allowed customers from all walks of life: everyone who could afford a few pennies for a dish of coffee. No coffeehouse was safe from criminals, thugs and unsavoury soldiers. And when the stories ran out, Americans had no difficulty in exaggerating stories of their own. When British regulars began to patrol colonial cities during the tax crisis, and after the 'bloody massacre' in Boston on the night of 5 March 1770, John Hancock stated in his published oration, 'Our streets nightly resounded with the noise of their riot and debauchery; our peaceful citizens were hourly exposed to shameful insults, and often felt the effects of their violence and outrage … Hence, impious oaths and blasphemies so often tortur'd your unaccustomed ear.'[6] In the end, it mattered little to these colonists whether the actual incident that night was a trumped-up story; what mattered was that the corruption to their city had already taken place. They had a proprietary right to a free and voluntary public sphere, and it was being violated by the Quartering Acts.

When viewed in transatlantic perspective, several patterns in male coffeehouse social behaviour come to light. Firstly, both Londoners and Anglo-Americans knew better than to see coffeehouses as safe spaces. They were far from the benign sanctuaries of placid and refined republicanism with such undesirables. Politeness and gentility notwithstanding, coffeehouses brought with them crime. Many were places of extreme violence and impolite social behaviour which incommoded middling customers and officers alike. What historians today consider passive and benign coffee social intercourse, a contemporary would have considered quite dangerous. There was a disturbance in the very air of pleasure. Even under the most polite of circumstances, a gentleman coffeehouse customer might turn to his friend and say, 'Let me alone for that: Come Will. quick, quick! your Coat and Apron; take you my Vest, Hat, Perriwig and Sword.'[7] The implements of male politeness were also the implements of personal strife. A coffeehouse discussion often ending with 'He throws a Dish of Coffee in his face, and so they fight ... Coff. Mr. and Servants thrusts' em all out of doors ... they are nuizances to sober company in as high a degree, as they are scandalous to true Gallantry.'[8] Although caricatures, these scenes depict a world of coffee more dangerous than history remembers.

Secondly, coffeehouse conversation was inevitably the result of masculine notions of pleasure, fair play and honour. Even for polite members of the officer class, coffeehouse discourse was bound up in the new transatlantic urban experience of 'trifling'. Military officers attempted to articulate a polite style of sociability in their clubs and correspondence, but their recreations were extremely volatile. Nowhere was this more the case than at the card table, where the stakes represented not just a person's credit and good name but also their honour and rank. Games of chance often ended in affairs of honour.[9] Politeness did not necessarily discourage violent male encounters; it only added a protocol for honourable murder and often intensified the risks of personal conflicts. Furthermore, duelling never entirely replaced other more rancorous forms of personal assault because often officers played at cards and had other social dealings with more middling coffeehouse customers. If they did not personally associate with the lower sorts in the coffeehouses, the men under their command certainly did. Coffeehouse brawls persisted even though duelling was preferred among the officers.[10] Even coffeehouse proprietors were ruthlessly murdered in these brutal quarrels between coffeehouse customers.

Thirdly, the presence of the state in many of the empire's coffeehouses increased both the scope of violence and its effects. As the state began a violent campaign to root out its many enemies in the coffeehouses, it channelled male notions of honour among the officer class into a language of service to the state.[11] During the eighteenth century, the navy realized that in order to maintain its transatlantic influence more effectively, it must issue orders, receive commissions and offer promotions through the coffeehouse postal service. Very quickly, coffeehouses like Will's, the Jamaica and many others were home to a military hierarchy of command, which frowned on frivolous quarrels over honour and expected a respectful order to male interaction. The navy attempted to moderate violent encounters in coffeehouses, because they hindered the organization of maritime supplies and also tainted the honour of aspiring officers. Despite the navy's best efforts, coffeehouses remained infested with thug gangs and became meeting places for the enemies of the state.[12] Indeed, the law was primarily interested in the Joyce case because of its possible connections to the Rye House Plot. During the Jacobite rebellions, coffeehouses were hideouts for secret subversive societies, and a counter-campaign of rooting them out was conducted in coffeehouses by loyal informants. Espionage and revolution convulsed London's coffeehouse life. In times of war, coffeehouses were full of spies, making it dangerous to voice state secrets. When a man entered a coffeehouse, he was taking his life into his own hands, not knowing what or whom he should meet there and whether or not he would be forced to defend his personal honour or the honour of his country.

The public sphere: Polite or violent?

What might an officer expect to find when he asked his fellow, 'Conduct me to mine host?'[13] A broadside in 1691 entitled *Murther Upon Murther* pointed out the dreadful situation in which coffeehouse and alehouse proprietors found themselves. With the advent of coffee culture in London came a world of sudden and senseless murder. The remainder of the broadside's title summarized the sordid tale: *Being a Full and True Relation of a Horrid and Bloody Murther, Committed Upon the Bodies of Mrs. Sarah Hodges, Wife of Mr. Thamas Hodges, Mrs. Elizabeth Smith and Hannah Williams, the Loyal Coffee-House near Well-Gose at the end of East-Smith-field*. The Loyal Coffeehouse was evidently an ale house and a place of lodgings, for when an ale woman came to the house at about twelve noon on 7 January, she expected to find the house full of talkative boarders. She mysteriously found no one stirring. The downstairs room was in a disorderly state and no fire had been lit. She called out if all was well, but no one answered. A throng of neighbours, wanting to see what had happened, pushed their way through a few front rooms, and there, in the back bedchamber lay the body of Sarah Hodge. She had suffered a blow to the neck. In another room, they found a lodger named Elizabeth Smith dead in her bed with several blows to the head. The house maid lay beside her, with a wound across the throat. The murderers had evidently made off with a gold necklace, rings and earrings, and had plundered the house.[14] Here was a very devastating raid on a coffeehouse.

Americans read many similar accounts of violent London life and coffee disasters. The *New York Gazette* of 11 July 1726 told of a midnight affair in which a rogue told the hackney coachman of a lady's carriage to stand and deliver. The hackney rounded the corner of King Street, Goldsquare and rushed on at full speed through Westminster. As it did so, the highwayman discharged a round through the shutters of Lane's coffeehouse. The coach got through and, presumably, the ball sunk harmlessly into the opposite wall of the coffeehouse.[15] In another equally illustrative episode, a bank forger, William Hall, was seized at a coffeehouse and was committed to Newgate for forging a £6,400 note.[16] American readers were left speechless. How could such crimes so easily escape the law? This was the sort of lurid crime literature of the metropolis which would become so popular with British and American readers nearly one hundred and fifty years later. Coffeehouse crimes crossed geopolitical boundaries and united kindred peoples with an eager interest in London social life. Nor was coffee safer on the high seas. Stories of coffee frequently being lost at sea or damaged were everyday business affairs for American merchants reading the gazettes. Americans studied very carefully the tactics of London merchants who did not hesitate to burn in protest thirty-eight chests of damaged tea and five chests of damaged coffee in the presence of many customs officers and East India Company officials.[17] Coffee was known all over the empire for being a dangerous and risky urban product.

It was this sort of raucousness which in a caricatured account of Johnathan's Coffeehouse provoked one ruffian merchant at the bar to exclaim, 'I have heard of English Bedlam before, but never could believe there could be so many people all together quite mad.'[18] The caricature of Jonathan's continued, 'Jonathan's Coffee-house never afforded one theme ... But as Scandal is the grossest, and most savage appetite, and the opposite to true taste, we may easily imagine, what Connoisseurs the public is composed of, that they can so greedily devour the very offals of obscenity.'[19] As connoisseurship coincided with emerging outlets for pleasure and greed, coffee culture often ran counter to civility and taste. Why then did so many officers and other gentlemen view the coffeehouse as the ideal place for conversation? Nowhere else did male friendship and gaming or some other pleasure meet with an atmosphere completely devoted to male conviviality. Gentlemen of every stripe felt at home in a world which had no safety net other than mutual trust and personal honour. Francis Flight, a 'specularist' in London in the 1760s, had the more favourable experience of this sort of companionship. He related, 'My friend met me in the coffee-room, all spirits, shook me by the hand, said I was the honestest fellow in England, seated me in the box close to the window, threw up the sash.'[20] This quality of fraternal fellowship men of the age is called 'sociality', or the companionship of good fellows engaged in pleasant conversation.[21] Good spirits and honest companionship were the highest aspirations of gentlemen visiting the coffeehouse, but very often they met with disaster.

Nowhere were the 'offals of obscenity' more plainly seen than in the coffeehouse gaming culture sponsored by the officers. Although violence threatened the language of deference which held the martial hierarchy together, officers often protracted the violence in coffeehouses and personally defended their honour at the cost of social order. Card games were popular among officers for the very reason that they discriminated between men of lesser and greater status. The masculine connotations behind enforcing the boundaries of social space are what is particularly striking about frequent outbreaks of violence at the card table. Unfortunately, scholarship has placed more emphasis on political motivations of violence in coffeehouses, from Jacobites to Jacobins, but social friction was far more often the cause for violence in a coffeehouse.[22] Unlike balls, where gentry freely mixed in a fluid company, card games were meant to be private. Lord Mark Ker, a gambling gentleman in a London coffeehouse, certainly thought so. *The Aberdeen Magazine* printed Lord Mark Ker's incident as an example of manners typical during the Duke of Marlborough's wars. In other words, it was representative of Addison's London. Mark Ker was busy at the card table when an unwanted stranger decided to pester him and his partner with questions. Mark Ker responded by throwing the dice in order to choose which one would duel the unwanted stranger. When Mark Ker's partner won the toss, Mark Ker replied, 'You have been always more fortunate in life than me.'[23] Such an answer indicates that there was gentlemanly honour involved in maintaining the boundaries of social space between strangers in coffeehouses.

Coffeehouse men usually wished to find some form of genteel amusement from the coffeehouse, whether it took on high-life or low-life manifestations, and they guarded that pursuit ferociously. At St James's, Steele was accosted by a few well-dressed men who took offence at the social criticism in one of the *Tatler's* first issues and threatened to correct his manners by ending his ability to speak forever. Among the company of accusers were Lord Forbes and some other high-ranking officers, who obviously believed that the *Tatler* threatened the elite male order in the army. The coffeehouse was almost exclusively a male environment, as coffeehouse card tables proved. Some coffeehouses were wholly given over to gambling, like the Greyhound Coffee House in London, with its billiards table. Women would have played little part in such games. Others like Mary-le-Bone Gardens Coffee House catered to the high life and the more elegant social world of the gentry. It was furnished with a lavish ballroom which, as one observer described, 'was illuminated in an elegant manner with colored lamps: at one end of it women attended selling orgeat, lemondae, and other cooling liquors. This was intended as a representation of the English Coffee-house at Paris.'[24] But this was the exception to the rule; a coffeehouse in a pleasure garden was different from a coffeehouse in Covent Garden. Generally, London's coffeehouses were less successful than French salons at integrating women into the public sphere, since the social dangers involved particularly concerned male notions of honour. Frequent affairs of honour and 'loose women' such as at the Rose Coffee House, would have offended the social graces of many respectable middling and elite ladies.[25]

The unequal social status among men and women in coffeehouses is further evidenced by the practice of eligible bachelors posting announcements for suitable ladies. One advertisement in the *Daily Advertiser* in 1777 ran, 'a Lady, between 18 and 25 ... good Education ... Fortune not less than 5000 l ... Five Feet Four Inches without her Shoes; not fat, nor yet too lean; a clear Skin ... not very talkative, nor one that is deemed a Scold ... not over fond of Dress ... direct for Y.Z. at the Baptist's Head Coffee-House.'[26] Complexion, smarts and silence were this person's ideal, and ladies fitting the description were simply expected to 'direct' for the job, very much like domestic service. The coffeehouse in this sense was a mere way station: a brief rendezvous between interviewer and interviewee. It was clear that the coffee room served as the public office of this male inquirer's many varied business affairs, and seeking a wife was one of the many business issues which occupied coffeehouse men. Similar advertisements ran on behalf of gentlemen in King Street Coffee House, Somerset House and Will's Coffee House. One male solicitor described the application in gambling terms as an extension of his passion for games of chance.[27] How many suitable young ladies answered such advertisements is unknown. What is clear is that men, not women, were conducting the coffeehouse interviews. Women simply applied for the job, if they ever saw clear of the danger of such an application.

That the pleasurable world of 'polite' London, or anywhere else, for that matter involved such dangerous encounters between men and women has not been duly recognized by historians. In fact, the dangers of eighteenth-century urbanization have been obscured by a very useful, but also limiting form of analysis, known as public sphere theory. Politeness was a very real idiom of the long eighteenth century and was the language of the urban arena. Its extent, however, may be questioned. As important as politeness is to interpreting public conversation in the eighteenth century, John and Linda Pelzer notice that many contemporaries believed coffeehouses rarely lived up to expectations. The public sphere was a two-sided concept, where the crowd functioned as either a rational voice or a chaotic mob. Both Jonathan Swift and Richard Steele noted that the great literary conversation once had at Will's Coffeehouse when John Dryden, Samuel Pepys and Alexander Pope debated *Paradise Lost* and classical epic poetry had very much declined after the days of Dryden. The great patriarchs were scattered and their leader dead. Card tables replaced the literary discourse of a seeming bygone age, and gaming brought in a very different audience. Pelzer and Pelzer assert that the solution to changing coffeehouse clientele was the formation of formal clubs among the literary elites. They argue that coffeehouses were overrun with thieves, rakes, highwaymen, sharpers and quacks.[28] The journal of club and coffeehouse satirist Edward Ward in 1700 bears this out:

> There was a rabble going hither and thither, reminding me of a swarm of rats in a ruinous cheese-store. Some came, others went; some were scribbling, others were talking; some were drinking (coffee), some smoking, and some arguing; the whole place stank of tobacco like the cabin of a barge. On the corner of a long table, close by the armchair, was lying a Bible. Beside it were earthenware pitchers [along] clay pipes, a little fire on the hearth, and over it the huge coffee-pot. Beneath a small book-shelf, on which were bottles, cups, and an advertisement for the beautifier to improve the complexion, was hanging a parliamentary ordinance against drinking and the use of bad language. The walls were decorated with gilt frames, much as a smithy is decorated with horseshoes. In the frames were arities; phials of a yellowish elixir, favorite pills and hair-tonics, packets of snuff, tooth-power made of coffee-grounds, caramels and cough lozenges ... Had not my friend told me that he had brought me to a coffee-house, I would have regarded the place as the big booth of a cheap-jack.[29]

In a world where a Bible and a complexion advertiser lay together and nameless faces bought tonics and coffee-ground toothpaste from countless quacks, atrocities such as the murders at the Loyal Coffeehouse were part of the risks of the trade. Certain coffeehouses attempted to rise above the din of the crowd, but were often entangled in the larger world of coffee crowds for no other reason than the doors of a coffeehouse were always open to all. 'Even in the city's most respectable coffee-houses, the lawless were present,'[30] state Pelzer and Pelzer. Coffeehouse proprietors and customers alike were never really safe.

The public sphere was a sphere of pleasure seekers, and violence was its downside. Although crimes were abundant in coffeehouses, the most frequent form of violent conflicts in coffeehouses was interpersonal conflict rather than outright mob violence. Edward Ward specially took note of this in his satirical poem *The School of Politicks*

(1698). Conversants were heated both by arguments and by coffee, almost synonymous in Ward's portrayal, and conflict erupted between individuals locked in personal conversation.[31] One gentleman called out, 'At present – Pox this Coffee scalds my Throat.'[32] The gentlemen burned themselves on the coffee, disagreed over their tastes in wine and beer, and resorted to their swords as the final arbiter. Said one gentleman to another, 'Your Sword and mine shall be at mortal odds ... I'll make't High Treason for my Friends to taste it.'[33] Ward provided a unique insight into the tension between intense conversation and hot drink. Name-calling set gentlemen to reach for their swords, but sometimes finding them not there, they transformed their drinks from heated arguments into literal weapons. Ward described the transition from duel to brawl thus:

> You wear no Sword, I see, and 'twould be base
> To draw upon a naked Man,
> But here's my Dish of Coffee in your Face.
> T'other, though scalded, would not be
> Behind hand with him in Civility,
> But flung a Glass of Mum so pat.
> It spoild both Perriwig and Point Cravat:
> On this a Quarrel soon began,
> Till Constable, with pacifying Staff,
> Appeas'd the Fray, and the Contenders have
> Some respite, one his Face to cure,
> And t'other to refresh his Garniture.[34]

The gentlemanly argument descended into a food fight. Periwig and cravat were tarnished by the 'civility' of defending one's honour, as affairs of honour spoiled the very carriage of a gentleman. Ward was actually asking a profound question amid the humorous spontaneity of conflict; when did a duel with words or swords become an embarrassing brawl? Was there any respectability at all in duelling, either in word or deed? Certainly, it would have been a disgrace to have a coffee-man break up the fight. Ward reversed the imagery of arguing and duelling to demonstrate that men were blinded by passion rather than bound together by moderated discourse. Or, as he himself concluded, 'which vainly foolish, and unthinking I have spent in what we falsely call Good Company'.[35] By this he meant distinctly male company. In the coffeehouse, the duel and the brawl were perhaps closer than most gentlemen realized.

Nowhere was duelling and brawling more similar than at the gambling tables and parlours of coffeehouses in London and in British North America. The reality was not far off from Ward's satirical representation. Defending social space often became complicated and ugly, as Colonel Walker's experience in an undesignated American coffeehouse reveals. On a cold winter's night, Walker, an officer in America, carelessly left his cane in one chair and his gloves on another chair and hoped they would be in the same place when he returned. An officer came in and drew up one of the chairs close to the fire. When Walker returned to find one of his chairs missing, he declared 'that his dignity and himself were insulted'.[36] The officer replied, 'Sir, if you say another word on the subject, I'll throw you behind the fire.'[37] Walker decided that his life was worth more than his honour and backed down. Evidently, American coffeehouses were sometimes no safer than London coffeehouses.

The incident reveals the delicate and explosive nature of protocols for public conversation in the eighteenth century. There were limits to how far individuals could intrude on each other, even in a coffeehouse, and these limits were maintained by force on both sides of the Atlantic. Colonel Walker and the aforementioned Lord Mark Ker, a gambling gentleman in London, had remarkably similar and disturbing experiences in protecting their persons. Coffeehouses were not free-for-all. They often exploded into violence when gentlemen, and particularly men of the officer class, believed their personal spaces had been violated. The coffeehouse was a very unpredictable and risky place, but guarded by male honour. Until the advent of the Royal Navy, this notion of honour was unofficial and based exclusively on breeding rather than merit.

The rise of the navy and the art of self-deprecation

Officers were not merely concerned about quartering and victualling their own men. They also hoped to transform the coffeehouse from a chaotic and violent institution into a safe place for purchasing supplies and issuing orders. Violence hampered a dependable transatlantic shipping network which was simultaneously arising with coffee culture. 'Trifling' only got in the way of the navy's need to extend naval information across the coffeehouses of the empire.[38] Yet, masculinity and coffeehouse conflicts were also *negotiated* within a transatlantic system of communication. By providing a definite hierarchy of merit, the Royal Navy institutionalized male sociability and gendered coffeehouse public space as no other social force in the coffeehouses. Naval correspondence posted from coffeehouses did much to shape a masculine form of British discourse in London coffeehouses. Although this gendered discourse of male honour was at the heart of much of the interpersonal violence in coffeehouses, the navy successfully avoided male conflict by incorporating coffee's transatlantic connections into a system of command.[39]

Naval command offered promotions on the basis of sound references, respect for senior officers and an impeccable record of service. Here, the coffeehouses were ideal. They were connected to the major shipping contracts of the British Atlantic world. They even provided a postal network. This was noticeable to Samuel Pepys, who used the commercial connections and postal service of coffeehouses in the 1660s to negotiate supply contracts, rendezvous with his superiors in the Navy Office and transfer his duties as 'Clerk of the Acts' to the Naval Board.[40] By the eighteenth century, coffeehouses served as naval headquarters for ordering ship supplies, reporting on naval engagements, issuing orders and requesting transfers or promotions of rank.[41] The success or failure of a naval supply contract often depended upon personal coffeehouse connections. Officers assembled transatlantic resources from all over the world in light of credible contacts in London coffeehouses. As naval activity increased in the eighteenth century, naval command established bureaucratic associations of coffeehouse clientele which relied on the coffeehouse postal services to review performance at sea and to process requests of transfer. Officers seeking promotion were expected to adopt an unassuming and self-deprecating salutary style. Behind these requests was the insistence of personal honour and rank, resulting from longtime service to the British state abroad. Officers most successful at gaining patronage or recognition from superior officers mastered this martial language of respect and self-deprecation.[42] Soon enough, naval customers of coffee had created a hierarchical community of men with their own linguistic codes of honour and recommendation. This was quite independent of the linguistic reforms of Shaftesbury and Chesterfield but followed the same sorts of rules. Inside London's coffeehouses, a fellowship of imperially minded officers emerged, which recognized merit according to masculine virtues of bravery, duty and service. Together, they tried to make safer the shipping routes of empire and also articulated a masculine pattern for British coffeehouse sociability for an entire century.

The navy solicited human resources directly from coffeehouses and such solicitations often depended upon third-party references. Here again, a language of sociability emerged in the coffeehouse post, a language with a grammar of masculine virtues. In 1783, Mr Brodie, of Chapter Coffee House, St Paul's, requested employment as a navy surgeon in the following manner:

Sir

I had the honor some time age of being recommended to you by the Noble Mr. Wemyss and very lately by Mr. Campbell.

Although I am sensible that there are Surgeons older than myself at present employed yet I am led to hope than when you know I have had the *Cutter* searched twelve months and consider that my Expenses for Instruments … you will be pleased to think of employing me again.

I am fortunate in not being appointed a surgeon to a ship till upwards of two years … I must think it still more unfortunate when after having carried in her in the worst Sea all last winter & just myself to a great Expense, now to loose her, more especially as others who have been in Ships only twelve months are told they are to be continued for three years.

I hoped to have been equally fortunate and relying on the Recommendation I have had to you and on your Virtue and Candour I still hope tho' I understand the *Cutter* is given away to have no cause to complain or to Wish myself exempted from the general Rule.

I have the honor to be with Esteem

Sir

Your obedient humble servant.[43]

Brodie's request depended upon three aspects: personal recommendations, losses at sea and availability. He hoped that his references and familiarity with a particular ship would be more important to his prospective employer than seniority. He believed his hardships at sea a rite of passage for future employment. Still, he was not at all sure that his employer would agree. He appealed to a mutual sense of courage and camaraderie, 'Virtue and Candour'. All hardened seamen knew how rough and unpredictable voyages might be. Courage was Brodie's recommending virtue. Ultimately, however, it was in the hands of the officers. This coffeehouse exchange was one of many similar solicitations for surgeons. When the captain of the *Defiance* found himself without a ship's surgeon in 1778, he wrote from Will's Coffeehouse, asking his superior officer for a warrant to appoint a recommended surgeon Mr Stuart to his ship. Stuart was already serving aboard the store-ship *Dromedary*, so the request involved a transfer.[44] Once contracted, these surgeons were very much at the mercy of their superior officers. They were on call even while off duty in the coffeehouse. David Ramsay Karr, surgeon of Portsmouth Yard, had to gain official permission to extend his leave of absence at Will's Coffeehouse, while in town on private business.[45] The chain of command among naval officers imposed a form of social etiquette in the coffeehouses dependent upon personal male relationships. Referrals, requests of leave, transfers and warrants were all ingredients of the sociable language of naval contractors in the coffeehouses.

Merit in the navy often depended on patronage within the naval coffeehouses of London. Allan Auld, a navy assignee to the shipwright Joseph Charnock Port Royal, Jamaica, even had to request from the 'Honorable Commissioners' something as elementary as his pay. Considering his pay a gentleman's agreement, Auld's begged, 'the favor of an Order for his monthly money to be paid me at Deptford'.[46] Although his pay for service in the navy was an obligatory part of his assignment in Jamaica, Auld chose not to exhaust the good pleasure of his superiors, because he knew that the continuance of his position was at the mercy of the officers. In a sense, the conditions for employment depended upon a simultaneous, transregional affiliation in both London and Jamaica. Writing from the Sword Blade Coffee House in 1772, Auld was maintaining a transatlantic career through the London coffeehouse post. The merit of his post depended upon both his performance as an assignee in the New World and his London high command. The coffeehouse was the transatlantic link between them. Transatlantic correspondence was a prerequisite to naval service in the colonies, and in the navy, only those who revealed their dependence on superior officers continued their good standing.

Rather than self-reliance, masculinity in the Royal Navy was expressed through dependence upon one's reception among superiors. In naval coffeehouses, officers refined a British linguistic art form of recommending themselves by self-deprecation and politeness. Mr Brodie exercised this unique mode of communication in the passage above with calculated phrases like, 'I *hoped* to have been equally fortunate and relying on the Recommendation' and 'I still *hope* … to have no cause to complain or to Wish myself exempted from the general Rule.'[47] In so doing, they revealed a respect for higher officers, knowing that promotion of rank was only achieved by pleasing social superiors and honouring their standards for law and order within the navy. Like contractual agreements, naval performance reviews were based on a sociable language of mutual respect and a gentleman's agreement to the codes of male honour. In an exceptional example of heroic self-deprecating style, Marine Captain David Johnstone asked his superior officer if he might gain permission to get his wound examined at a surgeon's hall. Although in great need of medical attention, Captain Johnstone chose to downplay his heroism and stated with extraordinary reserve, 'I am now to request the favor of you to refer my Letter of the 10th to them, or to give such other direction thereon as you may Judge proper; I have the honor to be with great Respect.'[48] As if the burden of asking his superior's favour was of more consequence than his own condition, Captain Johnstone maintained his dignity in not showing haste or emotion in asking for a response from higher command.

Masculine honour was very dependent upon the emerging realization of global time and its implications for a hierarchy of command. The navy depended upon the news, time schedules and social circles of merchants in London coffeehouses to supply the colonies with naval commissions. Merchants and naval officers assembled a transatlantic understanding of time and materials through a coffeehouse chain of command. William Morland, purveyor, solicited the aid of Commander Isaac Drake, headed for Genoa and Leghorn aboard the *Duck*, Commander Joseph Shank aboard the Westmorland galley and Commander John Sharock aboard the Tuscany galley in 1733 to carry naval stores to Gibraltar and Portmahon. Morland had to organize his local time schedule around a prearranged London schedule. As no ship was actually bound for the ports in need of provisions, he explained, 'The following masers have promis'd to wait on your honors: at the time appointed.'[49] Morland balanced the convenience of his superiors and the availability of ships. If syncopating naval supplies for the highly interconnected Mediterranean world was difficult, resupplying American colonial bases often waited for months at a time. Morland believed his best opportunity of finding the soonest ship bound for Virginia was among the transatlantic merchants of the Virginia Coffeehouse. He explained to his superiors, 'I cannot find any Ships going to Virginia; and am told at the Virginia Coffey House, that there will not be any ready to proceed on that Voyage for a month or two.'[50] In like manner, W. Boswell, after touring the maritime coffeehouses and the merchant shipwrights' yards, called a meeting to assemble a fleet of volunteer transports. This meeting was a coffeehouse-style discussion on how best to collectively manage transatlantic supply on a large scale. Among those who attended the meeting in 1733 were Captain Edward Smith, master of a twenty-four-gun Jamaican frigate. Two other notables were to arrive from another coffeehouse: 'Mr. Godman will likewise come on account of Sir John Thomson and himself, for two ships, but I presume they are from Buttons, if they will do.'[51] The hope was that Sir John Thomson's coffeehouse circle of captain friends at Buttons would translate into real naval supply for colonial stations. These scheduled coffeehouse meetings determined the navy's ability to extend their material presence throughout the colonies. Arranging such matters involved synchronizing world time with London time. Thus, the navy developed a transatlantic consciousness of time which took into account colonial material and communication routes. Sociable officers in the coffeehouses of London measured the success and reliability of nautical performance on the high seas.

There was great risk in disregarding martial manners and personal procedures in the navy. Much like corporate audits today, the navy took status reports as an opportunity for performance review. Negligent officers were liable, even to the law, for mishandling property in their trust. Cementing and maintaining trust relationships by frequent and respectful updates saved many a captain from public disgrace. Runaways did not fare so well. Captain J. Vaughan sent the following report from Wills' Coffeehouse on 27 March 1749: 'Inclosed are two Ticketts belonging to two men who were turn'd over from His Majesty's armed vessel the *York* onboard His Majesty's Ship *Solebay* then under my Command but Run away from Her which I beg you will please to own the Record of. I am with great Respect.'[52] These runaways were marked men and Captain Vaughan might have been held responsible since they were under his charge. An apology was normally in order. Alexander Macpherson of Will's Coffeehouse gave a typical apology for not keeping his service records in the East Indies up to usual standards, stating, 'I am affray'd they are not kept in the Regular Method usual to his Majesty's Service, However, as I have used all my Endeavors for that Purpose, I hope they prove to the satisfaction of the Noble Board.'[53] The Navy Board was especially keen to investigate losses at sea. In one instance, purveyor John Bowyer proposed an investigation by the Board into why no remuneration for damages done to a timber supply were offered by the owners of the holding barges. Those responsible for the lost property held meetings at a local coffeehouse.[54]

In London, Thomas Taylor, proprietor of Lloyd's Coffeehouse, incorporated his coffeehouse into naval intelligence by becoming an official auditor of performance review. Taylor reported in 1790 that 'Capt. Dowsland of the ship *Betsey* arrived yesterday in the River from Petersburg had 11 days passage says that 11 Russian Men of War with their yards & Fapmaits struck were safe up at Reval for the Winter'.[55] Coffeehouse audits of performance review had very real impact on the reputations of officers serving throughout the empire. If officers showed initiative, honesty and polite humility they might find their superiors favourably disposed to their service and forgiving of the mistakes which inevitably arose from a world of global communication dependent upon ships of sail. The coffeehouses were particularly helpful in this regard, because like no other institution, they offered a gendered environment in which men could freely communicate about their honour.

The state's futile struggle for control of the coffeehouse public sphere

Despite the linguistic changes in coffeehouse sociability throughout the eighteenth century as a result of the military's increased presence, the state never gained control of the coffeehouse public sphere. The state could not even root out its many enemies and its very presence protracted violent encounters. The government had good reason to fear public opinion. Henry Ball with the Letter Office kept close watch over the letters and false rumours which sailors spread in coffeehouses in relation to the king's unpopular pro-French policy in 1673. The secretary of state moved to establish spy rings to watch for sedition, but in Yarmouth, nonconformists actually used the law against the government's intelligencer William Bower, closing down his coffeehouse in 1667 for spying on the free people of England.⁵⁶ Once the military set up in coffeehouses, it would be forever at war with coffeehouse frequenters who operated outside of the law. And taverns and coffeehouses were certainly syndicates of sedition. Paul Monod argues that Jacobites erected a network of disaffected taverns and coffeehouses in London as early as the 1690s. This network utilized pre-existing Roman Catholic taverns, but also included newer coffeehouses or secret coffee sellers. Original Bromfield was closed down by the government in 1690 but sold coffee in his home to Jacobite informants. In the 1714 rebellion, mainline Tory coffeehouses hosted Jacobite clients. Even Jonathan Swift's old haunt, Ozinda's Coffeehouse, was involved in the plot. By 1723, recruiters for the 'Pretender' used dozens of taverns in London, Westminster, and provincial towns like Chester and Stafford. In preparation of the 1745 rebellion, eleven public houses were identified by a London spy as Jacobite. Hamilton's Coffeehouse and Patrick Hoare's at Charing Cross harboured Jacobites fleeing from France. Mrs Leslie's Coffeehouse was the centre of much Jacobite correspondence. Jacobite agent William Fuller was nabbed in Cheapside at the Half-Moon tavern. Although the Cocoa Tree Club and the Honorable Board of Loyal Brotherhood were clubs for Tory Londoners and not specifically Jacobite, they contained Jacobites.⁵⁷ Yet the fact that these activities did not greatly implicate the large mercantile coffeehouses or the renowned literary houses suggests that Jacobites believed the lesser coffeehouses would allow them sufficient access to London news without the certainty of being discovered.

James Butler, the Duke of Ormond, lodged at Burton's Coffeehouse near St James's and organized a Jacobite smuggling ring during the 1720s. In 21 May 1722, Charles Quitwell [Quittwell] and a Jacobite merchant by the name of Cane received several barrels of wine through a chain of middlemen, and discussed selling bonds for the construction of a warehouse. Quitwell's greatest achievement was sending the Pretender's declarations via the French post on to key recipients in the coffeehouses. Baker employed Mr Jamison as an under-agent to receive letters at Burton's and presumably cover his tracks. The syndicate also included Mr Sanford at the British Coffeehouse near Charing Cross and Anthony Sanders at Will's Coffeehouse. Quitwell, although successful at his wine shipments, failed to secure funds to vital Swedish partners in a 'Madagascar Company'.⁵⁸ This chain reveals that sedition even touched the more well-known coffeehouses, but involved great care for secrecy. The correspondence reveals one very important aspect about subversive activity in coffeehouses: it had to conform to certain social rules of correspondence in order to be considered a benign business exchange. Some correspondents referred to the closure of mail in certain areas because of the likelihood of a plot against the government.⁵⁹ They knew they were being watched.

In one Jacobite exchange between Francis Sempill and Mr Sempill of Clair's Coffeehouse involving coded names, the writers replicated relational coffeehouse discussion. Francis Sempill wrote, 'Several attempts have been made to gain the Gentleman you mentioned in your last but none can succeed while his Brother lives. The great Intimacy you remark between Mr. Hill and Woodbe's father is remarkable; is it impossible to penetrate into the origin of it by Something more authentic than our Conjectures?'⁶⁰ In the Sempill exchange, Standwell stood for James Francis Edward

Stuart, Thomas for the Ministry, Bernard for Parliament, Stafford for the Duke of Argyll and Mr Houlder for the Duke of Ormond. The use of names for even political associations allowed the Sempills to transform sedition into a sociable narrative of familial honour and duties, clumsy though it was.

Thus, one passage ran almost like a private household letter among family relations:

> I doubt not but your many private Conferences between Hill, Smoothways & others tend to Thompson's overthrow … my Father may let Standwell know the Danger of a Change in the Managers, for I thing 'tis plain that if Stafford be preferred as well as Walker his affections and his views will be very different from what they are at this time.[61]

There was a sort of civility to this language of treason. Alexander Gordon wrote to James Johnson at Will's from Boulogue in exactly the same style: 'had a visit from a Gentleman … he was very much out of humor that you had not call'd for him, and seem'd to blame your going the way you went very much'.[62] A Jacobite letter sent to a Paris banker regarding credit sent to Will's read, 'I am very glad to hear that all Friends are well and extremely obliged to them for their friendly concern which I shall always endeavour to deserve, the Letter of Credit you mention is a favor that I could not reasonably expect or hope for, and will come safe either to Mr. Wilkins at Will's Coffee House Convent Gardens.'[63] And so on it ran. Jacobites imitated sociable conversation to throw the government and coffeehouse spies off their trail.

Thus, the government coffeehouse ring only had very limited success in protracting a war against violent insurrectionists. Yet, the state took a proactive role in coffeehouse social life. Wills' Coffeehouse and the Jamaica Coffeehouse featured prominently in naval command and both accommodated the state's attempt to root out its enemies. Troopships headed for Jamaica were organized from the Jamaica Coffeehouse. In this coffeehouse, James Potts offered his 330 ton ship *Louisa* to the navy in 1787 to transport troops and stores to the West Indies.[64] From Will's, Captain Philip Durell requested that the *Richard* and the *Thomas Tender* be attached to the *Eltham*, serving in the English Channel, and so strengthen the naval watch on Jacobite pirates and spies going to France in 1744. 'I beg you would give the necessary orders,' Captain Durell asked of high command.[65] Will's was a centre of activity during the Jacobite Rising of 1744–5. The navy had a strong presence at Will's probably after having discovered prominent Jacobite captains in the 1720s, like Captain Kelly who had connections in Paris and the support of Lord Lansdowne at home. Finding and reporting on prisoners in London coffeehouses was not uncommon. E. Carleton wrote to Captain Leeves at the Tennis Court Coffeehouse in Whitehall, informing him in 1746 of a list of rebel prisoners and an assessment of the strength of their guard. In this affair, Captain John Moorey, master of the Willing Wind Sloop, testified against the shipowner Ibbotson for convincing him to bring two gentlemen and the ship-owner's servant to Boulogne, presumably on criminal business. Ibbotson and the two gentlemen were imprisoned at Hastings.[66] Thus, coffeehouse naval correspondence was at the heart of not only securing a transatlantic chain of command but also removing internal threats to the state.

Will's Coffeehouse in Scotland Yard also became a centre for assessing a war with France from 1744 to 1746, in which orders, news and status reports depended upon the interpersonal relationships forged through naval coffeehouse networks. Two years after Captain Durell requested aid to the *Eltham*, the *Eltham* was operating in British North America to protect against the French Catholic invasion of the Eastern seaboard. The Admiralty kept an account of ships' records and their general musters through a coffeehouse postal exchange in London. Junior officers, like Captain Calmady at Will's Coffeehouse, were personally responsible for keeping track of lost ships. In the campaign against the French fortress of Louisbourg, the *Eltham* carried a record of the general muster, slop books and monthly books from the foundered ship *Weymouth* and brought them to London by order of Captain Calmady. In April 1746, Captain John Calmady wrote from Will's Coffeehouse and assured the Navy Board that his records were 'complete to the time of the Ship's being lost, and have satisfied the Lords of the Admiralty to that purpose'. However, his duties in finding a clerk were still unclear, and he thought it prudent to add, 'If you do not think proper to make them out at your Office, I will endeavour to hire a proper Person to make them out.'[67] Processing such information required finding trustworthy people in an information network, possibly among the coffeehouse milieu, and certainly included getting permission from high command through the coffeehouse post. In May, Calmady received the *Eltham's* records of the *Weymouth* and sent them on to the Admiralty Office along with a certificate of the activities of the *Weymouth's* company after the ship's loss and their recovering its furniture and provisions.[68] Calmady's reputation and rank depended upon how thorough his coffeehouse information was. Calmady's records of the *Weymouth* demonstrate the interconnectedness of the Admiralty and colonial naval officers through the coffeehouses of London.

Increasingly, the military complex endued transatlantic coffeehouse discourse with male notions of loyalty and merit. The state's presence encouraged a new channel for male chivalry inside coffeehouses. Ultimately, honour rested in service to the state. Such was the case with Major John Pigot who believed that his many long years of service spent in uncomfortable conditions had earned him some recognition. He defended his self-worth by the fact that he had for so many years set it aside. Now, Pigot demanded the rights of a gentlemen of state. Writing from the prestigious Parliament Street Coffeehouse in Westminster in 1793, Major Pigot explained,

> I did myself the Honor to write to you, some time ago, in ... of a letter which I received from Lord Grenville, wherein he retired me to you, as I have never had the honor of an answer to my letter, I should be happy to know if I have any favor to expect, in consequence of the exertions which I made for Government, and the many disagreeable situations in which I was involved on that accounts, Lord Grenville engaged me to undertake an employment ... as a most degrading, for a gentleman, but with pleasure I undertook, my thing that I conceived could render a service to the King and government, at that critical period.[69]

Although he hoped for a favourable reply, Major Pigot did not presume to demand veteran's pay, and yet he hinted at his right to it. He put himself at the leisure of his superiors and from a posture of servitude asked, not demanded, a just recognition for his service. Manly endurance in the service of the state was the true mark of a gentleman. Long suffering had been Major Pigot's virtue in life, as he saw it, and any gentleman might expect at least an answer to his inquiries as to veteran's pay.

Indeed, Pigot was referring to a previous gentleman's exchange between him and Lord Grenville about his identifying disaffected persons after his service in the 80th Regiment. Pigot asked for formal employment in the service and to be put on full captain's pay. The year before, he had exposed an 'underhand business' of Frenchmen who were hiding out in the suburbs. Pigot ran in the finest coffeehouse circles and kept a close eye on political affairs in Westminster and London. He commented on the rejection of Thomas Paine's revolutionary ideas among prominent brokers of the Stock Exchange and believed that the tobacconist Freybourg was 'incendiary' for holding the view that it was unconstitutional to suspend *Habeas Corpus* in times of war. Pigot also knew the standing reputations of the leaders of party debate and referred to a loss of popularity in Charles James Fox among the people of Westminster.[70] Thus, Pigot not only advanced his personal status through military service but worked hard to cement his reputation of loyalty to the state by engaging in political discussion in the coffeehouse social sphere of Westminster. The fact that he was on speaking terms with Lord Grenville was proof enough, but it may not have been sufficient to secure for him a permanent place in the army.

The safest course for respectable coffeehouse proprietors and notable coffee customers was to become an arm of the law. In some cases, the army directly set up at a coffeehouse to supervise recruiting procedures at the grassroots level. Such was the case with Lieutenant William Nedham in 1793, who posted a formal request from the York Coffeehouse to the undersecretary Evan Nepean, requesting earliest notice if any regiments were to be raised, since he desired to inform their commanding officers. Similarly, Captain J. Hollwell of the Prince of Wales established a rendezvous from Will's Coffeehouse to raise seamen in 1770.[71] In other cases, coffeehouse proprietors and informants worked informally to root out plots. David Lloyd, proprietor of Lloyd's, informed the government in March 1719 of a rumour he heard from his neighbour that arms were secretly being stored at the alehouse in Mint Street, Southwark. This must have been a double win for Lloyd: a discovery of armed treason in the making and the vindication of a large financial coffeehouse's reputation over a seedy alehouse.[72] Yet, Lloyd's had already had a reputation for overseeing justice. In 1703, one of Lloyd's customers exposed a certain Gipson, who had tricked many merchants at the Exchange to allow him to illegally negotiate an exchange of fifty prisoners between Holland and France. In the 1790s, Thomas Taylor, master of Lloyd's, took this a step further and became a naval correspondent for the government.[73] It was in Taylor's best interest to do so, for in 1792, an anonymous memorandum identified a filigree worker at the *Blue Posts*, some hairdressers and a shoemaker at the *Lion and Goat*, and one Randall at Garraway's, orator and formerly a writer for *Parker's General Advisor*, all engaged in seditious acts.[74] Sedition was a very real aspect of coffeehouse social life and proprietors had to go out of their way to root them out. The military could never fully expel traitors from the coffeehouse public sphere. Violence and instability in coffeehouse discussion continued throughout the eighteenth century.

Conclusion

Officers unsuccessfully confronted violence in coffeehouses and left it a much more violent place. The boundaries of social space in coffeehouses, as in the army and navy, were bound up in pre-existing concerns for male honour, especially among elites. Officers hoped to navigate London's new social world with honour and politeness and use the coffeehouses as places to organize the empire, but their sense of superiority and their masculinity often ended in impolite and violent behaviour. Officers participated in the gaming culture of coffeehouses with the same ferocity which average merchants did. New urban amusements intensified, rather than contracted, the possibilities for misunderstanding and threatened the delicate maritime infrastructure which had constructed the coffeehouse public sphere and upon which the navy depended for supplies. Coffeehouses were volatile places for pleasure seekers, where the misplacing of a glove or a false word at the gambling table could mean a death threat. Coffeehouse owners were often killed by soldiers and criminals or else dragged into the disputes of their customers. Policing social space was mostly in the hands of the individual male patrons.

Male violence was widespread in the coffeehouses and would have minimized gender mixing among London's more informal houses to the lower classes. Those establishments associated with other social venues, like operas and concerts in the public gardens, enjoyed marginal success with civil relations between genders, but their range was limited due to their decentralization and proximity to 'loose' living in a commercial society. Coffeehouses like Jonathan's and the Rose were downright scandalous. But it was not just the establishments in disrepute which signalled danger to the average visitor, male or female. Even those institutions like St James's and Will's which were the paragons of the printed language of civility were often hotbeds for personal and ideological conflict, as male writers and fighters defended their honour intellectually or physically. Of course, male congeniality was the main objective, whether it was manifested at the card table, over billiards or in a ring of social critics. Male frequenters of coffeehouses staked their personal territory in a coffee-room and advertised for business and even marriage partners in the press. There were levels and conditions to polite masculine behaviour in the coffeehouse.

The navy did much to harness this unique sense of male honour in coffeehouses and reshaped coffeehouse discourse by offering rewards to servants of the state. Coffeehouses served as headquarters for the navy where sociable exchanges of resources, men and commissions were daily features. The colonial project of harvesting American lumber for shipbuilding and getting masts and sails up to standard involved a review process through the coffeehouse post. In coffeehouses like Will's and Jamaica, officers orchestrated a command structure based on merit and supervised colonial naval supply stations. Yet, unlike the very dense network of British naval support through the narrow Straights of Gibraltar, news from the Atlantic was often months apart. Distance across so unpredictable a sea led to uncertainty among captains and their officers as to who was personally responsible for naval inventories. The navy required that a meticulous ship's record of slop books and monthly books be turned in to naval officers through the coffeehouse postal service. Still, the process of review was highly personal and any captain suddenly held financially responsible for losses at sea might also be considered disloyal, inept or negligent. Captains often justified their own actions as loyal, brave or reasonable under conditions of uncertainty.

Justifying one's rank or actions was a delicate balance. Captains made sure not to convey disrespect to their officers by adopting self-deprecating suggestions of worth or personal intimacy. Thus, requests like 'I beg leave', 'I hope to have your favor', 'the favor of an Order' or 'I have the honor to be respectfully' were standard modes of address among officers in the coffeehouses of London. These forms implied masculine notions of honour, candour, deference and, most importantly, rank. Officers learned to report everything and get as much granted permission as possible for every commission, lest they be held solely responsible for any mishaps on the way. It was this very overfamiliar language of fawning and self-deprecation which Steele set out to root out of everyday usage in *Tatler* No. 78, where he asserted that 'with great truth and esteem my humble servant' was better rendered 'am with great respect'.[75] Nevertheless, both captains and naval superiors daily reinforced this deprecating habit through constant correspondence and social networking in coffeehouses. The navy grew accustomed not only to reviewing ships and supplies but also certifying wounds and punishing runaways. Naval review in coffeehouses grew into a massive human resources department, judging performance on the basis of masculinity and service to the state. As this developed, captains and naval seamen exposed their persons and reputations to the constant judgement of their superiors. Coffeehouses were places where social hierarchy was a very real force.

Part II

Polishing communities and negotiating empire

4

Coffee-women, licensure and a polite public sphere

Coffeehouse scholarship generally acknowledges a transition from coffee's exotic and uncertain origins to its civic importance and its connection with polite society. Brian Cowan has called it 'civilizing the coffeehouse'. This turn roughly parallels the history of the latter Stuarts, the 1688 Revolution and the subsequent rise of constitutional monarchy, free discourse and the 'rage of party' during the late seventeenth and early eighteenth centuries.[1] Cowan, Pincus and Klein have argued that the evolution of 'civility' began with Restoration-era anxieties to find a rational control over public conversation. This civilizing ethos intensified during the post-Revolutionary era, the result of club rules and discourse among the coffeehouse *virtuosity*. John Barrel has argued that the definitive feature of British coffeehouse life was politics and news.[2] Through the eighteenth century, political coffeehouse clubs grew in importance and by the second half of the century, the term 'coffee-house politicians' signified the shared association of men in the coffeehouse public sphere.[3] Both Klein and Pincus similarly place coffeehouse life within a middling urban world of news, polite connoisseurs, clubs and worldly conversation. The resonance left behind by the politicization of coffee was indelibly marked in the minds of most political journals of the era. There was an aspiration towards public influence among many of the so-called coffeehouse 'wits', and their discourse was keenly felt by readers who often read of stylized caricatures of them in political satires. Coffeehouses were naturally suited to free political discourse, since they were only governed by the classical notions of taste and refinement.[4] Copley attempts to diversify the political narrative of coffee with the inclusion of commercialization but adopts Steele and Addison's definition for politeness. Berry contrasts this sort of politeness with Moll King's *impolite* coffeehouse.[5] That coffeehouse life in the eighteenth century involved politeness and politics seems incontrovertible, and although the Whigs never fully controlled coffeehouse discourse, Addison and Steele somehow diffused a language of manners throughout coffeehouse literature which gave the illusion of Whig consensus.[6]

Behind such an approach remains the assumption, not fully realized within our rendering of coffeehouses, that licenced coffee dealers agreed with the implementation of club politics and politeness. They somehow mysteriously evolved with the clubbable aspect of coffeehouse life in the eighteenth century. The mysterious agency of coffeehouse owners on both sides of the Atlantic requires closer examination. Having established coffee's propensity to institutionalize pleasure as a new category within British urban life and its intensification of the violent aspects of leisure and association, we now must turn to the varied social responses which propelled coffee into public life.

Coffeehouse proprietors in London felt the influence which coffeehouse merchants had in encouraging a consumer culture across the Atlantic and tried their best to ease their customers into a cosmopolitan world of free enterprise. This inevitably involved negotiating the terms of economic empire across the Atlantic. Coffee did not take a monolithic path towards acculturation. Rather, the effort to reform the coffeehouses represents the struggles of both coffee suppliers and consumers to rationalize and enhance its social use. Only a few of the coffeehouses of London gained financial stability and social respectability by incorporating both the financial and political news of investors into their houses. Thus, the reputation for politeness only came to rest upon certain coffeehouses after they had gained the support of enterprising British elites involved in Atlantic trade, governance and journalism. Owners with transatlantic customers and financial elites replaced violence in their coffeehouses with the new consumer ethos of taste. These houses appealed to an increasingly urban middling public, embedding their idiom of politeness into the eighteenth-century public sphere and simultaneously laying the foundations for an Enlightened understanding for the British Atlantic system of exchange which exonerated the right of association. If Georgian Britain was considered an 'empire of goods', then those coffeehouses with transatlantic connections negotiated the meaning of Anglicization.[7]

Proprietors transformed coffeehouses into safer places for urban elites first by rearranging the spatial dimensions of coffeehouses to cater to the private discussions of transatlantic financial investors and second by carefully cultivating polite discussion and newsprint. This in turn encouraged the rise of clubs during Queen Anne's time and beyond.[8] The risks of coffee were most immediately felt by coffeehouse proprietors, who carried the full financial responsibility of presenting coffee to the public. Therefore, it is to them that primary agency for implementing politeness into the coffeehouse public sphere belongs. They were politeness's final arbiters, even if they were not its source. Coffeehouse owners chose to accept the idiom of polite news culture because they desired to climb the social ladder of sociability and construct a middling public sphere at a time when merchants were increasingly participating in the material cultures of taste. Politeness seemed the most advantageous way of purging their houses of crime and disorder and appealed to all those who could afford some measure of aristocratic taste. As coffeehouse proprietors had to pay for damages caused by public raucousness (both financially and morally), it follows that they would be prompt in orchestrating social protocols within their houses. Their reforming efforts simultaneously saved 'conspicuous society' throughout the Anglo coffeehouse world from violence and prepared the way for a political print culture which would allow transatlantic travellers of aristocratic or middling means to construct 'remote neighborhoods' of friends who read their local news while abroad. Attracting transatlantic investors also strengthened their bargaining power with the government in obtaining more reliable routes to the coffee trade. Especially in America, coffeehouse proprietors were at the end of a long chain of credit and unreliable supply of coffee. Therefore, they had every incentive to join hands with lobbyists and journalists in creating an imperial idiom of coffee as a polite drink.[9]

Because hospitality was largely understood as predominantly a feminine virtue by both Protestant morality and Enlightenment sociability (where sensibility and love were increasingly playing a role in epistolary culture), women were central to the development of middling coffeehouse publics in the eighteenth century. They were the second group to take on the violence of coffeehouse life and were among the first to actually succeed in implanting a polite public in the coffeehouses. Yet, as many coffeehouses were run by women who were largely excluded from coffeehouse conversation, the attempt to reveal female agency in enforcing standards of behaviour is riddled with questions. Historians of coffeehouses are very much divided on the exact roles of women, if any, in the coffeehouses of London.[10] Colonial coffee-women, however, did actively encourage social standards of politeness and taste during the age of Enlightenment, as Swift said they would, and, upon licensure, agreed to uphold civic rules of godly behaviour.[11] From the gazette advertisements and the fashionable stores which sprung up around their coffeehouses, it may safely be surmised that many colonial women succeeded in gaining gentrified colonial customers and advanced their social status in the public sphere.[12] There is, then, some area of comparative analysis which can be made between coffee-women in London and America and the salon-keepers of France and Germany. The most basic principle that can be drawn is that coffee-women throughout the century were concerned with politeness, although their ability to refine conversation along those lines depended greatly upon either the social status of their families or the civic roles local male authorities gave them. It is perhaps to enlightened women, rather than the classical ideals of male intellectuals, that the historian must first turn for any real social solution to the question of whether politeness ever actually existed in the coffeehouse public sphere.

And yet, the Enlightened understanding of coffee as a polite and associational drink cannot be ignored. Right to association undergirded the entire clubbable male atmosphere of coffeehouse life. Regardless of the social upheavals which coffeehouses brought to the Anglo-sphere, somehow, news and coffee enjoyed a successful marriage throughout the eighteenth century, due to the rise of clubs and their demand for coffee conversation rooted in urban experience. Addison and Steele's popularization of the gentleman's editorial column actualized the participatory public sphere by giving a voice to the average coffeehouse customer 'trifling' about London. Through the standardization of coffee and news grew the 'associational society' of London's clubs, endlessly emulated by colonial American elites and disseminated by middling merchants.[13] The rise of the clubs was no small moment in coffeehouse history. Clubs transformed certain coffeehouses into the public arenas of political debate. Yet, the sheer diversity of clubs is enough to dispel the notion that they were ever entirely monopolized by Whigs. There were beefsteak clubs, scientific societies, merchant associations, marine insurance journals and finally political clubs, both Whig and otherwise. Behind the emphasis on experiential knowledge within the coffeehouse clubs remained the continuing discourse of refining manners in accord with taste and personal choice, forever immortalized in *Spectator*. Political coffeehouse discussion was merely a social solution to reforming public manners, avoiding the unpleasantries of coffeehouses and releasing the creative power of connoisseurs through print. Hence, *Spectator* presents an idealized view of coffeehouse discussion, which, although filled with its own social controversies, still maintains an imaginative classical ethos which naturally guides human interactions towards taste and order.[14] The power of such an imagination quickly merged with the actual cultural understanding of coffee itself, as news and the coffeehouse joined hands on both sides of the Atlantic. It was a union which sounded more stable than it really was. Coffee-women and coffee-men dealt with their chaotic social worlds by adopting the classical style and attracting male clubs as their most important clientele.

The murders pictured in the preceding chapter suggest that coffee-women were often threatened by their customers, who shut them out of their conversations but involved them in their quarrels. These women responded by imposing a polite standard for male social behaviour. Women insisted on gentlemanly, polite conduct to encourage 'conspicuous society' but could rarely achieve this by themselves. This was especially the case in the North American colonies, where women worked alongside legislatures and city governments to actualize respectable sociability.[15] All too often, the debate over gender and the coffeehouses assumes a false distinction between coffeehouse men and women outside the public sphere, but the truth is that women also worked at refining male social behaviour from *within* the coffeehouse, though not as active participants in the common conversation.[16] Gender was an important component, if not the defining factor, in the formation of polite public spaces.

The eighteenth century was an interesting time for women. Generally, women were barred from publishing books of most sorts, had less access to formal classical education than men and were not allowed entrance into many public social events. However, these roles shifted ever so slightly during the eighteenth century. That women gained important social roles in articulating polite sociability is undeniable. Particularly in France, ladies of the court hosted conversation for courtiers and the *philosophes* in salon parlours, but these ladies had connections to prominent families. Even home life was changing and often involved new public responsibilities. Through the late seventeenth and early eighteenth centuries, trade brought new and exciting household goods within the reach of middling families, and women with means were expected to visit these shops for the good of their families. Life was no longer either subsistence or the court. The cottage industry, although very much alive in the eighteenth century, was not entirely confined to the home. The domestic sphere grew to include certain features of the public sphere. Middling women primarily entered London's social life through shopping, which was believed to be a polite alternative to the masculine public sphere of the coffeehouses.[17] Although women were never fully or overtly ousted from public coffeehouse life, they took many personal risks whenever they infringed upon public male sociability in the coffeehouses. The overwhelming impression from British coffeehouse literature of the eighteenth century is that women were not allowed to visit coffeehouses, but there are sporadic references of women doing so.[18] It was known among coffeehouse customers that women occasionally broke the rules.

A great many women, often widows, opened coffeehouses or continued the businesses of their deceased husbands. Cowan estimates that more than 20 per cent of all coffeehouses in London in the late seventeenth century were kept by women.[19] These did more than serve coffee; they moderated discussion and in most cases sought a respectable clientele. Across the British Atlantic world, women opened coffeehouses in accord with generally accepted male behaviour in their establishments, but their exact place in coffeehouse discussion remains vague. There were some cases of women encouraging low-life talk and prostitution in their houses, but these houses never attracted a reputation beyond those who lurked in dark alleys in London. The sinfulness of such houses was obvious to coffeehouse proprietors and customers alike. 'What Solomon says in respect of the Harlot, is but too applicable to Taverns, Alehouses, Coffee-Houses, and Brandy-Shops,' warned one Christian critic, 'Let not thine Heart decline to their Ways; go not astray in their "Paths" … their Houses are the Way to Hell, going down to the Chamber of Death.'[20] Colonial American city officials were more insistent on the point than in London. Particularly in America, coffee-women applying for licensure did so on the authority of their Christian character and respectable reputations. Holiness was a prerequisite for women opening coffeehouses in North American cities. Especially in Quaker societies, civic leaders trusted Christian womanhood to the task of providing a public sphere of chaste hospitality.[21] Yet the influence of these women was sporadic. A coffee-woman was more often a censor than a participant in the male world of coffeehouse conversation.

Feminine sociability and middling coffeehouse publics

In the popular mind, Jane Austen's world of Regency sociability is still remembered for its etiquette, but this was the result of more than a century of development. The power of that era rested on the success of female sociability during the age of Enlightenment. Whiggish notions of taste were behind it. Reinke-Williams argues that women's sociability changed with the institutional structure of London in the eighteenth century. The growth of England's victualling industry necessitated spousal cooperation. Husbands and wives ran public accommodations together, and widows continued these businesses. In London, more street sellers moved into indoor shops, providing genteel and middling girls with work and polite customers of both genders with places to buy fashionable goods. Women were allowed to help facilitate rules of etiquette in the world of fashion; hats, bonnets, lace and China tea services. Domestic management, or the proper maintenances of household subordinates, was the primary mode of judging a woman's reputation. Women began displaying their domestic spheres in the public life of the town in order to advance their social status, as reputation increasingly depended upon the honour of one's occupational identity. For middling to upper-class urbanites, the dowry increasingly became a pressing logistic in a marriage, as the generational interplay between family finances and motherhood determined one's status in society.[22]

Shops were no small aspect of polite middling sociability in the eighteenth century, and shopping was the primary way for middling women to associate in polite society. Berry argues that shopping was governed by the middling model of politeness. She includes shopping into the range of leisurely activities which Langford, John Brewer and Peter Borsay identified as generating an age of polite consumption in Georgian England. Shopping ought to be considered a social ritual of everyday consumer experience. Berry states, 'shopping, unlike assembly-going, parading in pleasure gardens, conversing in coffee houses or dancing at balls, is seldom described by historians of the eighteenth century as a distinctively "polite" activity, yet it was a constituent element of, and of itself produced, a polite lifestyle'.[23] Young girls of higher social status shopped in groups, usually accompanied by a servant. These trips to the shops were often conducted in the morning when men were away at their businesses. Ladies reinforced politeness by leisurely browsing fine wares and discussing their social value. London had four exclusive shopping streets – the Strand, Fleet Street, Cheapside and Cornhill: at least two out of the four corresponding to coffeehouse districts of the city. Expensive books, fine China, alabaster and gold clocks, glass crystal and expensive jewellery filled the windows of these shops, primarily aimed at the passing eyes of the ladies. Although mud and muck still sat in the streets, shoppers could glimpse in a shop window one fleeting vision of glory which they might implant in their parlours. Berry explains, 'The cleanliness and convenience of the environment, and civil sociability of shopkeepers, helped to make browsing a polite activity.'[24] It was this culture of shopping which Josiah Wedgwood created for the higher middling sorts in manufacturing trinkets of every sort. He chose exclusive places for his shops, refused to issue trade cards and hung noble crests over the doorway of his warehouses to give the illusion that his customers were entering a space reserved for the ruling classes. Similarly, shops across London arranged their high-quality wares with matching high-quality accessories. For instance, jewellers often placed expensive jewellery in great, glass-windowed cabinets. Like a theatre with changing scenes, customers could pass each shop and glimpse a particular aura of urban comfort. Bow-fronted windows came in by the late eighteenth century, extending the fantasy of consumer space out into the street.[25] Such aspects of eighteenth-century retail forced shops out into the sociable experiences of every browsing passer-by, primarily female, and reinforced a polite experience to leisure.

In North America, eighteenth-century shops and items of taste signalled the rise of the middling merchants in American life, their newfound wealth and the transatlantic exchange of ideas and goods which brought increasing numbers of clients into the coffeehouses. Colonial America was, for all its ostentation, really a realm in which the richest aristocrats and the lowest peasants played little or no part. It was an enterprising economy which depended on slavery and indentured servitude, but involved little of the permanent landed hierarchies and nothing of the lavish courts of Europe. Therefore, gentrification was entirely manufactured in America, as middling peoples imagined themselves to be emerging aristocrats. Class and culture were two integral parts of American consumer society. Simon Middleton and Billy G. Smith's work has envisioned class in colonial America as a pre-modern cultural exchange in which the linguistic constructions of collective identity including religious, ethnic and family ties to the Old World were riddled with the ever-changing contingencies of colonial conditions. They have harmonized class analysis with gender studies, postmodern scepticism of class determinism and the 'linguistic turn'. New social history and Pierre Bourdieu's notion of a 'subject class' in which linguistic conditions naturalize the symbolic framework for constructing a collective identity, or 'a sense of one's place', impose new demands on class analysis as a mode of historical inquiry.[26] Class can no longer be seen as class conflict determinism, nor can it be isolated from the gendered linguistic development of a cosmopolitan culture of taste in the eighteenth century. Yet, because America possessed a porous social strata relative to Europe, and social mobility was at least structurally possible if not actually so, the interplay between class and the culture of politeness is essential to an investigation of the changing nature of colonial coffeehouse clientele. It is that very interplay which transitioned coffeehouses from violent social experiments into largely non-violent and dynamic transatlantic consumer spheres.

What is clear from new class analysis is that the middling sorts rose to the top and increasingly dominated colonial American social life in the eighteenth century. The immediate effect of the rise of middling wealth in America was a widening of social spaces for lower middling shopowners and artisans who aspired to polite society, while simultaneously reinforcing their inferiority to enterprising transatlantic investors, aristocratic merchants and English governors serving in the New World. In their search for 'genteel associations and friendships', middling ladies and gentlemen marked the shops and coffeehouses in America as places for displaying status. It was this very sociological shift which stabilized the coffeehouse as an institution for polite modes of burgeoning discourse and moved it away from its turbulent past. As Middleton and Smith argue, 'Pursuing genteel lives in the burgeoning consumer empire, this new middling sort ... sharpened distinctions in colonial communities and nurtured resentment among those who lacked the wherewithal to acquire the trappings of respectability'.[27] Rather than obliterating social distinctions, the middling peoples of America cultivated a language of respectability in their manuals and private letters which, as Konstantin Dierks states, paid deference to 'persons of quality' and aided 'literate young middling men pursuing service occupations to navigate a commercializing economy and an elite social realm with which they were already intersecting'.[28] Technical manuals gave middling folk to understand that they were of 'ordinary Learning & Capacity', who were maintaining markets for their social superiors in colonial government and in their transatlantic communications with the English gentry. In developing such a language of polite commerce, middling Americans both reinforced social hierarchies and also diversified middling occupations, making room for bookshop owners, furniture shopkeepers and printers to imagine their climb towards the realm of gentility. Dierks asserts that in this climb, 'they commercialized the transatlantic economy'.[29] Above all, they used the coffeehouse as a public arena to correspond with their betters through print or in person. Some made it to a form of genteel position, others did not; but all were in some way adjacent to it, providing the genteel public sphere with cultured literature or the material products necessary to arrange a world of taste.

Arranging that world of taste was a highly personal and class-sensitive project, dependent upon emerging gendered economic relationships between gentlemen merchants and household wives. Thus, the middling effect on American society was to infuse business friendships into nearly every aspect of life. Jennifer L. Goloboy has argued that specifically transatlantic friendships, maintained by an epistolary culture of politeness and mutual obligation, ensured the success of a middling society in Charleston, South Carolina. Young men sought older patrons in vertical social networks on both sides of the Atlantic and horizontal relationships among their peers.

This required travel and coffeehouses increasingly serving the transatlantic demands of the middling sort in America. Goloboy mentions George Nelson, who between 1784 and 1798, lived in Charleston, London, New York and Philadelphia.[30] Andrew M. Schocket claims that transatlantic flows of information and capital were critical for Philadelphian bankers and grain exporters like Robert Morris, Thomas Willing, William Bingham and Thomas Fitzsimmons. These sorts of men were almost rootless, transcending local ties, but their mobility was no less personal. They subscribed to the London *Gentleman's Magazine* and other coffeehouse news outlets like *Every Man His Own Broker: or, A Guide to Exchange-Alley* .... They were members of a fraternal bourgeois with a universal standard of polite values which reinforced their varying degrees of economic, political and cultural influence.[31] Goloboy illustrates the transatlantic nature of this personal exchange of sensibilities, both middling and aristocratic, between merchants and patrons. 'Using shared experiences to sustain long-distance business friendships,' she states, 'merchants reinforced transatlantic similarities in middle-class culture. These men helped insure that middle-class culture was a child of the Atlantic World.'[32] Yet transatlantic merchant friendships only amounted to the supply of polite consumption in America. Household wives were the ones actually tasked with the duty of buying these goods, and they extended their domestic spheres into the very cultural process of shopping. Middling society depended upon friendships, between gentlemen exchangers of goods and partnerships in the coffeehouse and between ladies and gentlemen in the domestic atmosphere of the shop.

In London, the coffeehouse was very often the extension of a similar domestic sphere, although it was never as respectable an institution as the shop. The wives of deceased husbands were to be found everywhere operating coffeehouses, but with sometimes seemingly less intentional reasons of reinforcing politeness. Indeed, in some cases, women lowered the morality of London coffeehouses. The Finish Coffeehouse in Covent Garden was overrun with 'dissipation and debauchery ... of depravity and infamy', as a contemporary called it. This contemporary knew his sin in going there.[33] The Rose Coffeehouse, also in Covent Garden, had a reputation for loose women. Taylor's Coffeehouse in the Southwark Mint housed the riffraff of 'insolvent debtors, ... thieves, prostitutes, and lawless'.[34] Ram Alley was the most infamous street in London for women of ill repute. Its taverns and particularly the Maidenhead Coffeehouse drew much censorship from the inquests of the ward mote.[35] Clearly, despite its continuance, citizens in London denounced the Maidenhead as sinful. Hardly any written account of these houses applauded their use and all were either euphemistic, subversive or guilty about their real purposes or else obviously derogatory. Here, both God and man alike 'gave them up to uncleanness through the lusts of their own hearts, to dishonour their own bodies between themselves'.[36] So the sermons ran. A writer to the *Spectator* remarked, 'I cannot but complain to you that there are, in six or seven Places of this City, Coffee-houses kept by Persons of that Sisterhood. These Idols sit and receive all day long the Adoration of the Youth within such and such districts.'[37]

One such place was Tom King's Coffeehouse of Covent Garden, started by Tom King and his wife Moll, who ran a secret house of prostitution. After Tom's death in 1737, widow Moll made the establishment more public, promoting 'flash talk', a low-life form of subversive communication.³⁸ Flash talk exonerated the underworld of thieves with street slang quips, as in this passage from Fielding's *Life and Character of Moll King, Late Mistress of King's Coffee-House in Covent-Garden* (1747): 'There's a Grunter's Gig, is a Si-Buxom; two Cat's Heads, a Win; a Double Gage of Rum Slobber, is Thrums; and a Quartern of Max, is three Megs: – That makes a Traveller all but a Meg.'³⁹ This was unintelligible to even literate readers of the eighteenth century. Much like the criminal slang of 'cant', which Johnson defined as 'a corrupt dialect used by beggars and vagabonds', Berry describes flash talk as a 'secretive and exclusive … denoted entry into a counter-culture of libertines and wits rather than one of the ancient universities'.⁴⁰

In a word, this form of sociability was the opposite of polite letters, or the journalistic reforms of the eighteenth-century enlightenment in London. Its secrecy connoted illegitimacy. The 'conspicuous society' of the high Enlightenment stood for an entirely different form of sociability: one of politeness, wit, regulated and controlled amorous courtships, and scholarly pursuits. Although a genre of literature existed which celebrated impolite behaviour, like *The Life and Intrigues of the late Celebrated Mrs Mary Parrimore* (1729), such fascination was limited by the infamy of 'intrigue' and sin surrounding such lives.⁴¹ Fielding knew that he was dealing with one of the most infamous coffeehouses in London. He remarked in his *Covent Garden Tragedy* (1732), 'What rake is ignorant of King's Coffee-House … A Place in Covent-Garden Market, well known to all Gentlemen to whom Beds are unknown.'⁴² Indeed, according to Lillywhite's directory of London coffeehouses, Moll was repeatedly fined by the city for disorderly conduct. The city took a dim view of such establishments, although it rarely closed them down outright. Still, of the 2,034 coffeehouses catalogued by Lillywhite, only four were identified under prostitution.⁴³ If we take the *Spectator* as our authority, the number of bawdy coffeehouses in London increases to seven. Surely, the possibilities for more coffeehouse prostitution abounded, but the contemporary editorial commentary and catalogued record bears out a different story. Coffeehouse prostitution was confined to the back alleys because it was sinful. Most of those alleys were soaked in gin, not coffee, for gin had far more carousers to its name than coffee.

Puritan New England took an even dimmer view of such public coffeehouse establishments and initially entrusted coffeehouses only to godly women. Women's place in the colonial coffeehouses originated with the Puritan morality of the 1670s. Unlike London taverns which were licenced by the Society of Vintners, municipal authorities directly policed coffeehouses in America.⁴⁴ James Davis claims that the Puritans in Boston prohibited men from operating taverns, because it encouraged idleness. Women were exempt from this rule, as public hospitality was considered part of a woman's role. In 1670, Dorothy Jones was the first licenced proprietor of coffee in Boston, followed closely by Mary Gutteridge. Davis states, 'Operating under the watchful eyes of the authorities, the women kept an iron rule over their taverns, and encouraged coffee as an alternative to imported liquors and high prices. The coffeehouses stayed orderly: patrons gossiped, bought insurance, and kept track of news.'⁴⁵ More than politeness, Puritan authorities were concerned about building a public morality of free enterprise. The Protestant emphasis of free enterprise and local exchange, or the middling sensibility, in the town coffeehouse remained a feature of Boston's cityscape for over a century, and women were often in charge of what might be said in these houses. This was the case until the Free Masons took ownership of the coffeehouse tavern Green Dragon, playing host to the Sons of Liberty and Massachusetts statesmen like Paul Revere, Dr Joseph Warren, Samuel Adams, James Otis and John Adams. They ushered in male ownership and patriotic and ceremonial notions of coffee. For instance, in 1714 the Green Dragon hosted a ball in honour of the coronation of George I, hailed as the 'Supreme Lord of Massachusetts'.[46] With first an imperial and then republican pageantry, the moralizing force of women hostesses began to decline.

William Penn also believed that public victualling might threaten Christian morality and so regulated coffeehouse development in Philadelphia. Victualling licensure in Pennsylvania was the governor's sole authority, while the Provincial Council determined the rules of order for such establishments. When coffee entered Pennsylvania for the first time in the early 1660s, William Penn considered it too expensive. The price soon dropped and coffee was no longer generally believed to be too wasteful a product. Local entrepreneur Samuel Carpenter opened the first coffeehouse in Philadelphia, along with the first bakery, city crane and wharves. His reputation for being a hardworking and enterprising merchant was impeccable. By the mid-eighteenth century, printing took control of Philadelphia's coffeehouse culture. William Bradford opened the London Coffeehouse in 1754 with its printing house by subscription, encouraging a fraternity of male merchants to give their support for the endeavour to link polite letters and news with coffee conversation.[47] It was distinctly middling in its culture merged with the moralizing and non-violent literary interests of socially disposed Americans. In the northern colonies, Christian morality and enterprise controlled coffeehouse culture. And it was a task which involved a proprietary strategy for coffeehouse owners and their wives.

But what of lower-class women and servants tending the bars? Although many coffeehouses hired maids to tend to the bar and serve the coffee, their participation in coffeehouse conversation remained scanty at best, and though they often drew the unpleasant attention of coffeehouse rakes, their influences could be more benign.[48] The geniality of a good inn maid was forever memorialized in the English carol *Gloucestershire Wassail*:

> Be here any maids? I suppose here be some;
> Sure they will not let you men stand on the cold
> Sing hey O, maids? come troll back the pin,
> And the fairest maid in the house let us all in.[49]

Coffee maids were certainly admired and even courted, but rarely did they enter into male conversation as free members of discourse. Class and function separated them from their customers. These working women would have been even more at risk in a coffeehouse conversation than middling women, since their very presence would have been mistaken for an unsavoury invitation. Thus, Ward, Hogarth and others depicted coffeehouses such as the Denmark Coffeehouse on Bridges Street as being filled with the raucous of lewd women.[50] Definitely any woman in such company of flirtatious coffeehouse men had little reputation to begin with, for as one anonymous tract against coffeehouses in 1673 ran, 'Had Women any sense or spirit, they would remonstrate to his Majestie.'[51] We catch a glimpse of the average housewife in the play *Tarugo's Wiles: or, the Coffee-House* (1668), who ran to the coffeehouse to pull her husband back home from his hours spent with the society of his fellow *virtuosi*.[52] Similarly, in *The Maidens Complaint* (1663), Dorothy finds her husband 'at a Coffee-house, making a chimney of his noddle, where there is such an odious scent: fog, fog, fog, it makes my heart ache to think what a Jaques he makes of his brains ... I protest Ione there's a little comfort in Chocolate'.[53] The coffeehouse was filled with dangers for the average housewife and the sociable activity between men and women in such places was generally exploitive if more than a genial 'please' or 'thank you'.

It is to middling and aristocratic women that we must turn for any real possibility of female sociability in coffeehouse life. Steven Pincus questions the prevailing notion that women were excluded from coffeehouses and gives several examples of respectable ladies visiting coffeehouses. Thomas Bellingham gathered political news from women at the coffeehouse, but whether they were called specially or usually to be found there is not certain. Robert Hooke and Robert Boyle dined with Boyle's sister, Lady Ranelagh, at Man's Coffeehouse. Presumably, Ranelagh would not have gone without her respectable male chaperones. Pincus claims that Martha, Lady Giffard, sister to Sir William Temple, frequently visited the coffeehouses. However, he cites only a letter from Swift stating 'a gentlewoman from Lady Giffard's house had been at the Coffee House to inquire for her'.[54] This is certainly not enough to indicate that she was 'a habitué of coffeehouses'.[55] Furthermore, it is not clear whether she had a male chaperone like Lady Ranelagh or not. Pincus also quotes an article in the *City and Country Mercury* from 1667 which stated, ' "city ladies and citizens wives" were said to relish the opportunity for political discussion the coffeehouses provided'.[56] If so, the *City and Country Mercury* was alone in considering the 'coffeehouse politicians' not generally, or even exclusively, male. These were nothing more than interlopers in a male world. John Barrell explains,

> By the second quarter of the century, 'coffee house politicians,' as they came to be called, had become objects of satire – as men unnaturally preoccupied with public affairs at the expense of the private and domestic, as too concerned with the figure they cut in coffee-house conversation; most often as men in too low a sphere of life to take a legitimate interest in politics.[57]

If women did regularly mingle among them, they too would fall under the same censure of the satirical journalists, but no prevailing word remains of them; quite the reverse. Walter Scott's adage in *The Bride of Lammermoor* would make little sense without a coffeehouse gender divide: 'I hope to see the day ... when justice shall be open to Whig and Tory, and when these nick-names shall only be used among coffee-house politicians, as slut and jade are among apple-women, as cant terms of idle spite and rancour.'[58]

There are a few more notable instances of middling to upper-class women entering the coffeehouses: mostly for arts or society, not politics, and seemingly chaperoned by male acquaintances. Cowan argues that women went to coffeehouses for art auctions, but here they were simply acting in the interests of their domestic sphere. At one such auction in 1682, the Lady Rutland hired a principal (presumably male) to place the bids. Another exception was spinster Hester Pinney, who negotiated prices for lace at Garraway's and Jonathan's. Still, Pinney's father accused her of impropriety for lodging above a coffeehouse. Few spinsters would have been so willing to tarnish their reputations by pursuing wholesale lace in merchant coffeehouses. Clearly, Pinney was one woman who frequently broke the rules of both class and gender. In Bath, the 'coffee rooms' served ladies in the spa-houses, but here mixed company was a prerequisite to sociability. Ladies were very much under the guidance of their chaperones. Cowan's only other examples include James Brydges's wife, who dropped her companion off at the coffeehouse while making her own calls around the town and a few examples of female travellers lodging in coffeehouse rooms. Yet there is no evidence that women actually joined men in the public room for conversation. Most of the activity of women in coffeehouse lodgings was suspect. Cowan argues that the city records of London document that most female patrons were regularly accused of adultery and money laundering. Middling and aristocratic women who did run or visit such establishments were clearly breaking social rules. That the government took such matters seriously is evidence that unaccompanied women would have been discouraged from visiting coffeehouses.[59] Respectable ladies would have had every reason to solicit a male guardian when the necessity arose to enter a coffeehouse. Without one, she would have been risking her reputation for no reason.

Art exhibitions were the few occasions when it was excusable for ladies to find themselves in coffeehouses. Larry Stuart claims that ladies came out to the Exchange coffeehouses to see frequent scientific experiments and expositions put on by the Royal Society.[60] Subscription libraries seem also to have been the result of both men and women subscribers. The *Liverpool Chronicle* issued the following library proposal in February 1758:

> To all Gentlemen and Ladies, who desire to encourage the progress of Useful Knowledge, to procure for themselves a rational entertainment and to do a great deal of good at a small expense, the following Scheme is proposed. The Two Reading Societies who meet at the Merchants Coffee House and the Talbot being willing to make their plans as extensively useful as possible, and sensible how much some public provision of this kind is wanted here, mutually propose to unite their present Stock of Books into one and thereby to lay the foundation of a Public Library.[61]

Whether ladies and gentlemen were involved in the reading discussion at the Merchants Coffeehouse is unclear from the announcement, but since there appeared to be two societies, it may reasonably be assumed that if ladies were permitted, one society was for men and the other for women. Subscription libraries like these were often to be found in provincial towns, as in Newcastle, where admissions were set at £5.5s. and annual fees at £2.2s. These reading assemblies hosted critical debate on certain novels, plays, newspapers, pamphlets and books.[62] In such cases, the event or project drew ladies into coffeehouse areas under certain conditions, rather than to the general conversation of the place itself, a phenomenon which was even more true of coffeehouse galas. Ladies often entered coffeehouses with ballrooms or pleasure gardens for formal events, such as at Mary-le-Bone Gardens Coffeehouse and the Ranelagh Gardens Rotunda. Such places served not only coffee but also tea for the ladies, perpetuating the gendered social habit epitomized in Fielding's *Coffee-House Politician* (1730): 'Coffee with a Politician, Tea with a fine Lady, or "Rack Punch with a fine Gentleman".'[63]

Coffeehouse ballrooms were even more important in provincial or colonial areas where little other social arenas existed for country dances. In all the North American colonies, the Annapolis Coffeehouse was perhaps the finest example of a ballroom. Here, the governor's social circle dined and nowhere was there a finer example of 'conspicuous society' in a coffeehouse, save perhaps in Paris. Women were allowed in during special occasions, but no evidence exists to say that they frequented the coffee-room during business hours when it was used by the merchants. The patrons and patronesses of the Annapolis coffeehouse enacted a pageant of polite society in courtly masquerades and dinner parties. American courtly habits were completely imaginary, as no real historic chivalry ever existed in America. Colonial governors of royal colonies like Virginia and Maryland were at liberty to let fancy have free rein. On one occasion, the governor of Maryland threw a lavish December night ball at the coffeehouse for the ladies and gentlemen of the city. His dinner order consisted of beef, chickens, turkeys, tongues, loaves of bread, custards, tarts, cheese cakes, four gallons of spirits, eight gallons of wine, plus £10s10 worth of punch and grog on tap. Twenty-nine forks and thirty-five knives were lost in the mayhem of festivities, and the colony recompensed the owner for the loss.[64]

The ladies were peculiarly on display in Maryland. According R. Lee Van Horn,

> The Maryland Gazette tells us that numerous beautiful women, making a most brilliant appearance, were present [at a gala at the Stadt House]. The ladies of Annapolis had always enjoyed an enviable position among the women of the province of Maryland and the other colonies. Their reputation for grace, charm and beauty extended far and wide. Contemporary writers were continually extolling their charms to the world.[65]

Similar celebrations were held in Boston, and during the Federal era, in the grand chandeliered coffeehouse ballrooms of New Orleans.[66] In such affairs, the lower middling sort, the riff-raff of shopkeepers, tradesmen and local artisans, who were increasingly being accommodated in most other American coffeehouses, played no part whatsoever.

This love for social display and its corresponding aristocracy did not end with the revolutionary era; rather, ironically enough, it was heightened by the republican pageantry of George Washington's generalship. He was the toast of the coffeehouses throughout the colonies, and wherever he went, ladies and gentlemen hosted balls and celebrations in his honour.[67] Upon his retirement, he was greeted in Fredericksburg, Virginia, in 1784 as a conquering republican consul. Twenty-one artillery rounds saluted his arrival and an assembly of notable gentlemen greeted him with honour, some of them were undoubtedly veteran officers. Thirteen toasts accompanied dinner at the coffeehouse, including toasts to the 'Sovereign States', 'American Congress', 'our late and virtuous army', 'The Order of Cincinnati' and 'our gallant heroes who have bravely fallen in defence of American liberty'. One newspaper recorded that 'On the evening, an elegant ball was given at the Town-Hall, where a numerous and brilliant company of ladies assembled, who now in turn received the pleasure of beholding their great protector and virtuous defender'.[68] Coffee served new republic ceremonies, in which an aristocracy of virtuous officers, patriots and their ladies played host.

Gentility and refinement were more important guides of social behaviour in the coffeehouses of the colonial American south than in the north. This was due in part to the aristocratic planters, who, as the English gentry would have seen them, were still middling. It is necessary to delineate between the imaginative middling culture of politeness, which certainly contained an affectation of aristocratic tastes, and the enterprising colonial conditions which upheld American public life. Female proprietors of southern coffeehouses came to understand this distinction. The trick lay in marketing the coffeehouse as if it was not a market. It was a polite forum for leisurely gentlemen. Its customers imagined they *were* gentlemen for no other reason than that they were participating in the world of polite letters as gentlemen were in England. These southern coffeehouse proprietors appealed to the eighteenth-century notion of politeness as a means of gaining respectable male clientele. Yet ownership did not necessarily project female voices into the public sphere. The most that can be said for ownership is that women policed male notions of politeness as prerequisites for licensure. They did so in accord with the established social rules of middling respectability. When Meredith Muse opened her coffeehouses on Main Street in Fredericksburg in 1777, she advertised it as a place 'where gentlemen may be genteelly accommodated with lodging'.[69] Most likely, this was the very coffeehouse which hosted Washington in 1784. Its prominent position would have particularly catered to the men of business in the city. Similarly, Teresa Pearse's coffeehouse opened in Norfolk in 1773, 'for the Accommodation of Travellers and others; supported by a Society of Gentlemen'. It was 'under the Direction and Management of Teresa Pearse' but financially upheld by a board of gentleman subscribers.[70]

In such cases, women had to prove their moral characters as respectable hostesses to the colonial governments. The process of licencing middling mercantile establishments also involved the gendered notion of domesticity. It has already been demonstrated that godliness was a large factor in determining licensure in Boston and Philadelphia. This was also the case in the south. When Mary Newell asked the governor and council of Maryland for a coffeehouse licence, she distinguished her coffeehouse from 'a Tipling House or any Thing tending to Excess and Intemperance'.[71] She argued that it was a necessary extension of her domestic livelihood. Her petition stated that she had worked many years supporting herself 'by her drudgery' and that 'She finds old Age and Impotency has much impeded her that she cannot longer scuffle in the world so to provide herself with Necessaries as formerly'. The petition appealed to the chivalry of the male statesmen for the provision of widows, calling them to 'out of your Abundance of ... Consideration and Pity will be pleased to grant Relief'.[72] Female coffeehouse ownership and licensure assumed service to a male public sphere, with gendered responsibilities for both proprietors and patrons to maintain godliness and middling respectability in their ventures.

But middling publics of America increasingly merged the material cultures of both men and women, combining the domestic sphere of women with the public mercantile worlds of men. The lines between male and female sociability blurred when shops combined with coffeehouses to draw 'ladies and gentlemen' into their premises. Hugh Walker, & Co. advertised coffee alongside men and women's shoes in the *Virginia Gazette*. Joseph Northup solicited 'Ladies and Gentlemen, and the public in general' at his shop in Norfolk near the American Coffeehouse which sold dresses, stockings, ribbons, silks and scarlets.[73] In the south, plantation families came to town together on designated days for business and domestic supplies, so it made perfect sense to advertise for both genders. Milliner Mary Dickinson saw opportunity in linking female shopping interests with male coffeehouse visitors. She moved her jewellery and fine millinery store in Williamsburg to quarters above the coffeehouse across from the Capital building.[74] In this way, she captured the attention of the wealthy burgesses, who would be most likely to buy her imported commodities from London. It was a successful experiment and probably even gained the patronage of the governor's circle. After just six months in her new location, Dickinson was advertising 'a GENTEEL and very elegant Assortment' and offered her 'thanks to those Gentlemen and Ladies who have favored me with their Custom'.[75] It was a cash-only business, making it exclusively for those who purchased only for the status and taste gained by buying such wares. Buying and selling opened the public sphere to middling women, who in turn worked to enforce politeness even in exclusively male domains, like the coffeehouse.

For every good reason to surmise that women were regularly active in coffeehouse life there is an equally good reason to argue that they were barred from doing so. Because coffee drew in political and commercial discussion, men reserved these public places for themselves. As Ellis states, 'In effect, coffee-houses were almost more than anywhere else male-oriented, gendered almost exclusively masculine.' Women were often owners and servers of coffee, the subjects of observation and comment, but rarely participants in the conversation of the common coffee tables. The places reserved for mixed company were theatres, parks and pleasure gardens but not coffeehouses.[76] Still, there were always interlopers. Ladies were frequently found in coffeehouses, but they were deliberately breaking assumed rules of social order. Although Swift referred to ladies investing in the Change Alley speculations during the South Sea Bubble, and so presumably at Garraway's Coffeehouse, nineteenth-century historian Edward Callow reasoned that because of the place's high standards for commercial culture and coffee comforts like well-aged vintage, mahogany boxes and well-dressed waiters, 'I do not suppose a woman ever entered the place during the present century.'[77] Perhaps the only way to settle such a question is to evaluate the discourse of coffee and gender in the eighteenth century and look for taboos in the language of coffeehouse sociability.

Whether women could enter a coffeehouse and the conditions for doing so was debated by the journalists and writers of the age. There were those who desired conversation from ladies of taste and propriety in the public sphere and lamented that coffeehouses did not offer more opportunity for platonic sociable exchanges with the ladies. The clearest example of this is found in Swift's *Hints Towards An*

Essay On Conversation (1713). Remarking on the deplorable state of conversation in coffeehouses like Will's, Swift believed that the ladies of Charles I's court had cultivated conversation in opening their houses to rational discourse but had since been displaced by the new trifles of London. Celebrated by the poets of that time, ladies had reinforced chaste conversation, but with the rise of public entertainments outside of the court's prerogative, their moderating influence was lifted and public life degenerated into lower pursuits. Swift argued, 'If there were no other use in the conversation of ladies, it is sufficient that it would lay a restraint upon those odious topics of immodesty and indecencies, into which the rudeness of our northern genius is so apt to fall.'[78] Like the Goths of old, Swift believed the historical imagination of the British peoples always possessed an impulse to plunder rather than civilize. Hence, 'This degeneracy of conversation, with the pernicious consequences thereof upon our humours and dispositions, hath been owing, among other causes, to the custom arisen, for sometime past, of excluding women from any share in our society, further than in parties at play, or dancing, or in the pursuit of an amour.'[79] Swift certainly did not believe coffeehouse conversation was mixed in any respect. Among the coffeehouse jests, women were just gossips outside the coffeehouse window, who went about 'scolding most comfortably in the street together'.[80]

Both Steele and Addison felt a similar tinge of regret and actively solicited their polite contributions to their editorial columns. Nevertheless, they reinforced the need for a male public sphere and *Spectator* excluded both artisans and women from their imagined club of intellectuals. Copley claims that *Spectator* actually perpetuated the scolding stereotype of widowhood by calling their conversation 'criminal'.[81] It was only ladies of respectable standing who deserved recognition, for 'You see in no Place of Conversation the Perfection of Speech so much as in an accomplish'd Woman,' wrote Steele.[82] This is why Steele asked that ladies send him any story of the personal acquaintances he could remodel into a satirical commentary of public manners.

There are only occasional citations of ladies in coffeehouses in Steele and Addison's writings. Writing from Will's Coffeehouse, Steele observed a lady called 'Sappho' who frequently soliloquized her own verses, sang, danced and baffled the crowd with her boldness. Steele commented that she 'can say and do whatever she pleases, without the imputation of any thing that can injure her character; for she is so well known to have no passion but self-love'.[83] Clearly, 'Sappho', by being a woman of wit in a coffeehouse, was breaking the rules. On nights when 'Sappho' was presumably absent from Will's, Harry Spondee conversed freely on the subject of winning female attention by speaking nonsense. He had no real ladies to contend with in this arena among his coffeehouse listeners, and Steele considered the remark most unfair.[84]

Steele knew he was caught in a world which discussed women but did not seriously permit their entrance. Yet, his age was one of enlightenment. In *Tatler* No. 42, he argued that Shakespeare's female dialogue was incomparable with the freedom of conversation among ladies of his age. He stated, 'There were not then among the ladies, shining wits, politicians, virtuosae, free-thinkers, and disputants; nay, there was then hardly such a creature even as a coquette: but vanity had quite another turn, and the most conspicuous woman at that time of day was only the best housewife.'[85] Ladies were legitimate participators in the great exchange of social knowledge, but they were all too often the direct objects of coffeehouse conversation rather than its agents. This basic paradox lay at the heart of Steele and Addison's discourse of women in their journals. The great power of social observation had been unleashed and mixed company was more instructional to the scientist of human manners than a tight crowd of familiars. As one writer in the *Guardian* expressed it, 'I pass my time in the principal glands of philosophers, poets, beaux, mathematicians, ladies, and statesmen ... Nor was it unpleasant entertainment, sometimes to descend from these sublime and magnificent ideas to the impertinences of a beau, the dry schemes of a coffee-house politician, or the tender images in the mind of a young lady.'[86] The coffeehouse did not usually contain all of these specimens of study. Of necessity then, Steele and Addison announced in the *Guardian* that ladies who did not care to drop their letters to the editor in the general mailbox on the west side of Button's coffeehouse could inquire for the coffee-man's little daughter, who would convey the letter to the receptacle. Certain ladies would rather trust a four-year-old girl, albeit 'virtuously educated', than approach the west side of the building.

Generalizations of female taste in the journals and gazettes created friction between men and women, because women were barred from much of the discourse about them. Women distrusted such coffeehouse banter. Franklin reinforced this point when he adopted the feminine pseudonyms Martha Careful and Caelia Shortface for a debate in *The American Mercury* in 1728. Franklin alerted the public to the great rift between men in coffeehouses and taverns and the real conditions of upstanding and industrious housewives. His 'Martha Careful' of Philadelphia both exposed and issued a challenge to Samuel Keimer for immodestly discussing women. She exclaimed,

> In behalf of my Self and many good modest Women in this City (who are almost out of Countenance) I Beg you will Publish this in your next Mercury, as a Warning to Samuel Keimer: That if he proceed farther to Expose the Secrets of our Sex, in That audacious manner, as he hath done in his Gazette, No. 5. under the Letters, A.B.O. To be read in all Taverns and Coffee-Houses, and by the Vulgar: I say if he Publish any more of that kind, which ought only to be in the Repositary of the Learned; my sister Molly and my Self, with some others, are Resolved to run the Hazard of taking him by the Beard, at the next Place we meet him, and make an Example of him for his Immodesty. I Subscribe on the behalf of the rest of my Agrieved Sex.[87]

In America at least, the controversy depended upon the Christian feminine virtue of modesty. Rarely was such a virtue mentioned in the Addisonian language of the London journalists, but in Quaker country, it made perfect sense to defend one's modesty. Franklin challenged Keimer on the basis of his immodesty with regard to discussing women. The real danger was that the gazettes spoke to a formidable crowd of men in the taverns and coffeehouses and women could not directly respond to such conversations. Men conversed immodestly about women in public because the world of letters and conversation was theirs alone. Franklin as 'Caelia Shortface' threatened 'to inform Thee of Our Resolution, which is that if thou proceed any further in that Scandalous manner, we intend very soon to have thy right Ear for it'.[88] In a curious twist, Franklin blamed coffeehouse men for being scolds; their twitching ears and gossiping tongues were insatiable. He knew all too well that the coffeehouses were the realm of men and that women entered them at their own risk only under the most extreme of circumstances.

Feminine sociability and the polite public sphere in the age of Enlightenment

Although it is difficult to connect women to coffeehouses directly, it is essential to see their role in the emerging polite sociability of the broader middling and aristocratic public spheres of the eighteenth century. Aristocratic women and their salons in Europe did more to define the sociable conditions for disseminating a culture of taste than any other factor. Every gentleman familiar with the great philosophical discourses of his day, from Voltaire to Montesquieu, was somehow indebted to a salon for their popular influence. In France, feminine sociability has been linked with the high Enlightenment, while in England, Whig salons constructed the more conservative political attitudes of the Regency period. French salons and British coffeehouses were very different in almost every respect. Salons were much closer to court patronage than a coffeehouse and also catered to higher class fashions. Still, both salons and coffeehouses included female hostesses, polite tastes and a politically active middling readership. Although men dominated the French 'republic of letters' in the academies, Dena Goodman and Deborah Hertz have demonstrated that women forged a sophisticated social infrastructure for public sociability and even carved out careers for themselves in the emerging public forums. The chief contribution of women of high social standing was to expand their social circles and expose them to Enlightenment philosophy in salon establishments. Goodman argues that rather than being places of traditional femininity, salons acted as social bases for the 'republic of letters' and salonnières in the mid-eighteenth century and, like Marie-Therese Geoffrin, Julie de Lespinasse and Suzanne Necker provided, political order to French sociability. They did so by integrating a Rococo aesthetic of casual and elegant discursive space and implementing politeness as the basis for equality. Such efforts involved a new form of public politeness. Necker wrote,

> Politeness has been regarded as a [kind of] servitude; while its origin, on the contrary, is found in consideration that force has given to weakness, to age, to women, to children ... Politeness conforms to the principle of equality that is so often spoken of; it is the rampart of those who cannot defend themselves, and that as well on which their praise and their merit are based. [89]

Although feminine, politeness was also liberating. Goodman argues that it was also a social method for reinstating balance between the strong and the weak, or the male and the female.

Salonnières pioneered a literary outlet for political discourse. Women maintained their social networks across great distances through an epistolary world in which private letters acted as mini narratives and were often recited as lavish love narratives before salon audiences. Women monopolized the ethos of this literary genre, implementing discipline through penmanship, orthographic rules and a style that celebrated love as rational choice.[90] In short, salonnières were career hostesses of a new expressive mode of reasoning. They transformed their salons into academic destinations where mixed company shared a free intercourse of intellectual and artistic accomplishments. Goodman states, '*Autonomy, exclusivity, social mobility*, and *reputation*, the key terms in *le monde*, were key terms in the Republic of Letters as well.'[91] As in the academies where men jockeyed for recognition through accomplishment, women managed the 'republic of letters' with the Enlightenment ethos of merit. Benedetta Craveri has added that the spirit of *le monde* emphasized emulation rather than discrimination, relying on merit as a social means of divining truth through politeness. Through polite conversation, *philosophes* such as Voltaire and Diderot hoped to achieve a social consensus in humanities and politics.[92]

It was this aristocratic and middling salon culture which birthed much of the civil service in Continental Europe. In Berlin, Deborah Hertz shows that Jewish salonnières such as Rahel Varnhagen Levin and Brendel ('Dorothea') Mendelssohn-Schlegel climbed the social ladder through strategic marriages, sustained a domestic area for Junker nobles visiting the city and pioneered a 'republic of scholars' ('Geilefrtenrepublik') for budding Romantic intellectuals. German authors tripled from 1760 to 1800, sparking a literary revolution.[93] Similarly, the Galles family in Vannes, France, advanced their social station from printers to aristocratic members of local government and the French army. They founded a salon which socially converged on the upper middling and aristocratic families and combined the classical Latin curriculum of Cicero, Virgil, Livy and Ovid with the French Enlightenment. Marriages in these intellectual salons founded a new aristocratic class of governing families and civil servants from middling backgrounds.[94]

Female salon sociability had its limits, marked by the social divide in the Enlightenment itself. According to Robert Darnton, overcrowding in the academies simply squeezed out an entire class of writers who gradually began to see the book market as an elaborate patronage network closely guarded by writers in high social circles. Royal pensions were only awarded to the established *le monde* academician social circles. This disparity created two levels within the French Enlightenment: the high-life *philosophes* inside the state-sponsored academies and the low-life writers in Grub Street. Books were already vested with privileges in journal guilds, and the emerging literary establishment removed from cafés into salons. Hatred for *le monde* society grew among Grub Street writers as the older generation of *philosophes* died and a new generation of writers collaborated with the *grands* in a mutual fusion of the *gens de lettres* with the *gens du monde*. Voltaire himself seemed to have fallen under the spell of this new social alliance when he argued in his entry 'Gens de lettres' in the *Encyclopedie* that only after the 'taste' of court life was acquired (in the aristocratic salons) could *philosophes* turn to the masses. Naturally, Grub Street writers resented this patronizing tone and those who did not make the *monde* fell back into the low life in Grub Street – a literary proletariat even in the book boom of the eighteenth century. However, literary hacks in the café underground formulated a resistance movement against the 'high enlightenment'. Countering the *Journal de Paris* and *Mercure*, Simon-Henri Linguet founded the *Republique de lettres et des arts* in which he and his fellow Grub Street writers frequently snipped back at the academicians. The disparity in French Enlightenment literary culture continued until the emergence of the Jacobin pamphleteers who hoped to destroy the 'aristocracy of the mind'.[95]

The French Revolution saw the sudden end of the salons, associated with the old regime and corrupt aristocracy. However, Joan B. Landes relates that revolutionary women reconstituted association in new public clubs with political objectives during the summer of 1791. The Society of the Friends of Truth, which had advocated for the establishment of the republic in response to the king's flight, also became the first political club to allow women and generally supported a campaign to end primogeniture, abolish spousal abuse and legalize divorce. Under Etta Palm's leadership, the women's section lobbied for physical protection under the law and the establishment of national women's clubs for a more organized system of civic education. Despite Condorcet's petition to grant women political recognition, women were consistently barred a political presence at the National Assembly. In the midst of the Terror in 1793, radical Jacobin women organized the Society of Revolutionary Republican Women to police the streets and monitor patriotic compliance to the Revolution. They adopted the 'red cap' male uniform of the Jacobins, displayed weapons openly and imposed social discipline in the club by formalizing rules and procedures. In October, market women revolted against the Society's efforts to enforce uniform compliance and the Jacobin state authorities turned against the club. The Committee of General Security issued an unfavourable report and the government responded by closing the Society and banning women from public associations of this sort. The last public outlet for women activism was swept away in a fury of resentment, suspicion and Jacobin terror.[96]

Meanwhile in England, Whig sociability developed in the late Georgian period and gave rise to a rhetorical regularity that has since become a trademark in English literature. Running through the Whig political salons of London such as Holland House, English conservative values culminated in the Regency era. Lady Holland's salon at Holland House, Kensington, became the centre of Whig culture from 1797, when Lord and Lady Holland married, to Lord Holland's death in 1840. Lady Holland dominated the Whig social sphere with a firm and imperious hand, which Susanne Schmid argues, 'cultivated the art of verbal combat'.[97] She held her own in public and to the utter astonishment and even dismay of her peers, Lady Holland created a miniature society of Whig cultural values, in which social elites visited her literary establishment during 'the season'. Lord Holland attracted a Whig political following because he was the nephew of the Whig reformer Lord Charles Fox, but Lady Holland refined this social circle through a strict adherence to the Whig values of 'taste', chaste politeness and moral liberty. So cultivated was Holland House that it became a place where dinner parties often evolved into impromptu cabinet meetings for the Whig political leader Thomas Creevey. Holland House also grew into a literary establishment, as it intersected with the creation of the *Edinburgh Review* and launched the literary careers of Lord Macaulay and Charles Dickens. Lady Holland carefully crafted an English rhetorical style of relaxed Whig morality, which she differentiated from the flirtatious sociability of Italy or the inflexible and corrupt hierarchy of Spain. She policed her social sphere with an austere sociability which many of her critics mistook for snobbishness. However the language of insider-jokes and self-disciplined superiority grew into a generic linguistic code in conventional English literature and society.[98]

Edmund Burke integrated this disposition into the political order. Burke agreed with Lady Holland about the need for a guiding aristocracy of virtue over public society. Burke articulated an English 'moral imagination' (a cultural persuasion of manners which tends towards natural law) and advocated 'little platoons' of voluntary association to preserve civic order. Thus arose a form of conservatism which eventually married Enlightened discourse, based on a right to association, with the grandeur of Regency politeness. As intellectual historian Russell Kirk has argued, Burke held to a politics of prescription, in which custom provided a spiritual continuity to reform. An entire century of coffeehouse and salon discourse stood behind it. Like Samuel Johnson, Burke believed that civilized people crafted social constitutions over time. This Whig view of society was very much at odds with the more radical reformers of France. Kirk stated of Burke,

> He detested 'abstraction' – by which he meant not *principle*, but rather vainglorious generalization without respect for human frailty and the particular circumstances of an age and a nation. Thus it was that while he believed in the rights of Englishmen and in certain natural laws of the universal application, he despised the 'Rights of Man' which Paine and the French doctrinaires were soon to proclaim inviolable. Edmund Burke believed in a kind of constitution of civilized peoples; with Samuel Johnson, he adhered to the doctrine of a universal human nature. But the exercise and extent of these rights can be determined only by prescription and local circumstances; in this Burke read Montesquieu much more faithfully than did the French reformers.[99]

Burke desired a cultivated aristocracy of the mind. England was a community of souls, founded upon social traditions which gave meaning to law. Burke's anchor point for spiritual continuity in society was the moral spirit of a gentleman.[100] The public sphere was a gentlemanly sphere, softened by sentiment. Burke mourned,

> I love a manly, moral, regulated liberty as well as any gentleman … But now all is to be changed. All the pleasing illusions which made power gentle and obedience liberal, which harmonized the different shades of life, and which by a bland assimilation incorporated into politics the sentiments which beautify and soften private society, are to be dissolved by this new conquering empire of light and reason … moral imagination, which the heart owns and the understanding ratifies, as necessary to cover the defects of our naked, shivering nature, and to raise it to dignity in our own estimation, are to be exploded, as a ridiculous, absurd, and antiquated fashion.[101]

By 'bland association' and 'private society' Burke implied that 'moral imagination' was best displayed in unfeigned conversation, in which both ladies and gentlemen played a part. Lady Holland put such thinking into action. If men discussed the moral order of Britain in their 'little platoons', they were indebted to England's ladies for embedding their 'little platoons' into mainstream political society.

The ideal of female etiquette matured during the Regency era. Burke set the stage for Regency and early Victorian literature that lauded social stability and public manners in an era when new enclosure laws entrenched the social power of the gentry as never before. Sir Walter Scott's *Waverley* (1814), Lord Macaulay's *History of England* (1848) and Jane Austen's novels epitomized the style. Austen did more than simply reinvigorate the moral imagination of Whig social discourse. She modified it. Austen confidently manoeuvred her female characters through the male-dominated social world and empowered them with private wit and social dignity. As Martin Price argued, Austin differentiated between moral passions (self-righteousness) and moral realism, or the realization that moralizing is itself a danger. In Austen's novels, moral balance is achieved only when it is contained within certain limits and tempered by experience. Describing Austen's difference between moral passion and moral imagination, Price stated,

> The comic sense [wit] is compatible with moral imagination if not moral passion ... it is also a recognition that the moral passions cannot trespass beyond certain limits. The effort to sustain moral consciousness at the same level of intensity in all our experience becomes a form of destructive anxiety. We may sense the consequences of the imperceptible choice and insist upon the fact of choice; yet we cannot always be bringing scruple and moral anxiety to each gesture of our lives ... There is at last a residual innocence we must grant to experience.[102]

With this unconscious morality rooted in experience, Austen gave full flower to the deprecating aversion which marked English high society. Portraying the morally overexuberant as ridiculous, Austen artfully positioned moralizers beneath the notice of the truly virtuous. This social dismissiveness reaffirmed the importance of manners as moral guides without succumbing to relentless rules.

In like manner, Holland House frequenters displayed a certain reticence for the Romantic Lake poets. Lady Holland expressed her distain for the Romantic rejection of the moral code by dismissing any claim the Romantics had on serious literary development with an air of austere deprecation. They were beneath her notice. In particular, Schmid relates a comical encounter between Lady Holland and Lord Byron in which 'Lady Holland ... seems to have scared the poet stiff in a very literal sense. His vision of metamorphosing from a graceful antelope into an item of food, that is, of consumption, mirrors his constant fear of being devoured by domineering women.'[103] Byron cowered before Lady Holland in a way not unlike Austen's own Mr Collins in the presence of Lady Catherine de Bourgh. Here, the power of the Regency Whig aristocracy was complete. Arguably, Lady Holland's social image was one which best exemplified Wollstonecraft's republican ideal for women as austere, self-disciplined public citizens, fully educated and endowed with reason and virtue.[104] Perhaps, Lady Holland's aristocratic airs comprised a new republican identity. In any case, the art of conversation had moved from mannered sociability to social dignity and empowerment. It was a dignity which presumed a place for women in public discourse. This place had been a century and a half in the making.

Conclusion

Women successfully implanted the sociability of the Enlightenment into their coffeehouses and salons, making public spaces safe for new urbanites to establish dispassionate discourse in negotiating trade and the civil service. Women actively expanded the polite culture of coffeehouse life to include middling aspirations towards gentility, making the coffeehouse more polite, commercial and transatlantic. Gender roles and class consciousness were mutually dependent concepts in coffeehouse ownership, and the middling publics who increasingly gained power of the Atlantic world from their coffeehouses soon saw the need to network with other prospective partners as 'ladies' and 'gentlemen' (politeness being both a gendered and a class concept). Shops catered to both the domestic aspects of middling households and the public aspects of polite culture which joined private life to the coffeehouses. Thus, the coffeehouse and the shop came closer and closer together, broadening coffeehouse publics to include lower middling artisans within their polite retinue and putting them in contact with transatlantic social superiors. Although deference was a critical part to social discourse, coffeehouses also invited every aspiring middling customer into a world of leisure, where he could imagine himself a gentleman in contact with European discussions of taste and refinement. Although intended for men, many of the polite coffeehouses in North America were opened by women, who dexterously managed to encourage the illusion of gentility and the allure of politeness for middling publics, both male and female, in shopping districts. Thus, politeness and non-violence followed coffeehouse owners with real social connections.

In court societies like France, ladies supervised the social exchange of polite letters by providing a platform for the high enlightenment to forge vital social networks with court patrons. They became the gatekeepers of 'conspicuous society' and its polite pageant of mixed sociability. In England, the salon came into its own with Whig hegemony of the government. Lady Holland fully embodied the Whig salonnièr, enforcing taste and polite sociability among a small group of invited statesmen and artists who supported the state. In the more popular enlightenment of gazettes and journals, coffeehouse conversation involved a more masculine social atmosphere of news and business. It was judged a persistent and unavoidable oddity to see women in the coffeehouses. When a woman did enter a coffeehouse, regardless of her social standing, she was expected to provide hospitality to a chased form of masculine sociability. The underworld of flash-talk was prosecuted by the state and was generally confined to the dark alleys of Covent Garden. Coffee-women in Boston and Philadelphia obliged the enterprising merchants of North America with a godly and chased form of public morality. Likewise in the south, coffeehouse hostesses opened polite houses for the gentlemen of the town. Their case for licensure depended upon their godly ability to host these men.

The eighteenth-century discourse of women is fraught with contradictions. Ladies appeared in lavish coffeehouse balls and pleasure gardens, escorted by men at special social events. They also organized literary campaigns under the watchful eye of literate gentlemen. This uneasy arrangement posed questions about unsolicited women in coffeehouses. From the sporadic references of women in coffeehouses, it is impossible to claim that men ever fully defended their own domain in all cases, but the women who did enter were almost universally seen as invaders. Swift, Steel and Addison understood that with the advent of social observation, the absence of general allowances for women in the coffeehouses plagued their journalistic experiments with unresolvable controversies. Women who talked freely were clearly inviting ridicule. But how were ladies of taste (perhaps the natural arbiters of such matters) to dispense public virtue in an age when more and more literate middling women actually followed the news and great events of the day? The London journalists desired women to participate in their editorial columns but did not formally allow them the social space to do so. As gazette culture dawned in America, Franklin argued that the gender imbalance actually invited immodest conversation. Men were tempted to play the role of gossip when modest women were completely absent from the city gates.

Figure 5 Gentlemen reading the news in their coffeehouse overlooking the New York harbour.

Contributor: Lebrecht Music & Arts/Alamy Stock Photo.

Figure 6 The General Post Office in London was conveniently situated adjacent to Lloyd's Coffeehouse.

Photo by The Print Collector/Getty Images.

Figure 7 The beginnings of the Wall Street Stock Exchange in the New York Tontine Coffeehouse.

Photo by DeAgostini/Getty Images.

Figure 8 Thomas Taylor, proprietor of perhaps the most successful coffeehouse of his time, Lloyd's of London.

Photo by The Print Collector/Getty Images.

5

Coffee-men, lobbyists and conmen of empire

In 1737, Virginians were ecstatic to hear that 'a large Body of Coffee Men [coffeehouse proprietors], of the Cities of London, and Westminster, waited on the Right Hon. Sir Robert Walpole; desiring his Assistance in the House of Commons, for Relief in the Act against Spirituous Liquors.'[1] Perhaps, thought Americans reading the *Virginia Gazette*, public protest in London would result in more beneficial laws for the trade. Their hopes seemed verified nine years later when the Crown passed several bills in parliament 'for encouraging the Growth of Coffee in his Majesty's Plantations in America; and … for the better securing and encouraging the Trade of his Majesty's Sugar Colonies in America'.[2] However, warehouse inspection procedures frustrated coffee merchants in both London and America throughout the century. In the wake of the repeal of the Stamp Act in 1766, a committee of West Indian and North American merchants met at the King's Arms tavern in Williamsburg and agreed to allow the importation of coffee, cocoa and sugar only into American ports with regular customs houses so that it might be 'deposited, free of duty, in the King's warehouses, until exported'.[3] Eventually, Americans would give up on warehouses altogether and police the trade by colonial committee according to certain non-importation and non-exportation agreements, but that was only after they had exhausted every legal precaution. The coffee-men of London had charted a path of public protest and appeal which later became vital to the Continental Congress.

In the early eighteenth century, coffeehouse lobbyists and proprietors were the third group to try to reform the coffeehouse. These men politicized their efforts and negotiated a more equitable and sociable system of empire across the Atlantic. Proprietors were foremost in lobbying for the political rights of transatlantic associations. They mobilized marine insurers, Exchange coffeehouse merchants and other coffeehouse political activists to stabilize Atlantic trade and provide fair standards for customs procedures. It was this struggle which set the long eighteenth century apart for being an era of political discourse and coffeehouse reform. One vital element about coffeehouse conversation is the significance which coffeehouse proprietors had in opening the political process up to the people in a time long before universal male suffrage. Proprietors had every incentive to impose moderating forms of discourse on their clientele and formalize the imperial importation process of coffee. Theirs was a world of violence and dissatisfied customer experience and the burden of proof rested upon their shoulders alone to demonstrate that coffee was truly a civil drink. Bankruptcy, murder and even sedition hung in the air. This is readily apparent in the cavalier way in which coffee customers called to their coffee-men in coffeehouse poetry and drama. The reputation of a proprietor's house depended on what clientele that proprietor sought and what social connections were available. If a coffeehouse became overrun with too many anonymous travellers or tradesmen, it may have disastrous results for attracting a respectable middling class of customers in connection with vital news outlets and business associations of the city. News was itself a complicated, delicate and expensive process. Historians have considered coffeehouse advertising culture and political pamphlets, but what is often missed is the language of conversation to be had in coffeehouses and the topics of conversation encouraged by coffeehouse proprietors. Nevertheless, evidence exists that coffeehouse owners in London actually banded together to enforce social protocols and make real political change.

Coffeehouse proprietors became the first to politicize the transatlantic process of acquiring coffee and joined hands with enterprising merchants, statesmen and newsmen to further encourage the growth of cosmopolitan coffeehouse development. Their language of protest and reform became the basis for an associational coffeehouse world of critical gazettes and transatlantic newsfeeds. These proprietors actualized the Enlightenment philosophy of right to association. They petitioned parliament and engaged journalists to regulate the coffee trade, formalize the demand for news of transatlantic trade and finance, and reform conversation within the coffeehouse. In London, coffeehouse proprietors of establishments like Lloyd's, Garraway's and the so-called Virginia and Maryland Coffeehouse aspired to provide highly specialized places for transatlantic clientele. They believed that their coffeehouses were havens for civic discourse and 'conspicuous society' but that the media and trade monopolies hampered the development of free association. It would not be until the mid-eighteenth century that the efforts of proprietors would fully realize the birth of an associational world of distinct 'remote neighborhoods' dependent upon a gazetting journalism celebrating right of association.[4]

In the early eighteenth century, very few London coffeehouses subscribed to colonial news outlets for the simple reason that not many colonial gazettes existed. They themselves had to begin the process of connecting news and markets across the Atlantic using informal means, such as letter campaigns to key individuals. In the meantime, proprietors had to deal with delicate credit structures and poor warehouse procedures which threatened their very existence. Corruption was rampant in the East India Company and investors in tea and coffee organized a campaign in the coffeehouses to curtail its power. Coffeehouse proprietors and merchants became some of parliament's earliest and most formidable lobbyists after the Protestant Succession and during the rise of the Whig ascendancy of the government. Coffeehouse petitions put a real interest group of transatlantic merchants behind government reforms of the British shipping and packing industries throughout the world.[5] In orchestrating a more imperialistic and centralized process for gaining dependable coffee supply, coffeehouse proprietors gained a more transatlantic clientele. They also united merchants on both sides of the Atlantic in a scepticism of the corrupt nature of monopolies and their harmfulness to free association. American investors began following the news of dissatisfied coffee investors who publicly burned their chests of damaged tea and coffee in the city square. Gradually, securing a competitive and equitable trade for coffee became a symbol for gaining the right to association (or 'assembly', as the American Bill of Rights would later have it). The coffeehouse then became the metaphor for free information in the gazettes and also for a dispassionate public sphere. Americans would later implement the same language of protest against the tea tax which London proprietors had once made regarding unfair coffee and tea policies.[6]

The personal pressures of extended credit and unpredictable supply

Coffeehouse proprietors were at the receiving end of a long train of colonial merchandizing which often threatened their credit. London shops alone carried more than 146 tonnes of tea in 1784. Large shops distributed tea, coffee, sugar, spices and tobacco to smaller shops with credit structures allowing even the English poor to invest a total of 10 per cent of their household budgets into sugar and tea. Customs officers inspected a total of 7,639,917 pounds of coffee per year in the early 1770s. About seven times that much legal tobacco circulated the British economy every year. The sheer amount of consumer goods encouraged shop owners to invent a 'visual culture' for these products. Troy Bickham argues that this was the result of food's relative greater availability in the seventeenth and eighteenth centuries.[7] Yet these items were not as easy for retailers to obtain as they were for consumers to purchase. The culture of consumption in London was incredibly deceptive. Unlike customers, retailers had to turn a profit in order to buy more and more tea and coffee. This was not always easy to do when their products depended upon shipments of tea, coffee, sugar and tobacco with no predictable schedule for shipment arrivals and departures. *Lloyd's List* kept a running tabulation of index prices, but nowhere was there a list of tea and coffee ships. All inventories were through personal orders and customs inspections. Therefore, coffeehouse proprietors had to watch the Customs Office closely for annual estimates of how many shipments were received and their pound weight. Because the market shifted greatly from year to year, last year's reports were not an accurate means of estimating annual supply, but it was the only means available to coffeehouse proprietors.

In 1718, several coffee merchants and traders in London petitioned the House of Commons for redress when the *Endeavour* pulled into port from Holland with only empty bales to show for its 2,325 pounds weight of registered coffee. The *London Merchant* left port with a shipment of 2,736 pounds weight of coffee for Holland. Frederich Bodzeco was in charge of a returning shipment of 2,325 pounds weight of coffee headed for London, but although the ship returned, the coffee was mysteriously missing. The importers who had ordered the shipment were incensed. It probably meant financial ruin.[8] Consumers were oblivious to these problems of supply when they visited a coffeehouse, but without dependable shipments of coffee, entire merchant associations and wholesalers might not be able to turn a profit. One way to solve the problem was to get a nominated value for the coffee. For his shipment aboard the *Princess Amelia*, Francis White wrote Thomas Woolley to send two East India Company directors to Customs and get a value of the coffee.[9] This was not the first time Woolley was held responsible for compliance with Customs Office procedures. Secretary of Customs Charles Carkesse had written to Woolley in September 1712 saying he was most displeased with the Company's lack of compliance with a recent act of parliament which mandated that all warehouse keepers give an exact account of every pound of tea and coffee brought into and cleared from their warehouse. Carkesse chided the Company for its surprising intransigence in refusing to weigh all their imported coffee and insisted that Woolley move immediately to get the directors to agree to maintaining procedure. This mercantilist approached was muddied by the fact that warehouse keepers rotated positions, and their records needed to be copied over. The East India Company complained that the Land-Waiters who had their coffee in custody had witnessed that it had been weighed out under a previous warehouse keeper. The issue was thrown into the courts, and while the East India Company avoided compliance, coffee merchants in London risked losing everything.[10] Warehouse inspection procedures needed stricter enforcement: a legal battle which would stretch a century.

There were certain members of the Company who were not to be trusted. One tidesman Robert Corner was dismissed from the Company for stealing coffee from the *Princess Anne*. The Commissions of the Customs led the prosecution against him and whoever else up the chain of command who might be suspected. Nine years after Carkesse's confrontation with Woolley over warehouse inspections, Carkesse again wrote to Woolley, requesting that the examination be widened to Captain Nicholas Luhorne and First Mate Charles Hudson in the case of Corner.[11] Carkesse's correspondence reveals that value for coffee was negotiated between customs officers, shipowners and corporate directors. Throughout the eighteenth century, wholesalers and retailers worked to embed into the legal process an accountability structure for the value of weighed coffee shipments and often prosecuted each other for violations. In 1770, a company of shipowners meeting at the Jerusalem Coffeehouse submitted to the Court several proposed amendments to their charter, clarifying loading procedures. It specified uniformity of wages for loading shipments, specific times for voyages starting from the Coast of Coromandel and the Malabar Coast, that all disputes regarding a ship be settled before it begins another voyage, that all outstanding accounts for materials be set at 5 per cent interest, that the managing owners have power to appoint their own officers, since the owners were responsible for them by law, that unloading time should be fixed and, most importantly, 'that freight be allowed for all goods carried out as the property of passengers and persons in India'.[12] This charter established clear transitions in rights of ownership for property in travel and supervisory authority over the chain of command.

Although parliament passed legislation in 1765 requiring stricter warehouse inspections and customs officers had cleared 282,119 pounds weight from South Sea Company warehouses in the year 1766 (valued at £36,035/6/6), coffeehouse proprietors had very little real power to lobby Customs until the Committee for the Management of the Concerns of Lloyd's Coffee House began a correspondence with

Lord Liverpool, requesting formal recognition from the Treasury. This, of course, was part of a war effort against France.[13] The East India Company, on the other hand, had a near monopoly on the eastern warehouses where inspections took place. They possessed a great amount of de facto power in negotiating the economics of the coffee trade. Indeed, too much power, or so thought New Englanders unloading ships in 1765, who complained against customs officers inspecting East India Company warehouses in America. As late as 1813, West Indian planters were stumbling to find a way to establish a system of trade which would allow them protection from the 'Company's Monopoly'. Coffeehouse proprietors were outclassed by the corporate power of the East India Company for much of the eighteenth century, and they knew it.

Thus, American colonials were not the first to protest the collaboration between the Customs Office and the East India Company as a corrupt bargain. The coffeehouse proprietors of London and their transatlantic clientele of investors were the first. They had previously seen corruption in foreign trade during the South Sea Company scandals at houses like Garraway's and Jonathan's, which had sold many of the South Sea Company's bonds in the 1720s. These coffeehouse lobbyists did not wait for Burke's eloquent tirade against the Company's control of India in 1788. They knew very well that the Company controlled a whole lot more than India; they controlled the very process by which goods were inspected in warehouses across British trade outposts.[14] Financial strain caused by corruption in the east was first felt by investors in London's coffeehouses before they reached parliament or the American colonies. Yet, Americans followed closely the protests and petitions made from coffeehouses and mimicked the tactics of coffeehouse proprietors. In 1727, New Yorkers read about angry coffee and tea merchants burning many chests of damaged tea and coffee in the heart of London, while customs officers and East India merchants watched in horror.[15] It was an eerie prelude to Boston.

Coffee-men were so insistent in their quest for fair trade because they had everything to lose. When merchants or coffeehouse owners lost their credit, they were sent to debtor's prison and forced to beg from the very persons who had once been patrons of their establishments. Financial loss meant the loss of one's personal freedom. Timothy Harris was one such unfortunate coffeehouse proprietor who described himself to Sir H. Sloane sometime around 1723 or 1724 as 'a poor, distressed Prisoner, now starving for want of relief of my debt … my very deplorable Condition, will influence your pious Heart, this Holy time of Lent, to commiserate my Distress'.[16] How many more coffeehouse proprietors fell into this strait is lost to the public record. Certainly, the coffeehouses which had less of a reputation suffered more when they went under, and the proprietors of these houses stood a much larger chance of closing. Coffeehouse proprietors must have kept a mental list of notable persons who would be of financial or personal assistance in times of trouble. It might be the only thing to bring them back into business. Likewise, they would have had to keep up personal relationships with prominent wholesalers of coffee, tea and sugar and possibly even talk with customs officers inspecting shipments. Wholesalers, customs officers and respectable customers were not only the economic basis of their trade, they were also the social basis for their class.

Colluding to organize a rational public sphere

Coffeehouse owners began establishing protocols of sociability and controlling consumer experience in order to gain a respectable reputation among notable customers and public critics. Some coffeehouses in London succeeded by appealing to fashion and leisure, others to convenience and trade. All of the notable houses began to link the increasingly politically active press with a stylized language of good taste and sociability. Klein states, 'As fashion shaped the objects, so taste defined the consumer … If consumption was a domain for the actuation of politeness, production had to gear itself to satisfy polite tastes.'[17] He argues that, in particular, coffee and tea became highly ritualized instruments of sociability, requiring very specific arrangements of equipment to aid in preparing and serving hot beverages.[18] Coffeehouse owners attempted to publicly order social intercourse and optimize the consumer experience. Theirs was a delicate balance of providing social cues without creating rules. As Ellis argues, coffeehouse life was not governed by formal rules but rather by implicit modes of behaviour which generally maintained an openness in conversation regardless of wealth, status or power.[19] One satirical notice ran,

> Enter, Sirs, freely, but first, if you please.
> Peruse our civil orders, which are these …
> Pre-eminence of place none here should mind,
> But take the next fit seat that he can find …
> He that shall any quarrel here begin,
> Shall give each man a dish t' atone the sin …
> Let noise of loud disputes be quite forborne,
> No maudlin lovers here in corners mourn,
> But all be brisk and talk, but none too much,
> On sacred things, let none presume to touch.[20]

This obviously glossed over the chaotic sides of coffee, but it did describe a culture. Furthermore, proprietors could expel customers from their common tables if conversation became violent. Proprietors took an eager notice in topics of discussion and began to segment their tables according to the clustering of conversing customers. Later, proprietors began installing wooden partitions and boxes to mark private spaces within coffeehouse conversation. As John Barrell has shown from a close inspection of various coffeehouse prints found in the British Museum, the standard coffeehouse design included a common room and various bookable private rooms. Every common room had a common table, not unlike a country inn, and also a more modern row of booths along the wall. Barrell argues that the very existence of segmented space in the common room delineated between public and private space inside the coffeehouse and emphasized a gentleman's right to private expression. Coffee-men began incorporating private space into their coffeehouses by installing private booths, curtains and reserved rooms for club meetings or private conversations. However, they still maintained the common room with a common table for free and open conversation.[21] The reputation of many a coffeehouse depended upon the protections they afforded polite gentlemen.

How well did the coffeehouse guard the sacred nature of polite conversation? Coffeehouses instituted right to privacy in a public place.

They also had a reputation to maintain with the critics. One such critic styled himself as 'Censor General' and published a pamphlet with his critical review of London social life in *The Connoisseur* (1754). He did not have the keenest appreciation for the coffeehouses of Change Alley, calling its inhabitance 'the unforeskinn'd race'.[22] Gamblers overran these coffeehouses with 'the many little artifices made use of to allure adventurers'.[23] Artifice, ever the enemy of the age of reason, was the vice which proved most destructive to a coffeehouse's reputation.[24] Gaming at Garraway's Coffeehouse drove the customers into furious passions and 'Bubble-Brokers' stood as still as statues, insensitive to humanity around them. Some places in Change Alley were even too horrid for censor George Colman to enter:

> FROM Garraway's it is but a short step to a gloomy class of mortals, not less intent on gain than the Stockjobber: I mean the dispensers of life and death, who flock together, like birds of prey watching for carcases, at Batson's. I never enter this place … Batson's has been reckon'd the seat of solemn stupidity: yet is it not totally devoid of taste and common sense. They have among them Physicians who can cope with the most eminent Lawyers or Divines; and Critic.[25]

Much like the coffeehouse politicians, the coffeehouse physicians were the quacks of the business. The only saving quality was the openness of coffeehouse life which put some doctors in close contact with lawyers and other respectable classes. Compared with Change Alley, Colman believed St Paul's Coffeehouse had a breath of fresh air, with its close connection to the clergy of the cathedral and the booksellers of Chapter Coffeehouse who were 'not the worst judges of merit'.[26] Nevertheless, they suffered from the delusion that the merit of a book was its sales rather than its content. This was the mediocre world of the tradesmen, who were not entirely devoid of a liberal knowledge of literature. Like Dante's Purgatorio, these shadows of wit refined themselves in the heat of the marketplace.[27]

From there, Colman ascended to a sort of literary Paradiso at the suburbs of the Temple and Covent Garden, where the patrons of the law, arts and humanities revolved in their respective celestial constellations. Here, everyone 'trifled', but with taste, leisure and gaiety. It had its coxcombs, but Colman stated that 'the Temple however is stock'd with its peculiar beaus, wits, poets, critics, and every character in the gay world'.[28] Still, Covent Garden held the title as 'the acknowledg'd region of gallantry, wit, and criticism'.[29] Literary men crowded into Bedford's Coffeehouse every night, discussing the merit of every new play and piece of writing from the London press. A 'polite scholar and a wit' presided over a talkative senate of critics, who shared jokes from box to box. Leaving Covent Garden, Colman proceeded to White's and the coffeehouses of Westminster where 'men of Quality' neither debated learning nor cluttered the leisurely atmosphere with business. They kept the 'politer amusements' of 'whist for the trifle of a thousand pounds'.[30] These coffeehouses fashionably displayed the lifestyles of their notable customers on their sleeve. Such was Humphry Kidney at the St James's Coffeehouse, who, as its 'major-domo', became something of an 'arbiter of taste'.[31] Leisure, politeness and customer satisfaction were measures of their reputation among the critics.

Coffeehouse proprietors increasingly discovered that the press could either help or damage their reputations. Several of the most successful coffeehouses in London banded together in 1728 to organize a consolidated news chain to spare the expense of buying many newspapers and to curtail gossip.[32] Under enormous personal and economic pressure, a coffeehouse owner never knew where the next problem to the trade was going to arise. If anyone had reason to formulate a dispassionate public sphere it was the proprietors of coffeehouses where discussion took place. News and coffee had never been complementary trades, and with the explosion of news in the early eighteenth century, coffee-men banded together to protect their interest. In 1728, coffeehouses in London and Westminster formed a sort of guild to institute rules of order for buying certain newspapers throughout their coffeehouses. The assemblies and meetings of the coffeehouse 'brethern' included the following signatories:

> James Ashley. Kent's Coffee-house, Chancery-Lane.
> Stephen Wiggan. Baker's Coffee-House, Change-Alley.
> William Braithwaite. Robin's Coffee-house, Old-Jury
> Thomas Johnson. Elford's Coffee-house, George Yard.
> Charles Molins. Anderson's Coffee-house, Fleet-street.
> Thomas Wills. Tom's Coffee-house, Wood-street.
> Lawr. Page. Will's Coffee-house, Lincolns-Inn Back-Gate.
> George Abington. Abiongton's Coffee-house, Helborn.
> John Morris. Garraway's Coffee-house, Change-Alley.
> William Fielder. John's Coffee-house, Sheer-Lane.
> Thomas Jemson. Lloyd's Coffee-house, Lombard-Street.[33]

Lloyd's issued circular letters, received subscription requests and took out an advertisement in the *Daily Post*, calling for a general meeting of all coffeehouse managers to meet at Tom's Coffeehouse in Wood Street, on the 30th of November. Their most pressing concern was that multiple newspapers were far too expensive for coffeehouse owners to maintain. Middling customers expected not one but the latest issues of all the city papers available in the common room of their coffeehouses, at no expense to themselves. The cost of a dish or two of coffee from each reader was all the remuneration coffeehouse subscribers received. The more papers coffee-men ordered, the less return they got from each dish of coffee.

To remedy the problem, coffee-men called for a guild for information. Coffeehouse papers would not be subject to market demand, for subscriptions were set at a flat rate of one guinea and a single paper cost three half-pence. This guild mentality was also cooperative. Coffee-men promised to divide the profits equally at regular intervals. Like all guilds, the coffeehouse press would moderate its newsfeed. Every subscriber was contractually obligated to keep a book with minutes recording all public 'matters and occurrences' (in classical republican terms, *res publica*) which were deemed 'proper' for public scrutiny. Determining the properness of information was every gentleman's civic responsibility in this republic of letters. Provision six mandated every coffeehouse subscriber 'fix up an Advertisement in his House, giving Notice to Gentlemen frequenting it of this Undertaking; and desiring them to acquaint him with such Events and Transactions, as they shall judge worthy of Publick Notice'.[34] Publishing news would depend on the normative judgement of a literate middling sort by personal solicitation, rather than spying. Time, increasingly the essence of middling life, would regulate the dissemination of news. Clerks were to regularly collect news twice a day from all the subscribing coffeehouses and release it to a designated complier, which brought it to print. Finally, advertising amounted to a standard rate of six pence per ad. Thus, coffee-men boasted that they would be most equipped to provide public news. Having direct access to the private letters of gentlemen who volunteered their information, coffee-men hoped to possess greater ties to foreign cities and domestic discussions. Coffeehouses were 'the Grand Magazines of Intelligence'.[35] News would be discursive, much like it had been in the glory days of coffee pamphleteering, only with a formal guild to protect it.

All the subscribers assembled at Tom's Coffeehouse at 3.00 pm of the 30th to hear Mr Fielder of John's Coffeehouse speak about their resolutions. Fielder identified gentlemanly sociability as the essential aspect of news. If the project was to succeed, it needed to establish a trust between coffeehouse subscribers and informative gentlemen who acted as public notaries to the news. Fielder distinguished between certain kinds of men, those 'Gentleman who are grave, generous, and undesigning, and Persons who are ludicrous, wanton, and Lovers of Mischief'.[36] False news, by its very object of bringing into 'contempt and ruin' the reputations of men customers of the town, depended upon antisocial traits such as 'Borlesque and Ridicule, and render'd of little or no Service, by the ungenerous, unmanly Conduct of Persons of this Turn'.[37] False news overturned that which was 'grave and useful' in the republic of letters, while unmanly and ungenerous men plagued the public sphere with vice. *Gravitas* was the central virtue of this public sphere and it depended upon the 'Credit, Reputation and Universality' of the public trust in the coffeehouse press.[38] Thus, news, like coffeehouse conversation, depended upon sociable traits of universal male fellowship. Fielder predicted 'greater Frequency of Company at their Houses; for a Fresh News-Paper being publish'd every Morning and Evening, the Week and the Year round, every Morning and Evening will Company resort to the Coffee-Houses to see the News ... This is pretty evident from the Custom of Gentlemen upon Post-Nights; who resort in greater Numbers.'[39] Better news would bring better company into coffeehouses and establish a more sociable society.

The resistance against the increasing pressures from news was futile. Political parties had unleased the power of the press. In the tumultuous decade of the 1670s, the court party disseminated broadsides and discussed news openly in the palaces, gardens, state offices and coffeehouses around Whitehall and St James's. Shaftsbury formed the Whig opposition party and showered the coffeehouses across the city with broadsides which favoured the exclusion of James, Duke of York, from the throne of England.[40] The debates during the subsequent Exclusion Crisis (1679–81) were only the beginning of free political debate. With the expiration of the Licensing Act of 1662 in 1695, London had become by default the only capital in Europe with a free press. Thereafter, newspapers and publishing houses sprang up from the gutters of London, in direct competition with coffeehouse broadsides. What had since become known as the golden age of print culture was the end of the coffee broadside news era, proper. London's first daily paper, the *Daily Courant*, began in 1702 and ran until 1735. The *Evening Post*, founded in 1706, was London's first evening newspaper. If these papers were the only dailies in London, coffee-men would have happily laid them on their common tables with the other broadsides and pamphlets. But they also had to subscribe to the *Daily Post* (launched 1719), the *London Evening Post* (1727–1806), *Daily Advisor* (1730–98), the *Gentleman's Magazine* (1731–1907) and so on.[41] Before this new freedom of the press, coffeehouse broadsides were very often the only bastions of public knowledge. Although evening news in particular would have greatly enhanced coffeehouse conversation, since many of the middling customers frequented the establishments in the evenings after going to the theatre, it fundamentally altered the broadside debates once found in coffeehouses. Rather than personal signatories of broadsides, where gentlemen could choose to duel in the 'republic of letters' if they so desired, the press was now incorporated and anonymous. Coffee-men felt the era of the ammeter was over and the reputations of their respectable customers were always at the mercy of an anonymous newsfeed.

A new era of public opinion dawned. Gazettes refined public conversation within coffeehouses and pushed it towards politics, economics and moral philosophy. As merchants looked towards coffee to connect them to markets, they looked to gazettes for political opinion. Many coffeehouse clubs rallied around new political parties for the very reason that the gazettes and magazines allowed their voices to be heard for the first time. Addison and Steele worked in Button's coffeehouse to bring the public into the centre of the political and social commentary, launching *The Guardian* (1713) to host letters to the editor on social issues. The success of this method inspired others to construct political newsfeeds of their own. Beginning in the 1720s, radical Whigs forged the 'Country' party alongside disaffected Tory squires who had borne much of the cost of the War of Spanish Succession (1701–14) with France. Under Lord Bolingbroke these political organizers effectively took politics 'out-of-doors' and into the coffeehouse gazetting public. *The Craftsman* (1726–46), the party's new trumpet, sold like hot cakes with 10,000–12,000 copies per issue. It simply dwarfed the earlier success of *Spectator*. Coffeehouse and tavern publics had found a new voice, especially in provincial towns, where oppositional papers were perhaps even more popular among Britain's middling elites. Papers such as the *Newcastle Courant, York Courant, Norwich Gazette, Gloucester Journal, Salisbury Journal* and *Farley's Bristol Journal* capitalized on the fear of successive Court Whig ministries among the nation's middling readers by publishing loads of oppositional letters and essays. By 1780, the 'nation' had politically mobilized. Thirty-five debating clubs existed in London with a total of 400–1,200 members registered under each club. The press grew from six London daily newspapers in 1746 to fourteen in 1790. These clubs took London gazettes and turned them into a national pastime. British readership increased from 2.5 million in 1713 to 16 million in 1801. John Cartwright's Society for Constitutional Information and the exclusively Female Parliament Society were counter-parliamentary debating offshoots of the radical movement.[42]

Radical opposition to print culture was perhaps most evident in provincial English coffeehouse clubs and journalism, where the public sphere was the only resource against corporate town oligarchies. In fact, because social life in these towns was less aristocratic and more open to an enterprising 'autonomous bourgeois public', provincial newspapers contrasted their civic-mindedness with London's chaotic and corrupt social life. Branches of political clubs sprouted in the provinces. The Duke of Newcastle, a member of the Hanover Club, in 1712 formed the Loyal Societies, or Mughouses, in London and policed political activity on the streets. Provincial authorities likewise formed 'loyal societies' in Bristol, Exeter and Norwich. The Artillery Company of Norwich openly confronted Tory opposition and the Loyal Society of Worsted Weavers. The Whig Constitution Club in Norwich and the Tory Recorder's Club in Newcastle rose above the fray and established London-style political clubs of civil discourse which held quarterly meetings and other social gatherings. Newspapers kept discourse in these clubs informed with political news from London. The *Newcastle Courant* and the *Newcastle Chronical* as well as numerous prints from London and York circulated through about 150 inns, taverns and coffeehouses. Provincial coffeehouses and clubs became centres for Wilkite radicalism and out-of-doors political campaigning during the latter half of the eighteenth century, when the Gordon riots and mob violence threatened to undo the civil public sphere of the earlier club culture.[43]

News abstracted coffee's 'conspicuous society' and allowed publics to extend their coffeehouse discussions into the imagined world of epistolary social critique. A great period of discursive coffeehouse life began when middling coffee customers and coffeehouse proprietors invited this new journalistic culture of politeness into their public resorts. Intellectually, this lasted through London's high enlightenment, from Addison to Thomas Paine's *Rights of Man*. In a process which Benedict Anderson has termed 'print-capitalism', coffeehouse readers bought news as though it were a consumer commodity. Readers could assemble new vernacular communities around books, newspapers and ideas.[44] Using such an interpretive lens, it may be argued that transatlantic subscription syndicates of local news in coffeehouses created new coffeehouse communities: 'remote neighborhoods' of colonial readers following London news and vice versa. Journalists and newspaper writers in London and colonial American cities believed they were engaged in an experiment to elevate the best aspects of urban life into a discussion of classical taste. In so doing they defined new civic duties and moderated the rational pursuit of 'conspicuous society'. Gazettes provided the Atlantic community with a newsfeed which spoke to the needs of merchants, officers and governors alike. These elites congregated in the coffeehouses to get the news straight off the ships and formed business associations which would carry their own news back to London. This journalism began a new era in coffeehouse culture, which celebrated news, *polite letters* and social commentary as the basis for urban sociability. They took political clubs engaged in the public sphere as their cue. Thus, the coffeehouse public sphere intentionally politicized, preparing the way for a transatlantic newsfeed of colonial gazettes which diversified coffeehouse communities into 'remote neighborhoods' of consumers who imagined they were buying the goods and habits of civilized urban life.

Colonial gazettes and their coffeehouse readers imitated the reforms of Addisonian commentary and still preserved their local or regional society columns. Although not all coffeehouse clubs were political, most of the notable ones followed the dispassionate, rationalizing language set forth by all the titles of the great editorial columns and episodic journals which flooded the news market: *The Tatler, The Trifler, The Connisuer, The Spectator, The Guardian, The Rambler, The Idler* and so on. They were not Whig in the primary political sense, but were marked by London's high enlightenment and the style of Addisonian journalism.[45] In reforming the literature read in coffeehouses, these journalists changed coffeehouse life. Violence, discomfort and poor credit continued to be unfortunate aspects of the lesser coffeehouses in London, but they were not consciously embraced by London journalists or American coffeehouses which matured along the London model in the 1760s. For these coffeehouses, a polite clientele came with the gentleman's magazine and editorial columns in the news. Though the issue of politeness and coffeehouse conversation remains controversial, the subject is unavoidable since some of London's most famous coffeehouses earned the reputation for being polite establishments. It was this very reputation which most American coffeehouses aspired to through cultural emulation of English social norms. Nevertheless, politeness cannot be seen as a monolithic evolution towards civility. It was rather a dynamic collision with the issues plaguing coffeehouses through the late seventeenth and early eighteenth centuries. Only the cultivation of *humane letters* would bring about the form of coffeehouse conversation we now remember as polite.[46]

The ethos of dispassionate journalism transformed the press and set the stage for political activism. Swift had argued in 1713, 'the little decorum and politeness we have are purely forced by art, and are so ready to lapse into barbarity'.[47] John Dunton first popularized the civilizing editorial style in his *Athenian Mercury* (1690s), soliciting letters to the editor on scientific, religious or even 'trifling' matters. He called it 'the Question Project' and started his own Athenian Society to adequately answer the questions of the letters. He situated his journal and society in James and Mary Smith's coffeehouse, obviously with the permission of the owners, who understood the significant 'linguistic turn' in discursive space which was taking place. Dunton's journalistic style became the inspiration for social commentary. Addison's and Steele's *Tatler* and *Spectator* were even more influential in laying the groundwork for the sort of dispassionate social commentary which magazines, advisers and gazettes would imitate, for they proved the public success of such a model. Colonial American gazettes like the *New England Courant* and the *New-York Weekly Journal* emulated the social cues of London's journalistic environment to actualize the Addisonian ideal for an editorial club of scholars. This Enlightenment had invented a new form of club.[48] The eighteenth-century journalists signalled a cultural change in the press, which made formalization of the coffeehouse public guild of information an impossibility.

Still, the decision to marry Addisonian gazettes (of whatever political persuasion) with coffeehouse discussion remained ultimately with coffeehouse proprietors. Would they agree to host the clubs and journalists of middling coffee-goers, or would they choose to identify with other interests, like landed elites, or the working poor who flooded 'gin lane'? Most coffeehouse proprietors soon gave up the struggle against expensive newsfeeds and did everything they could to reform their houses into respectable institutions, trusting to polite advertising culture to make up the difference in cost. Politeness was soft power in the eighteenth century which opened public places in cities to politically and socially important groups. Coffeehouse proprietors desired to use this soft power and consciously shifted the culture inside their coffeehouses. Daniel Button understood this when he decided to host Steele and Addison's editorial experiment at his coffeehouse. Indeed, Button used *The Guardian* as a means of improving the public sphere, an informal alternative to the guild method. He helped erect the lion's head to receive editorial commentary of sociable occurrences in the city which became a symbol of Steele and Addison's social reform.[49] He also entered the debate himself, publishing the following request to a notable critic:

> I have observed that this day you make mention of Will's coffee-house, as a place where people are too polite to hold a man in discourse, by the button [see footnote 10 in chapter 3 for 'button twisting']. Every body knows your honour frequents this house; therefore they will take an advantage against me, and say, if my company was as civil as that at Will's, you would say so: therefore pray your honour do not be afraid of doing me justice, because people would think it may be a conceit below you on this occasion to name the name of your humble servant.[50]

Button lobbied for public recognition in the press for being a polite coffeehouse. He understood the vital significance of politeness as a new consumer medium and was proactive in submitting a letter to the editor in *The Guardian*. It proved successful. Thirty years later, the critic Colman commented, 'Button's, the grand archetype of the Bedford, was frequented by Addison, Steele, Pope, and the rest of that celebrated set, who flourished at the beginning of this century, and was regarded with just deference on account of the real geniuses who frequented it.'[51] Coffeehouse owners could not afford to be silent in the press during the critical age of reason, since their own establishments were very much on trial in the press. Most of the notable coffeehouse proprietors actively encouraged a business or leisurely reputation for their coffeehouses. As certain coffeehouses gained specific associations (for literature, or politics, or games, or trade), the image of their customers changed from house to house. For instance, Colman wrote, 'I am a Scotchman at Forrester's, a Frenchman at Slaughter's, and at the Cocoa-Tree I am – an ENGLISHMAN. At the Robin Hood I am a Politician, a Logician, a Geometrician. ... or any thing – but an Atheist.'[52] Above all, critics used politeness and taste to judge the reputations of coffeehouse clientele. Proprietors could do nothing other than enter the public sphere as it was and advance their reputations according to the tastes of that age. They soon joined hands with the printers and gazette writers to forge a shared discursive space of politeness, open 'Country' politics (whether Whig or Tory), fair trade and free association across the Atlantic.

Colonial coffeehouse proprietors and transatlantic print culture

Gazette culture truly transformed coffee culture into an entangled discourse of manners and men across the Atlantic. Colonial gazettes encouraged a leisurely and polite coffeehouse readership by advertising coffee and by discussing manners. The purpose of the gazettes was to educate the populous and transform them into freer, civically minded and virtuous citizens. These included not just transatlantic merchants but actively solicited the input of literate farmers, tradesmen and artisans. In theory, anyone could write a letter to the editor in a gazette. The farmer's almanacs, a staple of American agricultural life until the advent of television, integrated the journalistic style of London's social commentaries with the more mundane aspects of seasonal lifestyles. Almanacs defined an imagined transatlantic discourse, while many of their readers never even made it beyond subsistence living. Yet as recent research suggests, the editors and printers upon which such a news culture depended certainly did rely on a traveling, educated news chain of transatlantic merchants, government officials and fellow printer kinship networks.[53]

The growth of colonial gazettes in the eighteenth century helped to strengthen a transatlantic culture of free association and Anglo habits of sociability into American society. From them, it is possible to deduce much about colonial American coffeehouse life. Much of the narrative of coffeehouses in the gazettes was shaped by the literary style of politeness coming from London's journalistic reforms. Gazettes gave coffee a philosophical trope of right of association and free trade, a meaning which was not lost on coffee customers in cities who went to read the gazettes. Since coffee culture in America grew simultaneously with the advent of gazettes, manners and coffee were almost synonymous terms. As Joseph Adelman states, 'To facilitate these conversations, printers placed their offices as close to the nerve centers of local commercial and political life ... near taverns and coffeehouses, the post office, a market or exchange, or town wharves. Such locations facilitated the easy handoff of essays by local luminaries.'[54] This being the case, the arrangement was a mutual one in which printer and coffeehouse owner cultivated a shared public culture of news for coffee-goers. The coffeehouse proprietor was no less an agent in this transition than the printer. The only reason why one is remembered and the other is very often neglected by the historical record is because the written word is our only remaining access point to their shared social networks. If we only had actual diaries of coffeehouse owners, the various social arrangements inside them might not be so mysterious. The literary imagination of Anglo coffeehouse life infused itself into the actual consumer experience of coffee and print, making it difficult to separate myth from reality. Yet, perhaps simply presenting what colonial Americans saw in their coffee is not disingenuous in this case. In short, colonial Americans saw a polite drink which was different from alcohol in its connection to *humane letters* and enterprising society. Coffee consumption in colonial America involved a balance between the universal theme of free association and the regional aspects of advertising coffee in real local environments.

What brought coffeehouses and printers together across the Atlantic was a shared discursive gazetting culture of discussion and journalism. This, in turn, increased the lobbying power of coffeehouse publics. The *Boston News-Letter* became America's first weekly newspaper in 1704 and Boston also became the first colonial city to establish its own gazette in 1719. By 1760, Boston ran four newspapers in addition to its five other printing houses, some of which were connected to coffeehouses. New York established its gazette in 1725, and among the Charleston urbanites, the *South Carolina Gazette* appeared in 1732. Philadelphia started the *Athenian Mercury* in 1719 and later the

Philadelphia Gazette. After gazettes in Britain began adding cultural commentaries of political events, history, science and society, Benjamin Franklin and David Hall pioneered an Addisonian style of social commentary and political satire for the *Philadelphia Gazette* in 1729.[55] Gazettes spoke the new empirical language of English social commentators. *The Maryland Gazette* headed its front page with the verse from the coffeehouse 'wit' John Dryden,

> Look round the habitable World how few
> Know their own Good! or knowing it pursue!
> How void of Reason are our Hopes and Fears!
> What in the Conduct of our Life appears.[56]

The charge was to observe the world and model life from experience. One of the paper's cultural columns began with the injunction to divert the mind 'from useless Trifles, and instead thereof to furnish their breasts with valuable knowledge'.[57] It promised to liberate minds through knowledge, reason and virtue and insisted on a culture of taste without decadence. The editors eventually shrank the social commentary column in favour of publishing translated Latin poetry from the College of William and Mary, news, parliamentary minutes and more advertising.[58] Evidently, it was easier to impart culture and politics through the news than it was to introspectively evaluate it. Annapolis, Williamsburg, Germantown, Portsmouth, Newport, New Haven and New London founded their gazettes after the same model. Local news was rarely on the agenda for colonial newspapers. Instead, readers preferred to believe that they were participating in a cultural discussion of civic manners and world events through foreign news in a sort of open and oppositional 'Country' style. Political monopoly of any sort was an abhorrence.[59]

Liberal learning was reinforced not only in the gazettes and book selection of coffeehouses in the coffeehouse printing press but also through book auctions held in coffeehouses. Colonial Americans read contemporary and classical literature and participated in the scholarly community of London coffeehouse readers. Booksellers were advertised in the colonial gazettes and read by book connoisseurs in coffeehouses. One such advertisement in the *Virginia Gazette* in 1777 included the Greek New Testament, Horace, Virgil, Plutarch, Shakespeare, Addison and Johnson's dictionary.[60] Booksellers connected various colonial regions together more directly through a universal language of knowledge. Subscriptions for *The Complete Surveyor of North American Lands* crossed boarders, including subscribers from the London Coffeehouse and the Union Library in Philadelphia, Boston, New York, Baltimore and many lesser cities.[61] Coffeehouses went into business with printers to further the culture of literacy and strengthen middling sponsorship of coffeehouse life. Boston printers B. Green and J. Allen and book-trader Nicholas Buttolph sold their books at the corner of Gutteridges Coffeehouse in 1700 and J. Mein founded the London Bookstore at the second door above the British Coffeehouse. In New York, Samuel Loudon and John Holt listed their publishing houses in 1773 simply 'near the coffeehouse'. Their works included theological subjects such as thanksgiving sermons and state reports including the minutes of the New York General Assembly.[62]

The Philadelphia coffeehouse presses were perhaps even more political and the city exploded with coffeehouse newsprints during the eighteenth century. Booksellers Rivington and Brown came from London and established bookstores across from the London Coffeehouse in Philadelphia and the Golden Key in New York. William and Thomas Bradford established their bookshop inside the London Coffeehouse and R. Aitken set up shop three doors from the coffeehouse in Market Street. Benjamin Towne sold his books in Front-street, near the coffeehouse there. Their books informed Philadelphian citizens of revisions to colonial charters, petitions and even manufacturing processes. The Bradfords and E. Oswald and D. Humphreys published regular reports and circular letters. These bookshops drew crowds who desired more public spaces devoted to civic discourse. Several 'respectable citizens' issued a proposal in 1790 for another coffeehouse at the corner of Market and Walter Streets.[63]

Colonial coffeehouse presses were full-orbed social entities in direct connection with Anglo-American critiques of both church and state. It was no secular ideal which infused the coffeehouse market with books, but rather one firmly rooted in the theology of the Reformation. Buttolph at Gutterides in Boston published books on the Gospel and Providence and Loudon on the doctrine of predestination.[64] This theological emphasis had once been the case even in London. From a 1687 auction catalogue at Wellingtons Coffeehouse, the three clerical subjects of theology, classics and philosophy dominated the list, although medicine, geography and astronomy also appeared. It included Latin New Testaments and commentaries from Geneva, *Ovidii Epistolae, Horatii, Juvenalis & Persil Poemata*, Calvin's *Institutes* (listed as *Calvini Institutio Religionis Christianae*), Calvin's sermons in French, the catechisms in the Prayer Book, the Westminster Confession, *Drury's Model of Church-Government* and an extensive range of Puritan devotionals and theological treatises from Thomas Watson to Richard Baxter. It was obvious to the auctioneer that these coffee-goers not only knew Latin but were fluent in the Reformed and classical disciplines of these works.[65]

As universal as this academic coffeehouse readership was, the gazettes reveal various regional responses to the growing service economy of coffee and print. The coffeehouse was a very practicable institution. Coffeehouses served the public locally in advancing useful knowledge, reflecting regional needs and intercolonial trade. For instance, the *Virginia Gazette* announced in 1779, 'A Very Valuable Iron Work, called Carlisle Iron Work' was 'To be Sold by publick vendue, at the coffeehouse in Philadelphia.'[66] Manufacturing interests in the North could more easily be linked with prosperous planters of the South through coffeehouses and gazettes. Boston, in particular, emphasized coffee's proximity to good business opportunities. When Daniel MacNeill came from Dublin with his saddler business in 1769, the *Boston Gazette* announced he set up shop close to the British Coffeehouse. Similarly, creditors announced that they would meet at the British Coffeehouse to settle the debts of the deceased sailmaker Isaac Wendell. The British Coffeehouse was certainly a place of much local financial importance. Just as small businesses in Boston noted their proximity to meeting houses, realizing the importance of these places in settling frequent small matters of public concern, the coffeehouse as an institution grew into the meeting houses of public life of the colony. Hot drinks were easily commercialized among Boston's small shops, such as John Goldsmith's 'choice chocolate' shop near John Hancock's wharf. Rather than obsess over chocolate's leisurely properties, Goldsmith emphasized its cheapness and quality; in short, Goldsmith was concerned with chocolate's commercial properties. He marketed it by simply promising, 'The chocolate will be warranted good, and sold at the cheapest rate. – Cash given for cocoa. Cocoa manufactured for Gentlemen in the Best Manner.'[67] Gentility and industry were thus inseparable. Benjamin Loring understood the character of the colony well when he announced 'that he has opened a Coffee House in Weymouth, near the Meeting House – Gentlemen Travellers, &c. will meet with kind Reception on very moderate Terms'.[68] Loring hoped his new coffeehouse would be an extension of the 'New England Way', where private gentlemen might go to discuss the town meetings and other business on their way to other nearby towns.

In the American South, lawmakers catered coffeehouse life to enterprising plantation elites, rather than leaving the clientele of coffeehouses up to chance. The colony controlled coffeehouse life through licensure. As early as 1690, Maryland passed a law requiring all coffee, sherbet, chocolate and tea retailers to obtain licences, 'for payment of his Duties of excise to the King by Recognizance; for which Licence, Security and Recognizance he shall pay 12 d. and no more, upon pain to forfeit 5 l. for every month he shall Retail without Licence'.[69] To prove one's soundness in the coffee business, one had to prove that one had a civil and polite clientele. In 1768, Maryland formally differentiated coffeehouses from inns and taverns, mandating each key city in Maryland to 'license any Person within the City of Annapolis, Chester Town, Baltimore Town or Frederick Town to keep one Coffee House within the said City and each of the said Towns for the Entertainment of Company and that such Person so licensed as aforesaid shall not be obliged to find and provide Beds for lodging Company or Stabling and Provender for Horses'.[70] Here, Maryland lawmakers were doing more than policing the coffeehouse; they were creating a coffeehouse public sphere. Separating common overnight guests from those who entertained a company in a coffeehouse during the day actually determined its social use and position in the city. The purposes of such licensure laws were to establish a city headquarters for short business meetings between plantation owners and their transatlantic merchants and encourage a civil and polite environment for discussion.

Colonial lawmakers did not intend to diminish the tavern from public life in reserving the coffeehouse for business; it merely wanted to provide a model for socializing which it hoped would then influence even the older taverns. In fact, taverns continued to flourish, and many colonists found that they were better places for informal discussion than the city coffeehouse. For instance, John Doncastle's tavern in Fredericksburg was outfitted with 'a very find London Billiard Table, and what Furniture they shou'd happen to want suitable for such Business; also a considerable Assortment of good Liquors. The House is well known, and us'd by most of the Gentlemen that come to the said Town.'[71] Such taverns became subjects for critical review in the *Virginia Gazette*. All readers knew that taverns were just as successful, if not more successful institutions in America as coffeehouses. In 1776, a debate ensued in the editorial column of the *Virginia Gazette*, between a tavern keeper and an 'enemy of imposition', who pointed out many indecencies of urban life. One writer made a distinction between good tavern owners and bad ones. He argued that the profession was an honourable one for men of merit who provided lawful places of assembly. For public houses that disturbed the peace, he reasoned, 'as publick grievances should be redressed by publick authority, and publick offenders make publick examples of, it is still expected the tavern-keeper who dare fly in the face of justice, in defiance of authority, will be punished according to his demerit'.[72] The argument presupposed London's enlightened civility of peaceful and dispassionate assembly. Law and order should enforce the natural hierarchy of merit among men; such was the prevailing view of the coffeehouse. An example of one such tavern was Raleigh's Tavern, which was closely linked to polite letters. Until 1752, it was the chief subscriber of the *Virginia Gazette* in the city of Williamsburg, and thus Virginian businessmen and statesmen often chose it as their place of assembly.[73] Josiah Chowning's reputation was not that far behind for having a well-furnished and polite tavern. Chowning's first advertisement in 1766 ran, 'their custom may depend upon the best of entertainment for themselves, servants, and horses and good pasture. Josiah Chowning'.[74]

That Virginian coffeehouses sponsored a peculiar form of polite leisure and that it was advertised in the gazettes cannot be doubted. Southern colonial coffee-men understood that taverns had a decided advantage in providing lodgings for its guests, although such a provision opened its clientele up to more than daytime businessmen. Unlike London, Williamsburg's richest businessmen were planters, who only came into town for business and pleasure. Thus, planters tended to conduct business in the most convenient setting, where they could stay the night. Coffee culture had taken longer to solidify in the colonial peripheries because of its social, economic and cultural distance from the London *core*. By mid-century, the coffee-men decided to go beyond the minimum requirement of the law and integrate their houses into the lodging culture of their neighbouring tavern establishments. This was a distinctive southern phenomenon, a regional necessity and reinforced the social mores of the leisurely planting elites. In this sense, American southern coffeehouses operated more as rural inns than their urban London counterparts. Yet, they embraced gentility and politeness, and advertised their establishments for polite gentlemen in the gazette. Such advertisements featured 'Private Lodgings … for seven or eight Gentlemen, during the Assembly, at the Coffeehouse, by the Capitol.'[75] The proprietor had obtained this coffeehouse a year before in 1771 in an estate sale at the Raleigh Tavern. It was telling that not even a coffeehouse excellently positioned next to the Capital Building of Williamsburg sold out at Raleigh's. Yet an advertisement in 1769 had stated that it 'has been long used by many Gentlemen, in assembly and court times'.[76] If so, it found formidable competition in Raleigh's. The planters and visiting statesmen needed lodgings and often resorted to the old and notable taverns of their cities. Arguably, it was not until the tax crisis and revolutionary period when colonial coffeehouses came into their own as meeting houses, but then the emphasis was not on cultural reform and polite letters but rather protest and war. In the meantime, coffeehouse proprietors in key Virginia cities built up their reputation through the 1760s and 1770s.[77] Richard Charlton opened his new coffeehouse for 'all Gentlemen travellers, and others, who may please to favour him with their company, that they will meet with the best entertainment and other accommodations, such as he hopes will merit a continuance of their custom'.[78] Charlton's announcement followed Chowning's first announcement by a year. His followed the same pattern. Charlton, borrowing from Enlightenment social philosophy, announced that his genteel accommodations would merit patronage by allowing free association. Coffee was the rational drink of a social meritocracy which honoured the civic minds of the planting elites. Terese Pearse of the King's Arms Coffeehouse in Norfolk was even more specific. Her coffeehouse was 'a very genteel and convenient INN and TAVERN (with good Stabling for Horses) for the Accommodation of Travellers and others; supported by a Society of Gentlemen'.[79] The clientele which colonial coffeehouse proprietors sought were those who were statesmen or businessmen who read the gazettes and discussed news.

So connected was coffee and polite letters that the subscriber of the *Virginia Gazette* in Fredericksburg actually purchased a coffeehouse.[80] One way to attract an enterprising and polite clientele of coffeehouse gazette readers was to tie coffeehouse establishments to the entertainments of the city and imported commodities. Although there is no evidence in the *Virginia Gazette* to suggest that the Williamsburg Theater solicited coffeehouse customers directly, it may well be imagined that since Shakespeare was regularly preformed and advertised in the gazettes, it infatuated coffeehouse news readers.[81] When Mary Dickinson moved her millinery shop above the coffeehouse near the Capital in Williamsburg, she announced in the *Virginia Gazette*, 'a GENTEEL and very elegant Assortment of JEWELLERY and MILLINERY' from London ready for 'those Gentlemen and Ladies who have favored me with their Custom'.[82] Evidently, polite consumption and elegant sociability came from the same source, the coffeehouse. As early as 1737, the *Virginia Gazette* assured coffee-men that an act of parliament to suppress gin would not have a great impact on coffeehouses because their clientele was different. The article claimed that 'the Design of the Act being only to prevent the pernicious Consequences of strong Liquors sold at Gin-shops among the common People … at no Coffee-houses of Reputation was there ever any Complain of its being drank to Excess, or any bad Consequences happened from the drinking that Salutary Liquor'.[83] The coffee culture which Americans chose to cultivate was sober, polite and literate, not the common people of the gin houses. It was more inclined to the business and social life of the middling sort. These customers could follow the gazettes for a cosmopolitan discussion of the entangled nature of their leisurely world.

Transatlantic lobbyists and the economics of empire

All this sociability translated into real political power in the eighteenth century. The reformed coffeehouse increasingly served transatlantic merchant lobbyists who were independently becoming more and more powerful with administrators in the Board of Trade. Alison Olson has noticed that coffeehouses were closer to the wharves in Atlantic cities, and as such, merchant lobbyists almost always received news from letters and agents from ship captains who dropped them off at merchant coffeehouses before the official reports were available to the government at Whitehall. This is an essential point in understanding the transatlantic political process in the eighteenth century. The coffeehouses with American interests were all located one block away from Cornhill, on Seething Lane, Threadneedle, Fish Land and Birchin Lane, in close proximity to both the Royal Exchange and the Post Office. The strongest of these were the Chesapeake merchants at the Virginia-Maryland Coffeehouse who met year-round almost daily. They actually brought the duties on tobacco down during the 1650s and alongside Anglican ministers in America, Virginia planters lobbied for a tobacco inspection act. By 1712, they were formally organized at the Exchange and created their own committee to draft petitions, manage dues and send representatives to meetings with the Board of Trade. By 1734, four distinct London-colonial merchant groups had formed their own clubs at their respective coffeehouses: the Chesapeake, Carolina, New England and New York lobbyists.[84] These groups had real power because of the coffeehouse mail service and the social networks behind it. Olson states, 'Coffee house patrons could assemble quickly, within a day or so if necessary, and decide which information to pass on to the government and what action to press before the government servants learned the news themselves.'[85] Their lobbying power reached a peak during the years 1721–54, when Sir Robert Walpole, the Duke of Newcastle, and Henry Pelham held successive and uninterrupted control of the government with close connections to both disaffected Protestant groups and American lobbyists. Through their efforts, a more open and responsive mercantilist system of trade was hammered out, in which the customs office grew by 30 per cent to match the growth in colonial trade. Maryland merchants in London even asked the Board of Trade to bar the government of Maryland from passing any commercial law in less than eighteen months, so that they had time to review its impact on the transatlantic trade.[86]

Nor was this system of lobbying confined to the coffeehouses of London. American merchants soon realized the vital importance of cementing a postal ring of lobbyists across American cities with London coffeehouses. Accordingly, they built merchant coffeehouses of their own. By 1720, colonial merchants had established at least one coffeehouse-tavern in Boston, New York, Philadelphia and Newport, where they received the mail; signed petitions; distributed broadsides; bought insurance; raised capital, securities and interest; and held public auctions. At the British Coffeehouse, Boston merchants formed a club in the 1750s which consisted of 146 members. New England Quakers lobbied against discrimination. From 1690 to 1717, the London-American Quaker lobby grew to become one of the most powerful provincial blocks. They even repeatedly barred passage of bills which would have reverted charter colonies back to the Crown. Boston, Gloucester and Marblehead merchants commissioned Christopher Kilby to sail to London and bar passage of the liquor tax. Since London merchant clubs had no corresponding committees to speak of, such actions had to be undertaken independently through private agents or letter-writing campaigns organized in local coffeehouses. At the Exchange in New York, merchants held meetings from 1753 onwards, Charles Town had about 200 such merchant activists and Philadelphia possessed about 260 merchants who all met in a tavern and coffeehouse closest to the marine post. Most of these colonial societies lobbied for foreign immigration to America which they hoped would increase consumer demand. Also of prime importance to these societies was the supply of paper money, since formal hard currency was in extreme short supply. Charles Town merchants wanted regulation on auctions to stop the practice of underselling and Philadelphians lobbied for more flour quality inspections and regulation on the dimensions of wooden staves. These coffeehouse communities changed the course of public policy across the Atlantic. What is plain from all the evidence from coffeehouse lobbyists is that they were activists supporting the mercantilist system and attempted to further their own interests within it. All supported bounties on their exports.[87]

Still, it is also plain that behind the mercantilist attitudes of transatlantic merchants who accepted the Board of Trade's legal prerogatives, a freer notion of trade and private association loomed. What is easy to miss is that the journalizing culture of coffeehouse life, reflective in the gazettes and the discussion of public manners in the eighteenth century, depended upon the moral necessity of a free press and public opinion. Sectarian though it was, coffeehouse lobbing embraced a culture of public *critique* of that which concerned the public good. The right to association or freedom of assembly was championed by all and morally validated the voices coming from the reformed coffeehouses. Polite, dispassionate discourse would open the world to a freer and more open fraternity of man, where competitive markets and morality represented the same public spirit. It might even abolish war itself! George Washington freely embraced the utopian aspiration of the age when he wrote to the Marquis de Lafayette in 1786,

> As a Philanthropist by character, and (if I may be allowed the expression) as a Citizen of the great republic of humanity at large; I cannot help turning my attention sometimes to this subject. I would be understood to mean, I cannot avoid reflecting with pleasure on the probable influence that commerce may hereafter have on human manners and society in general. On these occasions I consider how mankind may be connected like one great family in fraternal ties. I indulge a fond, perhaps an enthusiastic idea, that as the world is evidently much less barbarous than it has been, its melioration must still be progressive; that nations are becoming more humanized in their policy, that the subjects of ambition and causes for hostility are daily diminishing, and, in fine, that the period is not very remote, when the benefits of a liberal and free commerce will, pretty generally, succeed to the devastations and horrors of war. [88]

Only an eighteenth-century man acquainted with the gazetting language of freedom could have hoped for such an ameliorating influence of trade and public civility. For this reason, Washington encouraged gazettes and magazines (the upper-end society journals of eighteenth-century news culture) throughout every American city, town and village as the 'vehicles of knowledge, more happily calculated than any other, to preserve the liberty, stimulate the industry and meliorate the morals of an enlightened and free people'.[89] Washington believed he could preserve the civil social order across the Atlantic through free trade without British standards of fairness set by the Board of Trade and the civil service, but the reality was that radical factions from below were already separating American discursive spheres from British ones.[90] Independence forced the founders to make their choice between national sovereignty and the old Atlantic fraternity of gazetting politeness as a legitimate public sphere for politics. A year after Washington wrote these words, the Convention at Philadelphia signed the Constitution, which by 1789 had solved the legal disputes behind the American civil social order, but it also created a new public sphere which replaced the Atlantic one. Moral statesmanship would supersede moralizing journalism as the anchor point in American political order and jurisprudence. Yet, Washington still hung on to the utopian aspirations of coffeehouse lobbyists which had constructed a language of freedom for Atlantic merchants and civil servants.

The newfound freedom of coffeehouse lobbyists is particularly evidenced in the confidence of transatlantic merchants following the settlement of debts after the Seven Years' War (1756–63). The war forged new transatlantic financial associations which the Board of Trade ultimately failed in incorporating into the fiscal state. What began as a trade dispute on the frontier became a global war and ended in a frenzy of land speculations and tax protests. During the 1750s, the French constructed a series of forts in the Ohio to secure their fur trading and hunting rights in the *Pays d'en Haut* (Great Lakes region)[91] and the lands west of the Appalachians. French Captain Pierre-Joseph Celoron de Bainville took his Canadian regulars and their native allies through a tour of the Upper Ohio, securing key positions and opening trade negotiations with western tribes such as the Shawnee and Miami. Under the command of Charles-Michel Mouet de Langlade, two hundred Ojibwa and Ottawa warriors attacked and destroyed the British frontier village of Pickawillany in 1752. Celoron reinforced this victory with a series of forts north of the Mississippi, adding reinforcements to Niagara, and establishing armed detachments at Presque Isle, Venago and Fort Le Boeuf. Virtually every notable north-western tribe was on the side of the French, save the Iroquois Confederacy, which had official ties with the British to maintain neutrality, but frequently betrayed British colonial movements to the French. The Iroquois had successfully played British–French politics to their own advantage and had secured trading rights and land with both sides. What offset the delicate balance of power was the Hudson Bay Company's decision to invest in American lands west of the Appalachians and to enforce the charter of Virginia which claimed sovereignty. Settlers and surveyors moved into the Ohio region, and Governor Robert Dinwiddie backed up their rights to the area with the militia. George Washington was sent with a small force in 1753 to move the French off the Ohio area. He successfully routed a small French vanguard but was soon forced to surrender and compelled to take the blame for assassinating the French envoy.[92]

For Britain, France and eventually Austria, Prussia and Russia, the beginning of hostilities in the American frontier would present the much more alluring prospect of challenging the balance of power in Europe. Gaining more of a foothold in Europe was the prime objective, but that front turned out to be a disappointment for all sides. The map really changed only in the American, Pacific and Asian colonies. Immediately after hearing of Washington's defeat, Newcastle's government began war plans. In early 1755, General Braddock took two regiments into the Ohio to dislodge the French. Governor Shirley would take Niagara with a New England force. William Johnson was to lay siege against the French forts Carillon and Saint-Frédéric at Ticonderoga and Crown Point respectively with volunteers from New York. Finally, British regulars and colonials would venture to take Fort Beausejour near Nova Scotia. However, a lack of colonial coordination doomed British operations in America. Braddock did not know the terrain and British field tactics were unsuccessful in Ohio backcountry. Indian scouts alerted the French of the British position and the French harried the army long before they reached Fort Duquesne on the Ohio River. Braddock was killed and lost nearly two-thirds of his men, before Washington accomplished a retreat. Colonial governments began to debate whether a British army should be used at all in colonial wars. Yet, Shirley's and Johnson's colonial armies were no more successful. They struggled supplying their men and found the logistics of moving big armies throughout the American wilderness as difficult as Braddock had found it. Johnson stood still, transfixed at the prospect of moving on Ticonderoga or Crown Point. His success in defeating a disorganized French assault earned him a baronetcy, but it did not move American objectives forward. The only objective which was successful was the Nova Scotia campaign, in which Colonel Robert Monckton took Fort Beausejour as planned. The French Acadians in Nova Scotia were given one last chance to swear loyalty to the British Crown. Many refused, and thousands were deported to New France on the Canadian mainland, losing their homes and property. This act enraged the French Canadian population and forged their determination to continue the war.[93]

With Braddock's defeat, French and Indian raids ravaged the countryside in Pennsylvania, Maryland and Virginia, and the Iroquois plundered the New York backcountry. The capture of Fort Oswego encouraged both French and Indian fervour for the war. Unlike English armies, French settlers and Indians fought alongside each other, sharing the spoils. By 1756, British officers knew that a massive British campaign would be necessary to continue the war. Lord Loudoun was sent with two more regiments of British regulars to replace Braddock's failed attempt in the Ohio region. When Loudoun arrived, the French had just taken Fort Oswego in August 1756, and Loudoun tried to force colonial governments into raising and providing for a provincial army under his command. The governments of Pennsylvania, Virginia and Massachusetts resisted his attempts at raising a colonial force under British commanders with colonial money. Yet, Loudoun's strategy was tactically aggressive. He launched a direct assault at the centre of New France, along the St Lawrence, and requested a strong army and strong navy from England. Prime Minister William Pitt's new ministry quickly responded to Loudoun's demands by providing several thousand men and a navy. Their orders were to attack Louisburg on Ile Royale and Quebec. Historians are divided as to how effective the combination of British regulars and American colonials were as a fighting force. Certainly, Loudoun's brisk manner at Boston, Philadelphia and other colonial capitals only increased tensions. Yet, more recent military history sees the indispensableness of British regulars in winning the latter campaigns of the war. Average soldiers serving in the regular army adapted more quickly to light infantry and flanking tactics in America than had previously been acknowledged. Yet, quartering British regulars in American homes began a constitutional debate between Britain and her colonies over rights. Parliament had allowed the British army to be housed at all inns and public houses, but in America, most taverns had no stables. Loudoun accordingly began forcing private citizens to quarter his soldiers, and colonists protested that according to the Bill of Rights, private quartering was illegal. Loudoun complained that the colonies were protesting that parliament had no authority over them in the inn act but were using parliament's Bill of Rights on the other hand to argue against private quarter.[94]

Loudoun waited in Halifax for his new British army and navy longer than he expected. By the time all had arrived in July 1757, the French had similarly amassed a large fleet at Louisburg, and French General Montcalm had prepared a force of French and Indian allies to attack Fort William Henry on Lake George. In early August, Montcalm besieged the Fort William Henry on Lake George and within a week had compelled the British to surrender. Although Montcalm had promised quarter for British prisoners, the natives massacred many captured soldiers before Montcalm could put a stop to it. Loudoun understandably balked at attacking the heavily guarded French forts. Pitt's administration finally settled matters by qualifying colonial leaders with junior officer positions in the British army and replacing Loudoun with General Abercromby. Pitt's government promised a more active British military presence in the Americas and in Europe, one which cooperated with its allies and fellow colonists.[95]

In Europe, Fredrick's Prussian army met the French to the west, the Austrians to the south and the Russians to the east. Austria took Silesia back from Prussia after their defeat and loss of that territory in the War of the Austrian Succession. France invaded Hanover. Britain offered troops to Ferdinand in Hanover, but these only succeeded in keeping the French at bay. At first, the engagements seemed to go very well for Prussia. Although vastly outnumbered, Fredrick won the battles of Rossbach and Leuthen (1757), regaining much of Silesia and putting the Austro-French hold over Bohemia in jeopardy. Gradually, however, Fredrick's threadbare army began showing signs of wear. In the exhausting battle of Zorndorf (1758), Fredrick lost more men than he could afford, and the battles of Hochkirck (1758) and Kunersdorf (1759) ended in defeat. However, Russia and Austria did not follow these up with a decisive victory inside Prussia. The European theatre ended in deadlock and the treaty in 1763 returned European borders to their antebellum status. What did redound to Britain's favour was the campaign in India under the leadership of Robert Clive. Clive's victories in the north of India, particularly at Plassey (1757), secured Bengal for the British. However, the fighting in the south to subdue the French-backed Sepoy army at Pondicherry and Madras dragged on a while longer. The French gradually withdrew their naval support because of British naval strength, and the whole of India virtually fell into British hands.[96]

Meanwhile, the massacre at Fort William Henry increased the desire for war within New England. Whereas in Boston, Loudoun had struggled to get just 2,000 recruits, now 7,000 men volunteered for service. Connecticut raised 5,000 troops, New Hampshire raised 800, Rhode Island raised 1,000, New York raised 2,680 and Pennsylvania raised 2,700. The British planned a three-pronged attack: first on Louisburg and Quebec with 14 regular battalions and 5 American ranger companies (about 14,000 men) under General Amherst and a fleet; second on Montreal from New York with 9 regular regiments and colonials amounting to about 25,000 troops under command of Abercromby; and third on Fort Duquesne on the Ohio with Brigadier John Forbes's 2,000 regulars and 5,000 colonists. The British launched a successful assault on Louisburg in July 1758, but Amherst hesitated to invade Quebec. Abercromby failed in taking the fortress at Ticonderoga and retreated after losing about 1,967 regulars and provincials in the struggle. However, Abercromby's quartermaster, Colonel John Bradstreet, attacked the French at Frontenac on Lake Ontario and effectively separated the French supply chain from Canada into Louisiana. The third prong was also successful, and Forbes forced the French to surrender at Fort Duquesne in November 1758 with the unexpected support of more native allies. The changing nature of native alliances was a major factor in Britain's eventual victory over North America.[97]

From parliament's perspective, this was a war for the conquest of Canada and not merely the defence of its colonial claims in North America. It proposed a grand operation in Canada for the year 1759 with three main objectives. General Wolfe was commissioned with an amphibious force to strike Quebec City directly. Amherst would take command of Abercromby's New Yorkers and once and for all take Ticonderoga and Crown Point, and move into Montreal. Finally, Sir William Johnson and General Prideaux replaced the deceased Forbes with instructions to move through Niagara. On 4 June 1759, Wolfe's force reached Quebec City from Halifax and eventually scaled the Heights of Abraham, after looking for ten weeks for a chink in the French defences. Wolfe gained Quebec but lost his life in the battle. Johnson and Prideaux defeated the French at Niagara with the help of the Iroquois, who had renewed their Covenant with the British in late 1758. Montreal fell on 7 September 1760. This effectively ended war in the north, but fighting continued for a time in the Caribbean and the Pacific between France, Britain and Spain. Britain seized the islands of Martinique and Guadeloupe from the French and Havana, Cuba and Manila in the Philippines from the Spanish. This gave Britain a decided advantage in the peace talks in late 1762. France ceded all of Canada and Illinois in exchange for the return of their more profitable sugar islands. Likewise, Spain would surrender Florida in order to gain Cuba. France was forced to give away Louisiana to Spain, who wished a buffer zone between British North America and its western holdings. These successes ushered in a glittering era of British world supremacy, just as George III had newly ascended the throne in 1760.[98]

Yet even with the rise in British patriotism came colonial frustration and transatlantic financial chaos. British national debt totalled nearly £146 million, while annual revenues equalled less than £10 million, and future British administrations expected the Americans to pay a share. The ensuing tax crisis in America, resulting from Grenville's sugar and stamp taxes (1764–5), forever changed the relationship between Britain and her colonies. Of prime importance to Americans was their right to legislate for themselves and also to maintain their legal claims over the frontier, which had been their reason for beginning the war in the first place. In response to devastating Indian risings like the Cherokee War (1760–1) and Pontiac's War (1763–6), parliament passed the Proclamation of 1763, which prohibited any Anglo-American settlement west of the Appalachian Mountains. It was already too late, for American companies were buying up the land for themselves. The Ohio Company revived itself after the close of the war and invested in the settlement and trade which had been made possible by new military roads and secure forts. The Company sought for a licence from the Virginian lieutenant governor, Francis Fauquier, for ownership of the Pittsburgh area and the Forks of Ohio before Pennsylvanians could gain possession. Meanwhile, the Loyal Company asked Fauquier for an overlapping claim for southern Ohio. Fauquier promptly relayed the request on to the Board of Trade. The Board upheld Indian hunting rights to the area and discouraged settlement. Finally, the Ohio Company approached the Privy Council in London, with Colonel George Mercer acting as agent. Yet, the Company was not allowed to formally sell land until after 1763 and only in the Fort Cumberland area. Most of its settlers were already to be found up and down the Ohio without the protection of the law. Furthermore, American land claims in the wake of the war were now entangled in a transatlantic discourse for legal recognition, involving the Board of Trade and American companies.[99]

It is impossible to demonstrate that the war fundamentally altered Anglo-American consumer habits in any way, or else increased or decreased the spread of coffeehouse culture across the Atlantic. Yet, the war did set up a transatlantic fiscal crisis which would play out in the coffeehouses of London and across North America. American debt from the war cemented an unbreakable tie between coffeehouse communities who had invested in the debt and the British government, who could not escape the pressure which these lobbyists exerted from the merchant coffeehouses of London. The question of imperial revenue was a very serious one for the transatlantic merchant community, representing Britain's constitutional commitment to protect private property. War with France had not only left the British coffers dry but it heightened the transatlantic imperialism of merchant association based in London coffeehouses and operating in America, who demanded that the governments of Europe honour their debts. In this struggle international treaty agreements which settled war debts had an impact on the economics of transatlantic association. Merchants argued that if the Westminster government was not fiscally sound, then it would have devastating effects on American assets. One such case was the committee of proprietors and holders of Canada bills and reconnaissances in the Seven Years' War. They formally organized in 1765 in the New York Coffeehouse in London and resolved to accept from the British and French courts no less than 50 per cent of the worth of their bills of exchange and 25 per cent of all cards and ordinances. This amounted to about £100,000–£150,000, but they dropped their figures to £80,000–£120,000. The Court of France, although bound by treaty to honour the debts, did not agree to pay the full amount for any foreseeable future. In June 1766, the committee tallied an estimated 2,500,000 livres which had yet to be paid. In July, the committee displayed certificates for liquidation of the national debt. They formed a committee for the express purpose of liquidating Canada papers and petitioned the Lords Shelburne and Richmond for recognition in the House of Lords.[100]

The British Importer sealed the certificates of the committee as being lawful British property after the settlement with France over Canadian lands. The committee had some legal grounds for their case, but their cause would ultimately depend on the personal influence they could gain. Without patronage, their petitions meant little more than paper and could not force parliament to consider honouring their debts over other budgetary concerns. During the years 1767 and 1768, the committee resubmitted its claims individually by bill holder, but several claims were rejected and the government began converting reconnaissances into rent contract stocks. The committee begged Lord Waymouth for ministerial protection in 1768. Meanwhile, the French government declared in a subsequent treaty in 1767 that all bills delivered to the merchants in Canada for providing for French Troops would be paid, but as of 1769, they had not honoured the terms of the treaty. Furthermore, the committee faced opposition in the House of Lords. While petitioning the House of Lords, the committee switched addresses from the New York Coffeehouse to Tom's Coffeehouse, Cornhill. Their petition fell on deaf ears in April 1769 and the committee decided to withdraw their formal request and depend solely on Weymouth's personal pursuit of their case in the House.[101] A note to Weymouth in April 1769 stated, 'They have Come to the Resolution of dropping their Application to the House of Lords for this Session, remaining in the fullest Confidence that his Lordship will Exert his utmost Endeavors to procure them immediate and Effectual Redress for the Breaches of the Treaty they Complain of.'[102] The committee decided to hang the legality of their demands on their social influence with the nobility of England; a relationship which was truly a transatlantic one negotiated from the coffeehouses of London.

France had threatened to discount the value of all reconnaissances not honoured before October 1769. An estimated 2,567,587 livres, ten sous remained in question under British claims. Duc de Choiseul with the French government suggested that British proprietors should accept two million livres of the total claims and the British government agreed to settle for the two million. This was estimated to be almost a 20 per cent reduction of the capital in question. The Committee was concerned with some reason that the government was going over their own heads in deciding their own property. They complained to Weymouth, 'The Original Claim amounted to upwards of 23 Millions and were reduced on Liquidation to 7 Millions or thereabouts, and what with alarming Edicts, and other Chicanes made use of, the Proprietors have been frightened to part with so much of their Property as to reduce it to the Quantity above specified.'[103] However, the committee was ready in April to agree with Choiseul's plan of exempting British Canada reconnaissances from the terms of the 1767 treaty but insisted that the funds discussed in the treaty were only a portion of the outstanding bills in their possession. The committee asked Weymouth in May 1769 to go public in the papers and gazettes, publishing the news that the proprietors only had a certain amount of time to cash in on their reconnaissances. The committee also asked for complete payment on the interest and principal of their bills. The fact that France was honouring some of the bills in a limited time frame compressed the terms of the payments and the committee feared that British claims would be confused with French claims.[104] They told Weymouth, 'The treaty of Peace whereon the convention was founded always held the British property of Canada Paper separate & distinct from France's Property, it has always been understood in that Light and all the proofs required & Negotiations enter'd into have separated these two property's.'[105] The international nature of the claims and specifically France's demands spelled confusion for those merchants attempting to manage the value of these bills for the merchant economy in Canada.

This negotiation of value dragged on into the early 1770s. In 1770, the French court once again decided to skew the value by converting Canada reconnaissances into contract stocks and thereby reducing interest on them. The Canada proprietors asked Weymouth for assurances of payment for the year 1771. By July 1770, it looked like the outstanding papers were virtually worthless for not having been payed. 'The Situation is very critical,' exclaimed the merchants.[106] They told Weymouth, 'This cause will no longer be that of a few Individuals, but where the honor and dignity of the Nation shall be so interwoven with it.'[107] In other words, the debt was a matter of national honour.

Property was a constitutional right and could not be denied. William Tooke, deputy chairman of the Canada committee, wrote to Rockford, telling him that outstanding interest was a national degradation. He complained,

> Now it appears, That in that List, Reconnaissances to the Amount of about 60,000 Livres, are property, not Liquidated in Great Britain, tho' British property; The French have Continued to pay the Interest due on all the Sums Specified in that List, till January last, When they refused to pay the Interest due on these 60,000 Livres, This is a very great Hardship on the Holders of these particular Reconnaissances, because the Reconnaissances themselves, when taken by British Subjects, did bear no Mark of Distinction, Whether proved in Great Britain, or Not, And when the Interest was continued to be paid to the British Holders of these Reconnaissances under that Edict.[108]

This speech motivated action. Rochford came back with a settlement which the committee found more agreeable but still with a significant deficiency in value. They resorted to a lottery. The committee sent Weymouth with a list of 60,000 livres in outstanding claims. Rochford saw to it that final arrangements were made and the committee personally thanked him for overseeing the final payment. However, the French only complied half-way, and the committee found that 'their whole Claim has been about half a Million short of their List of 2,567,507 Livres'.[109] The coffeehouse debate ended there, with only partial fulfilment of the balance. The case of the Canada proprietors reveals a very significant aspect of the fiscal crisis which led up to the American Revolution. Problems of government revenue were prosecuted by transatlantic merchants in coffeehouses, who demanded their fair share from the costs of wars. The British treasury, pressured by merchants in America to honour its debts, began taxing the colonies when all else failed. But the mechanism for doing so depended upon two vital institutions: a new customs office for America and a mail service which connected government officials serving in America with the London government. Coincidently, the Crown's move to generate revenue from an American postal service began just as the Seven Years' War was beginning. And that effort involved tapping into the coffeehouse social network of America's most successful printer, Benjamin Franklin.

Conclusion

George Washington, addressing the United States in 1783 after honourably resigning from the Continental army, victoriously declared,

> The foundation of our Empire was not laid in the gloomy age of Ignorance and Superstition, but at an Epocha when the rights of mankind were better understood and more clearly defined, than at any former period, the researches of the human mind, after social happiness, have been carried to a great extent, the Treasures of knowledge, acquired by the labours of Philosophers, Sages and Legislatures,

through a long succession of years, are laid open for our use, and their collected wisdom may be happily applied in the Establishment of our forms of Government; the free cultivation of Letters, the unbounded extension of Commerce, the progressive refinement of Manners, the growing liberality of sentiment, and above all, the pure and benign light of Revelation, have had a meliorating influence on mankind and increased the blessings of Society. At this auspicious period, the United States came into existence as a Nation, and if their Citizens should not be completely free and happy, the fault will be intirely their own.[110]

When Washington spoke of a 'progressive refinement of manners' on equal terms with what some historians have called the 'high enlightenment', or the political philosophy of Locke, Hume, Voltaire, Montesquieu and Gibbon, he referred to the coffeehouse journalism which laid the foundations for clubbable sociability and classical taste. For Washington and a great many American Founders, this is what Independence was all about, saving the civil social order of fraternity from tyranny. Although Washington took issue with the secrecy and discrimination of club culture, a secrecy which led ultimately to faction or party, he was still indebted to the mannerism of gazette clubs in London coffeehouses for his understanding of a friendship which truly brought citizens together in a public fraternity.[111] Only when a people had realized this 'growing liberality of sentiment' towards each other could they be entrusted with a government of their own. That 'sentiment' and 'refinement of manners' came about only because coffeehouse proprietors chose to become active in the political culture of the day and turn their houses towards the consumer publics who desired more political and social influence.

Coffeehouse lobbyists and proprietors provided social order to coffeehouses and pushed for a fairer system of economic empire across the Atlantic world. Proprietors moderated coffeehouse supply and demand with a variety of approaches, but all with the end of making coffee more readily available and safer to consume in a free market. It is to the proprietors that we must give the primary credit for civilizing the coffeehouses and expanding their impact on the political process, for they served both conversation and coffee directly to the customer, according to the tastes and political interests of their diverse clientele. Coffee retail was a very dangerous business, where coffee shipments often were misplaced or damaged. Credit was hard to find. Supply was in the hands of giant stock companies, as were the warehouses. The state had more connections to the East India Company than to the coffeehouse proprietors, making any possibility of lobbying very difficult until the late eighteenth century. Lloyd's took the lead in establishing a network of lobbyists and creditors in close connection with the Treasury. The Customs Office bickered with the East India Company over warehouse inspection compliance, while coffeehouse proprietors suffered the losses for poor trade policies. American gazettes heroized the struggle and memorialized coffee's symbolic language of protest against the cruelties of monopoly and the tyranny of debt. When coffeehouse owners suffered a downturn and went under, they were likely sent to debtor's prison. Financial loss was personal loss. They therefore had every incentive to form lasting polite relationships with notable customers, in the event that they did eventually go under. These relationships became the basis for Britain's associational world.

In protecting the coffee trade, proprietors and coffeehouse lobbyists defended their right to association: the philosophy of cosmopolitan experience which undergirded 'conspicuous society'. They laid the groundwork for an entirely new gazetting journalism which combined right of association with financial and political news. Eighteenth-century journalism would capitalize on the politicization of coffee begun by the proprietors and enlarge its meaning to envision a united world of intercolonial news and gazetting sociability. Perhaps someday, all hoped, entire communities of remote neighbours might patronize their colonial city's news from a London coffeehouse. In the meantime, many of London's most notable houses entered into an agreement to form a polite alternative to the news. It depended on their own personal social networks, soliciting gentlemen of respectable characters to present 'proper' news. However, they did not have enough social connections to successfully compete with the established press of London. Reform came within the pre-existing system of news and coffee, which many coffeehouse owners felt had betrayed their financial interests. Nevertheless, some coffeehouse proprietors like Button decided to host editorial projects within their houses and, ignoring the expense of print culture, use it to lobby for a polite reputation. The real reputations of coffeehouses were based upon the varying types of urban experience within their houses: gaming, literary talk, political review, polite leisure and so on. Critics judged coffeehouse reputations on the basis of leisure and politeness. The most reputable coffeehouse proprietors chose to work with the critics rather than against a system which put them at an economic, social and political disadvantage.

The cumulative efforts of coffeehouse proprietors, printers and journalists transformed the public opinion on coffee and instituted the editorial system which permitted middling elites to construct new imagined communities in London and eventually across the Atlantic world through the gazettes. 'Print capitalism' enabled coffeehouse readers to critically review their society, politics and the flow of goods across the Atlantic. This society flourished during the second half of the eighteenth century in the coffeehouses of the Anglo Atlantic world. The great coffeehouse project of the British Empire depended upon an enlightened understanding of manners and men and free association. Enlightened coffeehouse publics imagined they were part of the same community of news and reform. Free association suddenly projected the voices of thousands of unknown merchants, journalists and proprietors into the political debates of the eighteenth century, all of whom were committed to fair trade and sociability across the Atlantic. The transatlantic news-circuit sustained a language of polite coffeehouse sociability and free association for emerging transregional communities of travellers. These in turn bought the goods of commercial empire, emulating British tastes. Their language of politeness would become the language of political reform. Gazette writers hoped that the faith, enterprise and social mobility of American literate urbanites would fully realize the civic and social ideals of British society. Simultaneously, colonial elites and civil servants were relying on coffeehouse newsfeeds to better understand and possibly even negotiate bureaucratic structures of commerce.

6

Transatlantic news feeds and imagined coffeehouse publics

In 1728, Robert Carter awaited the inevitable flood of opinions from Virginia merchants who had powerful friends in London when parliament proposed to lift its ban on the stemming of tobacco. 'I believe most of ye Gentm in Virginia are urgent with their correspondents to come into this good design,' he said.[1] He knew that the Virginian merchant community spanned the Atlantic and easily outpaced even the government in their postal coffeehouse news-ring. The torrent came. Not only did the Virginians send many urgent replies but they also appointed a colonial agent to work alongside their friends in London to make sure their voices were heard. Their efforts depended on a united community which worked together as one family. Increasingly, governments on both sides of the Atlantic understood that they faced serious consequences if they did not first get the support of these neighbourhoods traversing the Atlantic. When Governor Hunter ran afoul with the New York City merchants, Hunter wrote to the Board of Trade that their agent in London Samuel Baker spread copies of a grand jury address against him 'on the tables of most coffee houses in the city'.[2] After the South Carolina assembly rather too hastily passed a heaving increase on import duties in 1744, Robert Pringle knew that they had made a mistake. He reasoned, 'Every person here [in London] in the trade will write to their friends at home [in South Carolina] about said tax bill.'[3] All of these incidents reveal the strength of these merchant communities who all defended their right to trade and maintained their personal reputations from coffeehouses in order to construct a more equitable system of maritime exchange.

By the mid-eighteenth century, the news and private letters streaming across the Atlantic from coffeehouse to coffeehouse secured a ring of royal officers, governors, merchants and journalists who regularly wrote to their patrons, friends and financiers in London. Coffee patrons serving in official capacities invented their own postal system which forged new transatlantic communities. Coffee's proximity to Atlantic shipping, insurance, the London Exchange and naval correspondence made the coffeehouse an institution distinct from the generic tavern and a more dependable line of communication, although their patrons also spilled into taverns and other venues. It was not long before the government at Whitehall had to contend with powerful interest groups lobbying for their own financial security. Rather than merely capitulate to their demands, parliament embedded its official postal service inside preexisting coffeehouse news networks. Committees, societies and government officials institutionalized this communications network for marine insurance, naval protection and customs officers, carrying the goods of the empire to coastal cities.

Coffeehouse proprietors bought into the empire by purchasing gazettes from across the Atlantic for their readers. Transatlantic newsfeeds strengthened travel and transregional identities. Through 'print capitalism' London and British North America remotely shared coffee publics. Colonial travellers to London met in coffeehouses which catered to their own colony and purchased its gazette. Philadelphians in London read the *Pennsylvania Gazette* from the 'Pennsylvania Coffeehouse', Virginians followed their own news from the 'Virginia and Maryland Coffeehouse' and London merchants visiting Philadelphia read the *London Gazette* at the 'London Coffeehouse'. Increasingly, transatlantic travellers reassembled their own colonial identities in a porous social network. These we might call 'remote neighborhoods', or communities of travellers who organized their cosmopolitan experience from a regionally specific coffeehouse. The political newsfeeds became a language of sociability among British coffeehouse goers which celebrated trade as the foundation for a free associational world. The Addisonian model of a polite and literate public sphere served as one way to unite transatlantic merchants through a language of free exchange. American coffeehouse customers came for the social commentaries which united them with civilization in an age of Enlightenment. All the while, they were feeling more and more British. With this transatlantic discourse, coffeehouses finally matured into normative institutions for polite gazettes in an age when the consumer revolution and 'conspicuous society' were at their height.[4]

These 'remote neighborhoods' were porous indeed. Colonial merchants and statesmen set up mail and social networks in the corresponding London coffeehouse of their colony, but frequently changed their addresses to the coffeehouses which allowed them to maintain their London friendships. Reputations were made and broken in the coffeehouses of London and colonial America. Benjamin Franklin would become the archetypal American merchant in London. His meticulous study of coffeehouse gazettes in London allowed him to transplant a rhetorical style of conversational satire back to his fellow American printers. While in London, Franklin supervised a news network which extended out into many of the great colonial cities. Franklin personally constructed a social network of gazette culture across the coffeehouses of North America and linked them to London. Agents, merchants and social elites in these coffeehouse environs maintained imperial connections through personal contacts in England. They brought the British economic system of empire ever closer to America.[5]

Establishing a transatlantic news circuit: Franklin's experience with coffee

The British government commissioned Benjamin Franklin as deputy postmaster general of North America in 1753 because he understood as no one else that the coffeehouses could be put to use to organize a dependable post. Parliament decided to establish an official postal service in the 1750s with America so as to gain revenue and to control political news. Americans had availed themselves of postal loopholes which, as Adelman explains, allowed individuals to send private letters through friends without bearing the cost. The coffeehouse was one such avenue. Franklin hoped to achieve a solution which was in both American and British interests, but his efforts only led to divided loyalties. Still, the British government expected much from him. Franklin had lived among the coffeehouses of London as often as in America during the 1720s and had worked hard at establishing printing networks which brought Americans into the English world of letters.[6] After having launched his home-grown version of Addisonian rhetoric in the *Philadelphia Gazette* and *Poor Richard's Almanac*, Franklin took up residence in the Pennsylvania Coffeehouse, Birchin Lane, London, in 1757. There, he would meet other merchants in connection with his native colony and find dependable mail routes back to home.

This 'remote neighborhood' of Philadelphians in London maintained a transatlantic community which competed in London's highly associational coffeehouse world. Franklin knew that London was the capital of an experiment in a new journalist style of news and polite letters. He hoped to acquire its peculiar metropolitan flavour and adapt it to American industry and the British economic system. His greatest achievement was not only formalizing a formal postal service but also in embedding many of his agents into official governmental capacities in America. He got New York printer James Parker an appointment as a customs officer in 1765. Parker served both as secretary of the Northern American post office under Franklin and as a customs officer. Franklin set up post offices in New York, New Haven, Jamaica, Barbados, Antigua and Dominica. But Franklin was also responsive to the needs of colonial assemblies. He appointed Jon Green as clerk of the Maryland General Court, and at the request of the Carolinian assembly, he commissioned Louis Timothee to set up a post office in Charleston. John Hold of the *New-York Journal* relied on Franklin for gazette subscriptions from printers Richard Draper of Boston, Alexander Purdie and John Dixon of Williamsburg, Fredrick Green of Annapolis and John Dunlap of Philadelphia.[7] Not only was Franklin connecting American printers to London's world of print, he was also connecting gazettes and journals in America together in ways which would later prove invaluable to the American cause.

Franklin returned to London in the 1750s with the express intention of forging this transatlantic news and postal circuit. From the Pennsylvania Coffeehouse, Franklin could continue his career as a London journalist, while organizing a printing and mail delivery service in the colonies. His correspondence with Philadelphian printer David Hall indicated that he gave criticism to the content of the Philadelphia papers. Franklin connected Hall with Mr Karr at the Pennsylvania Coffeehouse in London. Hall now had a transatlantic following for the *Pennsylvania Gazette*, both marrying political commentary from Philadelphia with London and encouraging a transatlantic Pennsylvanian community with coffeehouse news. Hall's London agent and good friend William Strahan sent him regular subscriptions to newspapers and magazines like the *London Gazette* on monthly packet ships most likely sent from coffeehouse addresses. While Adelman acknowledges that David Hall possessed perhaps the best transatlantic contacts in America's printing world, he looks to Hall's career in Edinburgh rather than to the London coffeehouses. Almost certainly without Franklin's vital connections to

London's coffeehouses and their journals, Hall's monthly shipments would not have been so dependable. And Franklin certainly used his coffeehouse connections well. He outmanoeuvred Hall in the Stamp Act debates when Hall took the side of the government and Franklin became increasingly sceptical of British legislation. William Bradford of the London Coffeehouse in Philadelphia published the debate Franklin was having in the press over tax policies in the 1760s.[8] By 1766, Franklin was receiving mail from America at the New England Coffeehouse as well as the Pennsylvania, and received updates from friends in Boston. He had at least one correspondent at the New York Coffeehouse by 1770. In 1774, Franklin opened an address at the Georgia Coffeehouse, London. But this system was fraught with difficulties. James Parker in New York complained that letters were often carried off at the coffeehouse rather than being directed to their proper recipients. Franklin himself was concerned that certain letters attributed to him and read aloud in the coffeehouses were forgeries and thus weakened the credibility of the newsfeed from Pennsylvania to London.[9]

Before permanently taking up residence in London, Franklin, acquainted with Addison's style, created a similar culture of news and social commentary for Philadelphia in the hopes of formalizing mail delivery. Franklin never intended to institute a postal service fully independent of coffeehouse news; he merely meant to systematize the delivery of mail utilizing the domestic resources available to him, including the coffeehouse. His first move towards that end was getting an efficient stamp-issuing process in the coffeehouses and this would prove very controversial after the passage of the Stamp Act. As early as 1735, he worked with the retired postmaster of Pennsylvania, Henry Flower, to help settle his accounts for postage at 'the old Coffee-House in Philadelphia'.[10] Franklin then tackled the problem of delivery. From London in 1763, Franklin and John Foxcroft issued the following instructions to their post office:

> We hope the Continuance of the Packets will in a short time be as advantageous to the office, as it must be to the Commerce of Britain and the Colonies. Nothing in our Power shall be wanting to second the laudable Views with which that Continuance is order'd. It is already advertis'd, and we have order'd the Advertisement to be constantly inserted for twelve Months to come in all News Papers of America. The regular and punctual Dispatch of the Mails will greatly recommend the Use of the Packets to the Merchants; and we doubt not but the good Effect of that Regularity will soon appear in the great Increase of Letters. If some Method could be fallen upon effectually to oblige the Masters of Ships to deliver all their Letters into the Office, it would raise a great Sum in Aid and Support of the Packets. A Clause inserted in some Act of Parliament relating to the Revenue requiring an Oath of every Captain, to be taken at the Custom House when he enters, that he had sent his Letters to the Office; and making it penal to break Bulk till that was done; might possibly have a very good Effect. Or perhaps a Clause obliging all Coffee Houses where Bags are put up, to bring such Bags of Letters to the Post Office before they are sent away; to be seald and directed to the Post Office of the Port to which the Ship is bound; and allow the Coffee House a half penny per Letter, for their Trouble in Collecting them; might be of use. All Opening of Ship Bags,

at Coffeehouses or elsewhere by Persons not authorized from the Post Office, and distributing the Letters gratis to the Persons they are directed to, or others, should likewise be forbidden.[11]

For Franklin, organizing mail was organizing the commerce of the empire. Like customs, it depended upon inspection procedures, but Franklin was bent on utilizing the pre-existing domestic coffeehouse infrastructure of news. He wanted a sustainable American system which was in contact with transatlantic mail networks. Firstly, mail would be sent in regular packets at express intervals.[12] Secondly, the regular times of mail dispatches would be advertised in all American newspapers. Thus, customers of private mail read the public news in order to know when to expect their letters. Thirdly, sea captains, sworn in at a customs office, would convey all mail off ships to the post office, after arriving in port. Fourthly, all domestic and foreign mail collected at coffeehouses should be bagged and sent to the post office for delivery. Fifthly, all mail going out from coffeehouses should be sealed, and in the case of transatlantic mail, it should be lawfully carried to the post office of the port of exit. In that way, all coffeehouse addresses would be linked to the postal system.

What Franklin did not want was the continuation of unauthorized coffeehouse proprietors or customers receiving and distributing mail at will. He was not *laissez-faire* with news and believed very strongly in the importance of stamps, seals and postmasters in connection with the imperial customs system. For this reason, his printer network would come under attack by the Sons of Liberty in America for being tainted with the British customs system which enforced the Stamp Act tax. Not only did Franklin receive criticism from the British government for arguing for a fairer transatlantic system, his agents were targeted by the more radical patriots from his own side.[13] Yet he saw the need of integrating his system into the domestic habits and public institutions of coffeehouse mail recipients. He knew well that most Americans read the gazettes in taverns and coffeehouses and that merchants most frequently posted their letters through coffeehouses.

The Stamp Act controversy ended all such hopes of an integrated system of print, customs and the post. Pennsylvanian stamp distributer John Hughes informed Franklin in September 1765 saying that he may be forced out of office in light of the 'Presbyterian Rage' against his officiating the new stamp tax. The Presbyterian factions in the Assembly House were forming committees of petition and redress in every colony, in the hopes of forming a union. Fired by patriotic sermons and tracts, mobs of patriots lit the streets with their bonfires and torches. Hughes said, 'I for my Part am well-arm'd with Fire-Arms, and am determin'd to stand a Siege.' Some of his friends patrolled his house and the coffeehouse, lest a mob grab him or his mail on the spot. When the ministry changed, the 'rabble' in the streets seemed to die away, but only for a while.[14] The next year was the complete takeover of the official mail service by the patriots. The Sons of Liberty hijacked the official news service, finding it unconstitutional, and began overseeing the dispersal of mail in the coffeehouses. Franklin's mail service was suddenly dismantled and publishers on both sides of the tax crisis were in danger. Parker sent Franklin several updates from New York in the summer of 1766, informing him that one noted publisher in connection with the Sons of Liberty had been arrested and that his paper was at risk. The Sons of Liberty responded by taking control of information directly. Parker described the confusion thus:

> They think and find the Parliament have given Way in one Affair of Grievance, they begin to imagine both the Post-Office and Custom-House are like Grievances … The Moment a Vessel comes in, the Letters are seized by Force, and carried to the Coffee-House, where they are carried out, and delivered even before Mr. Colden's or my Face, and the Collector durst not, or will not refuse to enter any: I spoke to the Surveyor General and to the Collector about it, but could get no Satisfactory Answer … The Spirit of Independance is too prevalent.[15]

In detangling British control from domestic affairs, the Sons of Liberty had effectively privatized the news. They were tired of any and all interference. They decided to separate forever news from customs, but they had seized a thread which unravelled both, since the ships that carried goods also carried mail. Franklin's agents were at risk. Parker was made Land-Waiter by the Governor, Surveyor General and Commissioners of the Customs to check every ship in the city and make sure that nothing was loaded or unloaded without official permission. In Albany and New England, riots broke out. 'The Lives of Some were lost on both sides,' explained Parker.[16] Making matters worse, most captains seemed to take the side of the patriots. Parker despaired, 'That the Sons of Liberty finding themselves the Ruling Party, begin to take upon themselves the governing part also … they make the Captains of Vessels deliver their Letters at the Coffee-House after their old accustomed Manner.'[17] Of primary concern for both these Sons of Liberty and Franklin's mail officials was control over information during the Stamp Act Crisis, even more than commodities. Franklin knew that both were at risk if either Britain or America violated the balance between coffeehouse mail distribution habits and postal service procedures.

That balance had depended upon Franklin's reputation among high-ranking British officials and coffeehouse intellectuals in London. Before returning home to join the Congress in Philadelphia, Franklin cemented his reputation in the London coffeehouses for being a printer, satirist and amateur scientist. His coffeehouse connections increasingly linked him with British academic circles. He hoped to get some books on electricity from Dr Preistly through an intermediary at St Paul's Coffeehouse and joined their scientific club in 1767. In 1772, Franklin received an order through the Virginia Coffeehouse for one of his own invented orchestral instruments, the glass armonica.[18] Then, Franklin changed sides and soon lost his reputation among his London patrons. Franklin freely released his wit upon the London coffeehouse public. Always disguised in a witty pseudonym, he fired off statements like 'Thus much I thought it necessary to say in favour of an honest Set of Writers, whose comfortable Living depends on collecting and supplying the Printers with News … who always show their Regard to Truth … to the great Satisfaction and Improvement of us Coffee-house Students in History and Politics.'[19] Perhaps Franklin's greatest piece of satire at that time was his *Open Letter to Lord North* (1774), in which he assumed the character of a quack coffeehouse politician who foolishly supported the militaristic force behind the Ministry, and so played the best British argument for law and order against itself.

For this piece, he ironically appealed to his quack status to emphasize the absurdities of his satirical suggestions. He teased,

> I, my Lord, who have no mean Opinion of my Abilities, which is justified by the Attention that is paid to me when I harangue at the Smyrna and Old Slaughter's, am willing to contribute my Mite to the public Welfare; and have a Proposal to make to your Lordship, which I flatter myself will be approved of by the Ministry, and if carried into Execution, will quiet all the Disturbances in America, procure a decent Revenue from our Colonies, make our royal Master (at least there) a King de facto, as well as de jure ... My Scheme is, without Delay to introduce into North America a Government absolutely and entirely Military ... and though they are descended from British Ancestors, they are degenerated to such a Degree, that one born in Britain is equal to twenty Americans ... Let all the Colonists be enrolled in the Militia, subject of course to Martial Law.[20]

No coffeehouse politician had spoken so sharply or with more cunning. From this letter, it may be assumed that Franklin was quite confident in his reputation in the coffeehouse press of both London and America. That same year, Franklin worked alongside Edmund Burke organizing a petition at the Waghorn Coffeehouse, Westminster, for the relief of the colonies. At this coffeehouse, Franklin put American agents in connection with members of parliament.[21] It was the closest he ever came to entering the parliamentary sphere. But it was all to no avail, for petitions did not ultimately sway parliament from erecting an imperial bureaucracy to supervise transatlantic news, commodities and revenue. During the war, Franklin communicated with Thomas Digges at Nandos Coffeehouse, but Franklin's coffeehouse social life was a shadow of what he had intended it to be.[22] It remained very much an undercover association by virtue of political animosities with England.

Personal reputations in a transatlantic public sphere

Perhaps the informal coffeehouse social network was more successful at connecting people and goods across the Atlantic than the official network which the British government tried to erect. Here, personal reputations counted for everything. Patronage networks made and broke many a personal reputation. The two ingredients necessary to understand these communities of coffee-goers are conversation and news subscriptions. Coffeehouses and print culture crossed boundaries in a way which reflected regional concerns. Gazettes sustained an Enlightened public sphere of sociability alongside new 'remote neighborhoods' of transatlantic travellers. By mid-century, coffeehouse proprietors in London began realizing the coffee culture of America and their acquired journalizing taste. In 1766, John Richmond advertised the Virginia and Maryland Coffeehouse in Cornhill in the *Virginia Gazette*, stating that he 'begs Leave to acquaint the Merchants, Commanders, and other Gentlemen, that he will take the strictest Care to accommodate the best Manner all those Gentlemen that will please to honour him with their Favours'.[23] Richmond's desire was to build a Southern-style coffeehouse in London and attract a transatlantic clientele. In like manner, coffeehouse readers of the *Virginia Gazette* followed the discussion minutes of the Liverpool Conversation Club at the George's Coffeehouse. Liverpool and the south-eastern seaboard of America shared a maritime and slave interest, and the *Virginia Gazette* furthered the notion that they might share the same polite language of sociability. Subjects ranged from whether trade was beneficial to the British Empire, of prime importance to the port city of Liverpool and American colonies, to improving theatre design.[24] The coffeehouse public sphere was a truly multifaceted transatlantic discourse which negotiated regional rules of sociability from one city to another.

It is not an overstatement to say that royal governors in America were indebted to coffeehouse associations for the continuance of their positions (although their appointments were rarely the result of lobbyists). These groups regularly turned out reports which reviewed the economic performance of their colonial governors and forwarded these report on to the Board of Trade. Several governors lost their good standing with the government in London as a result. In New York, Governor Hunter found himself before a grand jury which indirectly published its statements against him in the coffeehouse news-ring in London via the New York City merchants. Far more devastating was the story of Governor Belcher in Massachusetts who displeased Bostonian merchants and New England merchants in London for opposing the opening of a silver bank and for opposing the land claims of several important merchants in New Hampshire. These three groups worked together to have him removed from office. The New Hampshire correspondent to London, John Tomlinson, set up his headquarters of opposition at the New England Coffeehouse. As a result, many London merchants threw their support for another candidate and in 1741 Belcher was replaced. His London support had entirely collapsed to the pressures of the coffeehouse lobbyists.[25]

Most merchants and activists put pre-emptive pressures on governors even before they formally took office. Such was the case with Governor Spotswood of Virginia who was greeted by a crowd as he got off the ship or Cornbury of New York who was mobbed by several interest parties on his first day in the colony. Governor Bellomont of New York and New England, while stopping in Barbados for repairs, was greeted by a Presbyterian minister who advised him to preserve the religious liberties of the powerful dissenter groups in New England. Yet sometimes, transatlantic interests opposed each other. When Joseph Dudley gained the position of governor over Massachusetts, he had the backing of the London New England merchants and the Bishop of St Asaph. Increase Mather's more popular choice for governor, nominee Phis, was passed over for Dudley. Similarly, when the Board of Trade recommended Tobias Bowles for governor of Maryland on the basis that he had the support of the merchants there, the Privy Council chose to ignore them. And so, many provincial interest groups chose to keep up pressures on the office and influence electoral support through coffeehouse club meetings and by forwarding their reports to the Board of Trade. Governors were thus doubly attentive to creating a congenial following of supporters in the coffeehouses and public assemblies, very often accepting the social invitations for food, lodgings and entertainments with influential spokesmen and hosting dinner parties of their own in return. They knew that news carried quickly over coffee's transatlantic environs and that their jobs would answer for their social participation in that public sphere.[26]

Yet, without rendering what actual patrons talked about in these gatherings, coffeehouse communities remain mysterious. Although transatlantic merchants catalogued their flow of goods, they seldom kept meticulous journals of what they did in port. Finding records of transatlantic coffeehouse exchanges is surprisingly difficult. There are sporadic references to merchants from America arriving in London coffeehouses of their colony, like Samuel Curwen's journal entry on 3 July 1775, in which he wrote simply, 'Arrived at Dover England from America. 4th July – Arrived at the New England Coffee House, Threadneedle Street at seven p.m.'[27] Curwen was a fleeing loyalist from Massachusetts and not an average merchant. He discussed colonial politics, read the New York paper and convened with fellow New Englanders in London.[28] In some cases, these connections were very remote: 'James Teal, a son of the widow of the late Gov. Belcher'.[29] His fear of betrayal limited his visiting the coffeehouses or utilizing its postal services. Still, he occasionally met friends at the coffeehouses, and mostly dropped by for an hour or two to get the news. Curwen longed for a more leisurely sociable atmosphere and generally enjoyed the coffeehouse with either the adjoining pleasure gardens or else with a club. Aside from a casual reference here and there to one of his friend's everyday affairs, Curwen did not offer a single transcribed coffeehouse conversation.[30] The most detail he provided on such occasions was when he found his friend Mr Frs Waldo, 'and accompanied him to Canon coffee-house, Spring Gardens, and took tea, where were joined by Jo Scott, and remained till eleven o'clock talking politics', or when he 'walked to New England Coffee-house ... from then to the Disputing Club at King's Arms'.[31] His circle was a remote neighbourhood in incubation. Curwen launched the American Thursday dinner club in 1782 at the New England Coffeehouse, a community of exiles who lamented the fall of a transatlantic public sphere of British North Americans.[32] Curwen's case reveals that the biographical record of transatlantic coffeehouse exchange is mostly confined to the experiences of the wealthy and literate statesmen and planters of colonial America, who kept personal diaries or maintained extensive connections through letters. Thus, our view of coffeehouse social life is somewhat slanted by the mere emphasis of written documents which favour the rich over the adventurous lower-middling merchant community. What is clear is that these wealthy individuals cared immensely about their personal reputations in social coffeehouse settings and relied upon the institution of the London club to advance their social standing among their American peers.

One famed and often cited example among historians of a transatlantic coffeehouse-going gentleman is the fabulously rich Virginian planter William Byrd II. His frequent visits to the London coffeehouses inspired him to transplant leisurely pursuits to coffeehouses in Virginia. His prime reason for patronizing the Williamsburg coffeehouse was to encourage a clubbable gaming culture among the notable citizens of the city. He gambled with his friends late into the night and lost £12 and 10s in one sitting. But this was not enough to ruin Byrd or soil his reputation. He used games as a leisurely escape from the affairs of the city and connected with other like-minded card players. Usually, these visits to the Williamsburg coffeehouse accompanied his visits to the governor's family. It is curious that Byrd would begin an evening with a roast beef dinner and bottle of claret at the Governor's Palace, and then finish the evening at a coffeehouse settling his accounts with naval officers and playing at cards. The Palace had a fine parlour for cards and a ballroom for dances. Why did he change a lavish mansion for the city coffeehouse? He did not give any indication that the governor followed him.[33] Byrd's coffeehouse experiences are mysterious for the reason that Byrd went to the coffeehouses to find leisurely entertainments but could have equally found them in higher social circles. Perhaps it was because of coffee's reputation for free association which brought him there and its remote neighbourhood of transatlantic naval officers.

The Annapolis Coffeehouse actually did host the governor's balls and an imagined aristocratic community of colonial elites, royal officers and their ladies. It was one of America's coffeehouse circuits which advanced the reputation of American statesmen through fine dining and leisurely entertainment. In August 1771, the Lower House of Assembly agreed to 'sit during the present Session in the Ball Room and will allow on the Journal of Accounts and pay for the Use of the said Room, two adjoining Apartments, and the Revenue Office for the Upper House, and the Governor, the Sum of four Pounds Common Money p Day'.[34] This was merely the formalization of a sociable sphere of statesmen who had, for decades, regularly discussed their affairs in the coffeehouse after session. George Washington found the coffeehouse indispensable among his circle of urban associates in Annapolis.[35] His diary entry for 11 May 1773 stated, 'Breakfasted at Mr. Igns. Digges. Dind at the Coffee Ho. in Annapolis & lodgd at the Govrs.'[36] On 5 October 1772, he wrote, 'Reachd Annapolis. Dined at the Coffee House with the Jocky Club & lodgd at the Govrs. after going to the Play.'[37] Washington was rarely a man of many words, but we can expect the talk to be of political society and the quality of the plays as in London. His time in the coffeehouses of Williamsburg were similarly spent. For Washington, the coffeehouse was usually a late afternoon or evening affair. He chose to dine at the Raleigh and sup in a coffeehouse.[38]

So well acquainted was Washington with coffeehouse leisure that he considered hiring a German valet de Chambre who had come to offer fine accommodations to Philadelphians in the coffee rooms of the New Theater. However, Philadelphians were not as extravagant in their display of fashion as in Annapolis. The Theater never got underway and the valet was forced to open a hair-dressing shop inside Hyde's Tontine Coffeehouse. What he really wanted was to be a gentleman's butler, and Washington might just be the man. His personal reference Tobias Lear wrote to Washington, giving the following description:

> He is a tolerably well sized & well made man of about 5 feet 8 or 9 inches – and about 30 years of age – a German by birth – speaks the french language well – dresses Ladies' & Gentlemen's hair very well ... He says he understands the duties of a Butler well – and can set out a table in as handsome a manner as any man: But he is not acquainted with marketing or providing for a family – He would prefer acting as Valet & Butler to having the duty of one only. He would not undertake the business for less than two hundred & fifty dollars per year. Thus far the man says of & for himself. His price I tell him puts him out of the question; if every thing else should answer.[39]

That the New Theater and Hyde Tontine Coffeehouse, both examples of the many lesser coffeehouses in Philadelphia, played host to a remote neighbourhood of European travellers from the courts of Europe looking for new opportunities is simply astounding. The American coffeehouse circuit encouraged leisure and extravagance, and drew some of the finest domestic servants from Europe, although their fees were personally impracticable for anything less than nobility. Still, Americans felt that they were fully connected with the world of taste, advancing personal connections by judging the value of the public service industry.

The coffeehouse was at the centre of a community of men who jealously guarded their transactions with the British government upon the grounds of personal honour. What happened in a coffeehouse could have implications for one's standing with the British government. Doctor David Ross, who had victualled and served the officers of the British army in Maryland in 1758, disclosed to the governor that he had had a falling out with General Forbes over vouchers for his care of the army. Ross's orders for compensation had been deferred to Mr Howell, who paid Ross and billed Ross's creditors. Somehow a confusion ensued over billing and Ross was left entirely at the mercy of his creditors in New York and Philadelphia.[40] The argument found its way into the coffeehouse. Ross told the governor, 'I went to the Coffee house to go from thence to Reese Merediths, before dinner he informed that Mr Howell had been with him, and persuade me to deliver up the Bills.'[41] After discussing what amount of the bill was still outstanding, Howell and Ross decided to set out for New York to settle one bill with a certain Mr Kirby. Privacy was of the utmost importance for Ross, for if once the affair were leaked out, his reputation would be in shambles. Ross explained, 'I requested of him to call for me at the Coffe House ... he would not mention the affair to any person ... Gentlemen you are masters of your own business and no body shall know or hear any thing of it from me.'[42] Yet somehow the business got out and Ross was placed under watch by the sheriff. One of the few places he could resort to was the coffeehouse, but there, he made shipwreck of his reputation. In an illuminating passage of tit-for-tat, Ross narrated the coffeehouse conversation which brought himself and Howell to a point of falling-out:

> Mr Chew had talked very freely of the treatment I had received from Mr Howel, I observed that the Eyes of most people in the Coffee House were turned upon us as we sat in the Box, and I took notice of it to Mr Howel, and begged he would Step up with me into a private Room, where we could talk with more freedom, which he refused to do alledging he did a great deal of business in that publick manner. As I saw his intention seemed to be to fret and teaze me, and I was resolved to possess myself, I left the Box as decently as I could, lest my resentment and passion should carry me beyond the bounds of decency due to such a crowded Company of people who were strangers to me, Mr Howel went soon afterwards up Stairs, and I think Mr Israel Pemberton and Mr Meredith went along with him ... Mr Peters, I understood, did apply to Mr Howel, but the Express coming in that forenoon from General Amherst upon the Surrender of Louisburgh prevented my knowing what was the Event, I saw Mr Howel that Evening at the Coffee House but he took no notice of me. next day I waited on Mr Peters, but he was ill and confined to his

Room and I believe he wrote or sent for Mr Howel to come to him, but still I heard nothing from Mr Howel, and as I understood the affair was now publickly talked of and that several Reports which had formerly been spread with regard to my character in negotiating the affair gained ground with the Quakers in particular, I bethought myself of applying to Israel Pemberton and went to wait on him that afternoon, at first he seemed averse to looking into the Affair and told me that Mr Howel had informed him of it lately as he had observed us both talking together with great earnestness at the Coffee House. I told him I was very glad to hear it, and if he pleased to look into my papers he would be master of both sides of the affair, and that it would be an Act of Humanity to give some assistance to me who was so much a Stranger in Philadelphia ... I met with him at the Coffe House, he asked me if I had not received a Letter from the General, I told him I had.[43]

Ross had clearly been humiliated and was embarrassed. His complaint was that his financial reputation inside the remote neighbourhood of the coffeehouse creditors had been threatened. His accounts involved the war finances of a British general, creditors in New York and Philadelphia, statesmen in Maryland and countless other agents and officers from throughout the British Empire. The hinge in this vast web of accounts centred on one particular coffeehouse conversation in which gentlemen differed not just on the issue at hand but over how to express themselves in a public place. Had the spirit of gentlemanly association between Ross and Howell been violated by Howell's refusal to move from a box in the common room into a private apartment? Coffeehouse historian John Barrell observes that in the case of John Frost who was accused of uttering sedition in a coffeehouse in 1792, his innocence or guilt depended upon the gentlemanly rules of spatial etiquette in a coffeehouse. Frost's defence claimed that his conversation was directed to his friends, regardless of who else heard, and so was subject to the trust relationship between gentlemen and not part of the public matter. His accusers asserted that all conversation in the common room of a coffeehouse was public, regardless of to whom it was privately directed. Coffeehouses were public places which were regulated by an idea of a private and friendly discourse: private, not secret.[44] Barrell claims, 'Whatever else it was, the trial became a debate between Erskine and Sir John Scott, the new attorney general, on exactly what kind of a space a coffee house was ... Customers in the public coffee-room who were willing to engage in promiscuous conversation with men unknown to them signaled as much by sitting not in a box but at the main table.'[45]

Ross's incident with Howell illuminates the spatial references of British coffeehouses without the distortion of government espionage and radicalization of the public sphere. Defining the egalitarian rhetoric of the French Revolutionary era, Thomas Paine had claimed that coffeehouses were the primary places for finding public political opinion. The Society for Constitutional Information had contacts all across the coffeehouses of London. The question of treason in Frost's case rather distorts the social rules of the coffeehouse. Before that time, gentlemen like Ross and Howell operated under the clubbable rules of politeness. Ross and Howell were already sitting in a box and engaging in what Barrell considers a private conversation, but what Ross was painfully aware of in a way that only a contemporary could have experienced was that his sensitive conversation with Howell was still audible to the crowd in the common room and drew attention to itself by its very controversial nature. Private boxes only gave the illusion of private conversation in a coffeehouse; it did not isolate two conversants from the coffeehouse crowd. It was still part of the common room. As one gentleman to another, Ross asked Howell for a private room (above or below the common room). These private rooms, coffeehouse proprietors installed for just such purposes. Ross was not asking for removal from the public convenience of the coffeehouse, only for temporary removal from its public quarters to a private section. Howell's refusal signalled a scepticism in Ross's intentions over so meticulous a matter of accounts which had dragged on for some time. Howell was ready to settle the matter without further delay, but his refusal to grant Ross a private conversation about it in person was mistaken for an insult. Personal negotiations broke off at this point, and Ross referred to a higher authority, not only to provide him with the human resources necessary in settling his accounts but also in restoring his public character as a gentlemen in his public resort: an 'act of humanity'.[46]

Perhaps had Ross been in a southern coffeehouse among the planting gentry rather than in a Philadelphian coffeehouse, he would have had better success. The southern coffeehouses were known for being generally sociable and polite, perhaps more formal than in the north. Upon arriving in Virginia in 1774, John Adams, being a staunch New Englander, was impressed with his newfound friends in the southern coffeehouses. He wrote,

> Dined at Mr. Thom. Mifflins with Mr. Lynch, Mr. Middleton, and the two Rutledges with their Ladies. The two Rutledges are good Lawyers. Govr. Hopkins and Govr. Ward were in Company. Mr. Lynch gave us a Sentiment 'The brave Dantzickers, who declare they will be free in the face of the greatest Monarch in Europe.' – We were very sociable, and happy. After Coffee We went to the Tavern, where we were introduced to Peyton Randolph Esqr., Speaker of Virginia, Coll. Harrison, Richard Henry Lee Esq., and Coll. Bland. Randolph is a large, well looking Man. Lee is a tall, spare Man. Bland is a learned, bookish Man. These Gentlemen from Virginia appear to be the most spirited and consistent, of any.[47]

Although primarily referring to the spirit of their political ideals, Adams noted that the Southern gentlemen possessed a natural disposition towards sociability. It was this faculty which invigorated a community able to be entrusted with the public good. These coffeehouse-goers were a far cry from the Merchants Club in the British Coffeehouse near the Boston Wharfe, where Sam Adams, James Otis, John Pitts, Josiah Quincy, Dr Warren and Mr Molineux brooded in secret and organized plots for the Sons of Liberty. These encounters often ended in violence, as when James Otis was personally assaulted by John Robinson for his political views.[48] What is plain is that gentlemen successfully or unsuccessfully fought to secure their public reputations in coffeehouses across the Anglo world.

Still, before the American Revolution, middling colonial Americans rarely got the chance to experience Europe's coffee culture outside of the Anglo world. With the War for Independence came the need to commission American diplomats across not only London coffeehouses but also European coffeehouses more generally. Diplomats like John Adams were expected to secure their public reputations in these coffeehouses as citizens of the world. Representing the American cause involved being comfortable in European public circles and having a knack for avoiding the sort of confrontations which Ross and Otis had experienced in American coffeehouses. But exposure to European court coffeehouses also nuanced the views of many American Founders abroad, equipping them with cultural experiences which would allow them to differentiate the American civil social order from Europe and at the same time distance themselves from the revolution from below inside America. John Adams's lifelong obsession with the deterioration of manners serves as an example. John Adams's coffeehouse experiences became more cosmopolitan when he toured Europe's coffeehouses as an American diplomat. Politics was his entrance into Europe's finest urban resorts. European social life intrigued Adams, but it did not impress him. Adams refused to go along with the social expectations of French aristocrats. He grew disenchanted with France, and this perhaps more than any other reason made it difficult for Adams to secure real support for the American cause. At the French court, he found a whirling new world of 'Beggars, Servants, Garçons, Filles, Decroteurs, Blanchisseuses. Barges, Batteaux, Bargemen. Coffee houses, Taverns. Servants at the Gates of Woods and Walks. Fruit, Cakes. Ice Creams. Spectacles. Tailors for setting a Stitch in Cloaths. Waiters for running with Errands, Cards &c. Cabbin Boys. Coach Hire. Walking Canes. Pamphlets. Ordonances. Carts.'[49] Adams saw through the veil of court pageantry and, preferring the isolated coffee society of home, declared, 'Hospitality and Sociability are no Characteristicks here.'[50] No one played by the Addisonian rules. In Amsterdam, Adams found a stockjobbing society of merchants who conducted business in the coffeehouses constantly, not observing the Sabbath and reading the news with anxious faces at the prospect of war with England. In 1782, Adams wrote from Amsterdam, 'The Merchants of the American Coffee House have proposed a public Dinner here, but I have begged to be excused.'[51] Regardless of his hesitancy to enter Europe's social world, it was undeniable that John Adams was forming an extensive international network of information in coffeehouses which was necessary to establish his reputation as a diplomat. He even had a meticulous agent in London, Thomas Digges, who collected correspondence from Paris at Nandoes Coffeehouse, Temple Bar and informed Adams of the effect of the American war on stocks sold at Lloyds Coffeehouse.[52] That Digges could connect the news from two distinct London coffeehouses and forward it to Paris demonstrates the solidity of the coffeehouse news circuit across the remote neighbourhoods of European coffeehouse travellers.

As an American diplomat to Europe, Adams had to steer a middle course between the revolution from below and the revolution from without. Obsessed with American mores, Adams tried his best to reclaim America's Founding from natural rights theorists and radical patriots who saw that the Declaration and Constitution were radical departures from the old colonial assemblies and the English common law. Before Paine's *Rights of Man* (1791), natural rights had been articulated through the principles of common law and mixed government in Blackstone and Sidney. This was true of Boston's circulars of 11 February 1768 and 13 May 1774, Otis's *Considerations of Behalf of the Colonists* (1765), Jefferson's *A Summary View of the Rights of British North America* (1774), Hamilton's *The Farmer Refuted* (1775), Adam's *Notes for an Oration at Braintree* (1772) and even the Declaration of Independence itself, which contrasted natural rights with violations against the 'unwritten constitution' of England. Adams knew, however, that in reaching for Independence, Americans would inevitably think their experience was exceptional. Revolution would have a corrupting influence upon the manners and mores of Americans, bending them against old prejudices and prescriptive duties. 'We have it in our power to begin the world over again,' exclaimed Paine in *Common Sense* (1776). In conservative fashion, Adams set his whole career against those words. Adams would engage the metaphysics of the American revolution in two principal works. *A Defense of the Constitutions of Government of the United States of America* (1787–8) argued that the Constitution was the outworking of principles of government expressed in earlier colonial charters, the English commonwealth and the Roman Republic. *Discourses on Devilia* (1790) set about to challenge the democratic interpretation of the revolution. Finally, *Letters of Publicola* (1791) denounced abstract theorizing behind the philosophical origins of the American Founding. But by 1804, Adams believed that the revolution from below had triumphed and that mixed government was a thing too complicated for Americans to grasp. Adams called his age 'the Age of Folly, Vice, Frenzy Fury, Brutality, Daemons, Buonaparte, Tom Paine, or the Age of The burning Brand from the bottomless Pitt: or any thing but the age of Reason'. Where his father had despaired, John Quincy Adams decided to embrace the age as an opportunity for reviving republican manners. Lambasting Paine, John Quincy said, 'Happy, thrice happy the people of America! Whose gentleness of manners and habits of virtue are still sufficient to reconcile the enjoyment of their natural rights, with the peace and tranquility of their country ... not upon the metaphysical speculations of fanciful politicians.' John Quincy believed that the revolution from below and the French Revolution stemmed from two different sources, and that religious liberty would save the American republic from abstraction. He brought Friedrich Gentz's Prussian work on the essential difference into English translation in 1800, furthering Gentz's argument that the American Revolution, like Burke's assessment of the 1688 Revolution, was 'a revolution not made, but prevented'.[53] This view the Adamses forged after having personally joined the European public sphere and republic of letters as American diplomats. Their cosmopolitan experiences would serve as a guide to how to steer the American republic through the internationally disruptive decade of the 1790s.

John Quincy was perhaps a more natural fit to critique manners, since he was an American diplomat to the Russian court at the early age of fourteen years and a natural fit within European coffeehouse communities. He was eloquently suited to a society based on remote neighbourhoods of traveling associates, being conversant in several languages. Arriving with his father in Europe, John Quincy, although quite young, found himself in as vital a diplomatic role as his father.[54] While staying at the Swedish court in January and February 1783, John Quincy was the toast of the Swedish coffeehouses. He socialized with counts and other nobility, the French Consul and other influential diplomats, dining with them in their coffeehouses.[55] In his most detailed account of any coffeehouse, John Quincy Adams said in his diary on 1 January 1783:

> We found here Mr. Schiebe a gentleman who left Stockholm about a week before us.
> Norrkiöping is distant from Stockholm eighteen swedish miles or 120. English. Its situation is exceeding fine, at present every thing is covered with Snow; but it is in the midst of a plain which is bordered all round at about 6. or 8 English Miles from the town by high mountains from which you at first discover the city and in summer it seems to be in the midst of a large garden.
> After having dined I went to the [Swedish] coffee house, and found there Mr. Charles Bernard Wadström a gentleman whom I knew in Stockholm and whom I owed a great many obligations during my stay there; he presented me to all his family which was assembled together at one of his brother's, where I stay'd and supped.[56]

John Quincy was enchanted with the beauty of Norrkiöping's mountainous situation, its lush valley and almost storybook quality. Never before had he found such a beautiful coffeehouse. Its rural landscape must have given him a vision for coffee culture beyond the strict urban experience of Anglo coffee, trade and news. Then, leaving for London in November, John Quincy dined with a Maryland merchant and American commissioner, enjoyed an evening among the Royal Society and supped at the London Coffeehouse with its club. Staying on as a diplomat in London until after the Treaty of Paris, John Quincy reported to his father on parliamentary affairs and the affairs of fellow American diplomats like John Jay, while maintaining social connections in the coffeehouses.[57] In 1785, he returned to American shores, sailed up Long Island, met the French Consul and dined with a prominent Son of Liberty in a coffeehouse. But his European contacts had not gone away. He delivered messages to Governor Clinton and received news from his father in England. He was back among the taverns and coffeehouses of liberty in Boston and said simply, 'Dined with the delegates from Massachusetts.'[58] Like any other merchant in Boston, he turned in early; 'Went in the Evening to the Coffee house and at about 9 o'clock returned home.'[59] But his life had been fundamentally changed. He had toured the greatest coffeehouses of Europe and came back again to the merchant coffeehouses of America in a matter of a few years, seemingly taking for granted the coffeehouses which had hosted a seamless flow of ambassadors and courtiers for his company. Unfortunately, the Adams Papers do not return any account of his coffeehouse conversations and he did not offer any commentary on the differences among coffeehouses throughout the world. But if a historian could ask anyone for his cosmopolitan coffeehouse experience during the heyday of coffee culture in Europe and America, we could not find a more fitting person than John Quincy. His impressions are lost to us forever.

That the Founding Fathers were transformed by the coffee culture in Europe is undeniable. Benjamin Franklin described his coffee experience at Passy in these terms:

> The Comte du Nord, came to Mr. Vergennes while we were drinking Coffee after Dinner. He appears lively and active, with a sensible spirited Countenance. – There

was an Opera at Night for his Entertainment. The House being richly finish'd with abundance of Carving and Gilding, well Illuminated with Wax Tapers, and the Company all superbly drest, many of the Men in Cloth of Tissue, and the Ladies sparkling with Diamonds, form'd alltogether the most splendid Spectacle my Eyes ever beheld.[60]

If Adams was sceptical, and John Quincy was dexterous, Franklin was simply swept off his feet by the sparkle of coffee ceremony. That sparkle was perhaps most evident in his preference for Mocca coffee over cheaper West Indian coffee after being more intimately exposed to European sociability. It was not until after cementing a correspondence from the French cafes in the 1770s that Franklin took an eager interest in eastern coffee.[61] While in Passy, Franklin employed a French servant to keep track of expenses. In March and April of 1785, Franklin placed two orders for six livres of mocha coffee.[62] However, Franklin never did permanently enter French cafe society, although he had correspondents in them. He was a man riddled with contradictions, and his American philosophy of hard work cast a shadow of doubt on his experiences. Writing from Passy to Benjamin Vaughan, Franklin stated, 'Look round the World and see the Millions employ'd in doing nothing … What is the Bulk of Commerce, for which we fight and destroy each other but the Toil of Millions for Superfluities … for Tea and for Coffee, to the West Indies for Sugar, to America for Tobacco! … our Ancestors lived very comfortably without them.'[63] He knew that he himself was falling under his own condemnation. Washington also ordered fifty pounds of Mocha in 1799 on the basis that 'Coffee from the Red Sea city of Mokha was considered the best.'[64] As the American Founders established diplomatic relationships with Europeans beyond their own remote coffeehouse neighbourhoods, their tastes changed. More importantly, they forged vital connections which brought American interests to Europe and provided yet another vantage point to contemplating the meaning of the American cause.

Conclusion

With the growth of a merchant empire in the eighteenth century, coffee gained a transatlantic clientele with peculiar British habits of taste, leisure and business. Coffee's 'remote neighborhoods' wove the empire closer together in a shared culture of taste, emulation and sociability. Both transatlantic merchants and the British government increasingly made use of coffeehouse postal networks which had been created through newsfeeds and 'print capitalism'. Benjamin Franklin understood that news and coffee were forever linked and began formalizing a system of coffee print culture from London, which embedded American printers into the imperial customs and postal networks. Franklin's orchestration of the news depended upon personal coffeehouse connections with printers, agents and statesmen from both sides of the Atlantic. Accordingly, he tapped into a pre-existing 'remote neighborhood' in the colonial coffeehouses of London, where merchants from America assembled their peculiar local friendships and interest in London's metropolis. Transatlantic coffee customers like Curwen and Byrd demonstrated that coffee culture exhibited similar British traits for news and leisure on both sides of the Atlantic.

Over time, coffeehouses became one of the many playing fields for settling matters of transatlantic imperial interest. The fiscal crisis of the 1760s and 1770s involved more stakeholders than just the government of Westminster. It entailed a transatlantic community of merchants who controlled the fasted news-ring in the Atlantic world, lobbied for its own appointees and demanded the settlement of their debts. While the Canada reconnaissances were being settled in the coffeehouses of London, the government of Westminster was creating an imperial system of revenue through these very coffeehouses which eventually brought America into war and many of the Founding Fathers abroad as diplomats among the coffeehouses of the courts of Europe. In Europe, the Adamses and Franklin adopted a more cosmopolitan view of coffee culture, adapting their news circuits to the coffee protocols of Europe and gaining a taste for Eastern coffee. Colonial governors, diplomats, merchants and lobbyists alike knew that they were all tied together in often very porous social networks of coffeehouse neighbourhoods which drew them into the interests of the economic system of empire. The social experiment of 'trifling' in coffee's dynamic environs had evolved into a shared social space of political activism, replete with a political ideology of free association all its own. Coffee represented more than just entertainment; it came to embody the stakes in playing the game of empire and protecting one's own social status on both sides of the British Atlantic world.

Part III

Empire and revolution

7

Empire, free association and slavery

Here, readers should pause and reflect on the peculiar irony of the Atlantic coffee culture of the eighteenth century. Coffeehouse customers became connoisseurs of the emerging political and economic system of empire and defended their right to the material culture of the entire world through the language of free association. The irony was that transatlantic coffeehouse society was anything but free. Whole coffeehouse audiences were devoted to rejoicing over the odd spoils of war which had secured them their 'empire of goods'. Indigenous material cultures on display in coffeehouses from all over the world afforded transatlantic travellers the exciting prospect of diversifying their tastes and celebrating a new world of luxury and conquest. Scientific experiments conducted in coffeehouses only fuelled the engines of progress which captured the vital material resources of other lands and enslaved millions of labourers who cultivated vast plantations of sugar and coffee. Slavery featured little in its civic culture but dominated its mercantile culture. Slaves were bought and sold in coffeehouses across the Atlantic world, but discussing slavery in the many coffeehouse clubs seemed almost forbidden by common consent. Acknowledging slavery would undermine the very legitimacy of coffeehouse publics, since it contradicted their emerging political ideas of right to association and rule by consent. The very material culture of coffee which was believed to birth a free discursive sphere brought about imperial exploitation of the very cultures which invigorated taste and eventually led to political revolution. The discussion of natural rights in the revolutionary era would later fracture coffeehouse publics.

Coffeehouse life included more than its caricaturized social sphere of literate men. It included slave auctions and the exotic arrangement of cultural artefacts from all over the world. Coffeehouse owners and their customers celebrated connoisseurship in acquiring knowledge, amateur pursuits of learning and material displays of cosmopolitan experiences. These displays often emphasized the exotic nature of world commerce and travel in artefact exhibits and scientific experiments. The new empiricism and classicism of the eighteenth century provided a cosmopolitan framework for comprehending these artefacts as statements of taste and culture. This coffeehouse discourse sustained 'remote neighborhoods' of transatlantic connoisseurs through a moral philosophy of rational leisure and a new material culture of diversity. Artefacts from other areas of the world gave visual life to subcultures within the empire and allowed transatlantic travellers to imagine regional identities with greater clarity. Yet behind cosmopolitan coffee experience loomed the ethos of empire, the systematic plunder of the knowledge, wealth, tastes of the world and the assembly of those resources in new European urban settings. Coffee connoisseurs went to the coffeehouses not just to taste foreign commodities but to marvel at the collision of cultures which had brought so many trophies to London and America. If, as Bickham asserts, the foreignness of coffee allowed it to transcend geography, gender and class in ways that domestic goods could not, then it is equally true that its foreignness drew hard distinctions between the conquerors and the conquered.[1]

Although coffee was an imperial commodity, the practice of imperial connoisseurship conflicted with the imperial symbolism of eastern luxury of coffee in its advertising culture. Helen Berry and Brian Cowan argue that travel literature of the sixteenth and seventeenth centuries portrayed coffee as an exotic drink, with special healing properties among the Egyptian, Arabian and Turkish peoples. As coffee entered London in Greek coffeehouses, the eastern narrative of the 'Turkish berry' continued. The Latin Jew who founded Nando's coffeehouse hung Spanish tapestries in his coffeehouse.[2] The imperialist message of coffee was most apparent in the material displays of coffeehouses.

However, as coffee became a colonial product in the West Indies, the advertising of coffee did not seem to include slavery or shift from its mysterious eastern qualities. Yet, coffeehouse customers were daily confronted with the labour system behind imperial products in the daily business of their coffeehouses. Slave auctions were held in the Jamaica Coffeehouse. In Liverpool and New Orleans, coffeehouses functioned as slave markets, undercutting the White male discourse of British civil liberty. Regardless of how hard they tried to ignore it, coffeehouse-goers frequently ran into slavery, even if they never voluntarily chose to talk about it in the coffeehouse. The Virginia and Maryland gazettes published runaway slave notices in every issue. As these gazettes were read in coffeehouses throughout the American south, slavery and coffee converged in the coffeehouses across the empire. Nevertheless, in British advertisements of coffee, slavery is rarely a feature. Although coffee increasingly relied on the plantation slavery, it remained advertised as an eastern imperial commodity. Anglo consumers of coffee preferred to bathe coffee in eastern luxury over the slave labour of coffee plantations in the West. It was an intentional masking of the truth.

Science and imperial connoisseurship

Science intersected with the tropes of empire in the coffeehouses of London, and coffee connoisseurs celebrated the advancement of geographical knowledge by categorizing cultural experiences from various regions. Thus, coffeehouse bore names and artefacts of various cultures, like the Grecian, Turk and so on. It was the intent of both the proprietors of the Grecian and the learned classicists who frequented the Grecian to link that coffeehouse with learning and classical philosophy. It served as the public face to the private scientific discoveries of the Royal Society. The 'learned club' which included many Royal Society fellows like Sir Isaac Newton (president of the club), Sir Hans Sloane and Professor Halley took up regular meetings there. At the Grecian, scholars reinforced a culture of Greek language and neoclassical culture in opposition to Turkish tyranny. Jonathan Harris argues that the Grecian provided coffee customers with an eastern trope which critiqued the troublesome politics of Turkey, from whence the drink hailed. Other scientists like Hodgson and Hauksbee presented on experimental philosophy at the cosmopolitan coffeehouse Marine. There, under the shadow of the Exchange, Humphrey Ditton, a student of Newton, lectured on mathematics. Robert Arnold lectured on mathematics and astronomy at the Swan, near the Exchange. These scientists had an eager audience of imperialists. The merchants and marine insurers of the Exchange coffeehouses had every interest in natural and experimental philosophy, since they were keeping the ships of empire afloat and regularly discovering environmental difficulties of trade routes. These merchants found scientific knowledge useful.[3] Larry Stewart explains an intimate connection between science, geography and trade in these coffeehouses, stating,

> Uniquely situated, and thus different from the polite and political interchange that was increasingly held in Covent Garden, the Exchange coffee-houses existed where the convergence of commodity and credibility would ultimately produce a dynamic consumer society. In many instances, as Rob Iliffe puts it, 'Coffee houses were spaces of exchange ... [while] such sites, like the Royal Society, were in practice barred to all but the most successful craftsmen and tradesmen.' Even the cultivation of astronomy, and the pretense of philosophical learning that went with it, might give to ladies as well as gentlemen a cachet of politeness. But the power of politeness was likewise a complex affection adopted by Augustan essayists who could glory in cartography and astronomy and in the public virtues of private opportunities provided by a trading nation. Polite culture was unable to sustain a separation from the ideology of productivity, for commerce thus encouraged polite conviviality and exchange.[4]

Politeness intersected with the Augustan political discourse of global exchange and thus became imperialistic. Civility in itself did not create an ethos for empire, but when it became possessive of the various routes of exchange between Turk, Greek, English and American, it grew into an imperialistic display of cultural superiority. While drinking tea and coffee according to polite rules was not inherently imperialistic, consuming tea and coffee as trophies of a geographical domination of social protocols was imperialistic. Insofar as coffee was consumed in light of its 'foreignness', it was an imperialistic ritual. The Augustan coffee culture of taste was a direct product of the imperial and scientific ethos of its British consumers and traders. What might have been a domestic discourse on social mores and classical taste was transformed by the science of geography and natural history into a conquest of foreign consumer beverages.

The British transformed the 'foreignness' of various colonial products into national symbols of civility. Troy Bickham asserts that taste arose from the gastronomical interest in refining the pallet or, as Stephen Mennell called it, the 'British obsession with politeness, taste, and luxury'.[5] Bickham provides three reasons why politeness and ritualistic table etiquette were displayed primarily through foreign foods like tea and sugar rather than domestic foods. Firstly, foreign foods lacked a dietary history in

Britain and so were less rooted in the class and gender discourse of daily consumption. Secondly, because Britain could not produce mass quantities of foreign foods, they were all the more incorporated into the national consumer economy. They were marketed as a national expression of imperial attitudes. Thirdly, the economic efficiency of getting these goods to market through only a few ports and a couple of middlemen disestablished them from regional economic relationships.[6] In other words, tea, coffee, sugar, tobacco and spices were national concepts for polite or sociable exchanges of imperial goods.

British consumers of these goods maintained a tension between a national celebration of civility and a cosmopolitan discussion of the proliferating variety of peoples in contact with the empire. Bickham states,

> A number of these foods became linked with the empire and the peoples associated with it. African slavery, the East India Company, Virginian plantations, American Indians and China all became associated with special foods. Ultimately, an examination of food in this way underlines the case for recognizing the empire's pervasive presence in Britons' lives, and it reveals how the consumption of imperial goods shaped perceptions of the empire and the peoples connected to it by trade.[7]

These products were advertised in very specific ways, emphasizing certain colonial producers and nationalities over others. Advertising prints reinforced imperial origin myths. And visual culture was very much a part of eighteenth-century British newspapers. By 1770, newspapers included 251,470 legal advertisements per year. These advertisements almost always told an idealistic story of origin and the product's journey from the field to the shop. Although these prints circulated the coffeehouses, grocers primarily chose to purchase trading cards from various suppliers for their advertising, rather than newspapers. British tobacco smokers constructed an imperialistic narrative of healthy and industrious southern plantation slavery and peaceful relationships with Native American tribal leaders. Tobacco brands did not shy away from slavery; instead, they civilized it. In tobacco advertisements, slaves planted and harvested tobacco in a gradual and orderly fashion, under the protection and moderating influence of paternal White overseers. Thus, tobacco smokers were lulled into the racist myth that the product represented a fair paternal relationship between black producers and White consumers and that the quality of their tobacco had been verified by White male overseers. Similarly, advertisements idealized tobacco's civilizing influence on Native Americans. In the latter half of the eighteenth century, the ideal Indian chief became the symbol for colonial America, akin to Britain's *Britannia*. Tobacco advertising of this period depicted Native Americans passively smoking together or passing around the peace pipe with White British colonials. Here was the imperial ideal of the American civilization personified; Americans organized the natural resources and native peoples of the New World into an orderly system of friendship, work and trade. Planting, harvesting and smoking tobacco involved a British ritual of putting the African to good use and taming the savage.[8]

Tea and coffee were even more ritualized products in Britain than tobacco, and both had eastern cultural connotations associated with them which emphasized the great divide between the east and west. This was due largely to the fact that the great Turkish and Chinese societies with which the East India Company and the Levant Company did business were civilizations with imperial interests of their own and not always within the reach of formal European imperial control during much of the eighteenth century. In some respects, the ritualization of eastern tea and coffee embodied an appreciation for the artistic accomplishments of eastern civilizations on their own terms, even if it was an orientalist and exotic image. And still, the archetypal place of tea and coffee in Britain's so-called civilizing mission was unmistakable, though it was uncertain which of these two products would come to dominate social life in Britain. Tea was often associated with parlour etiquette, whereas coffee was the favoured drink of public urban sociability, and Daniel Button purchased four times less tea than coffee.[9] Still, tea and tobacco were visually advertised by grocers far more than coffee. Tax laws also favoured tea over coffee after the early eighteenth century. As trading cards began to gain favour among grocers in the 1740s, tea was unmistakably gaining ground as Britain's drink. By 1784, Bickham estimates that tea was consumed seventeen times more than coffee. Because tea was served at home and bought at the grocers, it more readily adapted to the retail culture of visual tropes than coffee. Tea was branded by certain bona fide clearing houses and London retail. Since tea came exclusively from the east, and particularly from China, the East India Company held a monopoly on the official trade, and the East India House at Leadenhall Street was London's main tea warehouse. In retail, family Twining in the Strand took the lead as London's most recognized brand. Trading cards at such shops often displayed male Chinese peasants loading tea crates with mock-Chinese writing onto ships. Tea services across the British Empire, unlike plainer coffee utensils, were most often stencilled in the traditional willow pattern, with Chinese pagodas and sweeping eastern landscapes.[10] Today, Twining's tea shop still displays two richly coloured Chinamen above its doors and tea connoisseurs are ushered into a museum of exotic British ritual. Family portraits, lavish antique tea sets done in floral and English pastoral designs, tea manuals, and vintage newsprints and notices fill the long hall, while tea tasters may sit at a bar and enjoy the latest brew. Still profoundly British and yet cosmopolitan, tea finds a ready audience among London's tourists.[11]

Coffee was a much plainer imperial drink than tea, but it still had what Bickham calls an imperial stereotype: the sign of the Turk with his Turban hung over many coffeehouse doors.[12] Yet, if it was imperial, the Turk was an orientalist image which referenced the Ottoman Empire: a formidably imperial Mediterranean power of wealth and prestige outside of Britain's formal control, although generally considered by British consumers to be corrupt and in decline. The Turk celebrated Britain's contact with the luxurious wealth of this vast empire, but it also hinted at the danger of going native. For many early coffeehouse goers in London, there was much doubt as to whether the importation of Ottoman coffee would not transform Englishmen into Turks or Africans, and the advertising culture was not very reassuring. Coffee's imperial discourse was entangled with eastern tropes which corresponded to a real competitive force with a rival imperial power. Interestingly enough, when Britain gained a foothold in the coffee colonies of the West Indies, it did not craft an imperial narrative for West Indian coffee. Perhaps, this was because coffee's luxurious connotations were still widely popular, although controversial. Also, the origin of the bean was often confused in London coffee shops. Coffee was sold in two blends, 'Turkish' and 'Plantation', or 'Bourbon', because of its French colonial origins. In other words, British consumers were under no illusion that the colonial production of coffee, or indeed the colonization of the West Indies, was fundamentally tied to Anglo institutions and settlement. It represented a purely competitive venture and the overwhelming population of these islands were slaves. It did not make for a very wholesome sales narrative. According to Kay Dian Kriz, British art usually ignored or idealized slavery. Although it was no secret that sugar was dependent on the slave trade, Bickham states that sugar was often marketed according to its consumer standards for weight and quality of refinement rather than by its geographical origin. Although coffee and sugar became British colonial products and as much a part of the empire as American tobacco, they did not encourage a cultural interest in the West Indies among consumers, who probably felt that the West Indies was the dirty underbelly of the empire. The image of the Turk was far more sociable. Yet, according to Bickham, coffee, tea and tobacco trading cards all tended to portray British merchant vessels, emphasizing Britain's commercial and naval presence on the world stage.[13]

Coffeehouses were the starting places for journeys and the exotic display of idealized distant lands. It was the drink of adventure. As the Rev. Andrew Burnaby explained, his *Travels through the middle settlements in North America, in the years 1759 and 1760* began 'in a coffee-house with some friends, and discoursing of things relative to that country'.[14] Yet as will coffee advertising, it seems that moralists in eighteenth-century gentlemen's magazines looked everywhere around the world for social origins of coffee, except to the slave plantations of the West Indies: no doubt, an intentional reluctance on the part of social commentators to mention the inconsistencies of coffee. Instead, commentators and coffeehouse owners alike constructed a myth of exoticism around the drink which would literally stimulate and enhance social intercourse. M. de Moncrif, an agent of affairs for the king of France, referenced the emperor of Abyssinia as part of a wider Arabic community, who 'are content with smoking, drinking coffee, and reposing on carpets'.[15] Luxury was the obvious connotation. In *Elegant Anecdotes* (1790), travel writer John Adams commented that the cities of Cairo, Damascus and Aleppo were full of exotic baths and coffeehouses, where 'in a large room, filled with smoke, seated on ragged mats, the wealthier class of people pass whole days in smoking their pipes, talking of business in concise phrases ... and frequently in saying nothing. Sometimes the dullness of this silent assembly is relieved by the entrance of a singer, some dancing girls, or one of those storytellers'.[16] Oriental trappings were original with the very first coffeehouses in England at Oxford. In July 1673, the Oxford City Council granted the apothecary William Ball to hang a sign depicting a 'Turke filling coffee' across from Bragg's coffee house. Similar licences were then given to James Hall on the corner of Turl and Broad Street and Dorothy Day on High Street near Tillyard's Coffee House.[17] Turkish typology was an elaborate charade, an orientalism which masked the far more unpleasant details of Atlantic production of coffee on slave plantations and posed the east as a distant source of exotic origin. In fact, nothing could signal the advent of public amusement more than the commodification of coffee in this manner. The 'Turke' gave a visual brand name to the idea of the public consumption of coffee, celebrating fine service at a time when Europeans were opening coffee to new urban markets and moving it away from Near Eastern monopolies, transplanting it to the West Indies. Of all the exotic artefacts and displays to be found among the coffeehouses of London, including elaborate Cherokee and Ottawa war clubs and waxworks, the material culture of African Americans seems strangely absent.[18] The process of coffee production seems to have influenced the coffeehouse culture in Atlantic cities very little, due to an avoidance of the subject in print culture until the Abolitionist movement. Yet, the silence must have been deafening for Atlantic merchants visiting London who had sugar holdings in Barbados or Jamaica.

The displays of artefacts in London coffeehouses deserve close examination for no other reason than that they demonstrated an imperial interest in other cultures and lands. Artefacts on display were trophies of cultural and in some cases military conquest. Don Saltero's Coffeehouse provides an excellent case study of the kinds of displays held in coffeehouses. These artefacts were notorious for being fakes, and yet Don Saltero's collection of 'Various Curiosities' was wildly popular. Listed as an amateur tooth-drawer and barber of Chelsea village in the *Tatler*, Don Saltero was for Steele a great fraud. Although Steele found Saltero a man with irresistible humour and good nature, surrounded by a crowd of barber shop companions 'under the title of Odd Fellows', Steele decried Saltero's quack trade.[19] He said of Saltero,

> The particularity of this man put me into a deep thought, whence it should proceed, that of all the lower order, barbers should go further in hitting the ridiculous than any other set of men ... Though I go thus far in favor of Don Saltero's great merit, I cannot allow a liberty he takes of imposing several names (without my license) on the collections he has made, to the abuse of the good people of England; one of which is particularly calculated to deceive religious persons, to the great scandal of the well-disposed, and may introduce heterodox opinions. He shows you a straw-hat, which I know to be made by Madge Peskad, within three miles of Bedford; and tells you, 'It is Pontius Pilate's wife's chambermaid's sister's hat ... half the politicians about him, he may observe, are, by their place in nature, of the class of tooth-drawers.[20]

Saltero's coffeehouse was a syndicate of tradesmen who came to the coffeehouse for chatter and made their living by entertaining others. This pageant of gossip and news would have been indistinguishable from any other coffeehouse had it not been for its extraordinary collection. Indeed, Steele had good reason to call it out in the *Tatler*, for as late as 1795, a *Catalogue Descriptive of the Various Curiosities to be seen at Don Saltero's Coffee House* listed hundreds of artefacts from all over the world.[21] The sheer quantity of such a published list testifies to the fact that many connoisseurs in London came to the coffeehouse to view imperial trophies.

The coffeehouse experience of empire was not always 'enlightened' and, in some cases, was a throwback to medieval superstition. What is perhaps most strikingly obvious is just how many Church relics are to be found among the collection. Relics made a fitting backdrop for the orientalist exoticism of eastern imperial trophies. In Africa, North America and India, trophies of war indicate an interest in celebrating

British imperial moments. The king of Morocco's sword of state and tobacco pipe were obvious statements of imperialism, as was the rupee from the capture of Nabob. Most of the artefacts from Africa featured mythicized Ancient Egyptian objects. Among the Indian trophies of war were decorative utensils, like the hookah pipe, representing a cultural imperialism. Turkish artefacts were geological, biological or mercantile, enriching the imperial experience of coffee. Similarly, China's artefacts were largely personal accessories or highly decorative works of literature, music and visual art. Their culture was exoticized for British consumer tastes. The Chinese played at cards, read philosophy and news, played highly crafted musical instruments, smoked, fanned themselves, wore shoes and possessed a monetary standard tied to British monetary value.[22]

American artefacts in the *Catalogue* celebrated the abundance of natural resources in connection with Britain's emerging consumer empire. Beaver, buffalo, raccoon, porcupine, hickory nut, walnut, Jamaican Casada bread, Tequila pepper and mallegator and dagilla bark represented a vast new world of practical, if not so exotic natural resources, over which Britain could lay claim.[23] Mutual survival in a new world transformed unilateral imperialism into a multilateral dialogue for influence, resources and power. These resources functioned as diplomatic symbols of imperial relationships with native peoples. For instance, Indian wampum beads were more than curiosities; they were a currency of goodwill between chiefs and settlers. Native cloths and tools, like moccasins and canoes, were just as vital to colonizing settlers as to their Indian neighbours. Even native weapons like tomahawks and arrows represented what historians have called a 'middle ground', or a mixed identity shared between colonists and Native Americans and nurtured through consumer culture.[24] The selection of North American artefacts in the *Catalog* bespoke of the interconnectedness of frontier survival. American artefacts attested to dynamic collisions and frustrated relationships. Much like the English relationship with Jacobite Highlanders, the American relationship was one both of conquest and brotherhood. Thus, Don Saltero's Coffeehouse featured the 'Target of Tee-Yee Been Hogo-Row, Indian Emperor of the six nations' and 'an Indian belt of wampum, a present from one Indian king to another, as a pledge of friendship', similar to the 'Scotch Highlander's target' and 'Scotch dirk'.[25] The mythical depiction of 'an iron bolt, shot red hot at Fort William, by the rebels, in 1745' was strikingly similar to the representations of ingenious frontier weapons common to both settlers and Indians, including darts, arrows, canoes and the 'Indian tomahawk taken in the field of battle at Quebec'.[26] These trophies represented contested relationships.

Slavery in the coffeehouses

The colonial slave trade was just as entangled with coffee as British imperial artefacts were, but while slavery was decried by many coffeehouse journalists, very few actually acknowledged that slavery lay at the root of coffee culture. Slavery was always distant for them and had no actual bearing on *how* British people consumed their coffee. Nevertheless, African slavery undoubtedly flowed through the coffeehouses in much the same way that imperial financial interests were connected to both coffee and slavery. Slaves were sold in coffeehouses in London, Liverpool, Bristol, Philadelphia, New York and Virginia.[27] The market forces behind coffee and slavery shaped how coffee customers viewed slaves. C. John Sommerville has described the vendible coffeehouse world noting, 'There were ads for every conceivable item and service – auctions of the paintings or furniture of the great, telescopes, birdcages, wheelchairs, shoe polish, rental properties, slaves, wigs and sales of positions in the church, with tales of domestic strife in notices of runaway husbands and apprentices.'[28] Slaves were made to seem like just one sort of commodity among many by White advertisers. A standard advertisement posted in the *Weekly Post Boy* of New York in 1750 ran, 'Just imported, a parcel of likely negros, to be sold at public vendue tomorrow at Ten o'clock at the Merchant's Coffee House.'[29] These slaves bore daily witness to the injustices of coffee's social world. Yet, despite the constant intrusion of slaves into the 'polite' world of coffee, the coffeehouse journalists did not generally see slavery as a moral blight to coffee culture. It was the cruelty of highly regionalized working conditions in distant parts of the empire that they blamed: most often, the slave sugar refineries in the West Indies. Samuel Johnson said that Jamaica 'continues to this day a place of great wealth and dreadful wickedness, a den of tyrants, and a dungeon of slaves'.[30] Similarly, *Spectator* No. 11 related a pitiful story of an adventurer arriving in Barbados:

> When a vessel from the main arrives in that island, it seems the planters come down to the shore, where there is an immediate market of the Indians and other slaves, as with us of horses and oxen. 'To be short, Mr. Thomas Inkle now coming into English territories, began seriously to reflect upon his loss of time, and to weigh with himself how many days' interest of his money he had lost during his stay with Yarico. This thought made the young man pensive, and careful what account he should be able to give his friends of his voyage. Upon which consideration, the prudent and frugal young man sold Yarico to a Barbadian merchant; notwithstanding the poor girl, to incline him to commiserate her condition, told him that she was with child by him: but he only made use of that information, to rise in his demands upon the purchaser.[31]

As coffeehouse literature in the eighteenth century interpreted them, Jamaica and Barbados were places where greed, corruption and exploitation were daily atrocities, but they were not representative of coffee culture in Britain. Although *Spectator* only represents distant echoes of a colonial slave society, its readership was very much internally connected to the trade. In London, slaves were sold at the Jamaica Coffeehouse along with other West Indian interests.[32] Coffeehouse customers simply turned their backs to the evils at home.

As the sugar interests were chiefly to be had in Bristol and Liverpool, slaves were auctioned off to English buyers in the coffeehouses of these cities in greater quantities than in London. Liverpool was in particular a bustling city full of colonial interests. In 1740 and 1751, sugar prices at Bristol and Liverpool were three shillings higher than the London market.[33] Slaves were one part of that proliferating coffee culture. F. E.

Smith has identified the variety of cultural experience in the Liverpool coffeehouses with the following delineations:

> Merchants Coffee House, West Indian cotton.
> George's Coffee House in Liverpool with slaves.
> Pontacks Coffee House, Theatre Royal ticket.
> George's – Conversation Club
> Merchants – Most Noble Order of British Bucks.
> Exchange – Ugly Face Club
> Merchants – Reading Society
> Bath Coffee House – recreational bathing with an indoor pool, dressing-rooms, and fireplaces.[34]

Thus, maritime interests encouraged a society of leisure and refinement, carefully covering up the cruelty of slavery. Liverpool elites considered trade and culture two sides of the same coin, and if a glance at their coffeehouse life were truly representative of their social experience, it would prove them right, but not in the way they preferred to see themselves. Their social experience involved exploitation. Thomas Henley, president of a merchant club at the Neptune Coffee Houses, wrote to The Marine Society of London in 1757, stating,

> In our Club (which is a Company of Tradesmen who frequently meet in the evenings at the sign of the Neptune in this town) some time ago, the subject of our conversation turned on the great utility and true patriot spirit of the design of your Society, whereon it was proposed and unanimously agreed to open a subscription amongst us.[35]

Attributing its 'patriotism' to the mythical power of the seas, the Marine Society gave no mention of slavery as its source. Wealthy Liverpool merchants ignored that it lay at the root of all their coffeehouse refinements. And these abounded. The Exchange Coffeehouse of Liverpool sold periwigs and had five Raphael paintings on exhibition captured from a French war. Book auctions at the Exchange included Addison, Milton, Pope, Family Bibles, Maps, prints and pamphlets. Woodchurch Manor, near Birkenhead, was sold here for £8,030 in December 1766.[36]

Slavery linked the coffeehouses' most notable commodity, conversation, with the rest of the empire. The very air of reform in the clubs was infused with slavery, and for that very reason, the issue of slavery was intentionally ignored in the moral commentaries of published coffeehouse clubs. Perhaps for this reason, the *Virginia Gazette* chose to follow the reforming clubs in Liverpool, rather than that of London. Saint George's Coffeehouse was home to both slaves and England's premier transatlantic coffeehouse club, the Conversation Club. Meeting minutes of the Conversation Club on politics, morality and society were regularly published in the *Virginia Gazette*, a colonial newspaper which similarly advertised slaves alongside auctions for landed estates. Among the many topics published in Liverpool and Virginia from the Conversation Club, African slavery was not one of them. Elites failed to acknowledge openly that the system which brought them coffee, sugar and a public sphere of free association rested on the labour of a subjugated ethnic group.³⁷ Virginian coffeehouses and Liverpool coffeehouses were strikingly similar in this regard. Their coffeehouses were both dominated by a landed and mercantile social elite who sold land and slaves in coffeehouses. The culture of coffeehouse slavery united a coffeehouse rhetoric of enlightened morality which left slavery intact.

Still, the coffeehouse 'wits' were not about to blame the sociable coffeehouse culture for architecting the colonial slave system, although one day's listening to the conversation at the Jamaica, Marine or Lloyd's coffeehouses would have sufficiently proved the point. Their racist perceptions logically proceeded any argument about slavery. In his *The School of Politicks* (1698), Edward Ward blamed the exoticism of other racial groups for corrupting the manners of the English. He expressed coffee in the following couplet:

To drink a Liquor of infernal Race,
Black, scalding, and of most offensive smell.³⁸

This racial stereotyping was common to coffeehouse literature like John Fothergill's *A Botanical Description and the History of Coffee* (1774), which had associated Mecca coffeehouses with rebellious gaming; the coffeehouses at Syria, Damascus and Constantinople with politicians, elegant manners and public sociability; and the coffeehouses of Medina, Cairo and Yemen as studious.³⁹ Berry has noticed that the mock-heroic coffeehouse pamphlet *Tom K's: or, the Paphian Grove* (1738) associated coffee with a racial degeneracy in Semitic and African peoples: 'the boiled juice of the "Turkish Berry" ... "The Black Girl that attends with the Coffee."'⁴⁰ A scene from *Thomas St. Serfe, Tarugo's Wiles: or, the Coffee-House. A Comedy* (1668) may also be added to Berry's examples. In the play, a coffeehouse customer sang alongside a baboon to entertain the crowd. The coffeehouse cook told one customer named Alberto, 'That's nothing; I catch'd him one day in the Kitchin both Playing and Dancing with the Negro-wench.' Alberto replied, 'Yet in Italy when they are associate with Operators, they are then reckon'd in the number of the Vertuosi; and to try what you have said, bring out the Negro-Girl, and we'll have a Dance to see if he'll imitate us.'⁴¹ Serfe believed that the African kitchen maid was little better than the baboon. The mockery of this piece reveals something about the racist assumptions of many of the coffeehouse satirists. For them, the racial injustice in drinking coffee was not that it kept Africans and Turks *under* society but rather that it let barbarians *into* society, albeit as servants and sideshows. Coffee literally and metaphorically coloured English society black. Yet, nowhere in these passages were blacks ever referred to as slaves, although it was inferred that the 'blackness' of coffee referred to its plantation origins. Thus, the evils of the slave coffee were excused as the negative influence of 'blackness' on White English sociability. The opposite was true. The presence of blacks in coffeehouses posed a challenge to the racist narrative which relegated conversation and debate to White Europeans.

Because coffeehouse slave market nomenclature was universally racist, it varied with the commodification of each slave region. In plantation societies and in slave port cities, slaves were advertised according to the colonial regions and food stuffs where they had originated or previously worked. In London, the language was more remote and exotic. To obscure the foreignness of Africans in the language of eastern luxury, slaves were sold at the Jamaica Coffeehouse in London as 'black ivory'.[42] This was a world apart from the complete commodification of slaves in plantation societies like Virginia and Maryland. Slaves arrived from the West Indies alongside the very products that depended upon their labour. Thus, one advertisement in Virginia ran, 'for Sale Jamaica and Leeward Island Rum, Muscovado Sugar, Madeira and Port Wine, Coffee, Pimenta, a few Negroes'.[43] Virginians read about the sale of slaves alongside the harvest reports of sugar: 'They had a prospect of great crops of coffee next year; that there was great plenty of sugar at market … three Guineamen arrived there a few months since, and sold their slaves very well.'[44] Both slaves and island and coastal products like sugar were brought to market by profiteering ship captains. The same was true in Liverpool where an advertisement at St George's Coffeehouse ran, 'A very fine Negro girl about 8 years of age, very healthy and hath been some time from the Coast … Apply to Capt. Robert Syers and Mr. Bartley Hodgetts, Mercer and Draper near the Exchange.'[45] Because slaves were considered transatlantic commodities, they shared advertising space with transatlantic goods. Runaway slaves were posted in or near the advertisements section of the Virginia and Maryland gazettes, where readers looked for the latest colonial shipments and monitored tobacco prices.[46]

In Virginian coffeehouses, the word 'negro' was synonymous with 'slave' and was part of a much larger culture of material commodities of 'good value' and coffeehouse trade. Although slaves were sold primarily according to their experience like 'a good Hostler, Gardener, and House Servant', they were subsumed into the cruder material culture of the West Indies.[47] Nowhere was this more apparent than in slave dress. Advertisements for slave clothing included lists like 'For sale, best brown sugar, French rum and coffee, by the hogshead or bag, blue cloth suitable for negroes, and a few pipes of wine' or, even more potently, 'sundry Merchandises, viz. Fifty one Pieces of coarse Wollen Cloth, fit for Negroes, &c. 130 ready made Shirts … 14 Bags of Coffee, 12 Hhds. of Molosses, 30 Casks of Rum'.[48] This was a form of consumable wear which mirrored the consumable goods of the plantation system itself. Slave owners were dressing plantation slaves in ready-made clothing purchased from shops which retailed goods produced on southern and West Indian plantations. In commodifying the material culture of 'negroes', southern merchants were actually commodifying 'negroes' *as* slaves. The Norfolk coffeehouse advertised on 17 November 1768, 'SEVERAL VALUABLE SLAVES, some of which are good savers and house servants.'[49] Slave auctioneer William Woodford announced on 12 February 1779, 'To be sold to the highest bidder, for ready money, before the coffeehouse door in Fredericksburg, on Thursday the 21st day of February (being Spotsylvania court day) TWENTY VALUABLE NEGROES.'[50] Like any West Indian good, 'valuable slaves' were 'valuable negroes'; their race and economic function intentionally conflated into one commercial concept.

This was why slave auctioneers persistently sold prestigious estates alongside slaves in coffeehouses across the plantation societies of the American south. They were commodifying two ends of the same plantation way of life. An auction in the court house of Charles City, Virginia, sold 'sundry slaves, Consisting of men, women, and children. Also a TRACT of LAND, containing by estimation 6,000 acres'.[51] Presumably the slaves and estate were not the same plantation, but they represented the two most valuable resources in a plantation society. Inside the large Exchange Coffeehouse of New Orleans, the brig and sheriff sales of March 1809 featured a plantation near the Bayou St John, lots in the Faubourg Plaisance and 'a negro [sic] man named Grand Joseph'.[52] By 1809, the Exchange Coffeehouse in New Orleans had long held an unopposed reputation in the *Louisiana Gazette* and *Louisiana Courier* for being the commercial and material centre of the city, serving customers with 'abundance and taste'. It hosted the chamber of commerce and received bagged mail containing the maritime lists, newspapers and commercial information of all the regular merchants and captains of the city. Ladies and gentlemen danced under grand chandeliers in the same building where 'negroes' were sold.[53] New Orleans flaunted its 'negro' slave culture in the coffeehouses as no other state. By the time Andrew Jackson held his grand ball there in celebration of the victory of the battle of New Orleans, the coffeehouse included three boarder's rooms, a gallery, one large room, a back room, a small pantry, a second room, a small room between two vestibules and a dining room. The Exchange had all the room it needed to commodify 'negroes' and host the social life of the town. Both the wealth and the labour of slave plantations were put on display in coffeehouses like these.

Among the coffeehouse intellectuals, only Benjamin Franklin seems to have appreciated the dreadful irony of slavery and coffee culture. As he described the consumer revolution of the eighteenth century,

> When employed merely in transporting superfluities, it is a question whether the advantage of the employment it affords is equal to the mischief of hazarding so many lives on the ocean. But when employed in pillaging merchants and transporting slaves, it is clearly the means of augmenting the mass of human misery. It is amazing to think of the ships and lives risqued in fetching tea from China, coffee from Arabia, sugar and tobacco from America, all which our ancestors did well without. Sugar employs near one thousand ships, tobacco almost as many. For the utility of tobacco there is little to be said; and for that of sugar, how much more commendable would it be if we could give up the few minutes gratification afforded once or twice a day by the taste of sugar in our tea, rather than encourage the cruelties exercised in producing it. An eminent French moralist says, that when he considers the wars we excite in Africa to obtain slaves, the numbers necessarily slain in those wars, the many prisoners who perish at sea by sickness, bad provisions, foul air, &c. &c. in the transportation, and how many afterwards die from the hardships of slavery, he cannot look on a piece of sugar without conceiving it stained with spots of human blood![54]

Coffee was actually slavery. Franklin unmasked the politeness of the era as a system which depended on the misery of millions, deconstructing the narrative of commodification which had dehumanized slaves. The superficialities which gave pleasure to so many British and Anglo-American coffee connoisseurs were nothing more than the extracted blood of slaves. Sugar, tobacco, coffee, tea were all momentary gratifications for White consumers and endless toil for enslaved blacks. Thus, White landlords intentionally distanced themselves from the system as soon as possible to hide themselves away in a 'polite' society. Large-scale sugar estates were run by absentee landlords, who cared little for the suffering of their 240–250 slaves per 1,000 acres of land. Sugar imports almost doubled mid-century, from 38,725 to 70,320 tonnes. While most of the slaves worked on sugar plantations because it was more economical, half of the land in Jamaica was given over to coffee and 20 per cent of land in Dominica was coffee. S. D. Smith claims, 'a slave tending 1.5 acres with an average yield of 833 lb per acre ... Coffee was, therefore, a crop that featured a land and labour ratio similar to sugar and tobacco.'[55] The system was too entrenched to be easily stopped, but the abolitionists of the next century made it their mission to embed the evils of slavery symbolically into the material culture of everyday life, so that 'he cannot look on a piece of sugar without conceiving it stained with spots of human blood'!

Conclusion

The public consumption of coffee was constructed from the imperial and colonial tropes which its consumers gave to it. The Turkishness of coffee was elaborately disguised behind a vale of neoclassical thought and conversation. The rise of geographical and mathematical knowledge in London coffeehouses transformed the discourse of coffee into an imperial social force, uniting merchants with territorial acquisitions and underscoring the importance of regional diversity among the 'remote neighborhoods' of coffeehouse communities. These publics celebrated the material culture of imperialism as an expression of free association, but behind the curtain of this imperial pageant, the voices of the conquered whispered the injustices of European cosmopolitanism. Coffeehouses displayed artefacts and resources from all over the world, especially war trophies from Africa and India. Chinese and Turkish material culture revelled in the exotic and artistic. In America, the conflict of cultures for natural resources was represented by war clubs, arrows, knives and tomahawks. Samples of American vegetation and animal life promised coffeehouse viewers that America was a vast realm of colliding peoples and resources. The materialism of coffeehouse imperialism revealed the 'middle ground' of frontier survival.

Similarly, slavery in coffeehouses revealed the often confused search for human identities in the midst of commodification. Slavery was not a subject of coffeehouse conversation because it seemed to undermine the philosophical understanding of the coffeehouse as a place of free association. Nothing could be further from the truth for those slaves who were sold in coffeehouses. Slaves sent to the West Indies underwent the same process of commercialization that other West Indian goods like coffee and sugar underwent. Sugar, coffee and rum were sold together and associated with similar standards for determining 'value'. One way was to identify slaves with the resources which they were supposed to cultivate on plantations. Thus, coffee, sugar and slavery evolved commercial connotations in an interdependent language of commercialization. Behind this commercialization was the racist stereotype in coffeehouse literature which held that 'blackness' was tropical, and therefore African slaves were best suited to cultivate sugar and coffee. In London, the 'blackness' of Africans was marketed as exotic. In Liverpool, the commodification of slaves and the diversification of public coffeehouse life happened simultaneously, and shared the same public spaces. In slave societies, the process of slave commodification was connected to the plantation subculture. Southern gazettes published runaway slaves with advertisements for other plantation commodities. Slave auctions at coffeehouses advertised both plantation estate sales and slaves together. The great irony in the coffeehouse slave market was that discussions of sociability and discussions of slavery never intersected. Slavery was less of a noticeable commodity than coffee for White male club members, who chose to enjoy the taste and rational influence of coffee and ignore its many injustices. They preferred to bathe coffee in the mystique of empire, which emphasized the political objectives of coffee in a civil sphere around the Atlantic world. As coffee grew closer to the entangled nature of empire, political inconsistencies within the British system brought coffee culture to its eventual end, as disaffected groups began calling for rights and civil liberties. Coffeehouses were so deeply embedded into the systems of economic empire that they became places of political protest and eventually revolution in the 1760s and 1770s.

Figure 9 Bostonian patriots accosting a customs officer.
Photo by Interim Archives/Getty Images.

Figure 10 Revolutionaries gathering at a coffeehouse in Paris.
Photo by Universal History Archive/Universal Images Group via Getty Images.

Figure 11 Washington chose coffeehouses and taverns as places for public ceremonies and Republican pageantry.
Photo by PHAS/Universal Images Group via Getty Images.

Figure 12 The restored R. Charlton coffeehouse in colonial Williamsburg is the only functioning historic British coffeehouse of its kind in existence.

Contributor: Daniel Ladd/Alamy Stock Photo.

8

Bringing down the empire

American patriots who read the colonial gazettes in September 1768 could not help feeling a sense of foreboding at the news of British troop movements. That year, Boston was in an uproar. John Hancock's ship *Liberty* had been seized by customs officers on a charge that it was smuggling Madeira wine and the Sons of Liberty were plotting revenge. Major Moncrief had handed General Gage new dispatches in New York and Gage decided to deploy his men, ostensibly to St Augustine in Florida, but New Yorkers feared the destination was Boston. At this early stage of the crisis, Gage had no British naval support and was compelled to solicit the aid of private merchants in New York. Not only did they refuse him any transportation, but they sent a public message to all the merchants in the city to stay clear of the army or face certain ruin. As one letter from Philadelphia reprinted in the *Virginia Gazette* put it, 'In the evening of that day written advertisements were posted up at the coffee-house, and the corner of every street, that if any man dared to hire them a vessel destruction would ensue.'[1] The fact that the merchants of New York chose the coffeehouse to post their evening news suggests that American patriots found the coffeehouse indispensable to their protests and later to the war effort. The coffeehouse had long provided a dependable conduit for merchant correspondence and a setting where political ideas could be aired, debated and disseminated to the populace.

American coffeehouse revolutionaries questioned the economic imperialism of British consumer culture with the same political language which had once created unified coffeehouse publics dedicated to commercial empire. Although continuity in the American civil social order would exist in the Congress and later under the Constitution which affirmed the pre-existing legal structure under federalism, grassroots revolutionaries, fired by political sermons and patriotic propaganda in gazettes, seized control of the Atlantic civil service in America without waiting for legal authority. Mob rule was unleashed against what was perceived as foreign tyranny coming from Britain: the biggest reason why American radicals did not turn against their own governments. The civil order they rebelled against was primarily British in the beginning, although incidents like Shays' Rebellion (1786–7) and the Whiskey Rebellion (1791) proved that these tendencies were potentially dangerous to the survival of the American civil social order. What revolutionaries in America and in Europe did achieve, though they acted independently and often under different ideological assumptions, was the destruction of any unified civic discourse in the coffeehouse.

The age of revolution destroyed the British social pageant of coffee across the Atlantic and signalled the retreat of literate elites into private club quarters. Revolution closed the classical consensus of coffeehouse culture which had celebrated polite sociability as the right to associate. The egalitarian appeal to natural rights, which became a popular creed for Jefferson and Paine in the 1790s, implied that all men were entitled to free association regardless of whether they were polite, classically educated or even literate. The public sphere radicalized. Distinct revolutionary and national movements segmented coffeehouse publics and polarized discussion. In America, anti-British patriotic pageants were staged at coffeehouses to purge them of imperial meaning, and in England, coffeehouses were increasingly flooded with spies and government agents who monitored the public sphere. Political polarization of the coffeehouses discouraged the clubbable culture which had hitherto influenced rational coffeehouse discussion. The Revolutionary Society of London freely conversed with French revolutionary coffeehouse intellectuals. American and French spies pervaded the coffeehouses of London during the last decades of the eighteenth century and Pitt's government sent officials to report disloyalty. Clubs retreated into private enclaves.[2] The discourse which had formed a transatlantic public sphere in the coffeehouses of London and America was pulled apart to form a new nation on one side of the Atlantic and to construct a national sphere of influence in London to resist French revolutionary influence.

Radical change came first to the coffeehouses in America with the sudden and vehement protest to the Stamp Act. The Stamp Act crisis sparked a controversy over public access to news. Dissonant groups often hijacked postal services in port cities, tarred and feathered postal agents, robbed mail deliveries and dispensed mail freely in coffeehouses. Both the Sons of Liberty and colonial agencies feared that Britain had usurped colonial news by insisting on customs inspections of postal routes. They saw immediately the importance of maintaining a free revolutionary press in coffeehouses entirely separate from the British customs and postal officers appointed in America. As colonial legislatures formed committees to petition parliament, the colonial gazettes openly embraced political dissent. The Sons of Liberty not only determined how mail was dispersed but also ran many leading news prints. Colonial coffeehouse and tavern customers were increasingly inundated with a partisan news feed which pervaded social life in capital cities. The Sons of Liberty staged elaborate burnings in effigy of Lord North and his customs officers in front of taverns and coffeehouses. Committees of public safety enforced non-importation regulations violently at the local level. In so doing, they united both private consumption and public consumer spaces with political resistance. Throughout the war, American coffeehouses hosted elaborate balls for the Continental army and were sites of celebratory fireworks and bonfires. Coffeehouse discussion was systematically transformed into a patriotic public sphere distinctly American rather than British.[3]

Coffee's republican tradition and the political elements of the American Revolution

A long line of coffeehouse scholarship has asserted the rise of republican ideas in the coffeehouses of London and America. However, there has yet to be a differentiation between early seventeenth-century republicanism and the exuberant republican coffeehouse reactions to the Stamp Act rooted in political rights. Coffeehouse literature generally assumed that debate in coffeehouses was republican because it was open to all classes. The democratization of coffee rationalized political coffeehouse discussion. Take, for example, the following claims from early twentieth-century historian of coffee, William Ukers:

> 'Coffee and commonwealth ... came in together for a Reformation to make a free and sober nation ...' that liberty of speech should be allowed, 'where men of differing judgements crowd' ... The seventeenth-century coffee houses were sometimes referred to as the 'penny universities'; because they were great schools of conversation ... England's great struggle for political liberty was really fought and won in the coffee house.[4]

Ukers was therefore confident that democratic tendencies, liberty and Commonwealth were first disputed inside coffeehouses. The most often cited example of this republican coffeehouse public sphere is James Harrington's Rota Coffee Club at the Turk's Head, Westminster, with its ballot box for political opinion. Through this ballot box, Ukers claimed that the Rota rooted republican opinion into coffeehouse life.[5] Ukers is not alone in his claim that republican ideas were inseparable with the coffeehouse culture of the Commonwealth and Restoration. Ellis states that 'Coffee-houses represented the democratic foundation of the English constitution.'[6] The price was affordable for all men, seating and discussion in the open coffee-room was unregulated, and customers were always discussing the news together. Ellis argues that the Rota popularized Harrington's republican ideas, which quickly spread through the coffeehouses in an age of Stuart autocracy.[7] Macaulay had stated, 'Dreams of perfect forms of government made way for dreams of wings with which men were to fly from the Tower to the Abbey, and of doublekeeled ships which were never to founder in the fiercest storm. All classes were hurried along by the prevailing sentiment. Cavalier and Roundhead, Churchman and Puritan, were for once allied.'[8] For these historians, London citizens invented a social republic outside of the state during the latter seventeenth century, balancing all the interests and estates of the Commonwealth in the democratic institution of the coffeehouse. Tavern historian Edward Callow claimed that this republican process was not complete until Queen Anne's reign, when members of the governments founded their own clubs in coffeehouses.

Callow, like Macaulay, dated the beginnings of this republicanism to the clubs of the Commonwealth and Restoration. He mentioned a string of influential clubs, including the Calves' Head Club, the Rota Club (with Harrington, John Milton, Marvel, Cyriac, Skinner, Nevil and, tangentially, Samuel Pepys), Cocoa Tree (for the Tories of St James' Street), the Mug House Club (a sing-song club and forerunner to music hall), the Brothers or Scribblers Club (with Walpole, the Earl of Oxford, Dean Swift, Pope, Gay and Arbuthnot) and finally King's Head Protestant Club (which wore patriotic green ribbons in Queen Anne's time).[9] Although Stephen B. Pobranski questions whether John Milton was part of the Rota, he reasserts the republican atmosphere of seventeenth-century coffeehouses and argues vehemently against the assumption that coffeehouses were simply glorified taverns. He reveals that coffeehouses of the Puritan Commonwealth were barred from serving alcohol and that Milton himself was influenced by a new colloquialization of coffeehouse writing style. He claims, 'Coffee houses offered a popular alternative to taverns by the late 1650s, a period when Milton was writing publicly about salvaging the Commonwealth ... The pamphlets ... convey the houses' convivial atmosphere ... as centres of debate ... people striking up a conversation over coffee.'[10]

This was the sort of coffeehouse culture which Habermas found invaluable when he stated, 'The coffee house not merely made access to the relevant circles less formal and easier; it embraced the wider strata of the middle class, including craftsmen and shopkeepers.'[11] Perhaps the prominence of republican ideals in the Commonwealth coffeehouses explains why both coffeehouse clubs and Milton's theology appear again and again in Addison and Steele's *Spectator*, but it does not explain the influence of the Glorious Revolution on republican attitudes. Stephen Pincus demonstrates the fundamental significance of the dynamic events of 1688–9 on republican rhetoric. James II's statist policies launched the first popular revolution, as citizens in London, York, Hull Carlisle, Gloucester, Oxford and throughout Wales and Ulster took to the streets in protest. Parliament asked William and Mary to preside over a new constitutional settlement which secured the right to property (for the landholder), liberty of conscience (for Protestants only) and some measure of political accountability. Historians have been careful not to equate these reforms with democracy, although it did give birth to political stability and a language of liberty.[12] Pincus claims the political debate in the Exclusion crisis and the following Glorious Revolution marked a rise in pamphleteering which augmented the importance of coffeehouses in defining political opinion.[13]

Apart from failing to notice various alterations in British republican platforms in coffeehouses, scholars have yet to address the republicanism of the revolutions of the latter eighteenth century and the discussion of taxation, representation and natural rights. With the monopolizing of the American tea trade by the East India Company, Ukers assumed that the people of Boston drank coffee in place of tea and that this American choice lasted well into the next century. Ukers quoted Daniel Webster's statement that coffee became 'king of the American breakfast table'. For Ukers, to drink coffee was to resist tyranny. Such an assumption is unfounded. The tax on tea was only a momentary dispute of secondary importance to the much larger debate on freedom of assembly and legislative rights. New England coffeehouse taverns quickly became places of meeting for dissenters and republicans, who finally mobilized to protest tax. Ukers was correct in noting a change in the public sphere as a result of the tax disputes. Of the Bunch of Grapes in Boston, Ukers commented, 'Like the Green Dragon over the way, its patrons included unconditional freedom seekers, many coming from the British coffee house when things became too hot for them in that Tory atmosphere.'[14] The Green Dragon was, as Daniel Webster claimed, 'headquarters of the Revolution'. John Adams, Paul Revere and James Otis formed their committee here. These patriots clashed with British officials, loyalists and even redcoats who met at the Green Dragon. But the real radicals met in the Bunch of Grapes. In 1776, a Philadelphia delegate read the Declaration of Independence aloud from the balcony to an enthusiastic crowd below. They built a bonfire so close to the building that they almost burned down the coffeehouse in their excitement.[15]

Although Ukers did attempt to include the debate on taxes and its effects on American republican coffeehouse attitudes, he offered no rationale for the vigilante republicanism of the Sons of Liberty. James Davis also narrates the violent entrance of the Sons of Liberty with no other interpretive comment than, 'Tea was associated with Toryism and it has never shaken off the stigma.'[16] The political incentive for patriots to pervade the coffeehouses with plots against the government is in great need of re-examination. The exact nature of the American protest movement during the tax crisis remains hotly disputed among scholars of the revolutionary era. In *The Stamp Act Crisis* (1953), Helen and Edmund Morgan argued neither the colonies nor the parliament had adequately considered the rights of colonies until 1764, when the Stamp Act crisis forced both sides to define each other's rights and authority in light of their new differences. Oddly enough, although both colonial governors and dissenting colonial statesmen drew on English constitutionalism, questions of authority were often decided on the basis of trade and present stability rather than through ideological arguments over constitutional rights. Here, Morgan separated the rhetoric of the Revolutionary era, inspired by a Whig political discourse, from the atmosphere of riot and revolt in the wake of the tax crisis.[17]

The crisis provoked two separate visions of what connections colonies had to their mother country. Massachusetts governor Francis Bernard attempted to clarify the empire in his *Principles of Law and Rights Allied to the Government of the British Colonies in America*. In it, he proposed to restore colonial recognition of parliamentary authority by claiming that colonies had a right to representation in parliament because the Royal charters had only been temporary and parliament had gained constitutional prerogative. Legislator James Otis countered in his *The Rights of the British Colonies Asserted and Proved* that parliament had no right to tax without colonial representation. As tensions increased, colonists changed the terminology of their political position: from 'rights and liberties of the Colonists' to 'Principles of freedom' and from 'rights of Englishmen' to 'rights of man'. Likewise, those favourable to parliament justified parliamentary authority on new grounds. Daniel Dulany argued that the colonies already possessed 'virtual representation', resembling certain cities in England which were only represented by their boroughs.[18] The political ideology became more and more resolute and universal.

However, violence and logistical concerns increasingly dominated the political landscape. Morgan noted that critics of the Sugar Act actually spoke more about the adverse effects to trade than about rights. Riots tested not just parliamentary authority but also parliamentary power. The Sons of Liberty ransacked the houses of government officials, hijacked the press and local civil affairs, and eventually won backing in every colony. Rhode Island passed the first resolution claiming a right to resistance. Virginia passed a resolution stating that only the colonial assembly had legislative authority. Maryland and the Carolinas regularly ignored the tax duties. Parliament closed many colonial courts over liabilities suits, but popular protest forced open many of these courts. Furthermore, pressure from English merchants on parliament forced a repeal of the Stamp Act, rather than any concession on the constitutionality of colonial rights.[19]

Historians favouring republican explanations of the American Revolution include Bernard Bailyn, Jack Greene and Gordon Wood. Bailyn argued in *Ideological Origins of the American Revolution* (1967) that the American Revolution was the ideological culmination of classical Enlightenment rationalism, common law and Puritanism. It represented a movement in harmony with the 'country' party of the 1720s–1730s to restore a proportionate government against British power. Greene believes that the Revolution represented a conservative attempt to protect older colonial systems of government and law by dismantling the early modern imperial structures of British rule. Wood understands the Founders' rhetoric as republican, drawing on the neoclassical ideas of Commonwealth. Thomas Jefferson epitomized this view in arguing that the virtues of the republic rested with the yeomen farmers of America. Yet, Wood also admits a more egalitarian force in American ideology and believes that average Americans took matters into their own hands. He articulates the violent acts of many anti-British citizens who fought for a more just society. The result was a constitution which balanced the regional interests of American society.[20]

More recently, the republican view of Bailyn and Wood has been challenged by the neoliberal school of Joyce Appleby and T. H. Breen. Breen has successfully shown that behind the American response to the tax crisis was a cultural context of consumer habits. Breen argues that popular mobilization against taxes was not the result of a republican ethos to protect a balanced form of government but rather a movement to protect the right of consumer choice. For Breen, the Lockean influence over America was a liberal insistence on the right of human choice. Anglo-Americans understood the marketplace as a national identity of protest against British goods: the very manufactured goods with which they had once celebrated their Britishness, namely tea, China, imported silks and sugar. Breen believes that the 'revolution of manners' in the Anglo world was not a republican classical ideology but rather a consumer culture of new materials which Great Britain used to erect an 'empire of goods'. These materials defined rather than merely expressed the rise of British politeness and civility. They were tokens which revealed success, tastes and leisure. The Navigation Acts were self-congratulatory statements of British wealth, officially constraining American trade to Great Britain. American revolutionaries constructed an ideology of domestic economy in opposition to the 'luxuries' of Great Britain. They wove together a national myth of homespun self-reliance.[21] Breen states, 'We can with reasonable confidence begin the investigation of the new commercial narrative in the early 1760s … Colonists first focused attention on why British authorities had redefined the rules that had governed the empire … In this context, the Sugar Act of 1764 seemed so precipitate, so destructive to the normal flow of trade.'[22] After the Townsend Acts of 1767 and the Tea Act of 1773, colonial legislatures attempted to erect a culture of protest by stopping merchants from purchasing British goods. These non-importation acts had mixed results. It was not until Congress established the Association in 1774 of local committees to inspect non-importation compliance that large-scale boycotting was achieved. These boycotts were a distinctly American revolutionary bourgeois invention, representing 'commercial rituals of shared sacrifice'.[23]

The Sugar Act was a tax on imports, but the Stamp Act placed taxes on the papers required to transact daily business. It came at a critical time when American merchants were suffering from a contracting domestic market, scarcity in the money supply brought on by the bankruptcy of European governments in the wake of the Seven Years' War and ever-increasing debt. Breen claims the Stamp Act was the spark which set off mass resistance against taxes as being violations of liberty and property (for Breen, consumer choice). The middling merchants, lawyers, planters and influential clergymen organized petition campaigns and formalized the Stamp Act Congress to voice colonial concerns. Villagers and townsfolk rioted in the streets and accosted tax agents, effigies of British officials were burned and the newspapers became viscerally ideological. In October 1765, two hundred New York merchants agreed to ban all British manufactured articles in the new year. Six weeks later, merchant assemblies in Boston, Philadelphia, Albany, Salem, Plymouth, Marblehead, Newburyport and Portsmouth had followed the New York plan. Both the *Pennsylvania Gazette* and the *New-London Gazette* asserted that British goods only served to destroy the local manufacturing economy and place the colonies in a state of dependence. Already, Americans were asserting a certain measure of independence. Breen asserts that the strategic importance of the wife's role in supporting the domestic household opened up the public forum to new, female voices. Women held spinning meetings, celebrated domestic production and even discarded their tea. In Boston, the newspapers published the news that hundreds of Boston ladies signed a couple agreement not to drink foreign tea. Women had a public, though not political role. Men enforced compliance through actual intimidation, exposing non-compliant merchants in the press threatening to forcibly remove foreign goods in cities like Boston, Philadelphia and New York. These activities were not entirely illegal, since in most cases they were sanctioned by town meeting and colonial assemblies, but equally, the politics of non-importation agreements changed the political status quo, placing more and more political power in the hands of local merchants who enforced the laws. In South Carolina, a dispute arose between two prominent planters who claimed to represent the mechanical interests of the colony and initiated separate non-importation agreements. Planters crafted a joint agreement at Charleston's Liberty Tree. With the Tea Act, the Sons of Liberty came into their own, enforcing non-importation with violence. Congress restored democratic procedures to law enforcement in setting up elections for trustworthy citizens to become members of the Association and monitor the local marketplace. From the Association, American citizens imagined an independent nation.[24]

Was the Revolution about ideas or goods, philosophy or experience? Coffeehouse research is particularly helpful here, because its methodology does not insist in an ideological hierarchy of goods but rather acknowledges the vital role of conversation and sociability in moderating consumption. Coffeehouses were arenas within which both ideas and goods, philosophies and experiences flowed, and in most cases became so entangled that it is impossible to separate one from another. The colonial coffeehouses were places where news, republican ideas and goods were discussed over food and drink. Although they were the critical intersection of news and consumption and featured among the chief public spaces during the tax crisis and American Revolution, historians of the revolutionary era have almost entirely ignored them. Breen provides only one example of a coffeehouse in New York which was used to assemble the public on the tea question.[25] Yet, coffeehouses were absolutely vital 'imperial spaces' and eventually became key arenas in establishing a revolutionary public sphere. The Sons of Liberty knew this well. Even before seizing tea, they seized the coffeehouse meeting rooms, newsprints and gazettes, knowing all too well that reclaiming thought and free discourse must also lead finally to the liberation of commerce and society from British power. Coffeehouse taverns often served as headquarters of public revolutionary sociability. Some talked, some wrote, some signed agreements not to buy British goods, but the patriots who gathered in coffeehouses actually fought to establish a public space of American liberty.

The politics of coffee: Revolutionary coffeehouses

Coffeehouse taverns (or taverns which sold coffee) were headquarters for revolutionary activity in two ways. Firstly, patriot groups took over certain coffeehouses in order to reclaim colonial control of the post, influence public opinion and organize violent activity against customs officers. Secondly, coffeehouses hosted Washington's army officers whenever they passed through, and in this way, they became the people's ballroom for revolution. In both aspects, they were the public sphere of the average citizen-soldier and not the forum for the founding statesmen in the Congress and later the Constitutional Assembly. Although the Founders frequently visited taverns and coffeehouses, they were busy constructing another legitimate sphere of authority and reconciling it with state and local governments. Their *res publica* was in the founding assemblies, not in the old coffeehouses which had once been the centres for civil service appointments, news and *critique*. But as critique became protest and protest became violence, the 'Founding' (so-called) happened in Independence Hall, among a small body of gifted statesmen, who effectively saved American institutions from the ruptures already taking place in the public sphere. Yet, reverberations of the Founding were felt across the coffeehouses in America, which birthed a martial pageant of protest and republican valour. The military pageantry of coffeehouse celebrations included cannon, gunfire, bonfires, and fifes and drums. It was gunpowder and not tea at Concord and Williamsburg which finally provoked the colonists to take up arms. Gunpowder and bonfires symbolized the moments of revolt. They were now set to the martial music of Washington's Anglo-American fife and drum repertoire, and the new pageant of modern republic was born.[26]

But coffee was not at all at first a recognized American product and as such the colonial legislatures debated whether or not it should be shunned like tea. Certainly, duties had been placed upon it, but such duties had long since been negotiated by transatlantic merchants. In 1737, Virginians followed closely the petitioning campaign of coffee-men in London and Westminster for easier laws relating to importing coffee. The next year, parliament passed an act which encouraged coffee alongside sugar.[27] Furthermore, coffee from the West Indies did not depend on the East India Company or a formalized British monopoly. In May 1766, a committee of West India and North American merchants decided the matter, agreeing that 'foreign sugars, coffee, and cocoa, be allowed to be imported … where regular custom-houses under the care of the King's officers … under such regulations as Administration may judge proper; if landed in Great Britain, to be deposited, free of duty, in the King's warehouses, until exported'.[28] Such a decision came just before the final repeal of the Stamp Act, which lifted all duties on imported coffee and pimento, lessened sugar duties to five shillings per hundred, reduced the duty on Madeira wine and declared all sugars, cocoa, coffee, indigo and cotton imports to North America intended for exportation to Great Britain free of duties.[29] Still, the colonial legislatures formed a secret committee which had been 'committed the care of suppressing luxury' and banned the importation of coffee, chocolate, rum and other liquors and imported textiles.[30]

It was the Declaratory Act of 1766 which lost England her colonies, and not the Tea Act. It gave parliament the right 'to bind the colonies and people of America, subjects of the crown of Great Britain, in all cases whatsoever'.[31] With these implied powers, the British parliament established a new American post office in 1774, a custom house, a new vice admiralty court, banned the intercolonial hat trade and put more duties on coffee, wine, sugar, tea and pimento. The gazettes concluded, 'Our liberties are SYSTEMATICALLY invaded.'[32] At the end of the year, the Continental Congress passed the following resolutions:

> Resolved, that from and after the 10th day of September, 1775, the exportation of all merchandise and ever commodity whatsoever to Great Britain, Ireland, and the West Indies ought to cease, unless the grievances of America are redressed before that time ...
>
> Resolved, that the committee appointed to prepare the form of an association, be directed to adopt the following clause, viz. that from and after the first day of December next, no molasses, coffee or pimenta, from the British plantations or from the Dominica, or wines from Madeira and the Western Islands, or foreign indigo be imported into these colonies ...
>
> Resolved, that a committee be appointed to prepare a letter to his Excellency General Gage ... that the soldiers under his Excellency's command, are frequently violating private property, and offering various insults to the people, which must irritate their minds, and if not put a stop to, involve all America in the horrors of a civil war. To entreat his Excellency, from the assurance we have of the peaceable disposition of the inhabitants of the town of Boston and the province of the Massachusetts Bay, to discontinue his fortifications, and that a free and safe communication be restored and continued.[33]

And so, America resolved to ban coffee. Coffee and trade represented communication, not commodification, and the ban on coffee was an acknowledgement of a broken relationship. Of prime concern to the Congress was the breach of trust between England and her colonies. Coffee, along with all British West Indian goods, was a part of the naval empire of Great Britain: the very arm which had allowed Britain to extend her armies and build military fortifications against colonial governments and their mobilizing militias.[34] On 3 March 1775, the General Assembly of New York formally declared the duties on molasses, coffee and pimento a grievance.[35] America was losing its relationship with the British plantation societies of the West Indies. Other nations were sympathetic. When the French colonial Hispaniola opened trade to North America in 1776, the *Virginia Gazette* interpreted it as the beginnings of a new diplomatic relationship with France, claiming, 'The French people in general are sorry for the unhappy times: Their constant toasts are General Washington and Lee.'[36]

Still, colonial coffeehouses continued to flourish during the 1770s, perhaps their most critical decade, and colonial port cities received bundles of coffee shipments. Non-importation of West Indian coffee was never successfully agreed upon or enforced. Perhaps this was because of the prevailing notion that although the Atlantic trade was policed by the British navy, it did not constitute direct dependence upon England, being a plantation society in its own right. Of course, most of the large-scale planters in the West Indies were absentee landlords living in England, but the work and resources required for the sugar and coffee trades did not involve the East India Company. The West Indies were closer to home: socially similar to slave plantations in the American south and geographically within reach of American merchant vessels. Franklin expressed the prevailing sentiment in *The Gazetteer and New Daily Advertiser* under the pseudonym, 'Homespun':

> But if Indian corn were as disagreeable and indigestible as the Stamp Act, does he imagine we can get nothing else for breakfast? Did he never hear that we have oatmeal in plenty, for water gruel or burgoo; as good wheat, rye, and barley as the world affords, to make frumenty; or toast and ale; that there is every where plenty of milk, butter, and cheese; that rice is one of our staple commodities; that for tea, we have sage and bawm in our gardens, the young leaves of the sweet white hickery or walnut, and, above all, the buds of our pine, infinitely preferable to any tea from the Indies; while the islands yield us plenty of coffee and chocolate?[37]

While the coffee trade was being debated, the debates actually inside colonial American coffeehouses were quite violent. William Bradford had gained a following of patriotic readers at the printing house in the London Coffeehouse. The Sons of Liberty began taking mail from the ships at port and dispensing it at the coffeehouses of New York. They constituted not only the 'ruling party' but also the 'governing part', as James Parker commented.[38] It disrupted the post-rider circuit from New York to New Haven, and probably involved both Philadelphia and Boston. Franklin informed his friend Thomas Cushing in 1771 that the mail from Boston was badly sealed, and appeared to be tampered with, doubtless the work of 'some prying Persons that use the Coffee-house here'.[39] So fearful was Parker of their power over the press and public sphere that he said,

> I think it not quite expedient to print a News-Paper myself yet a While: and for these Considerations: In the present unhappy Times, when the Sons of Liberty carry all before them ... who look with bad Aspect upon every King's Officer, and in particular on those of the Customs and Post-Office, I apprehend I should scarce be able to Stem the Torrent.[40]

Their power can be explained in the formal backing they received from many of the colonial legislatures. With the help of merchants decrying taxation, the Sons of Liberty had taken control of both the New York Exchange Coffeehouse and the Merchant's Coffeehouse, and the New York Assembly posted announcements in its coffeehouses in 1768, threatening destruction to any hired vessel, since it would almost undoubtedly be used by the military against Boston. Threatening advertisements directed at revenue officers lay on all the tables.[41] When tea arrived in 1773, the legislatures curtailed its use and, in some cases, placed a contraband on the tea. At the Merchant's Coffeehouse in May 1774, the Committee of Correspondence was founded to share intelligence with Boston and Philadelphia and gave their support for the First Continental Congress. This coffeehouse social network brought rebels together and colonial assemblies worked freely with them to protest taxation. Just before the Boston Tea Party, New York hosted a coffeehouse celebration for all the merchants who refused to transport tea. In October 1773 the General Assembly of Philadelphia passed a series of uncompromising acts which declared, among other resolutions, 'that whoever shall, directly or indirectly, countinence this Attempt, or in any Wise aid or abet in unloading, receiving, or sending the Tea sent, or to be sent out by the East India Company, while it remains subject to the Payment of a Duty here, is an Enemy to his Country'.[42] Since it was now a crime to take in tea at all, the coffeehouse mobs against tea and stamps had some measure of legitimate authority.

The mood in Boston that December was only too clear. The Boston coffeehouses had long been in patriot hands and the sudden intrusion of politics into the coffeehouse public sphere led to violence. Most news was to be found in the *Boston Gazette*, now firmly in the hands of Sam Adams, Paul Revere and his fellow Sons of Liberty. They held meetings and circulated its pages through the coffeehouse taverns of Boston: the Green Dragon, the Bunch of Grapes, the British Coffeehouse and so on. In Boston, the colonial legislators, gazette writers and coffeehouse conspirators were all intertwined. When Massachusetts representative James Otis expressed a personal criticism of John Robinson's political opinions in the *Boston Gazette*, Robinson challenged Otis to a duel in the British Coffeehouse. The *Boston Gazette* of 11 September 1769 gave the following story:

> After a Proposal on the Part of Mr. Otis to decide this Controversy by themselves abroad, or in a separate Room, the former was refused, but the latter seemed to be consented to by Mr. Robinson, but very unexpectedly to Mr. Otis, and while he was following, Mr. Robinson in the Presence of the publick Company in the Coffee-Room, suddenly turned and attempted to take him by the Nose; and failing in the Attempt, he immediately struck at him with his Cane, against which Mr. Otis defended himself, and returned the Compliment.[43]

At this point, the story became confused. The *Boston Gazette* claimed that Otis disarmed Robinson but was suddenly assaulted by a crowd of 'the Officers of the Army, Navy, and the Revenue' with swords and sticks and death threats. Otis left severely wounded.[44] The moral of the story was obvious; the British agents were going to force their political opinions at the point of the sword. However, the *Virginia Gazette* reprinted an account from the *Boston Chronicle* which expressly denied the use of swords or the exchange of death threats. It read, 'Several persons then interfered in behalf of Mr. Otis, one of whom laid hold of Mr. Robinson, tore his coat, and wrested his stick from him; but through the interposition of the company fair play was soon restored, and a ring formed, when a brisk manual exercise followed."[45] Whether the crowd restored order or aggravated the situation is hard to tell. But what the Otis affair does demonstrate is that political disputes were not only discussed but also physically determined in the social public sphere of the coffeehouse. Furthermore, coffeehouse crowds were forced to take sides. Patriots secured control of the British Coffeehouse in September 1770, when a committee of merchants met there to propose conciliatory measures for the general meeting at Faneuil-Hall, which would secure control of the warehouses to hold unwanted goods until they were re-shipped. Incidentally, the British Coffeehouse was renamed the American Coffeehouse by 1776, an indication that the coffeehouse officially recognized the patriot cause.[46] The transition had been a bloody one.

In Williamsburg, the coffeehouses were no less radical against stamps and tea. The *Virginia Gazette* scrupulously reprinted every patriotic event from the New York, Philadelphia and Boston gazettes. Tea was resisted and militias were at the ready. More than that, the patriot mobs were on the streets and in the coffeehouses from the very beginning of the tax crisis. In October 1766, George Mercer, the chief distributor of Stamps for Virginia, was due to arrive in Williamsburg from London and take up his new duties after a meeting with the governor. Arriving in the late afternoon, he made his way as far as the Capitol Building on his way to the Governor's Palace; Mercer was halted by a mob who demanded to know if he intended to proceed with his commission. Mercer tried his best to hold off the crowd until he could get to the protection of the governor and said that such an important question required the giving of his information to the governor and council. The crowd thought otherwise. When they got as far as the coffeehouse, they demanded an answer. The governor was also there at the coffeehouse to greet Mercer and try to rescue him from the crowd. He must have had the premonition that the angry citizens of his colony would force his new stamp distributor to surrender the commission before even taking it up. Unfortunately, the governor's presence was only a further provocation, and more and more citizens arrived at the coffeehouse to oppose the governor and his gentlemen-in-waiting standing by. Both sides now faced each other, and the coffeehouse mob asked once again of Mercer for his decision. Mercer wisely conceded the grounds for his answer but delayed the response. He promised to return to the Capitol at five o'clock that evening and give a formal declaration of his intent of service before a public crowd of citizens. The crowd gave him up to the governor and awaited the hour.[47]

All the notable merchants and gentlemen of the city turned out at the Capital for Mercer's reply. A hush fell on the crowd, as Mercer spoke:

Gentlemen, I now have met you agreeable to yesterday's promise, to give my county some assurances which I would have been glad I could with any tolerable propriety have long sooner. I flatter myself [no one] can blame me for accepting an office ... that was never disputed by any from whom I [can] be advised of the propriety or weight of the objections. I do acknowledge that ... before I left England ... I determined to know the real ... [opinions] of my countrymen from themselves... to say that those ... The commission so very disagreeable to my countrymen was solely obtained by the genteel recommendation of their representatives of General Assembly ... and though this is contradictory to publick report, which I am told charge me with assisting the ... Stamp Act ... Yet I hope it will meet with credit when I assure you I was so far from assisting it, or having any previous promise from the Ministry, that I did not know of my appointment until some time after my [voyage] ... from Ireland, where I was at the commencement of the session of Parliament, and for a long time after the act had passed. Thus, Gentlemen, am I circomstanced. I should be glad to act now in such a manner as would justify me to my friend and countrymen here, and the authority which appointed me, but the time you have allotted me for my answer is so very short that I have not yet been able to discover that happy medium, therefore must intreat you to be reserved to my future conduct, with the assurance in the mean time that I will not, directly or indirectly, by myself or deputies, proceed in the execution of the act until I receive further orders from England, and not then without the assent of the General Assembly of this colony; and that no man can more ardently and sincerely wish the prosperity thereof, or is more desirous of securing all its just rights and privileges then Gentlemen, Your sincere friend, and obliged humble servant, George Mercer.[48]

His assurances not to meddle in Virginian affairs without further instructions from England and the General Assembly were received favourably. In essence, Virginia would have no stamp commissioner, because the actual business of issuing stamps was indefinitely put on hold until the General Assembly decided what that actually looked like. What is obvious is that Mercer feared for his life and all the governor's horses and men could not assure Mercer of safety or secure the particulars of his commission beyond what the General Assembly (elected by the planters and merchants) would allow. Virginia's stamp collector had been forcibly encouraged to ignore the particulars of his post by a crowd of patriots at the coffeehouse.

Not all patriot activities in the coffeehouses were so violent, although they did become martial in their display of patriotic support of the American cause during the war for independence. Coffeehouses served as ballrooms and officer's clubs whenever Washington's army was in town. These were no mere copies of the British balls once thrown in honour of king and empire. They were new experiments in republican pageantry and owed much to the Stamp Act protests, public readings and bonfires outside the coffeehouses of colonial America. Indeed, in June 1766, patriots in Boston took occasion on the king's birthday to celebrate the repeal of the Stamp Act. The Royal salute was given, the gentlemen offered toasts inside the Bunch of Grapes, a ball was thrown at the King's Arms tavern for the ladies and gentlemen, and a bonfire lit outside.[49] Officially in honour of the king, the citizens of Boston actually celebrated the blessings of Providence on their resistance to tax laws. Although Tory governor Thomas Hutchinson held a more traditional ceremony for the king in 1771 with artillery salutes, toasts at the British Coffeehouse with all the naval officers and a ball at the concert hall, a subtle sense of self-determination undermined the royal pageantry of a bygone era whenever patriots organized their own events.[50] While royal governors fired a *feu de joie* for the king, the people mimicked British pageantry for their own revolt. As soon as Jamaica was assured by an issue of the *London Gazette* that the Stamp Act had been repealed, the people threw together a fantastic array of jubilations. One contemporary description ran,

> The Gentlemen Grenadiers, Light Infantry, and Half-Boot Blues, clothed in their uniforms, met on the occasion, and fired three vollies as a Feu de Joye. The Grenadiers and Light Infantry then retired to Rawleigh and Kemp's coffee house; and the Blues to Tilladam's, where they spent the evening with the greatest jollity. The Gentlemen of the Light Infantry had prepared an emblematical flag, representing Liberty Triumphant, and an odious Stampman imploring forgiveness for his many notorious oppressions and extortions during the exercise of his most detestable function; and also an effigy of the grant promoter and friend to the Stamp Law, which, after being ignominiously brought the Coffee House in a cart, was hum up to the sign post, while a bonfire was made in which he was consumed. The town was beautifully illuminated, many loyal toasts were drunk, and the evening concluded with the greatest harmony, decency, and decorum.[51]

In the stamp crisis, revolutionaries in the Americas believed themselves connected in a common struggle for economic self-defence against European power. The stamp-men and British officials were burned in effigy across North America.[52] Republican pageantry had its roots in the pageantry of tax protest.

Although fought over stamps, the patriotic pageantry was not fundamentally about stamps. It was about the American Protestant way of life. In October 1765, the chief justice held a public meeting at a coffeehouse, assuring the crowd that the change in parliamentary Ministry meant that the American way of life was saved; 'That there was not, the least Fear of an Alteration, of our Government; for that the Proprietors, had great Weight and Interest, with the present Ministers.'[53] A celebration ensued which ended in the attempted burning of several private homes suspected as housing advocates of the Stamp Act. The Watchmen put out the fires. There was merit in the gazettes explaining that certain events were 'concluded with the greatest harmony, decency, and decorum'. There was a fine line between the pageantry of protest and the violence of protest.

It is tempting to consider all American coffeehouses as solely under the control of the patriots, but that was not the case. Coffeehouses entertained British officers and were used as places to recruit American Tories into the British Army. From its occupation by the British army until 1783, the Merchant's Coffeehouse served as an officer's club. Officers of the Crown and richer citizens socialized at King's Head and the Indian Queen in Boston. Their very names conjured up loyalism and empire. In fact, when General Gage temporarily left Boston for London in June 1773, he was sent off by a gathering of army and artillery officers from Murray's Wharf, close to the coffeehouse.[54] Whenever the British army moved into a city, the patriot resistance went underground for a while. It never fully disappeared. By 1776, Americans were celebrating the anniversary of the founding of the Sons of Liberty with a pageantry which was complete with its own relics. On 14 August 1776, the Sons of Liberty gathered at Liberty Hall in Boston, stood on a pole and hoisted the 'Red Flag or Flag of

Defiance' on the stump of the old Liberty Tree which had been felled by Tories. They toasted liberty, hung more flags at the Bunch of Grapes and held a parade discharging thirteen artillery shots and giving three cheers.[55] Evidently, the patriot flags were displayed and removed at will, depending on who was in town.

Washington gave martial order to the pageantry of revolt. He insisted on Scripture being read at public functions. In March 1776, Washington and his officers met in chamber with the Council in Boston, proceeded to the old brick meeting house, listened to a sermon on Isaiah 33:20 about the peaceful festivals of Zion and dined at the Bunch of Grapes. While Washington was in Boston, nearby preaching included a sermon on 2 Kings 19:28, the controversy over kings and the origins of the war.[56] After the surrender at Yorktown, Washington's coffeehouse celebrations were more elaborate. Instead of feasting the birthday of a king, Americans celebrated the birthday of their republican general. In Fredericksburg, on 11 February 1780, Virginians celebrated the birthday of the 'Chief'. The *Virginia Gazette* stated,

> Two regiments of the Virginia line being detained there on account of bad weather, added much to the rejoicing of that day. At twelve o'clock (precisely) a great salute of 13 pieces of cannon were discharged, succeeded by a feu-de-joye, fired by the troops, who cut a very martial appearance, and went through their [fringe?] with the greatest regularity and good order. The evening was concluded with an elegant ball at the coffee house.[57]

Martial regularity and good order would become the two aspects of 'Hail to the Chief' ever since. They represented the 'newness' of the republic, as the red liberty flag. Thus, the elements of Fourth of July celebrations, bonfires, fireworks, gun salutes, parades, flags and liberty tokens all originated in the coffeehouses of American liberty. It was this flare of optimism which swept up even the sceptical John Adams in a feeling of ecstasy, when he charged all Americans to observe the day of the signing of the Declaration of Independence 'as the Day of Deliverance by solemn Acts of Devotion to God Almighty. It ought to be solemnized with Pomp and Parade, with Shews, Games, Sports, Guns, Bells, Bonfires and Illuminations from one End of this Continent to the other from this Time forward forever more.'[58]

The international effects of revolution: Radicalization of the coffeehouses

The American Revolution had a direct effect on the coffeehouses of Western Europe. While Americans were disputing taxation, radical Whigs in England believed that the voice of the people had been forgotten. Journalist John Wilks roused the people of England to new energy when Lord Bute was appointed head of the government against popular opinion. Wilkites formed new political associations like the Society of Supporters of the Bill of Rights to win back the electoral process for the people. Through electioneering and other out-of-door strategies, Wilkites pushed forward several reform proposals, including secret ballots and redistributing seats from 'rotten boroughs' across new population centres. Wilkite reforms ended in failure, but they did much to change the political climate in favour of popular sovereignty. Opposition candidates won seats in the 1774 election in Bristol, Bedford, Coventry, Dover, Middlesex and Rochester and challenged for the first time the oligarchy of Newcastle, as well as the political establishment in Portsmouth, Cambridge and Warwickshire. What is more, they brought about a change in the public sphere. When war broke out in America, anti-war riots swept the centres of deepest oppositional feeling. Coffeehouses were drawn into this oppositional political culture with the formation of radical Whig clubs like the Norwich Constitution Club. *The Newcastle Weekly Magazine* reprinted Paine's *Common Sense*, avidly read by many trade associations in its coffeehouses and inns. As historian Kathleen Wilson has concluded, 'the sense of the people' had been unleashed across England provincial public sphere.[59]

Tory refugee Samuel Curwen followed the gazettes with anxiety, while his transatlantic community of Philadelphians at the Pennsylvania Coffeehouse in London read with horror the transformation of Pennsylvania from a British colony into an independent American state.[60] More and more Tories would pour into England as a result of the war. But even in Paris, Franklin was causing a stir in the Parisian coffeehouses and coffee customers began taking sides. When he arrived in Nantes in December 1776, Lord Stormont told Weymouth that several French officers voiced in the coffeehouses that they had received private clearances from the Court to join Washington's Continental Army. Stormont worried that French officers were going rogue and supporting the fight against their old enemy. Furthermore, these notable persons had great sway over the coffeehouse public. 'He added that there will ever be such Men in all countries, who are ready to Run every Risk as they have nothing to lose,' said Stormont.[61] These French generals would later win the war for America. M de Vergennes instructed Jean Charles Pierre Lenoir to 'send his spies ... as they were call here, into all the coffee houses, and places of Public Resort, and if they found any Persons holding such Language immediately to secure them.'[62] Stormont feared the formation of international brigades from European coffeehouse publics, and according to Stormont's personal experience in the Parisian coffeehouses, the public opinion was very much against Britain. In January 1776, he told Weymouth,

> Our Coffee house Politicians, on the contrary, and those wits who take the lead in all Companies here, & who when they talk upon such subjects as these, may fairly be placed in the same line with the Politicians I have named, speak with great complacency of the late success of the Rebels in Canada. When I happen to be present, they moderate their language but cannot conceal their Joy. I think no step is to be laid upon, or conclusion drawn from the Language & Sentiments of men, who are incapable of distinguishing, sense, from sound, who are totally ignorant of the real Questions, who know nothing of Liberty, & Independence, but the name; and, who are eternally led astray by the Declamation, which they retail.[63]

Coffeehouse politicians no longer discussed only elections or parties but new ideas like liberty and independence. Stormont witnessed in 1776 the rise of a new form of popular political opinion which matured into a real social force in European coffeehouses during the 1790s and continued through the nineteenth century until the fateful year of 1848.

Revolution reverberated throughout the coffeehouses of England and France, as the new ideas of Thomas Paine and the social experiment of republican liberty was now underway in America. Many of the generals who had accompanied Washington now made their way back to France and knew that Europe was now an old world. Could it be remade in the image of the new? That was the question which drove revolutionary coffeehouse clubs in London and Paris to obsession. Ostensibly a society dedicated to the English constitutional principles of 1688, but actually a society which reconciled English nonconformity with the revolutionary ideas of Paine's natural rights, the Revolutionary Society began an international correspondence with French revolutionaries from 1788 to 1791. So divisive were their topics of conversation that they oscillated from one tavern to another, depending on the subject and purpose of the meeting. When commemorating the Glorious Revolution of 1688, the society met more or less openly in the London Tavern. But the centenary celebrations looked forward rather than backward and one lecturer spoke 'of the glorious example given in France to encourage other Nations to assent the unalienable rights of Mankind'.[64] Through the year 1790, the number of letters from French correspondents received and publicly read aloud increased. In 1791, the society founded a separate committee of correspondence to handle the French correspondence which met in St Paul's Coffeehouse. The Revolutionary Society's minute-book records at least three headquarters: the London Tavern, King's Head Tavern and St Paul's.[65] This was just the sort of club which government spies were looking for: expansive and subversive to the conservative government of William Pitt.

Conservatives noticed that revolution meant an alteration in the traditional relationship between the classes and they feared the people as a new social force in the coffeehouses of London. Major John Pigot felt inclined to have to justify his country against the prevailing popular criticism in the coffeehouses that suspension of habeas corpus in the war against France was really arbitrary power. Pigot found loyal friends among the prosperous bankers at the Stock Exchange, but the fact that he was compelled to dispel the 'incendiary' views of a tobacconist named Freybourg attested to the social force of revolutionary ideas. Never before did a major in His Majesty's Army believe that the word of a common working-class man deserved a reply, but the revolutionary arguments for the natural rights of man had implications for the class order. Writing from the Queen's Head Coffeehouse in 1792, William Butler told William Pitt that he denounced Mr Walters's reply in the press to the political opinions of his hairdresser. He exclaimed,

> This letter from a man of fortune to a man of the lower class, calling him Citizen, his equal, and stileing it in the first year of Equality, can certainly convey nothing but an Intention, to Inflame the minds of the people, and particularly the lower class who headed by such Villains would stop at nothing, but render the life and Property of every Individual at Stake, as nothing with me as a poor Individual is more earnestly wish'd for, than the abolition, and destitution, of such Inflammatory

Epistles, and every thing else. that then to subvert the good order of our present laudable Constitution and in order that such measures may be taken, as to you shall seem meet, I have taken the liberty of Transmitting it to you.[66]

It was a social constitution of which Butler spoke. Wealthy gentlemen who disciplined lower-class workers for supporting the French Revolution were succumbing to revolution within. Lecturing a hairdresser on the finer points of social equity and equality before the law suggested the moral force of the revolutionary spirit. The irony of it all was that Butler believed that this incident required discipline from a ruling class. There was more at stake in coffeehouse conversation during the age of revolution. Radicalization of the public sphere was the result of a new class consciousness. Populist politics and class consciousness brought down the older sociable experience of the London coffeehouse. Charles Moritz, a German Lutheran clergyman, traveling in England said this in 1782 of the once famed coffeehouses, 'There generally prevails a very decorous stillness and silence. Every one speaks softly to those only who sit next to him. The great part read the newspapers, and no one ever disturbs another.'[67] Because of revolution, rights and social divisions, news culture no longer had the charm to bring people together in dispassionate ways. It divided coffeehouse publics rather than uniting them and the resulting silence was deafening.

Conversational authority drifted into hardened ideological coalitions with real political power during the French Revolution, exerting even international influence. Evaluating French clubs through social networking and correspondence, Micah Alpaugh argues that British anti-slavery societies and activist clubs corresponded with the *Societé des amis des noirs* and eventually inspired the transnational formation of radical ideas in French Jacobin clubs. Beginning in 1787, anti-slavery societies ushered in a new era of sociopolitical activity in Britain, with freestanding grassroots divisions united in a national petitioning campaign. Parallel anti-slavery discussion groups emerged in France in 1779, called *musées*. Alpaugh even claims that the influence of the London Revolution Society on the French National Assembly led to the organization of an official Jacobin club network. As the National Assembly declared a common approach to civil and religious liberty between France and England, Jacobins in Paris founded the *Société de la Révolution*, or as it was later named, *Société des amis de la Constitution*. Jacobin clubs moved towards a platform of 'universal patriotism' as networking between the London Revolution Society and France increased through the *Paris Comité de correspondence*, necessitating a press industry capable to the task of informing regional clubs. Circulars kept clubs informed. The *Journal des sociétés-patriotiques francaises* (1790) was the first common newspaper, and later the *Journal des Clubs* created a common programme open for discussion in local clubs. Meanwhile, addresses from the London Revolution Society continued to pour into French Jacobin reading circles. The Strasbourg Jacobin club even credited England for the goals of the society, or '*Amis de la Constitution*'.[68] New revolutionary rhetoric found a home within the clubs of the public sphere.

However, revolutionary ideology narrowed the spontaneous phenomenon of voluntary association in clubs. As clubs became more ideological and tied to contemporary political issues, they also lost the moral autonomy of conversation.

Journals disseminated 'universal patriotism' defined by Revolutionary propaganda, not the casual conversation of the previous public sphere. Ironically, integrating the political goals of radical clubs into state revolutionary propaganda networks spelled their downfall. The presence of revolutionary ideology has sparked a historiographical debate on the value of sociability during the Romantic era of sentimentality. The debate culminated in a collection of essays entitled *Romantic Sociability* (2002) edited by Gillian Russell and Clara Tuite. These authors claim that Habermas, followed by Terry Eagleton and Jon Klancher, saw a decline in the importance of sociability as normative consensus during the Romantic period, stating, 'The consensual model of the public sphere was exploded from within, Eagleton argues, by the emergence in the 1790s of a counter public sphere of "the Corresponding Societies, the radical press, Owenism, Cobbett's *Political Register* and Paine's *Rights of Man*, feminism and the Dissenting churches, a whole oppositional network of journals, clubs."'[69] As bitter rivalries plagued the personal elements of the public sphere, Romantics turned criticism into solitary poetry. However, Russell and Tuite suggest that rather than a counter-public sphere, Romantic sociability expanded the boundaries of public life by intensifying political debate in the wake of the French Revolution.[70] Towards that end, James Epstein and Anne Janowitz offer particularly helpful insights into the nature of public discourse.

Epstein claims that coffeehouses were no longer impervious to other political and judicial spheres of influence, challenging the fixed ideal of civility as a protection for free speech. Government spies often rooted out Jacobin sympathies, as was the case with London Corresponding Society leaders Charles Pigott's and William Hodgson's arrests. Pit's administration made it clear that even public club and coffeehouse talk were liable for sedition. Under political pressure, clubs formalized the conditions for membership through the ceremony of toasting to various causes. These toasts, like duels, acted as personal challenges and counter-challenges within the public sphere. Walking into loyalist territory took courage. The 'Church and King' tavern read 'No Jacobins admitted here' above its doors, yet John Binns representing the London Corresponding Society did enter.[71] Thus, the boundaries of public space were fluid in the Revolutionary era but filled with great personal risks. The solution was the gentlemen's club for many among the upper middle classes. In 1790 the *Bee* journal in Edinburgh stated the coffeehouse may give way to the gentlemen's journal, replacing sociability with domesticity. To Epstein, coffeehouse clubs created passionate revolutionary political rhetoric during the 1790s that threatened the safety of the middle class. He claims 'as middle-class radicals retreated from the political fray... [and] the language of "equality" ... Crucial distinctions could no longer be maintained: the spaces and language of polite sociability and reform sentiment had to be more clearly demarcated from the raucous, dangerous places and tones of plebeian culture.'[72] Popular ideology from the lower classes frightened the middle classes and loosened the bonds of merchant politeness over the coffeehouses. Unlike Eagleton, Epstein sees that an expanding and more politically robust public sphere was the very reason for private withdrawal from it. Salons and gentlemen's clubs became the new refuges for intimate sociability, whereas the coffeehouses served as the seats of popular ideology and often political conflict. Intellectuals required a safer environment.

Certainly, even within high-literary societies, rhetoric hardened along popular ideological lines. Anne Janowitz describes the political hardening of Romantic activist literature through exposure to urban radical print culture in the 1790s. Explaining the literary career of Anna Aikin-Barbauld, who learned poetry in the Dissenting Academy at Warrington, Janowitz traces the evolution of Barbauld's poetic diction from a language of familiarity and amiability to a consciously Romantic and politically militant tone. Tutored at Warrington and eventually published by radical reformer Joseph Johnson, whose social circle included revolutionary Paine, feminist Mary Wollstonecraft and utilitarian journalist William Godwin, Barbauld's poetry was shaped by the Romantic ideals of the Warrington circle and reveals the hardening process of ideology. Her major debut was the publication of *Address to the Opposers of the Repeal* (1790) in which she linked religious toleration with the French Revolution, challenging the masculine politeness of the Enlightenment and positing the Revolutionary spirit as a universal step towards greater knowledge. Reinforcing her gender in 'To a Great Nation, Written by a Lady', Barbauld unabashedly claims that passionate analytical politics belongs equally to women as well as men. Nevertheless, Barbauld maintained her political objective of defending the rights of Dissenters, rather than blindly following the radicalism of Wollstonecraft. They often clashed over the direction of Romantic feminist goals. Janowitz comments, 'The different trajectories of the Aikins and the Wollstonecraft–Godwin–Shelleys mark out different lines in the politics of radicalism and republicanism in the late eighteenth and early nineteenth centuries.'[73] They also reveal the personal animosities brought on by Revolutionary ideology, the fragmentation of discursive patterns and the urge among middle-class activists to reconstitute public space along some recognizable creed. Amplified by revolutionary changes, the English clubs and salon societies of the late eighteenth and early nineteenth centuries reinforced a consistent creed of Whig values, outlining a national sociability of conservative reform. Lady Holland's Whig Club became the alternative to a free and open coffeehouse political discussion. There, upper-class Whig members of parliament rendezvoused during 'the season' and celebrated their withdrawal from the public sphere in a social net of disciplined, polite society and moral liberty.[74] The club culture of Whig salons celebrated upper-class values, even while the publics of the coffeehouses of London felt their new social power. The coffeehouse public sphere was sundered forever along class and ideological lines.

Conclusion

The age of polite coffeehouse association flourished until the last decade of the eighteenth century when revolution and war altered forever what had once been a transatlantic public sphere of Anglo sociability. During the tax crisis, revolutionary writers, like Franklin, Paine and Jefferson, mastered the metropolitan language of satire which had once celebrated the British commercial empire and turned it against itself with new egalitarian arguments. The egalitarianism of the revolutionary era dismantled the economic imperialism which had linked coffeehouse publics together. American coffeehouses nationalized into patriotic headquarters for protest and ceremonial pageants of republican values. The American coffeehouses were forever lost to Britain. In London, the radical ideas of Thomas Paine, war with France and government espionage heightened coffeehouse social tensions to a breaking point. Club elites retreated into their own club houses. White's was perhaps one of the first to close its doors in 1736. St James's and the Cocoa Tree were closed by the end of the century. The stock exchanges at New Lloyd's and New Jonathan's kept their coffee-rooms to themselves. During the revolutionary era, most of the rest of the clubs followed suit and fled to private club houses. The Foxite Whigs rallied around Lady Holland in her private estate. Travellers to London in the late eighteenth and early nineteenth centuries noted the deplorable state of social life in London and the almost deserted atmosphere of some of the old, famous coffeehouses. The London Enlightenment had ended. Likewise, the Edinburgh Enlightenment passed on into the stream of unionist nationalism. The American intellects and merchants were sundered forever by national independence and Britain's war with France.[75] Increasingly, French and American statesmen oversaw the new era of constitutions but from differing civil social contexts. American Founders preserved a pre-existing civil social order among free states, albeit losing some state sovereignty in the process; France overhauled its civil social order and began anew. Britain, however, would wait to reform its political structure until after the Napoleonic Wars. Yet conversation solidified into party ideologies, hardened in the process of revolution. Clubs, constitution societies and radical political discourse transformed the public sphere from polite sociability into revolutionary and counter-revolutionary factions during Pit's administration. Whig rhetoric grew into the conservative values of the Regency era, with its emphasis on social dignity and exclusivity rather than an open public sphere.

Conclusion

Old habits die hard. Despite heavy penalties from the law, merchants in London were still conveying boxes of private letters from coffeehouses to other port cities well into the nineteenth century. Post office solicitor Mark Beauchamp Peacock knew this well when he was called to testify before the House of Lords in February 1838 regarding the illicit conveyance of letters from coffeehouses. The merchant house of Baring, Brothers & Co. was accused of sending two hundred unstamped letters each week from London to American mail packets in Liverpool, and it seemed probable that they had the help of several coffeehouse owners. Peacock explained that separate legal actions had been taken against the proprietors of the Jerusalem Coffeehouse and the South American Coffeehouse for conveying letters to ships intended for Liverpool. However, the case became a difficult one to prove, since it was illegal only to send letters from one place in the UK to another and not exactly against the law to place letters aboard ships at the outports. The House pressed Peacock on the point:

Chairman:	'The Post-office have not seen it to be their duty to take any means for seizing or preventing such boxes being sent?'
Peacock:	'We have not since that evidence was given, certainly.'
Viscount Lowther:	'How did the prosecution against the coffee-house end?'
Peacock:	'They paid one penalty, I think, and I understood they gave an assurance that they would not continue it …'
Lowther:	'Have you ever adapted means to ascertain whether that practice was continued?'
Peacock:	'I am not aware of any steps …'
Lowther:	'You have not adopted any means to inform yourself whether that practice continues, or has to within a late period, at the coffee-houses in London?'
Peacock:	'Yes, we have at the coffeehouses; we have given them notice that they must not continue to send letters, but we have no evidence of their sending letters to Liverpool.'[1]

The post office's ambivalence in handling the coffeehouses attests to the power of an institution. Coffeehouses had long been the communication lines for the commerce of the British empire, but with increased government interference in the post during the late eighteenth and early nineteenth centuries, the transatlantic mercantile community was forced either to accept more bureaucracy or to go underground. Formalizing transatlantic mail conflicted with the previous institutional development of coffeehouse communities from 1650 to 1789.

Coffeehouses became important conduits of transatlantic marine correspondence and an important place to negotiate British corporate and governmental policy in the eighteenth century. Coffeehouse communities had bought into the British Atlantic system of empire on the principles of free association and conspicuous consumption and helped to launch revolutionary activity to free the press and public sphere from government regulations. Coffeehouses were specific cosmopolitan institutions which linked publics to cities across oceans through private and public postal services. Not only did coffeehouse customers eat and drink in coffeehouses, they set up private addresses with contacts to cities across the British Atlantic world. Indeed, even the eighteenth-century postal service made extensive use of the communication networks of coffeehouses to deliver its posts. The marine insurance agencies and Royal Navy formalized the coffeehouse postal network and institutionalized a command structure which transported the materials of the eighteenth-century British Empire around the globe. Such an empire demanded an efficient network of transatlantic communication, and in the eighteenth century, coffeehouses supplied that need, offering opportunities for insurance, business contracts and to negotiate fairer customs procedures.

Associations forged in coffeehouses patronized the free press and bought into a new transatlantic idea of news. Gazettes would provide local news across the cities of the Atlantic world in an Addisonian style of polite discourse, so that transatlantic travellers could reconstruct their own neighbourhoods remotely in coffeehouses while abroad in London or in the colonies. These transatlantic newsfeeds became the seeds of political social networks. Colonial governors formed social circles of powerful colonial elites and organized a civil service of customs officers from coffeehouses. But with the tax crisis (1764–5), a political counter-culture of protest radicalized the coffeehouse news press and severed the transatlantic communities from within the American coffeehouses. In the thirteen mainland colonies, coffeehouses provided one important site where patriots could work to disengage from an empire and forge a new nation.

The coffeehouse was among the most cosmopolitan of British urban institutions because it was dedicated to serving transatlantic travellers. Many of the elites of the eighteenth-century British Empire would emerge from these coffeehouses. The first coffeehouse communities organized social and business events to display their wealth and status and formed clubs which nurtured a 'conspicuous society' of business leisure in London and across British Atlantic cities. Coffeehouse 'triflers' defined a new form of urban sociability, combining politeness with leisure which David Hume and other Enlightenment philosophers recognized as an empirical discovery of human nature. Middling travellers with business interests self-consciously cultivated polite discourse around conspicuous consumption and expanded their social networks across urban communities. What made this possible was the connections which coffeehouses fostered between customers and shipping interests. Ships provided private postal services and expanded London social networks to include colonial elites.

Coffeehouse proprietors developed important elements of the system of economic empire inside coffeehouses, conveniently combining business with leisure. Proprietors linked hands with marine insurers and the Exchange coffeehouse merchants to stabilize British trade across the empire. They launched a successful petitioning campaign for warehouse inspections which brought transatlantic lobbyists into the political process in Westminster via the coffeehouses in Whitehall. Although they could never fully dismantle the monopolistic power of the East India Company, transatlantic coffeehouse publics did awaken a new political interest which waited until the revolutionary era to break the arm of central power and hinder the expansion of monopolized tea into another hemisphere of the world.

Coffeehouse lobbying came at a time when the navy was centralizing power across the empire through the London coffeehouse post. At the Admiralty Coffeehouse, the Sword Blade, Jerusalem, and Will's, naval officers maintained their transatlantic social networks through a masculine art of self-deprecation and martial honour. The coffeehouse connections Naval officers formed with agents in the West Indies and timber interests in Quebec enabled the Royal Navy to negotiate rank and manage transatlantic resources with the relative ease which allowed them to surpass all other naval powers. Coffeehouses provided marine insurance, shipping contracts and a communications infrastructure necessary for a global naval empire.

Coffeehouse proprietors instinctively understood the dramatic significance of cosmopolitan communities in their coffeehouses and did everything in their power to encourage their growth. Coffeehouse owners launched their own price currents and shipping news and even momentarily attempted a news syndicate which depended upon the social order of their clientele, but it could not compete with the free press. Proprietors chose to promote literacy through the free press, which bought up more and more readers in coffeehouses after the expiration of the Licensing Act of 1662 in 1695. The free press eventually became triumphant and carried the coffeehouse publics into a new era of transatlantic news which harmonized coffee culture with the political demands of transatlantic merchants.

The 'print capitalism' disseminated in coffeehouses and its transatlantic subscription syndicates ushered in a new coffeehouse community, the 'remote neighborhood'. These communities adopted the new manners of the society journals and brought into being a form of literature which held emerging civil service networks together across the British Atlantic. Journalism transformed public opinion on coffee, provided coffeehouse clubs with a pattern for sociability and instituted a journalistic editorial system which allowed middling readers a free hand in forming the transatlantic newsfeeds which linked them with 'imagined communities' across the Atlantic world. News journals and coffeehouse editorials delighted their readers with news from specific geographical locations and in an Addisonian style of taste and politeness. Distinct remote neighbourhoods of readers emerged in London, following their own local news in the Pennsylvania Coffeehouse of London, the Virginia and Maryland Coffeehouse, and the New England Coffeehouse. Likewise, the gazettes brought London news to the colonies and allowed colonists to engage in the discussion of social critique. Gazettes served the Atlantic world with a newsfeed which was at once universal to the transatlantic merchants, officers and royal governors and agents traversing the Atlantic. These new elites eagerly gathered in coffeehouses not just to get news but also to make news by forming business associations and buying into what Breen has called 'the empire of goods'.

Thus, London and British North America shared coffee publics in remote neighbourhoods. Pennsylvanians, Virginians and Marylanders all had a special place among London's coffeehouse urbanites. New York, Philadelphia, Annapolis and Williamsburg constructed city districts with public venues similar to London and linked them together through the coffeehouse. There, colonial middling elites could display their social status and fondness for London tastes and imagine they were aristocrats. In so imagining, they began to participate more and more in the transatlantic discourse of economic empire which provided them with the goods and habits of civilized urban life.

Because coffeehouses had served as an important focal point of economic empire in the British Atlantic world, they became a centre of political protest and revolutionary activity during America's War for Independence. Ironically, coffeehouse revolutionaries challenged economic imperialism with the same political language of critique which had been used to link coffeehouse publics across the Atlantic and encourage a consumer culture of emulation. Writers like Benjamin Franklin and Thomas Paine were masters of the cosmopolitan coffeehouse literary style of satire and used London's metropolitan language of critique to undo the empire from the coffeehouse presses in Philadelphia. Revolution caught like wildfire because it was so suited to the urbanization which middling coffeehouse publics had nurtured for the past half-century.

Arguments in the gazettes over representation and taxation sparked a counter-culture of protest in American coffeehouses. Counter-cultural groups like the Sons of Liberty violently stormed the coffeehouses, hijacked their transatlantic postal routes and transformed coffeehouses into patriot environs of propaganda. The War for Independence saw the complete transformation of coffeehouses from British cosmopolitan entities into American radical centres of revolt. The Sons of Liberty engineered a pageantry of liberty which encouraged public readings, burnings and martial celebrations. When the egalitarian rhetoric of Jefferson and Paine made its way to the coffeehouses of London and Paris, it forever changed the political activities of coffeehouse publics. It set the state against the people and those with government positions or holy orders against those with ordinary occupations. Clubs radicalized after the French Revolution. The gazetting communities which had once traversed the Atlantic would never resurface in the old Addisonian manner of taste, dispassionate discourse and polite association. Their transatlantic empire was forever dissolved.

Coffeehouse publics helped to make and break an empire. They used a language of social critique to encourage a new form of urban community which linked citizens together across political, cultural and economic networks. They later used much of that same language to pull these networks apart. Empire was facilitated from inside coffeehouses because of their superior connections to ports and the press. Colonial finance, marine insurance and the importation of an 'empire of goods' into the colonies intersected with coffeehouse communities. This new transatlantic perspective to coffeehouses, involving remote neighbourhoods, explains a lot about eighteenth-century social life and world affairs. It provides a cultural context for examining some of the century's most explosive conflicts and some of its most innovative systems. Historians investigating the imperialism of the Protestant succession in Britain, the Board of Trade, the customs offices, the East India Company and especially the Royal Navy must consider the transatlantic publics in coffeehouses. Perhaps most importantly, the history of American consumer tastes, the tax crisis and the Revolution should consider the protests made from coffeehouses. The 'empire of goods' was not just constructed between consumers and suppliers. It was negotiated in the coffeehouses across the Atlantic and eventually unravelled in the news culture peculiar to them.

Notes

Introduction

1. 'John Hughes to Franklin, Philada. Sept. 8. 1765, Sept. 10. 1765 and Sept. 10. 1765', in *The Papers of Benjamin Franklin* (Sponsored by The American Philosophical Society and Yale University Digital Edition by The Packard Humanities Institute), http://franklinpapers.org/franklin//framedVolumes.jsp, accessed 10 November 2017, http://franklinpapers.org/franklin/framedVolumes.jsp.
2. 'James Parker to Franklin, Wed, Jun 11, 1766', *Franklin Papers*, accessed 10 November 2017, http://franklinpapers.org/franklin/framedVolumes.jsp.
3. 'James Parker to Franklin, Tue, May 6, 1766', *Franklin Papers*, accessed 10 November 2017, http://franklinpapers.org/franklin/framedVolumes.jsp; 'James Parker to Franklin, Tue, Jul 15, 1766', *Franklin Papers*, accessed 10 November 2017, http://franklinpapers.org/franklin/framedVolumes.jsp.
4. 'James Parker to Franklin, Tue, Jul 1, 1766', *Franklin Papers*, accessed 10 November 2017, http://franklinpapers.org/franklin/framedVolumes.jsp.
5. Such concerns have already been addressed at great length in Brian Cowan, *The Social Life of Coffee: The Emergence of the British Coffeehouse* (New Haven, CT: Yale University Press, 2005) and Markman Ellis, *The Coffee House: A Cultural History* (London: Weidenfeld & Nicolson, 2004).
6. William Harrison Ukers, *All about Coffee* (New York: Tea and Coffee Trade Journal Company, 1922), 59–60; Stephen B. Pobranski, '"Where Men of Differing Judgements Croud": Milton and the Culture of the Coffee Houses', *Seventeenth Century*, vol. 9, no. 1 (1994): 35–9; John Barrell, 'Coffee-House Politicians', *Journal of British Studies*, vol. 43, no. 2 (April 2004): 210–20, accessed 7 March 2017, http://www.jstor.org/stable/10.1086/380950.
7. Bryant Lillywhite, *London Coffee Houses* (London: Georg Allen and Unwin, 1963), 216–20, 305–9, 551; Letter, Charles Carkesse to Thomas Woolley, 27 August 1712, India Office Records and Private Papers, IOR/E/1/4 ff. 193–195v, *Letters 110–111 Secretary Charles Carkesse at the Customs House in London to Thomas Woolley forwarding a copy of the Commissioners' minutes relating to the Company's Coffee. Related papers attached*, British Library; Letter, Charles Carkesse to Thomas Woolley, 26 September 1712, India Office Records and Private Papers, IOR/E/1/4 ff. 241–242v, *Letter 139 Secretary Charles Carkesse at the Customs House in London to Thomas Woolley concerning the coffee and tea in the Company's warehouses*, British Library.
8. *The New-York Gazette* (New York [N.Y.]), 25 December 1727, pg. 3, NYS Historic Newspapers, Image provided by: Syracuse University; *The New-York Gazette*, 1 March 1730, pg. 1; Parks, *Virginia Gazette*, 1 July 1737 – pg. 2, col. 2, Colonial Williamsburg Digital Library, Omohundro Institute of Early American History & Culture microfilm, 1950, http://research.history.org/DigitalLibrary/va-gazettes/; Parks, *Virginia Gazette*, 4 September 1746 – pg. 3, col. 1; Purdie, *Virginia Gazette*, 23 May 1766 – pg. 2, col. 3.

9. The names are derived from social columns in journals of the eighteenth century; 'Tatler, No. 15, Saturday, May 14, 1709', in Sir Richard Steele, *The Tatler: With Notes, and a General Index ... Complete in One Volume* (Philadelphia, PA: J.J. Woodward, 1831), 43; 'Idler, No. 64. Saturday, 7 July 1759', in Samuel Johnson, *The Yale Edition of the Works of Samuel Johnson, Volume II: The Idler and The Adventurer* (New Haven, CT: Yale University Press, 1963), 199; Nich. Nonentity, 'To the Author of The Trifler, Feb. 29. 1788', in *The aberdeen magazine, literary chronicle, and review; for The Year MDCCLXXXVIII. ...* vol. 1. 1788-90 Aberdeen, Eighteenth Century Collections Online, Gale, CMU Libraries – library.cmich.edu: 163-4, accessed 22 October 2016, http://find.galegroup.com.cmich.idm.oclc.org/ecco/infomark.do?&source=gale&prodId=ECCO&userGroupName=lom_cmichu&tabID=T001&docId=CW124930040&type=multipage&contentSet=ECCOArticles&version=1.0&docLevel=FASCIMILE.
10. Eric Hinderaker, *Boston's Massacre* (Cambridge, MA: Belknap Press of Harvard University Press, 2017), 78.
11. Barrell, 'Coffee-House Politicians', 210–20.
12. Lawrence E. Klein, 'Politeness and the Interpretation of the British Eighteenth Century', *Historical Journal*, vol. 45, no. 4 (December 2002): 873, accessed 29 October 2013, http://www.jstor.org/stable/3133532.
13. Ibid., 886–7.
14. Ibid., 879–80, 887.
15. Jürgen Habermas, *The Structural Transformation of the Public Sphere* (Cambridge, MA: MIT Press, 1991), 1–2, 10, 14–15, 22–3.
16. Robert Darnton, *The Literary Underground of the Old Regime* (Cambridge, MA: Harvard University Press, 1982), 2–12, 21–4; Dena Goodman, *The Republic of Letters: A Cultural History of the French Enlightenment* (Ithaca, NY: Cornell University Press, 1994), 53, 90–5, 99; Lawrence E. Klein, *Shaftesbury and the Culture of Politeness: Moral discourse and Cultural Politics in Early Eighteenth-Century England* (New York: Cambridge University Press, 1994), 5–21, 42, 138, 190.
17. Paul Langford, *A Polite and Commercial People: England, 1727–1783* (New York: Oxford University Press, 1994), 66, 69, 116–17, 199–203, 381; Lawrence E. Klein, 'Coffeehouse Civility, 1660–1714: An Aspect of Post-Courtly Culture in England', *Huntington Library Quarterly*, vol. 59, no. 1 (1996): 30–51, accessed 20 October 2016, http://www.jstor.org/stable/3817904; Brian Cowan, 'Mr. Spectator and the Coffeehouse Public Sphere', *Eighteenth-Century Studies*, vol. 37, no. 3 (Spring 2004): 345–66, accessed 20 October 2016, http://www.jstor.org/stable/25098064.
18. Klein, *Shaftesbury*, 5–21, 42, 138, 190; Klein, 'Politeness', 869–98; Klein, 'Coffeehouse Civility', 30–51.
19. Gillian Russell and Clara Tuite, 'Introducing Romantic Sociability', in *Romantic Sociability: Social Networks and Literary Culture in Britain, 1770–1840*, ed. Gillian Russell and Cara Tuite (Cambridge: Cambridge University Press, 2002), 5–6; Gillian Russell, *Women, Sociability and Theatre in Georgian London* (New York: Cambridge University Press, 2007), 5, 9, 66, 76, 93, 105, 107–17, 192; Tim Reinke-Williams, *Women, Work and Sociability in Early Modern London* (Basingstoke: Palgrave Macmillan, 2014), 107–17, 127, 135, 50.
20. Ukers, *All about Coffee*, xxvii, 73; Thomas Babington Macaulay, *The History of England from the Accession of James II*, vol. 1 (Project Gutenberg EBook, produced by Ken West and David Widger, 2013), 675; A. H. Arkle, 'The Early Coffee Houses of Liverpool', *Transactions of the Historical Society of Lancashire and Cheshire*, vol. 64

(1912): 1–16; Pobranski, '"Where Men of Differing Judgements Croud"', 35–9; John and Linda Pelzer, 'The Coffee Houses of Augustan London', *History Today*, vol. 32, no. 10 (October 1982): 40–7.
21. Steve Pincus, '"Coffee Politicians Does Create": Coffeehouses and Restoration Political Culture', *Journal of Modern History*, vol. 67, no. 4 (December 1995): 807–14.
22. Rudi Matthee, 'Exotic Substances: The Introduction and Global Spread of Tobacco, Coffee, Cocoa, Tea, and Distilled Liquor, Sixteenth to Eighteenth Centuries', in *Drugs and Narcotics in History*, ed. Roy Porter and Mikulas Teich (Cambridge: Cambridge University Press, 1995), 24–8; Gary S. de Krey, *A Fractured Society: The Politics of London in the First Age of Party 1688–1715* (New York: Oxford University Press, 1985), 221; Nicholas Rogers, *Whigs and Cities: Popular Politics in the Age of Walpole and Pitt* (New York: Oxford University Press, 1989), 401.
23. Peter Albrecht, 'Coffee-Drinking as a Symbol of Social Change in Continental Europe in the Seventeenth and Eighteenth Centuries', *Studies in Eighteenth-Century Culture*, vol. 18 (1988): 91–9; Jonathan Harris, 'The Grecian Coffee House and Political Debate in London 1688–1714', *London Journal a Review of Metropolitan Society Past and Present*, vol. 25, no. 1 (2000): 1–6.
24. Larry Stewart, 'Other centres of Calculation, or, Where the Royal Society Didn't Count: Commerce, Coffee-Houses and Natural Philosophy in Early Modern London', *British Journal for the History of Science*, vol. 32 (1999): 133–53.
25. Stephen Copley, 'Commerce, Conversation and Politeness in the Early Eighteenth-Century Periodical', *British Journal for Eighteenth-Century Studies*, vol. 18, no. 1 (Spring 1995): 63–6, 75.
26. Ellis, *The Coffee House*, 186–96.
27. Brian Cowan, 'The Rise of the Coffeehouse Reconsidered', *Historical Journal*, vol. 47, no. 1 (March 2004): 21–46, accessed 29 October 2013, http://www.jstor.org/stable/4091544; Cowan, 'Mr. Spectator and the Coffeehouse Public Sphere', 345–66; Cowan, *Social Life*, 87.
28. Brian Cowan, 'What Was Masculine about the Public Sphere? Gender and the Coffeehouse Milieu in Post-Restoration England', *History Workshop Journal*, vol. 51, no. 1 (Spring 2001): 127–57, accessed 20 October 2016, http://www.jstor.org/stable/4289724.
29. Cowan, *Social Life*, 101–2.
30. Helen Berry, 'Polite Consumption: Shopping in Eighteenth-Century England', *Transactions of the Royal Historical Society*, vol. 12 (2002): 375–7, accessed 20 October 2016, http://www.jstor.org/stable/3679353.
31. Helen Berry, 'Rethinking Politeness in Eighteenth-Century England: Moll King's Coffee House and the Significance of "Flash Talk": The Alexander Prize Lecture', *Transactions of the Royal Historical Society*, vol. 11 (2001): 65–81, accessed 20 October 2016, http://www.jstor.org/stable/3679414.
32. Gillian Russell and Clara Tuite, 'Introduction', in *Romantic Sociability*, 13–14; James Epstein, '"Equality and No King": Sociability and Sedition: The Case of John Frost', in *Romantic Sociability*, 43–8, 55–7; Anne Janowitz, 'Amiable and Radical Sociability: Anna Barbauld's "Free Familiar Conversation', in *Romantic Sociability*, 62–4, 72, 75–6.
33. Ukers, *All about Coffee*, 80–1; Lillywhite, '211. Button's Coffee House', in *London Coffee Houses*, 143–4, 503; Purdie, *Virginia Gazette*, 22 August 1777, pg. 3, col. 2; Hunter, *Virginia Gazette*, 17 November 1752, pg. 2, col. 2; Purdie and Dixon, *Virginia Gazette*, 16 May 1771, pg. 3, col. 1; James M. Davis, 'The Colonial Coffeehouse', *Early American Life*, vol. 9, no. 1 (1978): 27.

34. *The New-York gazette*, 8 November 1736, pg. 1, Image 1; *The New-York gazette*, 23 July 1739, pg. 2, Image 2; *The Maryland Gazette*, 7 January 1729, Number 69, 1, Archives of Maryland Online, *Maryland Gazette Collection*, 24 July 2009, http://aomol.msa.maryland.gov/html/mdgazette.html; David S. Shields, *Civil Tongues and Polite Letters in British America* (Chapel Hill: Published for the Institute of Early American History and Culture, Williamsburg, Virginia by University of North Carolina Press, 1997), 177–80, 199.

35. *Murther Upon Murther: Being a Full and True Relation of a Horrid and Bloody Murther, Committed Upon the Bodies of Mrs. Sarah Hodges, Wife of Mr. Thamas Hodges, Mrs. Elizabeth Smith and Hannah Williams, the Loyal Coffee-House near Well-Gose at the end of East-Smith-field, on Saturday the 17th. of this Instant January 1691* (London: Printed by G. Croom, at the Blue Ball in Thames-street, 1691), 3–4; Sir. J. Dalrymple, 'Historical and Biographical Anecdotes. [From the Second Volume of Sir J. Dalrymple's "Memoirs of Great Britain and Ireland", lately published.] Earl of Stair', in *The aberdeen magazine, literary chronicle, and review; for The Year MDCCLXXXVIII … vol. 1*. 1788–90, Eighteenth Century Collections Online, Gale, CMU Libraries – library.cmich.edu: 310, accessed 22 October 2016, http://find.galegroup.com.cmich.idm.oclc.org/ecco/infomark.do?&source=gale&pro dId=ECCO&userGroupName=lom_cmichu&tabID=T001&docId=CW124930 040&type=multipage&contentSet=ECCOArticles&version=1.0&docLevel=FASCIM ILE; 'Guardian, No. 171, Saturday, September 26, 1713', in Joseph Addison and Sir Richard Steele, *The Guardian, with Notes, and a General Index … Complete in One Volume* (Philadelphia, PA: J.J. Woodward, 1831), 229; *The New-York gazette*, 11 July 1726, pg. 2; *The New-York gazette*, 17 December 1728, pg. 2.

36. Letter, James Potts, the Jamaica Coffee House, 6 October 1787, ADM 106/1291/280, *James Potts, the Jamaica Coffee House. Offers the Louisa for transporting troops and …*, The National Archives, Kew; Letter, Captain Philip Durell, Wills Coffee House, 13 January 1744, ADM 106/989/8, *Captain Philip Durell, Wills Coffee House, London. Request that the Richard and Thomas …*, The National Archives, Kew.

37. Purdie, *Virginia Gazette*, 15 August 1777 – pg. 3, col. 2; Purdie and Dixon, *Virginia Gazette*, 6 May 1773 – pg. 3, col. 1; *Proceedings and Acts of the General Assembly*, September 1704–April 1706: volume 26, pg. 582, Archives of Maryland Online, http://aomol.msa.maryland.gov/000001/000026/html/am26--582.html; Shields, *Civil Tongues*, 55; Davis, 'The Colonial Coffeehouse', 27–8.

38. Western Manuscripts, Add MS 38340, Folio 98, *Vol. CLI (ff. 391). 1767,1768. includes:ff. 1–203 passim Navy; England: Various papers rel. to: 1766–1768. ff. 1–25 Admiralty: Papers rel. to: 1766–1767. f. 6 Brandy: Accompts of brandy imported, etc.: 1764-circ. 1785. f. 7 Rum: Imports of, to Grea …*, British Library; Letter, Managers of Lloyds Coffee House to the 1st Earl of Liverpool, 1798, Western Manuscripts, Add MS 38310, Folio 221, *Vol. CXXI (ff. 268). 23 July, 1787–31 Jan. 1799.includes:ff. 1, 31, 51, 232 Charles Jenkinson, 1st Earl of Liverpool: Correspondence with Marquis Cornwallis: 1779–1798.: Copies (except the first). ff. 1, 31, 51, 232 Charles Cornwallis, Viscount Brom*, British Library; Letter, Managers of Lloyds Coffee House to the 1st Earl of Liverpool, 1798, Western Manuscripts, Add MS 38232, Folios 60, 66, *Vol. XLIII (ff. 397). Apr.- Dec. 1798.Thomas Lack, Secretary to the Committee of the Privy Council for Trade: Letters to the 1st Earl of Liverpool: circ. 1793–1806.includes:ff. 1, 2, 8,53,150, 170, 199, 203, 210, 263, 304 b, 368 John de Blaquière, Li*, British Library; Letter, February 1718, India Office Records and Private Papers, IOR/E/1/9 ff. 80–81v, *Letter 47 Petition of several merchants and traders in coffee to the House of Commons*

concerning goods run on board the London Merchant, British Library; Letter, Charles Carkesse to Thomas Woolley, 27 August 1712, India Office Records and Private Papers, IOR/E/1/4 ff. 193–195v, *Letters 110–111 Secretary Charles Carkesse at the Customs House in London to Thomas Woolley forwarding a copy of the Commissioners' minutes relating to the Company's Coffee. Related papers attached*, British Library; Letter, Charles Carkesse to Thomas Woolley, 26 September 1712, India Office Records and Private Papers, IOR/E/1/4 ff. 241–242v, *Letter 139 Secretary Charles Carkesse at the Customs House in London to Thomas Woolley concerning the coffee and tea in the Company's warehouses*, British Library.

39. *The Boston-Gazette*, Monday, 31 July 1775, 4; *The Maryland Gazette*, 16 December 1728, Number 65, 1; Purdie and Dixon, *Virginia Gazette*, 25 June 1767 – pg. 3, col. 1; Purdie and Dixon, *Virginia Gazette*, 6 May 1773 – pg. 3, col. 1; Purdie, *Virginia Gazette*, 29 May 1778 – pg. 3, col. 1; Purdie and Dixon, *Virginia Gazette*, 30 April 1772 – pg. 3, col. 1; Purdie and Dixon, *Virginia Gazette*, 14 October 1773 – pg. 2, col. 3.

40. Samuel Curwen, *Journal and Letters of the Late Samuel Curwen Judge of Admiralty, Etc.*, ed. George Atkinson Ward, digitized by Bedford, MA: Applewood Books (New York: C. S. Francis, 1842), 30, 38, 42, 56, 100.

41. Arkle, 'The Early Coffee Houses of Liverpool', 1–6; Dixon and Hunter, *Virginia Gazette*, 14 March, 1777 – pg. 1, col. 2; Purdie and Dixon, *Virginia Gazette*, 17 November 1768 – pg. 2, col. 3, Purdie and Dixon, *Virginia Gazette*, 18 May 1769 – pg. 2, col. 1; Rind, *Virginia Gazette*, 1 December 1768 – pg. 1, col. 3; Rind, *Virginia Gazette*, 26 May 1768 – pg. 1, col. 4; Purdie and Dixon, *Virginia Gazette*, 23 June 1768 – pg. 1, col. 3; Troy Bickham, '"A Conviction of the Reality of Things": Material Culture, North American Indians and Empire in Eighteenth-Century Britain', *Eighteenth-Century Studies*, vol. 39, no. 1 (2005): 29–37; *Catalogue Descriptive of the Various Curiosities to be seen at Don Saltero's Coffee House and Tavern, in Chelsea. to which is prefixed, a complete List of the Donors thereof. The forty-sixth edition* (London, s.n., 1795?), 1–15.

42. *The New-York gazette*, 25 December 1727, pg. 3; *The New-York gazette*, 1 March 1730, pg. 1; Parks, *Virginia Gazette*, 1 July 1737 – pg. 2, col. 2; Parks, *Virginia Gazette*, 4 September 1746 – pg. 3, col. 1; Purdie, *Virginia Gazette*, 23 May 1766 – pg. 2, col. 3.

43. Parks, *Virginia Gazette*, 1 July 1737 – pg. 2, col. 2; Parks, *Virginia Gazette*, 14 July 1738 – pg. 2, col. 2; *The Boston-Gazette, and Country Journal*, 11 September 1769, volume 2, 658, The Annotated Newspapers of Harbottle Dorr, Jr, accessed 24 November 2017, http://www.masshist.org/dorr/volume/2/sequence/700?search Hit=1; Revolutionary Society minute-book, Western Manuscripts, Add MS 64814, *REVOLUTION SOCIETY: minute-book of the Revolution Society; 16 June 1788–4 Nov. 1791*, British Library; 'John Hughes to Franklin, Philada. Sept. 8. 1765, Sept. 10. 1765, and Sept. 10. 1765', *Franklin Papers*, accessed 10 November 2017, http://franklinpapers.org/franklin/framedVolumes.jsp; Dixon and Hunter, *Virginia Gazette*, 7 January 1775 – pg. 2, col. 3; Purdie and Dixon, *Virginia Gazette*, 2 December 1773 – pg. 1, col. 2; *The Boston-Gazette, and Country Journal*, Monday, 19 August 1776, pg. 2, col. 2, https://archive.org/stream/bostongazetteorc269bost#page/n209/mode/2up/search/grapes; Ukers, *All about Coffee*, 106–11.

44. Ukers, *All about Coffee*, 73; Barrell, 'Coffee-House Politicians', 207–8.

45. Ellis, *The Coffee House*, 106–7.

46. Ellis, *The Coffee House*, xii, 46–6, 86–8, 159–63.

47. Klein, 'Coffeehouse Civility', 31–51; Pincus, '"Coffee Politicians Does Create"', 815; Markman Ellis, 'Pasqua Rosee's Coffee-House, 1652–1666', *London Journal*, vol.

29, no. 1 (2004): 1–24; Helen Berry, 'Coffee Houses, Exoticism and the Evolution of Eighteenth-Century Culture' (master's thesis, V&A, 20 November 2003), 14–22; Berry, 'Rethinking Politeness', 65–81.
48. Letter, James Potts, the Jamaica Coffee House, 6 October 1787, ADM 106/1291/280, *James Potts, the Jamaica Coffee House. Offers the Louisa for transporting troops and …*, The National Archives, Kew; Letter, Captain Philip Durell, Wills Coffee House, 13 January 1744, ADM 106/989/8, *Captain Philip Durell, Wills Coffee House, London. Request that the Richard and Thomas …*, The National Archives, Kew.

1 'Trifling', an urban experience

1. Nich Nonentity, 'To the Author of The Trifler, Feb. 29. 1788', in *The aberdeen magazine*, vol. 1, 1788–1790, 163–4.
2. Works which have laid the groundwork for interpreting the Atlantic world include Bernard Bailyn, *Atlantic History: Concept and Contours* (London: Harvard University Press, 2005); Thomas Benjamin, *The Atlantic World: Europeans, Africans, Indians and Their Shared History, 1400–1900* (Cambridge: Cambridge University Press, 2009); Amy Turner Bushnell and Jack P. Greene, 'Peripheries, Centers, and the Construction of Early Modern American Empires', in *Negotiated Empires: Centers and Peripheries in the Americas, 1500–1820*, ed. Christine Daniels and Michael V. Kennedy (New York: Rutledge, 2002), 1–14; and David Armitage, 'Three Concepts of Atlantic History', in *The British Atlantic World, 1500–1800*, ed. David Artmitage and Michael J. Braddick (Houndmills: Palgrave Macmillan, 2002), 11–27.
3. Women shopped for tea in public, but most often bought it for parlour use. Coffee, however, was known as the politician's drink; Joan B. Landes, *Women and the Public Sphere: In the Age of the French Revolution* (Ithaca, NY: Cornell University Press, 1998), 40–5, 104–7, 113, 118–19, 140–6; Reinke-Williams, *Women, Work and Sociability*, 3, 41, 45, 66, 72, 74, 107, 117, 125, 127, 135; Markman Ellis, 'Coffee-Women, *The Spectator* and the Public Sphere in the Early Eighteenth Century', in *Women, Writing and the Public Sphere, 1700–1830*, ed. Elizabeth Edgar, Charlotte Grant, Clíona Ó Gallchoir and Penny Warburton (Cambridge: Cambridge University Press, 2001), 31–2; Berry, 'Polite Consumption', 375–7; Henry Fielding, *The Coffee-House Politician: or, the Justice caught in His Own Trap. A Comedy. As it is Acted at the Theatre-Royal in Lincoln's-Inn Fields Written by Mr. Fielding* (London: Printed for J. Watts, 1730), 8.
4. T. H. Breen, 'An Empire of Goods: The Anglicization of Colonial America, 1690–1776', *Journal of British Studies*, vol. 25, no. 4, Re-Viewing the Eighteenth Century (October 1986): 467–99, accessed 18 October 2014, http://www.jstor.org/stable/175565; Lorena S. Walsh, *Motives of Honor, Pleasure, and Profit: Plantation Management in the Colonial Chesapeake, 1607–1763* (Chapel Hill: University of North Carolina Press, 2010).
5. Robert O. Bucholz and Joseph R. Ward, *London: A Social and Cultural History, 1550–1750* (New York: Cambridge University Press, 2002), 1–8.
6. Ibid., 27–31, 56–67, 77–88, 122–5, 253–6.
7. Lillywhite, *London Coffee Houses*, 246, 363–4.
8. Jane Austen, *The Novels of Jane Austen, Persuasion* (Edinburgh: John Grant, 31 George IV. Bridge, 1905), 16, 18.

9. Lillywhite, *London Coffee Houses*, 216-20, 305-9, 551; Stephen C. Topik, 'Coffee', in *The Cambridge World History of Food*, vol. 1, ed. Kenneth F. Kiple and Kriemhild Conee Ornelas (Cambridge: Cambridge University Press, 2000), 643; Ellis, *The Coffee House*, 170-1, 179-80.
10. Kathleen Wilson, *The Sense of the People: Politics, Culture and Imperialism in England, 1715-1785* (New York: Cambridge University Press, 1995), 118-22.
11. Edward Callow, *Old London Taverns: Historical, Descriptive and Reminiscent with some Account of the Coffee Houses, Clubs, Etc.* (Downey & Co. Limited: London, 1899), 50, 248; Lillywhite, *London Coffee Houses*, 282-4, 289-91, 624-9; Letter, Christopher Jarvis Hurd, Jamaica coffeehouse, Nov. 6, 1751, ADM 106/1091/84, *Christopher Jarvis Hurd, Jamaica coffeehouse. Is sending a letter permitting me to go to …*, The National Archives, Kew.
12. Lillywhite, *London Coffee Houses*, 389-91, 444-5.
13. Lillywhite, *The London Coffee House*, 330-5, 395-7; John J. McCusker, 'The Business Press in England before 1775', *Library Sixth Series*, vol. 8, no. 3 (September 1986): 207, 224-5; John J. McCusker, 'The Early History of "Lloyd's List"', *Historical Research*, vol. 64, no. 155 (October 1991): 429; Ellis, *The Coffee House*, 178-9.
14. Lillywhite, *The London Coffee House*, 366, 581-2, 590-3, 655-9; Ellis, *The Coffee House*, 151-3.
15. 'Tatler, No. 1, Tuesday, April 12,1709', in *Tatler*, 11; Lillywhite, *London Coffee Houses*, 143, 639-43.
16. Lillywhite, *London Coffee Houses*, 641.
17. Anna Marion Smith, *Mother Goose and What Happened Next* (New York: E. P. Dutton, 1909), 96.
18. 'Spectator, No. 403, Thursday, June 12, 1712', in Joseph Addison and Sir Richard Steele, *The Works of Joseph Addison; Complete in Three Volumes, Embracing the Whole of the 'Spectator', etc.*, vol. 2 (New York: Harper & Brothers, 1845), 128; Lillywhite, *London Coffee Houses*, 500-1.
19. And Twining was making a substantial profit. According to Ellis, Twining charged Button between 5s 6d and 6s 8d per pound of coffee and between 16 shillings and 18 shillings for Bohea tea; Ukers, *All about Coffee*, 80-1; Lillywhite, '211. Button's Coffee House', in *London Coffee Houses*, 143-4, 503; Ellis, *The Coffee House*, 127.
20. Cowen, *Social Life*, 154; Ukers, *All about Coffee*, 107-12, 115-29.
21. Wilson, *The Sense of the People*, 12, 28, 30-1, 32, 228-52, 354-62.
22. Ibid., 140-50, 288-92, 303-5.
23. Davis, 'The Colonial Coffeehouse', 27-8; Ukers, *All about Coffee*, 115-30.
24. Nonentity, Nich. 'To the Author of The Trifler, Feb. 29. 1788', in *The aberdeen magazine*, vol. 1, 1788-90, 163-4; *The New-York gazette*, 8 November 1736, pg. 1, Image 1; *The New-York gazette*, 23 July 1739, pg. 2, Image 2; *The Maryland Gazette*, 7 January 1729, Number 69, 1; Shields, *Civil Tongues*, 177-80, 199.
25. James Boswell, *Boswell's London Journal, 1762-1763* (New York: McGraw Hill, 1950), 45, 47, 51-9, 61, 69, 71-6, 86, 104-7, 152-5.
26. Ibid., 91, 112.
27. Samuel Johnson, *The Works of Samuel Johnson, LL.D.: A New Edition, with an Essay On His Life and Genius, by Arthur Murphy, ESQ. in two volumes* (London: Henry G. Bohn, York Street, Convent Garden, 1850), 17.
28. E. Wesley Reynolds, III, 'London's Coffeehouse *Literati* and the Rise of the Public Man in the Eighteenth Century', *Studies in Burke and His Time*, vol. 30 (2021): 85-112;

Leo Damrosch, *The Club: Johnson, Boswell, and the Friends Who Shaped an Age* (New Haven, CT: Yale University Press, 2019), 1–3, 38–9, 124–35.
29. Johnson, *The Works*, 12.
30. See especially *Rambler* numbers 7, 10, 62, 78, and 89; ibid., 11–12, 17, 109, 135–6, 152–3.
31. *The Character of a Coffee-House, with the Symptoms of a Town-Wit* (London: Printed for Jonathan Edwin, at the three Roses in Lud-Gate-Street, 1673), 3.
32. *The Maidens Complaint Against Coffee. or, the Coffee-House Discovered, Besieged, Stormed, Taken, Untyled and laid Open to publick view, in a merry Conference between … Being Very pleasant and delightful for Old and Young, Lads and Lasses, Boys and Girles [Latin phrase] as the devout Ironmonger quotes it in his Annotations upon Toby and his Dog. Written by Merc. Democ. at his Chamber in the World in the Moon, for the benefit of all the mad-merry-conceited people under the Sun* (J. Jones: Royal Exchange, London, 1663), 1, 6.
33. *The character of a coffee-house wherein is contained a description of the persons usually frequenting it, with their discourse and humors, as also the admirable vertues of coffee / by an eye and ear witness. Eye and ear witness* (London: s.n., 1665, Ann Arbor, MI; Oxford, UK: Text Creation Partnership, 2006–2, EEBO-TCP Phase 1), 8, accessed 28 August 2017, http://name.umdl.umich.edu/A31685.0001.001.
34. Ellis, *The Coffee House*, 68–9, 115–22, 147.
35. The phrase originated with Sir George Sandys in this travel narratives of the Eastern Mediterranean world; *The Vertues of coffee set forth in the works of [brace] the Lord Bacon his Natural hist., Mr. Parkinson his Herbal, Sir George Sandys his Travails, James Howel Esq. his Epistles / collected and published for the satisfaction of the drinkers thereof* (London: Printed by W.G., 1663), 6.
36. *Coffee-houses Vindicated in Answer to the late Published Character of a Coffee-House Asserting From Reason, Experience, and good Authours, the Excellent Use, and Physical Vertues of that Liquor. With The grand Conveniency of such civil places of Resort and Ingenious Conversation* (London: Printed by I. Lock for I. Clarke, 1675), 1–2.
37. Ibid., 3–4.
38. Ibid., 4.
39. 'Idler, No. 64. Saturday, 7 July 1759', in *The Yale Edition of the Works of Samuel Johnson*, 199; For Johnson's arrival in London with David Garrick, see also Boswell, *Boswell's Life of Johnson, Abridged and edited, with an introduction by Charles Grosvenor Osgood* (New York: Charles Scribner's Sons, 1917), 24–7.
40. 'Tatler, No. 232, Tuesday, October 3, 1710', in *Tatler*, 382.
41. Ellis, *The Coffee House*, 76, 106, 178.

2 'Trifling' in the colonies

1. Quoted in Ukers, *All about Coffee*, 116.
2. Thomas M. A. Doerflinger, *Vigorous Spirit of Enterprise: Merchants and Economic Development in Revolutionary Philadelphia* (Chapel Hill: University of North Carolina Press, 1986), 21; Walsh, *Motives of Honor*, 171, 188, 200–1, 225–6, 238–9; P. J. Marshall, *Making and Unmaking: of Empires: Britain, India, and America c.1750–1783* (New York: Oxford University Press, 2005), 14–16, 42–3; Ian K. Steele, *English Atlantic, 1675–1740: An Exploration of Communication and Community* (New York: Oxford University Press, 1986), 78–90, 93, 213–28.

3. As economist Joel Mokyr has argued, the Age of Enlightenment was marked by a newfound national competition, or 'emulation', in which European societies employed scientists and engineers to craft better consumer products and so succeed in the pursuit of economic survival. European society grew because of its political fragmentation which encouraged competition and its cosmopolitan approach to empirical science. Americans also took part in the modern exchange of goods and ideas, as European intellectuals continued to engage in a pan-European pursuit of 'useful knowledge' through the lingua franca of Latin and gain economies of scale through the research and development of architects, clockmakers, engineers, physicians and printers who disseminated knowledge more or less freely. Joel Mokyr, *A Culture of Growth: The Origins of the Modern Economy* (Princeton, NJ: Princeton University Press, 2017), 42, 119, 129, 168–70, 228–9.
4. Walsh, *Motives of Honor*, 238–9; David Hancock, *Oceans of Wine: Madeira and the Emergence of American Trade and Taste* (New Haven, CT: Yale University Press, 2009), 275–9, 285, 294, 317–39, 387–9.
5. Toby L. Ditz first introduced the idea of trust as a mechanism to explain the public personas of merchant men doing business and securing credit; Toby L. Ditz, 'Secret Selves, Credible Personas: The Problematics of Trust and Public Display in the Writing of Eighteenth-Century Philadelphia Merchants', in *Possible Pasts: Becoming Colonial in Early America*, ed. Robert Blair St George (Ithaca, NY: Cornell University Press, 2000), 220–2, 226–8; Toby L. Ditz, 'Shipwrecked; or, Masculinity Imperiled: Mercantile Representations of Failure and the Gendered Self in Eighteenth-Century Philadelphia', *Journal of American History*, vol. 81, no. 1 (June 1994): 53–9, 61, 67; Alan Taylor, *American Revolutions: A Continental History, 1750–1804* (New York: W. W. Norton, 2016), 23–6; Thomas M. Doerflinger, *A Vigorous Spirit of Enterprise: Merchants and Economic Development in Revolutionary Philadelphia* (Chapel Hill: University of North Carolina Press, 1986), 18, 56, 85–6.
6. Daniel Vickers, 'The Northern Colonies: Economy and Society, 1600–1775' and Stanley L. Engerman and Robert E. Gallman, ed., *The Cambridge Economic History of the United States, Volume 1, The Colonial Era* (New York: Cambridge University Press, 1996), 245, 337–62; H. V. Bowen, *Elites, Enterprise and the Making of the British Overseas Empire 1688–1775* (New York: St. Martin's Press, 1996), 32–5.
7. T. H. Breen, *The Marketplace of Revolution: How Consumer Politics Shaped American Independence* (New York: Oxford University Press, 2004), 55, 78–9.
8. Joyce E. Chaplin, 'The British Atlantic', in *The Oxford Handbook of The Atlantic World c. 1450–c. 1850*, ed. Nicholas Canny and Philip Morgan (New York: Oxford University Press, 2011), 229–30.
9. Steele, *English Atlantic*, 213–28.
10. Davis, 'The Colonial Coffeehouse', 27; Ukers, *All about Coffee*, 126; Ellis, *The Coffee House*, 79.
11. Ellis, *The Coffee House*, 181; Ukers, *All about Coffee*, 126–30.
12. Billy G. Smith, 'Death and Life in a Colonial Immigrant City: a Demographic Analysis of Philadelphia', *Journal of Economic History*, vol. 37, no. 4 (December 1977): 865, accessed 9 September 2017, http://www.jstor.org.cmich.idm.oclc.org/stable/2119346; M. Dorothy George, *London Life in the 18th Century* (New York: Capricorn Books, 1965), 25.
13. Even though Bradford did publish at least some of the more popular literature of crime and scandal found in so many coffeehouses in London, he never quit publishing sermons and political essays of a more sober nature, as a close look at his book list

reveals: Clare A. Lyons, *Sex Among the Rabble: An Intimate History of Gender and Power in the Age of Revolution, Philadelphia 1730–1830* (Chapel Hill: University of North Carolina Press, 2006), 140–1.
14. Davis, 'The Colonial Coffeehouse', 27–8; Ukers, *All about Coffee*, 126–7; Some of Bradford's publications include the following and are available at the Library of Congress; *Directions for the Gulph and River of St. Lawrence, with some remarks* (Philadelphia: Printed by William and Thomas Bradford, at the London Coffee-house, 1774); Gervase Parker Bushe, *Case of Great-Britain and America* (London: Printed, Philadelphia, Re-Printed by William and Thomas Bradford, at the London Coffee-House, 1769); John Dickinson, *Address to the Committee of correspondance in Barbados* (Philadelphia: Printed and sold by William Bradford, at his bookstore in Market street, adjoining the London coffeehouse, 1766).
15. Ukers, *All about Coffee*, 127, 129–30.
16. Further discussion of the legal and social development of this holiness may be found in the following: David Thomas Konig, *Law and Society in Puritan Massachusetts: Essex County, 1626–1693* (Chapel Hill: University of North Carolina Press, 1979), 89–90, 96–7; David Thomas Konig, 'A Summary View of the Law of British America', *William and Mary Quarterly*, vol. 50, no. 1 (January 1993): 48–9; Cornelia Hughes Dayton, *Women before the Bar: Gender, Law, and Society in Connecticut, 1638–1789* (Chapel Hill: University of North Carolina Press, 1995), 2–13, 64–5; Cornelia Hughes Dayton, 'Was There a Calvinist Type of Patriarchy? New Haven Colony Reconsidered in the Early Modern Context', in *The Many Legalities of Early America*, ed. Christopher Tomlins and Bruce H. Mann (Chapel Hill: University of North Carolina Press, 2001), 338–43, 351; *Essays in the History of Early American Law*, ed. David H. Flaherty (Chapel Hill: University of North Carolina Press, 1969), 48, 58, 92–6, 176; David Thomas Konig, 'Dale's Laws' and the Non-Common Law Origins of Criminal Justice in Virginia', *American Journal of Legal History*, vol. 26, no. 4 (October 1982): 361–71; Cornelia Hughes Dayton, 'Excommunicating the Governor's Wife: Religious Dissent in the Puritan Colonies Before the Era of Rights Consciousness', in *Religious Conscience, the State, and the Law: Historical Contexts and Contemporary Significance*, ed. John McLaren and Harold Coward (Albany, NY: Suny University Press, 1999), 29–32, 40.
17. Lawrence Henry Gipson, 'Criminal Codes of Pennsylvania', *Journal of Criminal Law and Criminology*, vol. 6, no. 3, Article 2 (1915): 323–9.
18. Ellis, *The Coffee House*, 78–79, 181–3; Ukers, *All about Coffee*, 115–20; Davis, 'The Colonial Coffeehouse', 28.
19. Ukers, *All about Coffee*, 120–1.
20. Quoted in both Ukers, *All about Coffee*, 115–16 and in W. Harrison Bayles, *Old Taverns of New York* (Frank Allaben Genealogical Company, Forty-Second Street Building, New York, 1915), 275–8.
21. Ukers, *All about Coffee*, 124.
22. Mark Caldwell, *New York Night: The Mystique and Its History* (New York: Scribner, 2005), 44; John Lambert, 'From Travels through Canada, and the United States of North America in the Years 1806, 1807, 1808', in *Empire City: New York through the Centuries*, ed. Kenneth Jackson and David Dunbar (New York: Columbia University Press, 2002), 111–15.
23. William Ukers and Markman Ellis, while dedicating about fifteen to twenty-five pages each to Colonial American coffeehouses, do not name a single southern coffeehouse; Ukers, *All about Coffee*, 105–30; Ellis, *The Coffee House*, 76–9, 180–4, 202–3.

24. *Proceedings and Acts of the General Assembly, 1766–1768* (Maryland State Archives, copyright 31 October 2014), 481, accessed 18 Novemebr 2021, http://msa.maryland.gov/megafile/msa/speccol/sc2900/sc2908/000001/000061/html/am61--481.html.
25. *Proceedings and Acts of the General Assembly, 1771 to June–July, 1773* (Maryland State Archives, copyright 31 October 2014), 76, accessed 11 November 2021, http://aomol.msa.maryland.gov/000001/000063/html/am63--76.html; R. Lee Van Horn, *Out of the Past: Prince Georgeans and Their Land* (Riverdale, MD: Prince George's County Historical Society, 1976), 196.
26. Purdie and Dixon, *Virginia Gazette*, Jun. 25, 1767 – pg. 3, col. 1.
27. Purdie and Dixon, *Virginia Gazette*, May 9, 1771 – pg. 3, col. 2.
28. Dixon and Hunter, *Virginia Gazette*, Aug. 15, 1777 – pg. 6, col. 1.
29. Ukers, *All about Coffee*, 108–109; Ellis, *The Coffee House*, 76–8; Cotton Mather, *Everlasting gospel. The gospel of justification by the righteousness of God; as 'tis held and preached in the churches of New England: expressed in a brief discourse on that important article; made at Boston in the year, 1699. By Cotton Mather. And, asser* (Boston: Printed by B. Green, and J. Allen, for Nicholas Buttolph, and sold at the corner of Gutteridges coffee-house, 1700); John Ogilvie, *Providence, an allegorical poem* (Boston: Printed for and sold by J. Mein, at the London Book-store, second Door above the British Coffee-house, North-side of Kingstreet, 1766).
30. *A Conductor generalis, or, The office, duty and authority of justices of the peace, high-sheriffs, under-sheriffs, coroners, constables, gaolers, jury-men, and overseers of the poor: as also, the office of clerks of assize, and of the peace, &c. / compil* (Woodbridge, in New-Jersey: Printed for and sold by Garrat Noel, near the merchant's coffee House, in New-York, MDCCLXIV [1764]).
31. Ukers, *All about Coffee*, 109–13; Jack Quinan, 'The Boston Exchange Coffee Houses', *Journal of the Society of Architectural Historians*, vol. 38, no. 3 (1979): 256–62.
32. Alison G. Olson, 'The Board of Trade and London-American Interest Groups in the Eighteenth Century', *Journal of Imperial and Commonwealth History*, vol. 8, no. 2 (1980): 35.
33. Ibid., 33–4, 40–4.
34. Richard L. Bushman, *The Refinement of America: Persons, Houses, Cities* (New York: Vintage Books, 1992), xii–xvii.
35. Ibid., 140–55, 168.
36. Ibid., 161, 163.
37. Cynthia Adams Hoover, 'Music and Theater in the Lives of Eighteenth-Century Americans', in *Of Consuming Interests*, ed. Cary Carson, Ronal Hoffman and Peter J. Albert (Charlottesville: Published for the United States Capitol Historical Society by the University Press of Virginia, 1994), 310–21.
38. Doerflinger, *A Vigorous Spirit of Enterprise*, 23–6, 31–2, 42–3.
39. Taylor, *American Revolutions*, 23–6.
40. Marshall, *Making and Unmaking*, 16–17.
41. Taylor, *American Revolutions*, 23–6.
42. Marshall, *Making and Unmaking*, 43.
43. Marshall, *Making and Unmaking*, 43; Bushman, *The Refinement of America*, 9–10; Caroline Cox, *A Proper Sense of Honor: Service and Sacrifice in George Washington's Army* (Chapel Hill: University of North Carolina Press, 2004), 26–7.
44. Breen, *The Marketplace of Revolution*, 22–3, 55.
45. *The New-York Gazette*, 8 November 1736, pg. 1, Image 1.

46. John Phillips, *Horse-Flesh for The Observator: Being a Comment upon Gusman, ch. 4. v. 5. Held forth at Sam's Coffee-House // by T.D.B.D. chaplain to the Inferiour clergies guide* (London: Printed for R. Read, 1682), 9.
47. Johnson, *The Works of Samuel Johnson, LL.D.: A New Edition*, 17.
48. *The New-York Gazette*, 23 July 1739, pg. 2, Image 2.
49. Ibid.
50. Copley, 'Commerce', 65.
51. G. J. Barker-Benfield, *The Culture of Sensibility: Sex and Society in Eighteenth-Century Britain* (Chicago: University of Chicago Press, 1992), esp. chs. 2–4; Copley, 'Commerce', 64–6; Michael G. Ketcham, *Transparent Designs: Reading, Performance and Form in the Spectator Papers* (Athens: University of Georgia, 1985), 156; Jon Klancher, *The Making of English Reading Audiences 1790–1832* (Madison: University of Wisconsin Press, 1987), 19.
52. Copley, 'Commerce', 74.
53. Ibid., 74.
54. Ibid., 68.
55. 'Tatler, No. 15, Saturday, May 14, 1709', in *Tatler*, 43.
56. Washington Irving, *The Sketch-Book of Geoffrey Crayon, Gent* (New York: G. P. Putnam's Sons, 1882), 259.
57. 'Tatler, No. 15, Saturday, May 14, 1709', in *Tatler*, 43.
58. 'Guardian No. 35, Tuesday, April 21, 1713', *The Guardian: With Notes, and a General Index ... Complete in One Volume* (Philadelphia: J.J. Woodward, 1831), 52.
59. 'Tatler, No. 92, Tuesday, November 10, 1709', in *Tatler*, 190.
60. 'Tatler, No. 153, Saturday, April 1, 1710', in *Tatler*, 279.
61. 'Tatler No. 66, Saturday, September 10, 1709', in *Tatler*, 144.
62. 'Tatler, No. 21, Saturday, May 28, 1709', in *Tatler*, 53.
63. Ibid., 53–4.
64. 'Tatler, No. 230, Thursday, September 28, 1710', in *Tatler*, 379–80.
65. 'Tatler, No. 166, Tuesday, May 2, 1710', in *Tatler*, 298; 'Tatler, No. 180, Tuesday, June 3, 1710', in *Tatler*, 318.
66. Addison, *The Works of Joseph Addison*, vol. 1, 30.
67. Horn, *Out of the Past*, 177.
68. Shields, *Civil Tongues*, 199.
69. Ibid., 177–80.
70. William Byrd, '"October 9, 1710" and "November 22, 1711"', in *The Secret Diary of William Byrd of Westover, 1709–1712*, ed. Louis B. Wright and Marion Tinling (Richmond: Dietz Press, 1941, National Humanities Center, 2009), nationalhumanitiescenter.org/pds; Julia B. Curits, 'Chinese Export Porcelain in Eighteenth Century Tidewater Virginia', *Studies in Eighteenth-Century Culture*, vol. 17 (1987): 125.
71. Benjamin Franklin, 'Autobiography, Part 4', *Franklin Papers*; Benjamin Franklin and John Foxcroft to Anthony Todd, 10 June 1763, *Franklin Papers*; Benjamin Franklin to To Cadwalader Evans, 10 February 1773, *Franklin Papers*; Joseph Galloway to Benjamin Franklin, 17 October 1768, *Franklin Papers*.
72. *The Maryland Gazette*, 7 January 1729, Number 69, 1.
73. *The Maryland Gazette*, 3 December 1728, Number 69, 1; *The Maryland Gazette*, 24 December 1728, Number 69, 1; *The Maryland Gazette*, 7 January, 1729, Number 69, 1.
74. Bruce C. Daniels, 'Sober Mirth and Pleasant Poisons: Puritan Ambivalence toward Leisure and Recreation in Colonial New England', *American Studies*, vol. 34, no. 1 (Spring 1993): 123.

75. Increase Mather, *An Arrow Against Profane and Promiscuous Dancing, Drawn Out of the Quiver of the Scriptures* (Boston, 1684), 6.
76. Daniels, 'Sober Mirth', 124–34.
77. Purdie and Dixon, *The Virginia Gazette*, 1 June 1769 – pg. 1, col. 2.
78. Samuel Wales, 'The Dangers of our National Prosperity; and the Way to Avoid Them' (Hartford, 1785), in *Political Sermons of the American Founding Era, 1730–1805*, vol. 1, 2nd edn, ed. Ellis Sandoz (Indianapolis, IN: Liberty Fund, 1991), 853.
79. *The Boston Gazette, or Country Journal*, 12 February 1776, pg. 2.

3 Murders, officers and naval headquarters

1. Examination of James Joyce, Charles Hinton, 1685, Western Manuscripts, Add MS 41803, Folios 209, 213, *MIDDLETON PAPERS. Vol. I (ff. 338). Correspondence mainly addressed to Sir Leoline Jenkins, Robert Spencer, 2nd Earl of Sunderland, and Sidney Godolphin, 1st Lord Godolphin, [1st Earl of Godolphin 1706], in addition to Lord Middleton and Dr Owen Wynn*, British Library.
2. Ibid., Folio 209.
3. Ibid., Folio 213.
4. 'No. 291. *Sir John Cope trode the north right far*', in James C. Dick, *The Songs of Robert Burns: Now first printed with the Melodies for which they were written ...* (New York: Henry Frowde, London, Edinburgh, Glasgow and New York, 1903), 275.
5. *The New-York gazette*, 11 July 1726, pg. 2.
6. John Hancock, *An Oration*, 6, Monticello Digital Classroom, accessed 1 September 2018, https://classroom.monticello.org/media-item/john-hancocks-boston-massacre-oration/.
7. Thomas St Serfe, *Tarugo's Wiles: or, the Coffee-House. A Comedy: as it was acted at His Highness's the Duke of York's Theater / written by Tho. St Serfe, Gent* (London: Printed for Henry Herringman, 1668), 17.
8. Ibid., 27.
9. Sir. J. Dalrymple, 'Historical and Biographical Anecdotes. [From the Second Volume of Sir J. Dalrymple's "Memoirs of Great Britain and Ireland", lately published.] Earl of Stair', in *The aberdeen magazine*, 310; 'Change Alley Carricatur'd: Or, a Dream about Jonathan's Coffee-House', in *The beauties of all the magazines selected. For the Year 1762. Including the several original comic pieces. To be continued the middle of every month. ...* vol. 1, London, Mcxxlii [1762]–4, Eighteenth Century Collections Online, Gale, CMU Libraries – library.cmich.edu: 436, accessed 3 November 2016, http://find.galegroup.com.cmich.idm.oclc.org/ecco/infomark.do?&source=gale&prodId=ECCO&userGroupName=lom_cmichu&tabID=T001&docId=CW125781645&type=multipage&contentSet=ECCOArticles&version=1.0&docLevel=FASCIMILE.
10. Steele and Addison devoted much attention to the persistent incivility of duelling among gentlemen in coffeehouses. As many coffeehouse brawls and duels often began with the custom of twisting buttons off waistcoats, *The Guardian* set about to restore a space bubble around gentlemen coffeehouse customers. Duellers even clubbed together in coffeehouses in order to survive Steele and Addison's attacks in the press. 'Thomas Swaggar' of the very popular Terrible Club of coffeehouse youths had terrorized the gaming coffeehouses of Drury-lane and Covent Garden with their habit of displaying unusually long swords at their sides. *The Guardian* editorial

column eventually turned public opinion against them but could not fully root out the youths from their coffeehouses; 'Tatler, No. 38, Thursday, July 7, 1709', in *Tatler*, 89; 'Guardian, No. 84, Wednesday, June 17, 1713', in *Guardian*, 122–3; 'Guardian, No. 131, Tuesday, August 11, 1713', in *Guardian*, 178; 'Guardian, No. 171, Saturday, September 26, 1713', in *Guardian*, 229.
11. Letter, Major John Pigot to Lord Greenville, Parliament Street Coffee House, 1 March 1793, HO 42/25/4, Folios 7–8, *Letter [to Lord Grenville, foreign secretary] from Major John Pigot, late of …*, The National Archives, Kew; Letter, Major John Pigot, Parliament Street Coffee House, HO 42/23/199, Folios 446–7, *Letter from [Major] John Pigot at Parliament Street Coffee House noting …*, The National Archives, Kew.
12. Letter, Charles Freindenberg, Admiralty Coffee House, 20 October 1768, ADM 106/1164/226, *Charles Freidenberg, Admiralty Coffee House. I brought timber in the ship Elizabeth …*, The National Archives, Kew; Letter, William Applegarth, Jerusalem Coffee House, ADM 106/1255/131, *William Applegarth, Jerusalem Coffee House. Asks for a review of the claimed short …*, The National Archives, Kew; Letter, Mr Boswell, 27 October 1735, ADM 106/866/276, *Mr Boswell. Has been visiting merchants' yards and the Change, enquiring of ships …*, The National Archives, Kew; Letter, James Potts, the Jamaica Coffee House, 6 October 1787, ADM 106/1291/280, *James Potts, the Jamaica Coffee House. Offers the Louisa for transporting troops and …*, The National Archives, Kew; Letter, Captain Philip Durell, Wills Coffee House, 13 January 1744, ADM 106/989/8, *Captain Philip Durell, Wills Coffee House, London. Request that the Richard and Thomas …*, The National Archives, Kew; Letter, [?Jacobite] Charles Quitwell [Quittwell] to James Baker, 12 May 1722, SP 35/72/37, *Former Reference E37. [?Jacobite] Charles Quitwell [Quittwell] to James Baker, merchant, …*, The National Archives, Kew; Letter, [Jacobite] Cane to James Baker, 13 May 1722, SP 35/72/38, *Former Reference E38. [Jacobite] Cane to James Baker, merchant, Burton's coffee house, …*, The National Archives, Kew.
13. William Shakespeare, *The Tragedy of Macbeth* (New York: American Book, 1895), 30.
14. *Murther Upon Murther*, 3–4.
15. *The New-York gazette*, 11 July 1726, pg. 2.
16. *The New-York gazette*, 17 December 1728, pg. 2.
17. *The New-York gazette*, 25 December 1727, pg. 3; *The New-York gazette*, 1 March 1730, pg. 1.
18. 'Change Alley Carricatur'd', in *The beauties*, 436.
19. Ibid., 435.
20. 'The Adventures of a Speculist, in his Journey through London', in *The beauties of all the magazines selected. For the Year 1762. Including the several original comic pieces. To be continued the middle of every month … vol. 1. London, Mcxxlii [1762]–4*, Eighteenth Century Collections Online, Gale, CMU Libraries – library.cmich. edu: 294.
21. Ellis, *The Coffee House*, 56.
22. Nevertheless, scholars have also acknowledged an increase in the political intensity of coffeehouses during the French Revolution; Gillian Russell and Clara Tuite, 'Introduction', in *Romantic Sociability*, 13; James Epstein, '"Equality and No King": Sociability and Sedition: The Case of John Frost', in *Romantic Sociability*, 43–8, 55.
23. Sir. J. Dalrymple, 'Historical and Biographical Anecdotes. [From the Second Volume of Sir J. Dalrymple's 'Memoirs of Great Britain and Ireland,' lately published.] Earl of Stair', in *The aberdeen magazine*, 310.

24. I have taken these instances from the press to be literal rather than satirical. Yet, if the advertisements were ever written as satirical jokes, they reveal the gendered sensibilities of the male readers who found them humorous; Lillywhite, *London Coffee Houses*, 246, 363–4.
25. Ibid., 725.
26. Ibid., 106–7.
27. Ibid., 317, 538, 654.
28. John and Linda Pelzer, 'The Coffee Houses of Augustan London', 42, 47.
29. Ibid., 40–1.
30. Ibid., 47.
31. Edward Ward, *The School of Politicks: or, the Humours of a Coffee-House* (London, 1698), 15–22.
32. Ibid., 15.
33. Ibid., 16.
34. Ibid., 21–2.
35. Ibid., 23–4.
36. Thomas Anburey, *Travels through the interior parts of America; in a series of letters. By an officer. A new edition*, vol. 2, London, MDCCXCI. [1791], Eighteenth Century Collections Online, Gale, CMU Libraries – library.cmich.edu, 407–8.
37. Ibid., 408.
38. Letter, Marine Captain David Johnstone, Cecil Street Coffee House, 24 May 1780, ADM 106/1257/274, *Marine Captain David Johnstone, Cecil Street Coffee House. Asks for a direction for …*, The National Archives, Kew; Letter, W Boswell, 10 June 1734, ADM 106/854/180, *W Boswell. He has been at the coffee houses and most of the merchant shipwrights' yards …*, The National Archives, Kew.
39. Letter, Allan Auld, Sword Blade Coffee House, 8 January 1772, ADM 106/1207/2, *Allan Auld, Sword Blade Coffee House, Birchin Lane, London. Is assignee to Joseph …*, The National Archives, Kew.
40. Ellis, *The Coffee House*, 57–8.
41. Letter, Charles Freindenberg, Admiralty Coffee House, 20 October 1768, ADM 106/1164/226, *Charles Freidenberg, Admiralty Coffee House. I brought timber in the ship Elizabeth …*, The National Archives, Kew; Letter, William Applegarth, Jerusalem Coffee House, ADM 106/1255/131, *William Applegarth, Jerusalem Coffee House. Asks for a review of the claimed short …*, The National Archives, Kew; Letter, Mr Boswell, 27 October 1735, ADM 106/866/276, *Mr Boswell. Has been visiting merchants' yards and the Change, enquiring of ships …*, The National Archives, Kew.
42. Letter, Marine Captain David Johnstone, Cecil Street Coffee House, 24 May 1780, ADM 106/1257/274, *Marine Captain David Johnstone, Cecil Street Coffee House. Asks for a direction for …*, The National Archives, Kew; Letter, Major John Pigot, Parliament Street Coffee House, 8 July 1793, HO 42/26/23, Folios 54–5, *Letter from Major John Pigot at the Parliament Street Coffee House asking …*, The National Archives, Kew.
43. Mr Brodie, Chapter Coffee House, 13 June 1783, ADM 106/1275/229, *Mr. Brodie, Chapter Coffee House, St. Pauls. Request for employment as a Surgeon*, The National Archives, Kew.
44. Letter, Captain Goodall, Will's Coffee-House, 1 April 1778, ADM 106/1243/344, *Captain Goodall, the Defiance, Will's Coffee-house. As no Surgeon is appointed to the …*, The National Archives, Kew.

45. Letter, David Ramsay Karr, Will's Coffee House, 5 November 1770, ADM 106/1191/215, *David Ramsay Karr, Surgeon of Portsmouth Yard, Will's Coffee House, Scotland Yard. Came ...*, The National Archives, Kew.
46. Letter, Allan Auld, Sword Blade Coffee House, 8 January 1772, ADM 106/1207/2, *Allan Auld, Sword Blade Coffee House, Birchin Lane, London. Is assignee to Joseph ...*, The National Archives, Kew.
47. Mr Brodie, Chapter Coffee House, 13 June 1783, ADM 106/1275/229, *Mr. Brodie, Chapter Coffee House, St. Pauls. Request for employment as a Surgeon*, The National Archives, Kew.
48. Letter, Marine Captain David Johnstone, Cecil Street Coffee House, 24 May 1780, ADM 106/1257/274, *Marine Captain David Johnstone, Cecil Street Coffee House. Asks for a direction for ...*, The National Archives, Kew.
49. Letter, William Morland, 24 July 1733, ADM 106/849/241, *William Morland, Purveyor. Has enquired for any ships bound to the Streights to attend ...*, The National Archives, Kew.
50. Ibid.
51. Letter, W. Boswell, 10 June 1734, ADM 106/854/180, *W Boswell. He has been at the coffee houses and most of the merchant shipwrights' yards ...*, The National Archives, Kew.
52. Letter, Captain J. Vaughan, Wills Coffee House, 27 March 1749, ADM 106/1077/19, *Captain J. Vaughan, Wills Coffee House. Is sending tickets for two men transferred from ...*, The National Archives, Kew.
53. Letter, Alexander Macpherson, Wills Coffee House, 22 May 1752, ADM 106/1102/137, *Alexander Macpherson, Wills Coffee House. Is sending all his books, which are not kept ...*, The National Archives, Kew.
54. Letter, John Bowyer, 5 March 1696, ADM 106/481/316, *John Bowyer, Purveyor, Deptford at Reading with Roger Howard, John Burroughs and Robert ...*, The National Archives, Kew.
55. Letter Thomas Taylor, 2 November 1790, HO 42/17/36, Folio 63, *Note from [Thomas Tayler of Lloyds Coffee House] reporting the arrival from St ...*, The National Archives, Kew.
56. Ellis, *The Coffee House*, 89.
57. Paul Kleber Monod, *Jacobitism and the English People, 1688–1788* (New York: Cambridge University Press, 1993), 103–6, 294.
58. Letter, [?Jacobite] Charles Quitwell [Quittwell] to James Baker, 12 May 1722, SP 35/72/37, *Former Reference E37. [?Jacobite] Charles Quitwell [Quittwell] to James Baker, merchant, ...*, The National Archives, Kew; Letter, [Jacobite] Cane to James Baker, 13 May 1722, SP 35/72/38, *Former Reference E38. [Jacobite] Cane to James Baker, merchant, Burton's coffee house, ...*, The National Archives, Kew; Letter, Chittwood to Mr Jamison under the Cover of Mr James Baker, 13 May 1722, SP 35/72/51, *Former Reference E39. Copy letter from [?Jacobite] Chittwood to Jemison under cover of ...*, The National Archives, Kew; Letter, Anonymous to Mr Sandford, 18 July 1722, SP 35/37/27, *Former reference F27. Copy of anonymous letter to Mr Sandford at the British Coffee ...*, The National Archives, Kew; Letter, Mr Chivers to Mr Sandford, 20 May 1722, SP 35/37/22, *Former reference F22. Copy from Mr Chivers to Mr Sandford at the British Coffee House ...*, The National Archives, Kew; Letter, Mr Cane to Mr Sandford, 16 May 1722, SP 35/37/23, *Former reference F23. Copy from Mr Cane to Mr Sandford at the British Coffee House near ...*, The National Archives, Kew.

59. Letter, Mr Cane to Mr Sandford, 16 May 1722, SP 35/37/23, *Former reference F23. Copy from Mr Cane to Mr Sandford at the British Coffee House near …*, The National Archives, Kew; Letter, Anonymous to Mrs Sandford, 28 July 1722, SP 35/37/32, *Former reference F32. Copy of anonymous letter to Mrs Sandford at the British Coffee …*, The National Archives, Kew.
60. Letter, Francis Sempill to Mr Sempill, 13 June 1722, SP 35/38/20, *Former reference G1a. Copy from Francis Sempill to Mr Sempill at Clair's [or Clare's] …*, The National Archives, Kew.
61. Letter, Francis Sempill to Mr Sempill, 1 July 1722, SP 35/38/21, *Former reference G2b. Copy from Francis Sempill to Mr Sempill at Clair's [or Clare's] …*, The National Archives, Kew.
62. Letter, Alexander Gordon to James Johnson, 10 May 1722, Boulogne, SP 35/72/34, *Former Reference E34. Extract of a letter from Alexander Gordon to James Johnson [alias …*, The National Archives, Kew.
63. Letter, [Unknown] to Monsieur Maisonneuve, 19 July 1722, SP 35/72/59, *Former Reference E59. [Unknown] to Monsieur Maisonneuve, at Mr Waters, banker, Paris, …*, The National Archives, Kew.
64. Letter, James Potts, the Jamaica Coffee House, 6 October 1787, ADM 106/1291/280, *James Potts, the Jamaica Coffee House. Offers the Louisa for transporting troops and …*, The National Archives, Kew.
65. Letter, Captain Philip Durell, Wills Coffee House, 13 January 1744, ADM 106/989/8, *Captain Philip Durell, Wills Coffee House, London. Request that the Richard and Thomas …*, The National Archives, Kew.
66. Letter, Mr Crauford to Lord Carteret, 30 May 1722, SP 35/37/1, *Former reference F1. Extract from Mr Crauford to Lord Carteret. Captain Kelly frequents …*, The National Archives, Kew; Letter, E. Carleton to Captain Leeves, 2 February 1746, SP 36/81/1/22, Folios 22–3, *E. Carleton to Captain Leeves at the Tennis Court Coffee House, Whitehall ….*, The National Archives, Kew.
67. Letter, Captain John Chamady [Calmady?], Wills Coffee House, 7 April 1746, ADM 106/1026/186, *Captain John Chamady, Wills Coffee House. Receipt of letter to deliver the pay and slop …*, The National Archives, Kew.
68. Letter, Captain John Calmady, Wills Coffee House, 3 May 1746, ADM 106/1026/210, *Captain John Calmady, Wills Coffee House, Scotland Yard. Has sent the Weymouth's muster …*, The National Archives, Kew.
69. Letter, Major John Pigot, Parliament Street Coffee House, 8 July 1793, HO 42/26/23, Folios 54–5, *Letter from Major John Pigot at the Parliament Street Coffee House asking …*, The National Archives, Kew.
70. Letter, Major John Pigot to Lord Greenville, Parliament Street Coffee House, 1 March 1793, HO 42/25/4, Folios 7–8, *Letter [to Lord Grenville, foreign secretary] from Major John Pigot, late of …*, The National Archives, Kew; Letter, Major John Pigot, Parliament Street Coffee House, HO 42/23/199, Folios 446–7, *Letter from [Major] John Pigot at Parliament Street Coffee House noting …*, The National Archives, Kew.
71. Letter, [Lieutenant] William Nedham to Evan Nepean, 9 January 1793, HO 42/24/32, Folios 66–7, *Letter from [Lieutenant] William Nedham at York Coffee House, St James's …*, The National Archives, Kew; ADM 106/1188/250, 1 October 1770, *Captain J. Hollwell of the Prince of Wales, Wills Coffee House. John Cowling, his 1st …*, The National Archives, Kew.
72. SP 35/15/79, 12 March 1719, *Information of David Lloyd, coffee house keeper near Ludgate [London] reporting what …*, The National Archives, Kew.

73. Letter, RS to unknown, 10 March 1703, SP 42/7/25, 'A copy of a letter signed RS dated at Lloyd's Coffee House' ... objecting to the ..., The National Archives, Kew; HO 42/24/265, Folios 644–5, 24 February 1793, Letter from Thomas Tayler [master] of Lloyd's Coffee House reporting ..., The National Archives, Kew.
74. HO 42/23/307, Folios 663–4, 1792, Anonymous memorandum containing information about seditionists: Stewart, ..., The National Archives, Kew.
75. 'Tatler, No. 78, Saturday, 8 October 1709', in Tatler, 166–7.

4 Coffee-women, licensure and a polite public sphere

1. Cowan, *Social Life*, 113–20, 147–51; Lois G. Schwoerer, 'The Right to Resist: Whig Resistance Theory, 1688 to 1694', in *Political Discourse in Early Modern Britain*, ed. Nicholas Phillipson and Quentin Skinner (New York: Cambridge University Press, 1993), 240–1; Robert Oresko, 'The House of Savoy in Search for a Royal Crown in the Seventeenth Century', in *Royal and Republican Sovereignty in Early Modern Europe: Essays in Memory of Ragnhild Hatton*, ed. Robert Oresko, G. C. Gibbs and H. M. Scott (New York: Cambridge University Press, 1997), 349; James M. Rosenheim, *The Emergence of a Ruling Order: English Landed Society, 1650–1750* (New York: Longman, 1998), 9, 61, 74, 198, 256; Joad Raymond, *Pamphlets and Pamphleteering in Early Modern Britain* (New York: Cambridge University Press, 2003), 88, 134, 160, 362; Geoffrey Holmes, 'Introduction: Post-Revolution Britain and the Historian', in *Britain after the Glorious Revolution 1689–1714*, ed. Geoffrey Holmes (New York: Macmillan St. Martin's Press, 1969), 12–13; J. H. Plumb, *Origins of Political Stability: England 1675–1725* (Boston, MA: Houghton Mifflin, 1967), 36; G. V. Bennett, *The Tory Crisis in Church and State 1688–1730: The Career of Francis Atterbury Bishop of Rochester* (Oxford: Clarendon Press, 1975), 60; Tony Claydon, *Europe and the Making of England, 1660–1760* (New York: Cambridge University Press, 2007), 6, 28–9, 44–5, 220, 288.
2. Cowan, *Social Life*, 101–2, 199–24, 237, 242–6; Klein, *Shaftesbury and the Culture of Politeness*, 12; Pincus, ' "Coffee Politicians Does Create" ', 822–30; Klein, 'Coffeehouse Civility', 39.
3. Barrell, 'Coffee-House Politicians', 207–16.
4. Klein, 'Coffeehouse Civility', 30–51; Klein, 'Politeness', 875–94; Pincus, ' "Coffee Politicians Does Create" ', 807–14.
5. Copley, 'Commerce', 63–73; Berry, 'Rethinking Politeness', 65–81.
6. Cowan uses Addison and Steele's polite suggestions in *Spectator* to argue that Whigs worried that coffeehouse life was actually unruly and effeminate. Nevertheless, their entrance into the literary world of coffeehouse life left an enduring impression within the gazette culture of British coffeehouses; Cowan, *Social Life*, 225–30.
7. George Colman, *The Connoisseur. By Mr. Town, Critic and Censor-General, Numb. 1, Thursday, January 31, 1754* (London: Printed for R. Baldwin, 1755–6), 1–5; Lillywhite, *London Coffee House*, 143–5, 330–5, 395–7, 500–1, 503; Ukers, *All about Coffee*, 80–1; McCusker, 'The Business Press in England before 1775', 207, 224–5; McCusker, 'The Early History of "Lloyd's List" ', 429; Breen, *The Marketplace of Revolution*, 22–3, 55, 78–9, 166–8.
8. Ukers, *All about Coffee*, 73; Barrell, 'Coffee-House Politicians'; Barrell, 'Coffee-House Politicians', 206–10, 213–26; By a Coffee Man (n.d.), *The Case Between the Proprietors*

of News-papers, and the Coffee-men of London and Westminster, Fairly Stated ... (R. Walker at the White Hart, adjoyning to the Anodyne Necklace, without Temple Bar, 1729), 1–6, 19, 25–6.

9. *The New-York gazette*, 25 December 1727, pg. 3; *The New-York gazette*, 1 March 1730, pg. 1; Letter, Ship-owners at Jerusalem Coffee House to the Court, 7 June 1770, India Office Records and Private Papers, IOR/E/1/53 ff. 272–274v, *Letters 149–150 Proposed additions to Company charter parties submitted to the Court by several ship-owners meeting at the Jerusalem Coffee House in London*, British Library; Letter, February 1718, India Office Records and Private Papers, IOR/E/1/9 ff. 80–81v, *Letter 47 Petition of several merchants and traders in coffee to the House of Commons concerning goods run on board the London Merchant*, British Library.

10. Goodman, *Republic of Letters*, 74–5, 99, 101, 105; Dena Goodman, *Becoming a Woman in the Age of Letters* (Ithaca, NY: Cornell University Press, 2009), 8, 105–26, 133, 247, 274–5, 283–4, 295–301; Reinke-Williams, *Women, Work and Sociability*, 3, 41, 45, 66, 72, 74, 107, 117, 125, 127, 135; Berry, 'Polite Consumption', 375–7; Pincus, '"Coffee Politicians Does Create"', 815–16; Deborah Hertz, *Jewish High Society in Old Regime Berlin* (Syracuse, NY: Syracuse University Press, 2005), 1–2, 51–2, 81–2, 87, 99, 125–6, 131–3, 162, 177, 180, 186, 205.

11. Although the new sociability did alter the godly communalism of early Puritan morality, it did not fully dismantle the foundations of American social morality, for as David Konig states, 'the colony did not fall into chaos'. Moving from communalism to the male world of juries, litigation and chartered liberties, in Konig's words, 'saved them from Anglicanism and Stuart divine right monarchy on the one side and from social disintegration and Quaker or anabaptist heresy on the other'. Konig, *Law and Society in Puritan Massachusetts*, 89–90, 96–7.

12. Purdie, *Virginia Gazette*, 15 August 1777 – pg. 3, col. 2; Purdie and Dixon, *Virginia Gazette*, 6 May 1773 – pg. 3, col. 1; Purdie, *Virginia Gazette*, 5 July 1776 – pg. 3, col. 3; Rind, *Virginia Gazette*, 12 March 1772 – pg. 3, col. 1; *Proceedings and Acts of the General Assembly*, September 1704–April 1706: volume 26, pg. 582, Archives of Maryland Online, accessed 18 November 2021, http://aomol.msa.maryland.gov/000 001/000026/html/am26--582.html; Shields, *Civil Tongues*, 55; Davis, *The Colonial Coffeehouse*, 27–8.

13. J. G. A. Pocock, *The Machiavellian Moment: Florentine Political Thought and the Atlantic Republican Tradition* (Princeton, NJ: Princeton University Press, 1975), 4, 54, 56, 195–7, 211; James Von Horn Melton, *The Rise of the Public in Enlightenment Europe* (New York: Cambridge University Press, 2001), 20–1; Langford, *A Polite and Commercial People*, 66, 69, 116–17, 199–203, 381; Hancock, *Oceans of Wine*, 275–9, 285, 294, 317–39, 387–9.

14. Macaulay, *The History of England*, vol. 1, 472–3, 673; Peter Clark, *British Clubs and Societies, 1580–1800: The Origins of an Associational World* (Oxford: Clarendon Press, 2000), 1–3, 13, 40–1, 69–72, 114–29; Shields, *Civil Tongues*, 177–80; Lillywhite, *London Coffee House*, 209–12, 330–5, 363–6, 395–7, 718, 726–7.

15. Purdie, *Virginia Gazette*, 15 August 1777 – pg. 3, col. 2; Purdie and Dixon, *Virginia Gazette*, 6 May 1773 – pg. 3, col. 1; *Proceedings and Acts of the General Assembly*, September 1704–April 1706: volume 26, pg. 582, Archives of Maryland Online, accessed 11 November 2021, http://aomol.msa.maryland.gov/000001/000026/html/am26--582.html; Shields, *Civil Tongues*, 55; Davis, *The Colonial Coffeehouse*, 27–8.

16. Steven Pincus closed this debate by arguing that women moved fluidly through coffeehouse social life. Other scholars like Cowan find such an assertion too

ambitious, but the fact that women were somehow connected to coffeehouse life is now finally recognized; Pincus, '"Coffee Politicians Does Create"', 815–16; Lawrence E. Klein, 'Gender and the Public/Private Distinction in the Eighteenth Century: Some Questions about Evidence and Analytic Procedure', in *Eighteenth-Century Studies*, vol. 29, no. 1 (Fall 1995): 103–5; Cowan, *Social Life*, 246–54; Markman Ellis, 'Coffee-Women, *The Spectator* and the Public Sphere in the Early Eighteenth Century', in *Women, Writing and the Public Sphere, 1700–1830*, ed. Elizabeth Edgar, Charlotte Grant, Clíona Ó Gallchoir and Penny Warburton (Cambridge: Cambridge University Press, 2001), 31–2.

17. Goodman, *Republic of Letters*, 74–5, 99, 101, 105; Goodman, *Becoming a Woman*, 8, 105–26, 133, 247, 274–5, 283–4, 295–301; Reinke-Williams, *Women, Work and Sociability*, 3, 41, 45, 66, 72, 74, 107, 117, 125, 127, 135; Berry, 'Polite Consumption', 375–7.
18. Lillywhite, *London Coffee House*, 209–12, 363–6, 718, 726–7; Fielding, *The Coffee-House Politician*, 8; Pincus, '"Coffee Politicians Does Create"', 815–16; Barrell, 'Coffee-House Politicians', 211–12; Cowan, *Social Life*, 248–54.
19. Cowan, *Social Life*, 251.
20. *A Dissertation Upon Drunkenness*, 16.
21. Purdie, *Virginia Gazette*, 15 August 1777 – pg. 3, col. 2; Purdie and Dixon, *Virginia Gazette*, 6 May 1773 – pg. 3, col. 1; *Proceedings and Acts of the General Assembly*, September 1704–April 1706: volume 26, pg. 582, Archives of Maryland Online, accessed 18 November 2021, http://aomol.msa.maryland.gov/000001/000026/html/am26--582.html; Shields, *Civil Tongues*, 55; Davis, *The Colonial Coffeehouse*, 27–8.
22. Reinke-Williams, *Women, Work and Sociability*, 3, 41, 45, 66, 72, 74, 107, 117, 125, 127, 135; Ellis, 'Coffee-Women', 31–2; Mary Beth Norton, *Separated by Their Sex: Women in Public and Private in the Colonial Atlantic World* (Ithaca, NY: Cornell University Press, 2011), 3–5, 78–82, 91–2, 112–15; Dayton, *Women before the Bar*, 64–6, 137; Terry L. Snyder, *Brabbling Women: Disorderly Speech and the Law in Early Virginia* (Ithaca, NY: Cornell University Press, 2003), 10–14, 38, 143; Thomas A. Foster, *Sex and the Eighteenth-Century Man: Massachusetts and the History of Sexuality in America* (Boston, MA: Beacon Press, 2006), xix, 101–4, 114–15; Anne S. Lombard, *Making Manhood: Growing up Male in Colonial New England* (Cambridge, MA: Harvard University Press, 2003), 78–9, 103, 158.
23. Berry, *Polite Consumption*, 375–7.
24. Ibid., 379–83.
25. Ibid., 382–4.
26. Simon Middleton and Billy G. Smith, 'Introduction', in *Class Matters: Early North America and the Atlantic World*, ed. Simon Middleton and Billy G. Smith (Philadelphia: University of Pennsylvania Press, 2008), 1–15.
27. Ibid., 14.
28. Konstantin Dierks, 'Middle-Class Formation in Eighteenth-Century North America', in *Class Matters*, 104.
29. Ibid., 106–8.
30. Jennifer L. Goloboy, 'Business Friendships and Individualism in a Mercantile Class of Citizens in Charleston', in *Class Matters*, 111–12, 115.
31. Andrew M. Schocket, 'Corporations and the Coalescence of an Elite Class in Philadelphia'; and Goloboy, 'Business Friendships', 111, 124–7.
32. Goloboy, 'Business Friendships', 115.
33. Lillywhite, *London Coffee Houses*, 206.

34. Ibid., 488, 567.
35. Ibid., 713.
36. Romans 1:24 (King James).
37. 'Spectator, No. 87, Saturday, June 9, 1711', in *Spectator*, vol. 1, 140.
38. Lillywhite, *London Coffee Houses*, 596–7; Berry, 'Rethinking Politeness', 70–6.
39. Berry, 'Rethinking Politeness', 68, 75.
40. Ibid., 76.
41. Ibid., 68.
42. Quoted in Ellis, 'Coffee-Women', 35–6.
43. Lillywhite, *London Coffee Houses*, 488, 567, 597, 713.
44. Shields, *Civil Tongues*, 55; Davis, *The Colonial Coffeehouse*, 28.
45. Davis, *The Colonial Coffeehouse*, 28.
46. Ibid.
47. Ibid., 27.
48. As in the reference to 'Alderman Hodges's Cook-maid' in the Bowman Coffeehouse; Ellis, 'Pasqua Rosee's Coffee-House', 2.
49. Robert Bell, *The Annotated Edition of the English Poets* (London: John W. Parker and Son, West Strand, 1857), 184; Ellis, 'Coffee-Women', 31–9.
50. Ellis, 'Coffee-Women', 32, 37; Ellis, *The Coffee House*, 67.
51. *The Character of a Coffee-House, with the Symptoms of a Town-Wit*, 5.
52. Serfe, *Tarugo's Wiles*, 23–4.
53. *The Maidens Complaint against Coffee*, 3.
54. Pincus, '"Coffee Politicians Does Create"', 815–16; Julia G. Longe, ed., *Martha Lady Giffard: Her Life and Correspondence* (London: George Allen, 1911), 250–1.
55. Pincus, '"Coffee Politicians Does Create"', 816.
56. Ibid.
57. Barrell, 'Coffee-House Politicians', 211–12.
58. Barrell began his article with this adage; ibid., 206.
59. Cowan, *Social Life*, 248–54.
60. Stewart, 'Other Centres', 151.
61. Arkle, 'The Early Coffee Houses of Liverpool', 10.
62. Wilson, *The Sense of the People*, 47.
63. Lillywhite, *The London Coffee House*, 209–12, 363–6, 718, 726–7; Fielding, *The Coffee-House Politician*, 8.
64. Van Horn, *Out of the Past*, 501–3.
65. Ibid., 196.
66. Purdie and Dixon, *Virginia Gazette*, 4 July 1771 – pg. 1, col. 3; Samuel Wilson, Jr, 'Maspero's Exchange: Its Predecessors and Successors', *Louisiana History*, vol. 30 (1989): 197–200.
67. *The Boston-Gazette*, Monday, 1 April 1776, pg. 3, col. 2; *The Boston-Gazette*, Monday, 19 August 1776, pg. 2, col. 2; Purdie, *Virginia Gazette*, 13 June 1766 – pg. 2, col. 2.
68. *Virginia Gazette, or American Advertiser* (Richmond), 21 February 1784, *The Papers of George Washington Digital Edition*, accessed 5 August 2017, http://rotunda.upress.virginia.edu/founders/GEWN-01-03-02-0003-0010-0011.
69. Purdie, *Virginia Gazette*, 15 August 1777 – pg. 3, col. 2.
70. Purdie and Dixon, *Virginia Gazette*, 6 May 1773 – pg. 3, col. 1.
71. *Proceedings and Acts of the General Assembly*, September 1704–April 1706: volume 26, pg. 582, Archives of Maryland Online, accessed 18 November 2021, http://aomol.msa.maryland.gov/000001/000026/html/am26--582.html.

72. Ibid.
73. Purdie, *Virginia Gazette*, 5 July 1776 – pg. 3, col. 3; Rind, *Virginia Gazette*, 12 March 1772 – pg. 3, col. 1.
74. Purdie and Dixon, *Virginia Gazette*, 30 April 1772 – pg. 3, col. 1; Purdie and Dixon, *Virginia Gazette*, 14 October 1773 – pg. 2, col. 3.
75. Purdie and Dixon, *Virginia Gazette*, 14 October 1773 – pg. 2, col. 3.
76. Ellis, *The Coffee House*, 66–8.
77. Callow, *Old London Taverns*, 6–7.
78. Jonathan Swift, 'Modern History Sourcebook: Jonathan Swift (1667–1745): Hints Towards An Essay On Conversation, 1713', *Internet Modern History Sourcebook*, Paul Halsall, August 1998, Harvard Classics series, 1909, https://sourcebooks.fordham.edu/halsall/mod/1713swift-conversation.asp.
79. Ibid.
80. William Hickes, *Coffee-House Jests. By the Author of the Oxford-Jests. This may be printed. Mar. 30, 1677. Roger L'Estrange* (London: Printed for Benj. Thrale at the Bible in the Poultrey near Cheapside, 1677), 8.
81. Copley, 'Commerce', 73.
82. Ibid.
83. 'Tatler, No. 11, Thursday, May 5, 1709', in *Tatler*, 35; 'Tatler, No. 6, Saturday, April 23, 1709', in *Tatler*, 21.
84. 'Tatler, No. 60, Saturday, August 27, 1709', in *Tatler*, 132.
85. 'Tatler, No. 42, Saturday, July 16, 1709', in *Tatler*, 97.
86. 'Guardian, No. 35, Tuesday, April 21, 1713', in *Guardian*, 52.
87. 'Martha Careful and Caelia Shortface: Printed in *The American Weekly Mercury*, January 28, 1728/9', *Franklin Papers*; accessed 18 November 2021, https://franklinpapers.org/framedVolumes.jsp.
88. Ibid.
89. Goodman, *Republic of Letters*, 74–5, 99, 101, 105.
90. Goodman, *Republic of Letters*, 105; Goodman, *Becoming a Woman in the Age of Letters*, 8, 105–26, 133, 247, 274–5, 283–4, 295–301.
91. Goodman, *Republic of Letters*, 119, 130.
92. Benedetta Craveri, *The Age of Conversation*, trans. Teresa Waugh (New York: New York Review Books), 337–76.
93. Hertz, *Jewish High Society*, 1–2, 51–2, 81–2, 87, 99, 125–6, 131–3, 162, 177, 180, 186, 205.
94. Christopher H. Johnson, *Becoming Bourgeois: Love, Kinship, and Power in Provincial France, 1670–1880* (Ithaca, NY: Cornell University Press, 2015), 4, 31–6, 41–3, 50–1, 84, 98–9, 126, 264; R. R. Palmer, *The Age of the Democratic Revolution: A Political History of Europe and America, 1760–1800, the Challenge* (Princeton, NJ: Princeton University Press, 1959), 77–9.
95. Darnton, *Literary Underground*, 1–16, 20–6, 39.
96. Landes, *Women and the Public Sphere*, 40–5, 104–7, 113, 118–19, 140–6.
97. Susanne Schmid, *British Literary Salons of the Late Eighteenth and Earl Nineteenth Centuries* (New York: Palgrave Macmillan, 2013), 72, 76, 81.
98. Ibid., 72–6, 78–9, 82–6, 92–5, 98–102.
99. Russell Kirk, *The Conservative Mind: From Burke to Eliot*, 2nd edn (Washington, DC: Regnery, 1986; reprinted 2001), 20–2.
100. Benedict Anderson, *Imagined Communities: Reflections on the Origin and Spread of Nationalism* (New York: Verso, 1995), 7.

101. Edmund Burke, *Selected Writings and Speeches*, ed. Peter J. Stanlis (Washington DC: Regnery Gateway, 1963), 427, 458.
102. Martin Price, 'Manners, Morals, and Jane Austen', *Nineteenth-Century Fiction*, vol. 30, no. 3, Jane Austen 1775–1975 (December 1975): 278, accessed 19 March 2016, http://www.jstor.org.cmich.idm.oclc.org/stable/2933070.
103. Schmid, *British Literary Salons*, 103–4, 109–10.
104. Landes, *Women and the Public Sphere*, 127–33.

5 Coffee-men, lobbyists and conmen of empire

1. Parks, *Virginia Gazette*, 1 July 1737 – pg. 2, col. 2.
2. Parks, *Virginia Gazette*, 4 September 1746 – pg. 3, col. 1.
3. Purdie, *Virginia Gazette*, 23 May 1766 – pg. 2, col. 3.
4. Western Manuscripts, Add MS 38340, Folio 98, *Vol. CLI (ff. 391). 1767,1768. includes:ff. 1–203 passim Navy; England: Various papers rel. to: 1766–1768. ff. 1–25 Admiralty: Papers rel. to: 1766–1767. f. 6 Brandy: Accompts of brandy imported, etc.: 1764-circ. 1785. f. 7 Rum: Imports of, to Grea ...*, British Library; Letter, Managers of Lloyds Coffee House to the 1st Earl of Liverpool, 1798, Western Manuscripts, Add MS 38310, Folio 221, *Vol. CXXI (ff. 268). 23 July 1787–31 Jan. 1799.includes:ff. 1, 31, 51, 232 Charles Jenkinson, 1st Earl of Liverpool: Correspondence with Marquis Cornwallis: 1779–1798: Copies (except the first). ff. 1, 31, 51, 232 Charles Cornwallis, Viscount Brom*, British Library; Letter, Managers of Lloyds Coffee House to the 1st Earl of Liverpool, 1798; Western Manuscripts, Add MS 38232, Folios 60, 66, *Vol. XLIII (ff. 397). Apr.- Dec. 1798. Thomas Lack, Secretary to the Committee of the Privy Council for Trade: Letters to the 1st Earl of Liverpool: circ. 1793–1806.includes:ff. 1, 2, 8,53,150, 170, 199, 203, 210, 263, 304 b, 368 John de Blaquière, Li*, British Library; Letter, February 1718, India Office Records and Private Papers, IOR/E/1/9 ff. 80–81v, *Letter 47 Petition of several merchants and traders in coffee to the House of Commons concerning goods run on board the London Merchant*, British Library.
5. Letter, Charles Carkesse to Thomas Woolley, 27 August 1712, India Office Records and Private Papers, IOR/E/1/4 ff. 193–195v, *Letters 110–111 Secretary Charles Carkesse at the Customs House in London to Thomas Woolley forwarding a copy of the Commissioners' minutes relating to the Company's Coffee. Related papers attached*, British Library; Letter, Charles Carkesse to Thomas Woolley, 26 September 1712, India Office Records and Private Papers, IOR/E/1/4 ff. 241–242v, *Letter 139 Secretary Charles Carkesse at the Customs House in London to Thomas Woolley concerning the coffee and tea in the Company's warehouses*, British Library.
6. *The New-York gazette*, 25 December 1727, pg. 3; *The New-York gazette*, 1 March 1730, pg. 1; Parks, *Virginia Gazette*, 1 July 1737 – pg. 2, col. 2; Parks, *Virginia Gazette*, 4 September 1746 – pg. 3, col. 1; Purdie, *Virginia Gazette*, 23 May 1766 – pg. 2, col. 3.
7. Troy Bickham, 'Eating the Empire: Intersections of Food, Cookery and Imperialism in Eighteenth-Century Britain." *Past & Present*, vol. 198, no. 1 (2008): 73–7, 79, 81, 83.
8. Letter, February 1718, India Office Records and Private Papers, IOR/E/1/9 ff. 80–81v, *Letter 47 Petition of several merchants and traders in coffee to the House of Commons concerning goods run on board the London Merchant*, British Library.
9. Letter, Francis White to Thomas Woolley, 12 March 1718, India Office Records and Private Papers, IOR/E/1/9 ff. 128–128v, *Letter 76 Francis White in London to Thomas*

Woolley requesting he move two of the Directors to go to the Customs House to set a value to the coffee on board the Princess Amelia, British Library.
10. Letter, Charles Carkesse to Thomas Woolley, 27 August 1712, India Office Records and Private Papers, IOR/E/1/4 ff. 193–195v, *Letters 110–111 Secretary Charles Carkesse at the Customs House in London to Thomas Woolley forwarding a copy of the Commissioners' minutes relating to the Company's Coffee. Related papers attached*, British Library; Letter, Charles Carkesse to Thomas Woolley, 26 September 1712, India Office Records and Private Papers, IOR/E/1/4 ff. 241–242v, *Letter 139 Secretary Charles Carkesse at the Customs House in London to Thomas Woolley concerning the coffee and tea in the Company's warehouses*, British Library.
11. Letter, Charles Carkesse to Thomas Woolley, 21 June 1721, India Office Records and Private Papers, IOR/E/1/12 ff. 305–306v, *Letter 170 Secretary Charles Carkesse at the Customs House in London to Thomas Woolley requesting that Captain Nicholas Luhorne and his mate Charles Hudson attend the Commissioners of the Customs to be examined in the case of Robert Corner late tidesman who was dismissed on a complaint of stealing some coffee on board the Princess Anne*, British Library.
12. Letter, Ship-owners at Jerusalem Coffee House to the Court, 7 June 1770, India Office Records and Private Papers, IOR/E/1/53 ff. 272–274v, *Letters 149–150 Proposed additions to Company charter parties submitted to the Court by several ship-owners meeting at the Jerusalem Coffee House in London*, British Library.
13. Western Manuscripts, Add MS 38340, Folio 98, *Vol. CLI (ff. 391). 1767,1768. includes:ff. 1–203 passim Navy; England: Various papers rel. to: 1766–1768. ff. 1–25 Admiralty: Papers rel. to: 1766–1767. f. 6 Brandy: Accompts of brandy imported, etc.: 1764-circ. 1785. f. 7 Rum: Imports of, to Grea ...*, British Library; Letter, Managers of Lloyds Coffee House to the 1st Earl of Liverpool, 1798, Western Manuscripts, Add MS 38310, Folio 221, *Vol. CXXI (ff. 268). 23 July, 1787–31 Jan. 1799.includes:ff. 1, 31, 51, 232 Charles Jenkinson, 1st Earl of Liverpool: Correspondence with Marquis Cornwallis: 1779–1798.: Copies (except the first). ff. 1, 31, 51, 232 Charles Cornwallis, Viscount Brom*, British Library; Letter, Managers of Lloyds Coffee House to the 1st Earl of Liverpool, 1798; Western Manuscripts, Add MS 38232, Folios 60, 66, *Vol. XLIII (ff. 397). Apr.–Dec. 1798.Thomas Lack, Secretary to the Committee of the Privy Council for Trade: Letters to the 1st Earl of Liverpool: circ. 1793–1806.includes:ff. 1, 2, 8,53,150, 170, 199, 203, 210, 263, 304 b, 368 John de Blaquière, Li*, British Library; Letter, Feb. 1718, India Office Records and Private Papers, IOR/E/1/9 ff. 80–81v, *Letter 47 Petition of several merchants and traders in coffee to the House of Commons concerning goods run on board the London Merchant*, British Library.
14. Maya Jasanoff, *Liberty's Exiles: American Loyalists in the Revolutionary World* (New York: Vintage Books, 2012), 139–40, 241, 338, 348; Lillywhite, *London Coffee Houses*, 216–20, 305–9, 551.
15. *The New-York gazette*, 25 December 1727, pg. 3; *The New-York gazette*, 1 March 1730, pg. 1.
16. Letter, Timothy Harris, Keeper of the Coffee House in Ormond Street, London, and Prisoner in the King's Bench, Southwark to Sir H. Sloane, 1723/4, Western Manuscripts, Sloane MS 4047, Folio 155, *Sir Hans Sloane, Baronet: Original correspondence, chronologically arranged: 17th-18th centt.includes:f. 1 Jean François Le Feure, MD: Letters to Sir H. Sloane: 1723, and n.d.: Fr. f. 3 Thomas Hearne, antiquary: Letters to Sir H. Sloane: 1710–1731/2*, British Library.
17. Klein, 'Politeness', 883.
18. Ibid., 885.

19. Ellis, *The Coffee House*, 59–62, 66.
20. Ibid., 60; Ukers, *All about Coffee*, 73.
21. Barrell, 'Coffee-House Politicians', 206–10, 213–26.
22. Colman, *The Connoisseur*, 1.
23. By a Coffee Man, *The Case Between the Proprietors*, 10.
24. Colman, 'The Connoisseur, 1.
25. Ibid., 2.
26. Ibid., 2–3.
27. Ibid., 4.
28. Ibid., 5.
29. Ibid., 4.
30. Ibid., 4–5.
31. Ellis, *The Coffee House*, 115.
32. Cowan, *Social Life*, 173–4.
33. By a Coffee Man, *The Case Between the Proprietors*, 19, 25.
34. Ibid.
35. Ibid., 22.
36. Ibid., 27, 30.
37. Ibid., 29, 31.
38. Ibid., 29, 34.
39. Ibid., 34–5.
40. Ellis, *The Coffee House*, 90.
41. Melton, *The Rise of the Public*, 19–21; *Daily Post* (London, England: 1719), Library of Congress, accessed 18 November 2021, https://catalog.loc.gov/vwebv/holdingsInfo?searchId=21497&recCount=25&recPointer=1&bibId=17498315; *The London Evening-post*, Numb. [1] (12 December 1727) – Ceased with 13 March 1806 issue, (London [England]: Printed by R. Nutt, 1727–), Library of Congress, 18 November 2021r, https://catalog.loc.gov/vwebv/holdingsInfo?searchId=21581&recCount=25&recPointer=0&bibId=11337105; *Daily Advertiser*, London: Printed for J. Jenour, at No. 33, opposite St. Dunstan's Church, Fleet-Street. 3 February 1730- (September), 1798. 1743; 1796. On 3 reels, Gale microfilms, accessed 18 November 2021, https://catalog.loc.gov/vwebv/holdingsInfo?searchId=21607&recCount=25&recPointer=0&bibId=14642384; *The Gentleman's Magazine* (London: Printed by F. Jeffries, etc., 1731–1907), Hathi Trust Digital Library, accessed 19 September 2018, https://catalog.hathitrust.org/Record/000542092.
42. Melton, *The Rise of the Public*, 23, 27–8; Wilson, *The Sense of the People*, 41–2.
43. Wilson, *The Sense of the People*, 12–13, 28–41, 54–5, 62–4, 70, 229, 243, 259, 266–7, 315, 378–80.
44. Benedict Anderson, *Imagined Communities: Reflections on the Origin and Spread of Nationalism* (New York: Verso, 1995), 7, 33–40; Wilson, *The Sense of the People*, 40–1.
45. Pincus, ' "Coffee Does Politicians Create" ', 807–14; Harris, 'The Grecian', 1–2; Klein, 'Coffeehouse Civility', 31–4, 43–51; Copley, 'Commerce', 63–73; Berry, 'Rethinking Politeness', 65–81; Cowan, *Social Life*, 149.
46. Klein, 'Politeness', 873–5; Davis, 'The Colonial Coffeehouse', 27–8; Dixon and Hunter, *Virginia Gazette*, 15 August 1777 – pg. 6, col. 1.
47. Swift, of course, was a Tory, not a Whig; Swift, 'Hints Towards An Essay On Conversation'.
48. Mary Beth Norton seems to consider the term 'trifling' as an irritant to Dunton, a distraction from the more scholarly interests in the *Athenian Mercury*. However,

a close reading reveals that he desired to expand his audience to urban readers by discussing, however reluctantly, the behaviours of London's 'trifling' theater-goes and coffeehouse ramblers; Norton, *Separated by Their Sex*, 79–91, 120; Ellis, *The Coffee House*, 165.
49. 'Guardian, No. 140, Friday, August 21, 1713', in *Guardian*, 189–90.
50. 'Guardian, No. 85, Thursday, June 18, 1713', in *Guardian*, 124.
51. Colman, *The Connoisseur*, 4.
52. Ibid., 5.
53. Joseph M. Adelman, *Revolutionary Networks: The Business and Politics of Printing the News, 1763–1789* (Baltimore: Johns Hopkins University Press, 2019), 3–11, 21–43.
54. Ibid., 82.
55. Middleton and Lombard, *Colonial America: A History to 1763*, Fourth Edition (Malden: Wiley-Blackwell, 2011), 328–9.
56. *The Maryland Gazette*, 16 December 1728, Number 65, 1.
57. Ibid.
58. Middleton and Lombard, *Colonial America*, 328–9; *The Maryland Gazette*, 24 June 1729, Number 93.
59. Middleton and Lombard, *Colonial America*, 328–9.
60. Dixon and Hunter, *Virginia Gazette*, 10 October 1777 – pg. 3, col. 1.
61. Purdie and Dixon, *Virginia Gazette*, 22 July 1773 – pg. 3, col. 2.
62. Mather, *Everlasting Gospel*; John Ogilvie, *Providence; A guide to eternal glory…*; *Doctrine of absolute predestination stated and asserted: with a preliminary discourse on the divine attributes*; *A sermon, in which the union of the colonies is considered and recommended: and the bad consequences of divisions are represented: delivered on the public thanksgiving: November sixteenth, 1775* (New-York: Printed by Hodge and Shober, for Samuel Loudon, on Hunter's Key, 1773); *New York (Colony) General assembly, 1773* (New-York: Printed by John Holt, near the Coffee house, 1773).
63. James Rivington, *A catalogue of books, sold by Rivington and Brown, booksellers and stationers from London, at their stores, over against the Golden Key, in Hanover-square, New-York: and over against the London coffee-house, in Philadelphia …* (Philadelphia: Heinrich Miller?, 1762); *Speech intended to have been spoken by the Bishop of St. Asaph, on the bill for altering the charters of the colony of Massachusetts Bay …* (Philadelphia: London, printed: Philadelphia, Reprinted and Sold by Benjamin Towne, in Front-Street, near the Coffee-House, 1774); *A speech intended to have been spoken by the Bishop of St. Asaph, on the bill for altering the charters of the colony of Massachusetts Bay* (London, printed; Philadelphia: Reprinted and sold by Benjamin Towne, in Front-Street, near the Coffee-House, 1774); *Strictures on a pamphlet, entitled, a 'Friendly address to all reasonable Americans, on the subject of our political confusions.'* (Philadelphia: Printed and sold by William and Thomas Bradford, at the London coffee-house, 1774); *Proceedings of the Convention for the province of Pennsylvania, held at Philadelphia, January 23, 1775* (Philadelphia: Printed by William and Thomas Bradford, at the London coffee-house, 1775); Society of the Cincinnati, *Circular letter: addressed to the state societies of the Cincinnati, by the general meeting, convened at Philadelphia, May 3, 1784. Together with the institution, as altered and amended / Society of the Cincinnati* (Philadelphia: Printed by E. Oswald and D. Humphreys, at the Coffee-house, 1784); *Philadelphia, Nov. 10th, 1790: Sir, the wish of many respectable citizens … proposals for opening a coffee-house, corner of Market and Water Streets* (1790).

64. Mather, *Everlasting Gospel*; Ogilvie, *Providence*; *A guide to eternal glory* …; *Doctrine of absolute predestination*.
65. *A catalogue of Latin, French, and English books consisting of divinity, history, physick, travels, romances, volumes of plays, & which will be exposed … 1687, at Wellingtons Coffee-House* (1687), 37–40.
66. Dixon and Nicolson, *Virginia Gazette*, 2 October, 1779 – pg. 3, col. 2; *The process for extracting and refining salt-petre, according to the method practised at the Provincial Works in Philadelphia* (Printed by William and Thomas Bradford, at the London Coffee House, 1776).
67. *The Boston-Gazette, and Country Journal*, 11 September 1769; *The Boston-Gazette*, 11 September 1769, volume 2, 660.
68. *The Boston-Gazette*, Monday, 31 July 1775, 4.
69. *Dalton's The Country Justice, 1690*, volume 153, pg. 55, Archives of Maryland Online, accessed 18 November 2021, http://aomol.msa.maryland.gov/000001/000153/html/am153--55.html.
70. *Proceedings and Acts of the General Assembly, 1766–1768*, volume 61, pg. 481, Archives of Maryland Online, accessed 18 November 2021, http://aomol.msa.maryland.gov/000001/000061/html/am61--481.html.
71. Parks, *Virginia Gazette*, 12 September 1745 – pg. 4, col. 2.
72. Purdie, *Virginia Gazette*, 7 June 1776 – pg. 3, col. 3.
73. Hunter, *Virginia Gazette*, 17 November 1752.
74. Purdie, *Virginia Gazette*, 10 October 1766 – pg. 3, col. 3.
75. Rind, *Virginia Gazette*, 6 February 1772 – pg. 3, col. 3.
76. Rind, *Virginia Gazette*, 2 February 1769 – pg. 2, col. 3.
77. Such as in 1770, when coffeehouse and town meetings in Boston were called to enforce nonimportation; Rind, *Virginia Gazette*, 4 October 1770 – pg. 2, col. 1.
78. Purdie and Dixon, *Virginia Gazette*, 25 June 1767 – pg. 3, col. 1.
79. Purdie and Dixon, *Virginia Gazette*, 6 May 1773 – pg. 3, col. 1.
80. Purdie, *Virginia Gazette*, 29 May 1778 – pg. 3, col. 1.
81. Hunter, *Virginia Gazette*, 3 October 1751 – pg. 4, col. 1.
82. Purdie and Dixon, *Virginia Gazette*, 30 April 1772 – pg. 3, col. 1; Purdie and Dixon, *Virginia Gazette*, 14 October 1773 – pg. 2, col. 3.
83. Parks, *Virginia Gazette*, 14 January 1737 – pg. 3, col. 1.
84. Alison G. Olson, *Making the Empire Work: London and American Interest Groups, 1690–1790* (Cambridge, MA: Harvard University Press, 1992), 6, 21–2, 55, 57–8, 97–8.
85. Ibid., 58.
86. Ibid., 7, 55, 70, 94, 97, 108.
87. Ibid., 56, 64, 69–70, 110, 114–15.
88. 'Washington to Gilbert du Motier, Marquis de Lafayette, 15 August 1786, Mount Vernon', *National Archives: Founders Online*, accessed 4 February 2021, https://founders.archives.gov/documents/Washington/04-04-02-0200.
89. 'Washington to Mathew Carey, 25 June 1788, Mount Vernon', *National Archives: Founders Online*, accessed 4 February 2021, https://founders.archives.gov/documents/Washington/04-06-02-0317.
90. The argument for a radical revolution from below which differed from the Constitutional project was made by Gordon S. Wood in *The Radicalism of the American Revolution* (New York: Vintage Books, 1993), 229–70 and later by Woody Holton in *Forced Founders: Indians, Debtors, Slaves, and the Making of the American*

Revolution in Virginia (Chapel Hill: University of North Carolina Press, published for the Omohundro Institute of Early American History and Culture, 1999) and *Unruly Americans and the Origins of the Constitution* (New York: Hill and Wang, 2007) and Gary B. Nash in *The Unknown American Revolution: The Unruly Birth of Democracy and the Struggle to Create America* (New York: Viking, 2005).

91. Literally, 'Upper Country'.
92. Middleton and Lombard, *Colonial America*, 479–82; Fred Anderson, *The War that Made America: A Short History of the French and Indian War* (New York: Viking, 2005), 25–52; Fred Anderson, *Crucible of War: The Seven Years' War and the Fate of Empire in British North America, 1754–1766* (New York: Alfred A. Knopf, 2000), 2–65; Daniel Baugh, *The Global Seven Years War, 1754–1763: Britain and France in a Great Power Contest* (New York: Pearson, 2011), 35–71.
93. Middleton and Lombard, *Colonial America*, 484–5; Anderson, *Crucible*, 87–123; Anderson, *The War*, 64–87, 144–5; Baugh, *The Global*, 1–16, 117–40.
94. Middleton and Lombard, *Colonial America*, 487–92; Anderson, *Crucible*, 150–68, 179–84; Anderson, *The War*, 88–99; Baugh, *The Global*, 207–11, 250–60; Stephen Brumwell, *Redcoats: The British Soldier and War in the Americas, 1755–1763* (New York: Cambridge University Press, 2002), 1–10, 99–118, 227–36.
95. Middleton and Lombard, *Colonial America*, 492–4; Anderson, *Crucible*, 185–201, 208–26; Anderson, *The War*, 106–40; Baugh, *The Global*, 213–21, 236–7, 494–501.
96. Anderson, *The War*, 218–20, 228–9; Anderson, *Crucible*, 169–78; Baugh, *The Global*, 141–68, 271–81, 311–18, 462–83.
97. Anderson, *Crucible*, 227–85, 330–9; Anderson, *The War*, 141–76, 185–92; Baugh, *The Global*, 338–75; Middleton and Lombard, *Colonial America*, 494–5.
98. Anderson, *The War*, 193–217; Anderson, *Crucible*, 344–76; Baugh, *The Global*, 376–420, 421–52, 483–94, 598–609, 609–22; Middleton and Lombard, *Colonial America*, 495–501.
99. Anderson, *The War*, 231–50; Anderson, *Crucible*, 453–75, 524–6; Middleton and Lombard, *Colonial America*, 501–6.
100. Letter, Committee of the proprietors to Conway, New York Coffee House, Cleveland Row, 19 September 1765, SP 78/267/83, Folio 217, *Memorial from the committee of the proprietors or holders of the Canada bills …*, The National Archives, Kew; Letter, Committee of Canada merchants to Richmond, New York Coffee House, 2 June 1766, SP 78/270/32, Folio 82, *The committee of Canada merchants to Richmond, requesting him to order that …*, The National Archives, Kew; Letter, Robert Allen chairman of the committee of merchants to Henry Guinand, New York Coffee House, 24 July 1766, SP 78/270/97, Folio 233, *Memorial delivered by Henry Guinand on behalf of the committee of merchants, …*, The National Archives, Kew; Letter, Guinand to Roberts, New York Coffee House, 7 August 1766, SP 78/270/104, Folio 246, *Guinand to Roberts. The committee of Canada merchants asks to meet Shelburne …*, The National Archives, Kew.
101. Letter, Committee of merchants to Shelburne, New York Coffee House, 23 December 1766, SP 78/271/77, Folio 191, *Committee of merchants to Shelburne. It asks him to appoint Porten as …*, The National Archives, Kew; Letter, New York Coffee House, 15 January 1767, SP 78/272/17, Folio 39, *Details of settlement of claims to participate in the Canada paper …*, The National Archives, Kew; Minutes, New York Coffee House, 27 January 1768, SP 78/274/15, Folio 33, *Minutes of a general meeting of the proprietors of Canada bills, with names of …*, The National Archives, Kew; Letter, Committee of Canada merchants to Weymouth, New York Coffee House, 7

November 1768, SP 78/276/48, Folio 135, *Memorial from the committee of Canada merchants to Weymouth, protesting at …*, The National Archives, Kew; Letter, Holders of Canada reconnaissances to the House of Lords, Tom's Coffee House, 20 April 20, 1769, SP 78/278/12, Folio 27, *Humble petition of the holders of Canada reconnaissances to be placed before…*, The National Archives, Kew; Letter, Committee of Canada proprietors of reconnaissances to Weymouth, SP 78/278/25, Folio 54, 28 April 1769, *Note from the committee of Canada proprietors of reconnaissances to Weymouth ….*, The National Archives, Kew.

102. Letter, Committee of Canada proprietors of reconnaissances to Weymouth, SP 78/278/25, Folio 54, 28 April 1769, *Note from the committee of Canada proprietors of reconnaissances to Weymouth …*, The National Archives, Kew.

103. Letter, Canada bills committee to Weymouth, New York Coffee House, 11 January 1769, SP 78/277/20, Folio 53, *Memorial from the Canada bills committee to Weymouth. France threatens to …*, The National Archives, Kew.

104. Letter, Committee of Canada merchants, Tom's Coffee House, 26 April 1769, SP 78/278/23, Folio 50, *Note from the committee of Canada merchants. They approve Choiseul's proposal …*, The National Archives, Kew; Letter, Allen to [Wood], Tom's Coffee House, 19 May 1769, SP 78/278/37, Folio 103, Allen to [Wood], *Asks for Weymouth's permission to advertise in the public …*, The National Archives, Kew; Letter, Guinand to Weymouth, Tom's Coffee House, May 30, 1769, SP 78/278/44, Folio 115, *Guinand, by order of the committee [of Canada merchants] to Weymouth. The …*, The National Archives, Kew; Letter, Allen and Guinand to Weymouth, Tom's Coffee House, 13 June 13, 1769, SP 78/278/61, Folio 151, *Allen and Guinaud to Weymouth. The committee of Canada merchants has resolved …*, The National Archives, Kew; Letter, Guinand to Weymouth, Tom's Coffee House, 4 October 1769, SP 78/279/22, Folio 62, *Guinand to Weymouth. While being grateful that the proprietors of the Canada …*, The National Archives, Kew.

105. Letter, Guinand to Weymouth, Tom's Coffee House, 4 October 1769, SP 78/279/22, Folio 62, *Guinand to Weymouth. While being grateful that the proprietors of the Canada …*, The National Archives, Kew.

106. Letter, Robert Allen to Weymouth, Tom's Coffee House, 31 January 1770, *Robert Allen to Weymouth. Having no reply to SP 78/279 f.213 and having …*, The National Archives, Kew; Allen and Tooke [to Weymouth], Tom's Coffee House, 23 June 1770, SP 78/280/103, Folio 257, *Allen and Tooke [to Weymouth] on behalf of the proprietors of Canada …*, The National Archives, Kew; Letter, Allen to [Weymouth], Tom's Coffee House, 5 July 1770, SP 78/281/5, Folio 11, Allen to [Weymouth], *The members of the Canada committee are disappointed at …*, The National Archives, Kew.

107. Letter, Allen and Tooke to [Weymouth], Tom's Coffee House, 19 July 1770, SP 78/281/23, Folio 55, *Allen and Tooke to [Weymouth]. They protest at the French attitude towards the …*, The National Archives, Kew.

108. Letter, William Tooke to Rochford, Tom's Coffee House, 27 December 1771, SP 78/283/116, Folio 304, *William Tooke, deputy chairman of the Canada committee, to Rochford, querying …*, The National Archives, Kew.

109. Letter, Committee of Canada merchants to Rochford, Tom's Coffee House, 30 March 1772, SP 78/284/111, Folio 287, *The committee of Canada merchants to Rochford. They send a copy of their …*, The National Archives, Kew; Letter, Canada merchants' committee to Weymouth, Tom's Coffee House, 8 May 1772, SP 78/285/12, Folio 163, *List of 60,000 livres of claims submitted by the Canada merchants' committee …*, The National Archives, Kew; Letter, Allen and Tooke to Porten, Tom's Coffee House, 15

May 1772, SP 78/285/18, Folio 191, *Allen and Tooke from the committee of Canada merchants to Porten. Any ...*, The National Archives, Kew; Letter, Committee of British proprietors of Canada Reconnaissances to Rochford, Tom's Coffee House, 27 May 1772, SP 78/285/28, Folio 218, *Statement by the committee of British proprietors of Canada reconnaissances ...*, The National Archives, Kew; Letter, Committee of Canada reconnaissances to Rochford, Tom's Coffee House, 16 September 1772, SP 78/286/19, Folio 46, *Committee of Canada reconnaissances to Rochford. It asks that Blaquiere secure ...*, The National Archives, Kew.

110. George Washington, 'Circular to the States', *Founders' Constitution*, vol. 1, Chapter 7, Document 5 (University of Chicago Press, 1987), published 2000, accessed 20 October 2017, http://press-pubs.uchicago.edu/founders/documents/v1ch7s5.html.
111. 'Washington's Farewell Address 1796', *Lillian Goldman Law Library, The Avalon Project* (2008), accessed 20 October 2017, http://avalon.law.yale.edu/18th_century/washing.asp.

6 Transatlantic news feeds and imagined coffeehouse publics

1. Olson, *Making the Empire Work*, 116.
2. Ibid., 78.
3. Ibid., 115.
4. 'Diary of John Quincy Adams, Volume 1: Thursday Novr. 13th', 'Adams Family Correspondence, Volume 5: John Quincy Adams to John Adams, London May 20th. 1784', 'Adams Family Correspondence, Volume 5: John Quincy Adams to John Adams, London May 25th. 1784', 'Diary of John Quincy Adams, Volume 1: Sunday July 17th. 1785', and 'Diary of John Quincy Adams, Volume 1: 21st', *Founding Families: Digital Editions of the Papers of the Winthrops and the Adamses*, accessed 8 November 2017, http://www.masshist.org/publications/adams-papers/; Curwen, *Journal and Letters*, 30, 38, 42, 56, 100.
5. 'Franklin: Journal of the Peace Negotiations Thu, May 9, 1782', *Franklin Papers*, accessed 9 November 2017, https://franklinpapers.org/framedVolumes.jsp; 'Benjamin Franklin and John Foxcroft to Anthony Todd, Fri, Jun 10, 1763', *Franklin Papers*, accessed 10 November 2017, https://franklinpapers.org/framedVolumes.jsp; 'Richard Price to Franklin, Mon, Dec 15, 1766', *Franklin Papers*, accessed 10 November 2017, https://franklinpapers.org/framedVolumes.jsp; 'William Outram to Franklin, Fri, Jan 17, 1772', *Franklin Papers*, accessed 10 November 2017, https://franklinpapers.org/framedVolumes.jsp; 'From Caetanus d'Amraff (unpublished) Fri, Apr 17, 1778', *Franklin Papers*, accessed 9 November 2017, https://franklinpapers.org/framedVolumes.jsp; 'Diary of John Quincy Adams, Volume 1: Jany. 2d', 'Diary of John Quincy Adams, Volume 1: 4th', 'Diary of John Quincy Adams, Volume 1: 25th', and 'Diary of John Quincy Adams, Volume 1: 18th. Tuesd', *Founding Families: Digital Editions of the Papers of the Winthrops and the Adamses*, accessed 8 November 2017, http://www.masshist.org/publications/adams-papers/; Washington, 'Washington to Clement Biddle, 13 November 1799', *The Papers of George Washington Digital Edition*, accessed 9 November 2017, http://rotunda.upress.virginia.edu/founders/default.xqy?keys=GEWN-search-2-7&expandNote=on#match1; Cox, *A Proper Sense of Honor*, 1–28.

6. Adelman, *Revolutionary Networks*, 35, 43–5; 'Autobiography, Part 4', *Franklin Papers*, accessed 9 November 2017, https://franklinpapers.org/framedVolumes.jsp; 'Franklin to Samuel Ward, Thu, Mar 24, 1757' and 'Franklin to Jane Mecom Tue, Apr 19, 1757', *Franklin Papers*, accessed 9 November 2017, https://franklinpapers.org/framedVolumes.jsp.
7. Adelman, *Revolutionary Networks*, 33–9.
8. Ibid., 30, 36, 56; 'Franklin to David Hall Wed, Feb 22, 1758', *Franklin Papers*, accessed 9 November 2017, https://franklinpapers.org/framedVolumes.jsp; 'Franklin to David Hall Sat, Jan 12, 1765', *Franklin Papers*, accessed 9 November 2017, https://franklinpapers.org/framedVolumes.jsp; William Smith, *An Answer to Mr. Franklin's Remarks, on a Late Protest* (Philadelphia: Printed and Sold by William Bradford, at his Book-Store, in Market-street, adjoining the London Coffee-House. 1764).
9. 'Benjamin Kent to Franklin, September 1766', *Franklin Papers*, accessed 9 November 2017, https://franklinpapers.org/framedVolumes.jsp; 'Franklin to Samuel Wharton, Wed, Jan 10, 1770', *Franklin Papers*, accessed 9 November 2017, https://franklinpapers.org/framedVolumes.jsp; 'From the Georgia Commons House of Assembly Sun, Mar 13, 1774', *Franklin Papers*; 'James Parker to Franklin, Sat, Aug 8, 1767', *Franklin Papers*; 'Franklin to Joseph Galloway, London, Sept. 27. 1766', *Franklin Papers*, accessed 9 November 2017, https://franklinpapers.org/framedVolumes.jsp.
10. 'Extract from the Gazette, 1735 Sun, May 29, 1735', *Franklin Papers*, accessed 10 November 2017, https://franklinpapers.org/framedVolumes.jsp.
11. It should be noted that Franklin did not invent the post office in America, but he did desire to bring more consistency to mail delivery between American cities. David H. Flaherty argues that although the English Post Office Act of 1710 instituted the first postal system in America with regular scheduled deliveries, the routes did not extend very far into the interior and many continued the practice of sending their letters by designated travellers rather than through the official post; David H. Flaherty, *Privacy in Colonial New England* (Charlottesville: University Press of Virginia, 1972), 120–1.
12. 'Benjamin Franklin and John Foxcroft to Anthony Todd, Fri, Jun 10, 1763', *Franklin Papers*, accessed 10 November 2017, https://franklinpapers.org/framedVolumes.jsp.
13. Adelman, *Revolutionary Networks*, 62–6.
14. 'John Hughes to Franklin, Philada. Sept. 8. 1765, Sept. 10. 1765, and Sept. 10. 1765', *Franklin Papers*, accessed 10 November 2017, https://franklinpapers.org/framedVolumes.jsp.
15. 'James Parker to Franklin, Wed, Jun 11, 1766', *Franklin Papers*, accessed 10 November, 2017, https://franklinpapers.org/framedVolumes.jsp.
16. 'James Parker to Franklin, Tue, Jul 1, 1766', *Franklin Papers*, accessed 10 November 2017, https://franklinpapers.org/framedVolumes.jsp.
17. 'James Parker to Franklin, Tue, May 6, 1766', *Franklin Papers*, accessed 10 November 2017, https://franklinpapers.org/framedVolumes.jsp; 'James Parker to Franklin, Tue, Jul 15, 1766', *Franklin Papers*, accessed 10 November 2017, https://franklinpapers.org/framedVolumes.jsp.
18. 'Richard Price to Franklin, Mon, Dec 15, 1766', *Franklin Papers*, accessed 10 November 2017, https://franklinpapers.org/framedVolumes.jsp; 'William Outram to Franklin, Fri, Jan 17, 1772', *Franklin Papers*, accessed 10 November 2017, https://franklinpapers.org/framedVolumes.jsp.
19. '"A Traveller": News-Writers' Nonsense Mon, May 20, 1765', *Franklin Papers*, accessed 10 November 2017, https://franklinpapers.org/framedVolumes.jsp.

20. 'An Open Letter to Lord North, Tue, Apr 5, 1774', *Franklin Papers*, accessed 10 November 2017, https://franklinpapers.org/framedVolumes.jsp.
21. 'Franklin to Edmund Burke Mon, Dec 19, 1774', *Franklin Papers*, accessed 10 November 2017, https://franklinpapers.org/framedVolumes.jsp.
22. 'Thomas Digges to Franklin, Fri, Oct 8, 1779' and 'Thomas Digges to Franklin, Sun, Jan 9, 1780', *Franklin Papers*, accessed 10 November 2017, https://franklinpapers.org/framedVolumes.jsp.
23. Rind, *Virginia Gazette*, 25 December 1766 – pg. 3, col. 3.
24. Purdie and Dixon, *Virginia Gazette*, 9 February 1769 – pg. 2, col. 3; Rind, *Virginia Gazette*, 16 February 1769 – pg. 1, col. 3; Rind, *Virginia Gazette*, 9 March 1769 – pg. 1, col. 2; Purdie and Dixon, *Virginia Gazette*, 18 May 1769 – pg. 2, col. 1.
25. Olson *Making the Empire Work*, 77–8, 133.
26. Ibid., 77–8.
27. Lillywhite, *London Coffee Houses*, 389.
28. Curwen, *Journal and Letters*, 30, 38, 42, 56, 100.
29. Ibid., 30.
30. Ibid., 100, 143–4, 174, 202, 217, 235, 244, 275, 289, 293.
31. Ibid., 275, 293.
32. Ibid., 318, 346–8.
33. Curits, 'Chinese Export Porcelain', 125; Davis, 'The Colonial Coffeehouse', 26; William Byrd, '"October 9, 1710' and "November 22, 1711"', in *The Secret Diary*.
34. *Proceedings and Acts of the General Assembly, 1771 to June–July, 1773*: volume 63, pg. 86, accessed 18 November 2021, http://msa.maryland.gov/megafile/msa/speccol/sc2900/sc2908/000001/000063/html/am63--86.html.
35. 'Diary entry: 11 May 1773', *The Papers of George Washington Digital Edition*, accessed 5 August 2017, http://rotunda.upress.virginia.edu/founders/GEWN-01-03-02-0003-0010-0011; 'Diary entry: 23 September 1771', *The Papers of George Washington Digital Edition*, accessed 5 August 2017, http://rotunda.upress.virginia.edu/founders/GEWN-01-03-02-0001-0022-0023.
36. 'Diary entry: 11 May 1773', *The Papers of George Washington Digital Edition*, accessed 5 August 2017, http://rotunda.upress.virginia.edu/founders/GEWN-01-03-02-0003-0010-0011.
37. 'Diary entry: 5 October 1772', *The Papers of George Washington Digital Edition*, accessed 5 August 2017, http://rotunda.upress.virginia.edu/founders/GEWN-01-03-02-0002-0023-0005.
38. 'Diary entry: 26 October 1773', *The Papers of George Washington Digital Edition*, accessed 5 August 2017, http://rotunda.upress.virginia.edu/founders/GEWN-01-03-02-0003-0020-0026; 'Diary entry: 19 November 1773', *The Papers of George Washington Digital Edition*, accessed 5 August 2017, http://rotunda.upress.virginia.edu/founders/GEWN-01-03-02-0003-0022-0019.
39. 'From Tobias Lear, 9 November 1793', *The Papers of George Washington Digital Edition*, accessed 5 August 2017, http://rotunda.upress.virginia.edu/founders/GEWN-05-14-02-0239; Other instances of Washington's social life in coffeehouses may be found in his diaries; Washington, *The Diaries of George Washington*, vol. 3. ed. Donald Jackson, assoc. ed. Dorothy Twohig, The Papers of George Washington (Charlottesville: University Press of Virginia, 1978), 55, 178, 142–3.
40. *Correspondence of Governor Sharpe, 1757–1761*: volume 9, pgs 237, 246, 278–89, Copyright 31 October 2014, *Archives of Maryland Online*, https://msa.maryland.gov/megafile/msa/speccol/sc2900/sc2908/000001/000009/html/am9--237.html.

41. Ibid., 281–2.
42. Ibid., 284.
43. Ibid., 289–91.
44. Barrell, 'Coffee House Politicians', 206, 210–16.
45. Ibid., 214.
46. *Correspondence of Governor Sharpe, 1757–1761*: volume 9, pgs, 289–93.
47. 'Diary of John Adams, Volume 2: 1774. Fryday. Septr. 2', *Founding Families: Digital Editions of the Papers of the Winthrops and the Adamses*, ed. C. James Taylor, accessed 8 November 2017, http://www.masshist.org/publications/adams-papers/.
48. 'Diary of John Adams, Volume 1: 1769. Septr. 2. Saturday Night' and 'Diary of John Adams, Volume 2: August 13. or 14th. 1771', *Founding Families: Digital Editions of the Papers of the Winthrops and the Adamses*, ed. C. James Taylor, accessed 8 November 2017, http://www.masshist.org/publications/adams-papers/.
49. 'Diary of John Adams, Volume 2: 1779 Saturday [12 June]', *Founding Families: Digital Editions of the Papers of the Winthrops and the Adamses*, ed. C. James Taylor, accessed 8 November 2017, http://www.masshist.org/publications/adams-papers/.
50. 'Diary of John Adams, Volume 3: 1782 September 14. Saturday', *Founding Families: Digital Editions of the Papers of the Winthrops and the Adamses*, ed. C. James Taylor, accessed 8 November 2017, http://www.masshist.org/publications/adams-papers/.
51. 'Papers of John Adams, Volume 13: To C. W. F. Dumas, Amsterdam May 2d. 1782', and 'Papers of John Adams, Volume 10: To the President of Congress, No. 31, Amsterdam Decr. 2<6>5th. 1780', *Founding Families: Digital Editions of the Papers of the Winthrops and the Adamses*, ed. C. James Taylor, accessed 8 November 2017, http://www.masshist.org/publications/adams-papers/.
52. 'Papers of John Adams, Volume 9: From Thomas Digges to John Adams, London 3 Mar 1780', and 'Papers of John Adams, Volume 10: From Thomas Digges to John Adams, London Sepr. 26. 1780', *Founding Families: Digital Editions of the Papers of the Winthrops and the Adamses*, ed. C. James Taylor, accessed 8 November 2017, http://www.masshist.org/publications/adams-papers/.
53. I am indebted to Russell Kirk for the essential contrast between Paine and the Adamses over continuity in the American civil social order and the meaning of the American Founding; Russell Kirk, *The Roots of American Order* (Wilmington, Delaware: ISI Books, 1974, 2008), 393–403; 'From John Adams to Benjamin Waterhouse, 29 October 1805', *National Archives: Founders Online*, accessed 26 July 2021, https://founders.archives.gov/documents/Adams/99-02-02-5107.
54. Paul C. Nagel, *John Quincy Adams: A Public Life, a Private Life* (New York: Alfred A. Knopf, 1997), 1–34.
55. 'Diary of John Quincy Adams, Volume 1: Jany. 2d.', 'Diary of John Quincy Adams, Volume 1: 4th.', 'Diary of John Quincy Adams, Volume 1: 25th.', and 'Diary of John Quincy Adams, Volume 1: 18th. Tuesd.', *Founding Families: Digital Editions of the Papers of the Winthrops and the Adamses*, ed. C. James Taylor, accessed 8 November 2017, http://www.masshist.org/publications/adams-papers/.
56. 'Diary of John Quincy Adams, Volume 1: January 1st. 1783.', *Founding Families: Digital Editions of the Papers of the Winthrops and the Adamses*, ed. C. James Taylor, accessed 8 November 2017, http://www.masshist.org/publications/adams-papers/.
57. 'Diary of John Quincy Adams, Volume 1: Thursday Novr. 13th.', 'Adams Family Correspondence, Volume 5: John Quincy Adams to John Adams, London May 20th. 1784', 'Adams Family Correspondence, Volume 5: John Quincy Adams to John

Adams, London May 25th. 1784', 'Diary of John Quincy Adams, Volume 1: Sunday July 17th. 1785', and 'Diary of John Quincy Adams, Volume 1: 21st', *Founding Families: Digital Editions of the Papers of the Winthrops and the Adamses*, ed. C. James Taylor, accessed 8 November 2017, http://www.masshist.org/publications/adams-papers/.
58. 'Diary of John Quincy Adams, Volume 1: 21st', *Founding Families: Digital Editions of the Papers of the Winthrops and the Adamses*, ed. C. James Taylor, accessed 8 November 2017, http://www.masshist.org/publications/adams-papers/.
59. 'Diary of John Quincy Adams, Volume 1: 23d', *Founding Families: Digital Editions of the Papers of the Winthrops and the Adamses*, ed. C. James Taylor, accessed 8 November 2017, http://www.masshist.org/publications/adams-papers/.
60. 'Franklin: Journal of the Peace Negotiations Thu, May 9, 1782', *Franklin Papers*, accessed 9 November 2017, https://franklinpapers.org/framedVolumes.jsp.
61. 'From Caetanus d'Amraff (unpublished) Fri, Apr 17, 1778', *Franklin Papers*, accessed 9 November 2017, https://franklinpapers.org/framedVolumes.jsp.
62. 'From Jacques Finck (unpublished) Sat, Mar 19, 1785' and 'From Jacques Finck (unpublished) Sat, Apr 9, 1785', *Franklin Papers*, accessed 9 November 2017, https://franklinpapers.org/framedVolumes.jsp.
63. 'To Benjamin Vaughan (unpublished) Mon, Jul 26, 1784', *Franklin Papers*, accessed 9 November 2017, https://franklinpapers.org/framedVolumes.jsp.
64. 'Washington to Clement Biddle, 13 November 1799', *The Papers of George Washington Digital Edition*, accessed 9 November 2017, http://rotunda.upress.virginia.edu/founders/GEWN-01-03-02-0003-0010-0011.

7 Empire, free association and slavery

1. Bickham, 'Eating the Empire', 73.
2. Berry, 'Coffee Houses, Exoticism', 4, 10, 15–22; Cowan, *Social Life*, 113–20.
3. John and Linda Pelzer, 'The Coffee Houses', 42, 44; Harris, 'The Grecian', 1–6; Stewart, 'Other centres', 144–5.
4. Stewart, 'Other centres', 151.
5. Bickham, 'Eating the Empire', 79.
6. Ibid., 75, 79–81.
7. Ibid., 73.
8. Ibid., 81–8.
9. Ellis, *The Coffee House*, 125, 127.
10. Bickham, 'Eating the Empire', 88–9; S. D. Smith, 'Accounting for Taste: British Coffee Consumption in Historical Perspective', *Journal of Interdisciplinary History*, vol. 27, no. 2 (Autumn 1996): 196; Cowan, 'Social Life', 71–6.
11. I visited the museum on 15 January 2017.
12. Bickham, 'Eating the Empire', 89.
13. Ibid., 89–92.
14. Andrew Burnaby, *Travels through the middle settlements in North America, in the year 1759 and 1760; with observations upon the state of the colonies. By the Rev. Andrew Burnaby, D. D. Archdeacon of Leicester and Vicar of Greenwich. Edition the third; revised, corrected, and greatly enlarged, by the author, London, 1798*, Eighteenth Century Collections Online, Gale, CMU Libraries - library.cmich.edu: xiii.

15. M. de Moncrif, 'Extract of a Letter from Moka; written to M. PAbbc Teffier, by M. de Moncrif, Agent des Affairs for the King of France, in that City', in *The aberdeen magazine, literary chronicle, and review; for The Year MDCCLXXXVIII* ... Vol. 1. 1788-1790, Eighteenth Century Collections Online, Gale, CMU Libraries – library. cmich.edu: 492.
16. John Adams, *Elegant anecdotes, and bons-mots, of the greatest princes, politicians, philosophers, orators, and wits of modern times* ..., London, MDCCXC [1790], Eighteenth Century Collections Online, Gale, CMU Libraries – library.cmich. edu: 318.
17. Norma Aubertin-Potter and Alyx Bennett, *Oxford Coffee Houses, 1651–1800* (Kidlington: Hampden Press, 1987), 17, 30–31.
18. Bickham, '"A Conviction of the Reality of Things": Material Culture, North American Indians and Empire in Eighteenth-Century Britain', 29–37.
19. 'Tatler, No. 34, Tuesday, June 28, 1709', 'Tatler, No. 195, Saturday, July 8, 1710', and 'Tatler, No. 226, Tuesday, September 19, 1710', in *Tatler*, 81–3, 336–7, 76.
20. 'Tatler, No. 34, Tuesday, June 28, 1709', in *Tatler*, 82–3.
21. *Catalogue Descriptive of the Various Curiosities to be seen at Don Saltero's Coffee House and Tavern, in Chelsea. to which is prefixed, a complete List of the Donors thereof. The forty-sixth edition* (London, s.n., 1795?), 1–15.
22. Ibid.
23. Ibid.
24. Richard White coined the phrase in 1991 to describe the asymmetrical relationships forged in the Great Lakes region of North America. Richard White, *The Middle Ground: Indians, Empires, and Republics in the Great Lakes Region, 1650–1815* (New York: Cambridge University Press, 1991), XXXV–XXXVI; Timothy J. Shannon, 'Dressing for Success on the Mohawk Frontier: Hendrick, William Johnson, and the Indian Fashion', *William and Mary Quarterly*, vol. 53, no. 1 (January 1996): 42; Christopher L. Miller and George R. Hamell, 'A New Perspective on Indian-White Contact: Cultural Symbols and Colonial Trade', *Journal of American History*, vol. 73, no. 2 (September 1986): 315–16, 321.
25. *Catalogue Descriptive*, 10, 13–14.
26. Ibid., 8, 12, 14–15.
27. Callow, *Old London Taverns*, 51–2; Davis, 'The Colonial Coffeehouse', 27, 86; Purdie and Dixon, *Virginia Gazette*, 17 November 1768 – pg. 2, col. 3; Ellis, *The Coffee House*, 180.
28. C. John Sommerville, 'Surfing the Coffeehouse', *History Today*, vol. 47, no. 6 (June 1997): 8–10.
29. Ellis, *The Coffee House*, 180–1.
30. Johnson, 'From An Introduction to the Political State of Great-Britain. 1756. Original', in *The Yale Edition of the Works of Samuel Johnson, Volume X: Political Writings* (New Haven, CT: Yale University Press, 1977), 137.
31. 'Spectator, No. 11, Tuesday, March 13, 1710–11', in *Spectator*, vol. 1, 33.
32. Callow, *Old London Taverns*, 52.
33. Callow, *Old London Taverns*, 52; Richard Pares, 'The London Sugar Market, 1740–1769', *Economic History Review*, vol. 9, no. 2 (December 1956): 254.
34. F. E. Smith, 'Land and Ships Ere Sold over a Cup of Coffee', *Lancashire Life*, vol. 5, no. 5 (May 1957): 35.
35. Arkle, 'The Early Coffee Houses of Liverpool', 7.
36. Ibid., 1–6.

37. Arkle, 'The Early Coffee Houses of Liverpool', 1–6; Dixon and Hunter, *Virginia Gazette*, 14 March 1777 – pg. 1, col. 2; Purdie and Dixon, *Virginia Gazette*, 17 November 1768 – pg. 2, col. 3, Purdie and Dixon, *Virginia Gazette*, 18 May 1769 – pg. 2, col. 1; Rind, *Virginia Gazette*, 1 December 1768 – pg. 1, col. 3; Rind, *Virginia Gazette*, 26 May 1768 – pg. 1, col. 4; Purdie and Dixon, *Virginia Gazette*, 23 June 1768 – pg. 1, col. 3.
38. Ward, *The School of Politicks*, 1–2.
39. John Fothergill, *The Works of John Fothergill, M.D.* ... vol. 2, ed. John Cookley Lettsom (London: Printed for Charles Dilly, in the Poultry, 1783), 286–97.
40. Berry, 'Coffee Houses, Exoticism', 20–1.
41. Serfe, *Tarugo's Wiles*, 14.
42. Callow, *Old London Taverns*, 52.
43. Purdie and Dixon, *Virginia Gazette*, 3 February 1774 – pg. 3, col. 3.
44. Purdie and Dixon, *Virginia Gazette*, 2 July 1767 – pg. 3, col. 1.
45. Arkle, 'The Early Coffee Houses of Liverpool', 6.
46. Colonial Williamsburg's catalogued index of the *Virginia Gazette* returns over five hundred documented instances of issues with articles on runaway slaves. Williamsburg was seemingly by far among the highest areas for slave runaway advertisements, with seventy-one issues containing runaway notices; *Virginia Gazette Index: Slaves (cont'd)*, 'Slaves, runaway', Colonial Williamsburg Digital Library, accessed 18 November 2021, http://research.history.org/DigitalLibrary/va-gazettes/VGPPDetail.cfm?fileName=Slaves5.htm&first=Slaves%20(cont%27d)&last=; Purdie and Dixon, *Virginia Gazette*, 20 June 1771 – pg. 3, col. 3; *Maryland Gazette*, 22 April 1729, pg. 4.
47. Dixon and Hunter, *Virginia Gazette*, 30 March 1776 – pg. 3.
48. Dixon and Nicolson, *Virginia Gazette*, 2 April 1779 – pg. 2, col. 2; Dixon and Hunter, *Virginia Gazette*, 14 November 1777 – pg. 2, col. 2.
49. Purdie and Dixon, *Virginia Gazette*, 17 November 1768 – pg. 2, col. 3.
50. Dixon and Nicolson, *Virginia Gazette*, 12 February 1779 – pg. 4, col. 1.
51. Purdie and Dixon, *Virginia Gazette*, 13 August 1767 – pg. 2.
52. Wilson, 'Maspero's Exchange', 193.
53. Ibid., 191–200.
54. 'Franklin to Julien-David LeRoy (unpublished), [February 1784]', *Franklin Papers*, accessed 18 November 2017, http://franklinpapers.org/franklin/framedVolumes.jsp.
55. Pares, 'The London Sugar Market', 254; S. D. Smith, 'Sugar's Poor Relation: Coffee Planting in the British West Indies, 1720–1833', *Slavery & Abolition: A Journal of Slave and Post-Slave Studies*, vol. 19, no. 3 (1998): 68–9, 72, 75–6, 79.

8 Bringing down the empire

1. Purdie and Dixon, *Virginia Gazette*, 13 October 1768 – pg. 2, col. 2.
2. Dixon and Hunter, *Virginia Gazette*, 7 January 1775 – pg. 2, col. 3; Purdie and Dixon, *Virginia Gazette*, 2 December 1773 – pg. 1, col. 2; Purdie, *Virginia Gazette*, 13 June 1766 – pg. 2, col. 2; Purdie and Dixon, *Virginia Gazette*, 4 July 1771 – pg. 1, col. 3; Purdie, *Virginia Gazette*, 25 July 1766 – pg. 2, col. 2; Bickham, 'Eating the Empire', 73; Revolutionary Society minute-book, 16 June 1788–4 November 1791, Western

Manuscripts, Add MS 64814, *REVOLUTION SOCIETY: minute-book of the Revolution Society; 16 June 1788–4 Nov. 1791*, British Library.
3. 'Thomas Cushing to Franklin, Monday, June 10, 1771', *Franklin Papers*, accessed 24 November 2017, http://franklinpapers.org/franklin/framedVolumes.jsp; 'James Parker to Franklin, Tuesday, May 6, 1766', *Franklin Papers*, accessed 24 November 2017, franklinpapers.org/franklin/framedVolumes.jsp; Breen, *The Marketplace of Revolution*, 204, 218–25, 230–1, 254–60, 288, 300, 335; Dixon and Hunter, *Virginia Gazette*, 7 January 1775 – pg. 2, col. 3; Purdie and Dixon, *Virginia Gazette*, 2 December 1773 – pg. 1, col. 2; Purdie, *Virginia Gazette*, 13 June 13, 1766 – pg. 2, col. 2; Purdie and Dixon, *Virginia Gazette*, 4 July 1771 – pg. 1, col. 3; Purdie, *Virginia Gazette*, 25 July 1766 – pg. 2, col. 2; Dixon and Hunter, *Virginia Gazette*, 7 January 1775 – pg. 2, col. 3; Purdie and Dixon, *Virginia Gazette*, 2 December 1773 – pg. 1, col. 2; *The Boston-Gazette, and Country Journal*, Monday, 19 August 1776, pg. 2, col. 2, https://archive.org/stream/bostongazetteorc269bost#page/n209/mode/2up/search/grapes; *The Boston-Gazette, and Country Journal*, Monday, 1 April 1776, pg. 3, col. 2, https://archive.org/stream/bostongazetteorc269bost#page/n209/mode/2up/search/grapes; Dixon and Nicolson, *Virginia Gazette*, 26 February 1780 – pg. 2, col. 3.
4. Ukers, *All about Coffee*, 59, 73–4.
5. Ibid., 59–60.
6. Ellis, *The Coffee House*, 187.
7. Ibid., 187, 42–56, 59.
8. Macaulay, *History of England*, vol. 1, 738–9.
9. Callow, *Old London Taverns*, 248–51, 349.
10. Pobranski, '"Where Men of Differing Judgements Croud"', 35–8, 41.
11. Habermas, *Structural Transformation*, 33.
12. Pincus, *1688: The First Modern Revolution*, 50–4, 91, 122–5; John Miller, 'Crown, Parliament, and People', in *Liberty Secured? Britain Before and After 1688*, ed. J. R. Jones (Stanford, CA: Stanford University Press, 1992), 77–8; Julian Hoppit, *A Land of Liberty? England 1689–1727* (Oxford: Clarendon Press, 2000), 23–4; J. H. Plumb, *The Origins of Political Stability: England 1675–1725* (Boston, MA: Houghton Mifflin, 1967), xviii, 1–3.
13. Pincus, '"Coffee Politicians Does Create"', 811–14.
14. Ukers, *All about Coffee*, 111.
15. Ibid., 106–11.
16. Davis, 'The Colonial Coffeehouse', 29.
17. Edmund S. Morgan and Helen M. Morgan, *The Stamp Act Crisis: Prologue to Revolution* (Chapel Hill: University of North Carolina Press, 1953), 5–7, 15, 33, 39, 144, 271–6.
18. Ibid., 15, 99, 109, 112–13, 77.
19. Ibid., 33, 39, 91–9, 119, 126–7, 134, 144, 159–63, 178, 181–9, 199, 271–6.
20. Bernard Bailyn, *The Ideological Origins of the American Revolution*, fiftieth anniversary edition (Cambridge, MA: Belknap Press of Harvard University Press, 1967, reprinted 2017), 23–48, 140, 281–4, 303; Jack P. Greene, 'The American Revolution', *American Historical Review*, vol. 105, no. 1 (1 February 2000): 93, accessed 9 June 2018, https://doi.org/10.1086/ahr/105.1.93; Gordon Wood, *The American Revolution: A History* (New York: Modern Library, 2003), 55, 59. 91–105, 122, 129–30; Wood, *Radicalism*, 32, 56, 97, 145–6, 194–5, 235, 265, 303, 309, 330.
21. Joyce Appleby, *Liberalism and Republicanism in the Historical Imagination* (Cambridge, MA: Harvard University Press, 1992), 12–21, 90–4, 129, 141, 188–9,

196–9, 210, 217–18, 338; Breen, *The Marketplace of Revolution*, xi, xv–xviii, 9, 12, 18, 21–2, 36, 53, 78–9, 88, 190, 205.
22. Ibid., 11.
23. Ibid., xvi, 20, 26.
24. Ibid., 204, 218–25, 230–1, 254–60, 288, 300, 335.
25. Ibid., 248.
26. 'Thomas Cushing to Franklin, Monday, June 10, 1771', *Franklin Papers*, accessed 24 November 2017, http://franklinpapers.org/franklin/framedVolumes.jsp; 'James Parker to Franklin, Tuesday, May 6, 1766', *Franklin Papers*, accessed 24 November 2017, franklinpapers.org/franklin/framedVolumes.jsp; Purdie, *Virginia Gazette*, 13 June 1766 – pg. 2, col. 2; Purdie and Dixon, *Virginia Gazette*, 4 July 1771 – pg. 1, col. 3; Purdie, *Virginia Gazette*, 25 July 1766 – pg. 2, col. 2; Dixon and Hunter, *Virginia Gazette*, 7 January 1775 – pg. 2, col. 3; Purdie and Dixon, *Virginia Gazette*, 2 December 1773 – pg. 1, col. 2; *The Boston-Gazette, and Country Journal*, Monday, 19 August 1776, pg. 2, col. 2, https://archive.org/stream/bostongazetteorc269bost#page/n209/mode/2up/search/grapes; *The Boston-Gazette, and Country Journal*, Monday, 1 April 1776, pg. 3, col. 2, https://archive.org/stream/bostongazetteorc269bost#page/n209/mode/2up/search/grapes; Dixon and Nicolson, *Virginia Gazette*, 26 February 1780 – pg. 2, col. 3.
27. Parks, *Virginia Gazette*, 1 July 1737 – pg. 2, col. 2; Parks, *Virginia Gazette*, 14 July 1738 – pg. 2, col. 2.
28. Purdie, *Virginia Gazette*, 23 May 1766 – pg. 2, col. 3.
29. Purdie, *Virginia Gazette*, 13 June 1766 – pg. 2, col. 3.
30. Purdie, *Virginia Gazette*, 24 October 1766 – pg. 1, col. 3.
31. 'The Declaratory Act, March 18, 1766: An Act for the Better Securing the Dependency of His Majesty's Dominions in America upon the Crown and Parliament of Great Britain', *Constitution Society*, accessed 8 June 2018, https://constitution.org/2-Authors/bcp/decl_act.htm, taken from 6 George III, c. 12, *The Statutes at Large*, ed. Danby Pickering (London, 1767), xxvii, 19–20.
32. Rind, *Virginia Gazette*, 10 March 1774 – pg. 2, col. 3.
33. Dixon and Hunter, *Virginia Gazette*, 21 January 1775 – pg. 1, col. 3.
34. Purdie, *Virginia Gazette*, 7 June 1776 – pg. 3, col. 3.
35. Dixon and Hunter, *Virginia Gazette*, 8 April 1775 – pg. 2, col. 1.
36. Dixon and Hunter, *Virginia Gazette*, 1 June 1776 – pg. 2, col. 1.
37. "Homespun': Second Reply to 'Vindex Patriae' Thu, Jan 2, 1766', *Franklin Papers*, accessed 24 November 2017, http://franklinpapers.org/franklin/framedVolumes.jsp.
38. 'James Parker to Franklin, Tuesday, May 6, 1766', *Franklin Papers*, accessed 24 November 2017, franklinpapers.org/franklin/framedVolumes.jsp.
39. 'Thomas Cushing to Franklin, Monday, June 10, 1771', *Franklin Papers*, accessed 24 November 2017, http://franklinpapers.org/franklin/framedVolumes.jsp.
40. 'James Parker to Franklin, Tuesday, May 6, 1766', *Franklin Papers*, accessed 24 November 2017, franklinpapers.org/franklin/framedVolumes.jsp.
41. Ellis, *The Coffee House*, 202; Purdie and Dixon, *Virginia Gazette*, 13 October 1768 – pg. 2, col. 2.
42. Ellis, *The Coffee House*, 202–203; Purdie and Dixon, *Virginia Gazette*, 11 November 1773 – pg. 2, col. 1.
43. *The Boston-Gazette, and Country Journal*, 11 September 1769, volume 2, page 658, accessed 24 November 2017, http://www.masshist.org/publications/adams-papers/.
44. Ibid.

45. Purdie and Dixon, *Virginia Gazette*, 28 September 1769 – pg. 1, col. 2.
46. Rind, *Virginia Gazette*, 4 October 1770 – pg. 2, col. 1; *The Boston-Gazette, and Country Journal*, Monday, 9 September 1776, No. 1112, pg. 4, col. 3, https://archive.org/stream/bostongazetteorc269bost#page/n0/mode/2up/search/coffee.
47. The account in the *Virginia Gazette* is slightly different from the story now told by historical interpreters at the restored R. Charlton's coffeehouse in Colonial Williamsburg in two respects. Firstly, the crowd did not form up at the coffeehouse but rather forced Mercer to it as a place to relate the news, and secondly, the governor did not disperse the crowd but only encouraged more and more opponents. Mercer's promise to stand before his fellow citizens before commencing his duties was the only condition which induced the crowd to disperse. The *Virginia Gazette* stated,

> They attended him up as far as the Coffee House, where the Governour, most of the Council, and a great number of Gentlemen, were assembled; but soon after many more people got together, and insisted on a more speedy and satisfactory answer, declaring they would not depart without one. In some time, upon Mr. Mercer's promising them an answer by V o'clock this evening, they departed well pleased.

Royle, *Virginia Gazette*, 25 October 1765 – pg. 3, col. 2; A sample of the oral history now told in the restored coffeehouse may be found at 'Richard Charlton's Coffeehouse', *YouTube*, published 8 September 2016, accessed 24 November 2017, https://www.youtube.com/watch?v=WzFK_50Z8pE, 5:00–8:00.
48. Ibid.
49. Purdie, *Virginia Gazette*, 13 June 1766 – pg. 2, col. 2.
50. Purdie and Dixon, *Virginia Gazette*, 4 July 1771 – pg. 1, col. 3.
51. Purdie, *Virginia Gazette*, 25 July 1766 – pg. 2, col. 2.
52. Dixon and Hunter, *Virginia Gazette*, 7 January 1775 – pg. 2, col. 3; Purdie and Dixon, *Virginia Gazette*, 2 December 1773 – pg. 1, col. 2.
53. '[Samuel Wharton] to Franklin, Philada. Sun, 13 October 1765', *Franklin Papers*, accessed 24 November 2017, http://franklinpapers.org/franklin/framedVolumes.jsp.
54. Ukers, *All about Coffee*, 106–11; Purdie and Dixon, *Virginia Gazette*, 1 July 1773 – pg. 3, col. 2; Ellis, *The Coffee House*, 203.
55. *The Boston-Gazette, and Country Journal*, Monday, 19 August 776, pg. 2, col. 2, https://archive.org/stream/bostongazetteorc269bost#page/n209/mode/2up/search/grapes.
56. *The Boston-Gazette, and Country Journal*, Monday, 1 April 1776, pg. 3, col. 2, https://archive.org/stream/bostongazetteorc269bost#page/n209/mode/2up/search/grapes.
57. Dixon and Nicolson, *Virginia Gazette*, 26 February 1780 – pg. 2, col. 3.
58. 'John Adams to Abigail Adams, Philadelphia July 3d. 1776', *Adams Adams Family Correspondence, Volume 2*, Adams Papers, accessed 24 November 2017, http://www.masshist.org/publications/adams-papers/.
59. Wilson, *The Sense of the People*, 206–30, 240–4, 256–60, 290–5, 304–5, 315, 324–5, 342, 359, 379, 407.
60. See Chapter 9.
61. Letter, Stormont to Weymouth, Paris, Dec. 11, 1776, SP 78/300/155, *Stormont to Weymouth. Doctor Franklin has arrived at Nantes with his two …*, The National Archives, Kew.
62. Ibid.

63. Letter, Stormont to Weymouth, Paris, 3 January 1776, SP 78/298/4, *Stormont to Weymouth. Intelligence confirms the arming at Brest of 4 ships of ...*, The National Archives, Kew.
64. Revolutionary Society minute-book, 16 June 1788–4 November 1791, Western Manuscripts, Add MS 64814, *REVOLUTION SOCIETY: minute-book of the Revolution Society; 16 June 1788–4 Nov. 1791*, British Library.
65. Ibid.
66. Letter, William Butler to William Pitt, Queen's Head Coffee House, 23 November 1792, HO 42/22/196, Folios 494–5, *Letter to William Pitt from William Butler at the Queen's Head Coffee ...*, The National Archives, Kew.
67. Ellis, *The Coffee House*, 212.
68. Micah Alpaugh, 'The British Origins of the French Jacobins: Radical Sociability and the Development of Political Club Networks, 1787–1793', *European History Quarterly*, 44, no. 4 (October 2014): 594–7, 602–3, 611–12, accessed 7 September 7, 2015, http://ehq.sagepub.com.cmich.idm.oclc.org/content/44/4/593.full.pdf+html.
69. Russell and Tuite, 'Introduction', in *Romantic Sociability*, 13.
70. Ibid., 13–14.
71. Epstein, '"Equality and No King": Sociability and Sedition: The Case of John Frost', in *Romantic Sociability*, 43–8, 55.
72. Ibid., 56–7.
73. Anne Janowitz, 'Amiable and Radical Sociability: Anna Barbauld's "Free Familiar Conversation"', in *Romantic Sociability*, 62–4, 72, 75–6.
74. Schmid, *British Literary Salons*, 72–6, 78–9, 81–6, 92–5, 98–102.
75. Russell and Tuite, 'Introduction', in *Romantic Sociability*, 13; Schmid, *British Literary Salons*, 72–6, 78–9, 82–6, 92–5, 98–102; Graeme Morton, *Unionist Nationalism: Governing Urban Scotland, 1830–1860* (East Linton: Tuckwell Press, 1999), 156–65; Ellis, *The Coffee House*, 211–15.

Conclusion

1. *The Sessional Papers Printed by Order of the House of Lords ...*, vol. XXXIII (1838), 23–4.

Bibliography

Primary sources

Archives

British Library

IOR/E/1/4 ff. 193–5v
IOR/E/1/4 ff. 241–2v
IOR/E/1/9 ff. 80–1v
IOR/E/1/9 ff. 128–8v
IOR/E/1/12 ff. 305–6v
IOR/E/1/53 ff. 272–4v
Add MS 38232, Folios 60, 66
Add MS 38310, Folio 221
Add MS 38340, Folio 98
Add MS 41803, Folios 209, 213
Add MS 64814
Add MS 72899, Folios 93–5
Sloane MS 4047, Folio 155

The National Archives, Kew

ADM 106/481/316
ADM 106/849/241
ADM 106/854/180
ADM 106/866/276
ADM 106/989/8
ADM 106/1026/186
ADM 106/1026/210
ADM 106/1077/19
ADM 106/1102/137
ADM 106/1164/226
ADM 106/1188/250
ADM 106/1191/215
ADM 106/1207/2
ADM 106/1243/344
ADM 106/1255/131
ADM 106/1257/274
ADM 106/1275/229

ADM 106/1291/280
HO 42/17/36, Folio 63
HO 42/22/196, Folios 494–5
HO 42/23/199, Folios 446–7
HO 42/23/307, Folios 663–4
HO 42/24/32, Folios 66–7
HO 42/24/265, Folios 644–5
HO 42/25/4, Folios 7–8
HO 42/26/23, Folios 54–5
SP 35/15/79
SP 35/37/1
SP 35/37/22
SP 35/37/23
SP 35/37/27
SP 35/37/32
SP 35/38/20
SP 35/38/21
SP 35/72/34
SP 35/72/37
SP 35/72/38
SP 35/72/51
SP 35/72/59
SP 36/81/1/22, Folios 22–3
SP 42/7/25
SP 78/267/83, Folio 217
SP 78/270/32, Folio 82
SP 78/270/97, Folio 233
SP 78/270/104, Folio 246
SP 78/271/77, Folio 191
SP 78/272/17, Folio 39
SP 78/274/15, Folio 33
SP 78/276/48, Folio 135
SP 78/277/20, Folio 53
SP 78/278/12, Folio 27
SP 78/278/23, Folio 50
SP 78/278/25, Folio 54
SP 78/278/37, Folio 103
SP 78/278/44, Folio 115
SP 78/278/61, Folio 151
SP 78/279/22, Folio 62
SP 78/280/103, Folio 257
SP 78/281/5, Folio 11
SP 78/281/23, Folio 55
SP 78/283/116, Folio 304
SP 78/284/111, Folio 287

SP 78/285/12, Folio 163
SP 78/285/18, Folio 191
SP 78/285/28, Folio 218
SP 78/286/19, Folio 46
SP 78/298/4
SP 78/300/155

Newspapers

Daily Advertiser. London: Printed for J. Jenour, at No. 33, opposite St. Dunstan's Church, Fleet-Street. 3 February 1730–September 1798. 1743; 1796. On 3 reels, Gale microfilms. Accessed 19 September 2018. microformguides.gale.com/Data/Download/1003000A.pdf.
Daily Post. London, England, 1719. Library of Congress. Accessed 19 September 2018. https://catalog.loc.gov/vwebv/search?searchCode=LCCN&searchArg=sn%2093048038&searchType=1&permalink=y.
The Boston Gazette, and Country Journal. Accessed 18 November 2021. http://www.masshist.org/dorr/volume/2/sequence/700?searchHit=1.
The London Evening Post. Numb. [1]. 12 December 1727–Ceased with 13 March 1806 issue, London, England: Printed by R. Nutt, 1727–1806. Library of Congress. Accessed 19 September 2018. https://catalog.loc.gov/vwebv/search?searchCode=LCCN&searchArg=sn%2088088251&searchType=1&permalink=y.
The Maryland Gazette. Archives of Maryland Online, Maryland Gazette Collection, 24 July 2009. Accessed 18 November 2021. http://aomol.msa.maryland.gov/html/mdgazette.html.
The New-York Gazette. NYS Historic Newspapers. Image provided by: Syracuse University.
Virginia Gazette. Colonial Williamsburg Digital Library. Omohundro Institute of Early American History & Culture microfilm, 1950. Accessed 18 November 2021. https://research.colonialwilliamsburg.org/DigitalLibrary/va-gazettes/.

Papers

Founding Families: Digital Editions of the Papers of the Winthrops and the Adamses, edited by C. James Taylor. Boston: Massachusetts Historical Society, 2017. Accessed 18 November 2021. http://www.masshist.org/publications/adams-papers/.
Franklin Papers. Sponsored by The American Philosophical Society and Yale University Digital Edition by The Packard Humanities Institute. Published Online: 2006. Accessed 18 November 2021. https://franklinpapers.org/framedVolumes.jsp.
The Papers of George Washington Digital Edition. The University of Virginia Press, Copyright © 2008–17 by the Rector and Visitors of the University of Virginia.
The Sessional Papers Printed by Order of the House of Lords … vol. XXXIII. 1838.

Published works

A catalogue of Latin, French, and English books consisting of divinity, history, physick, travels, romances, volumes of plays, & which will be exposed … 1687, at Wellingtons Coffee-House. 1687.

A Conductor generalis, or, The office, duty and authority of justices of the peace, high-sheriffs, under-sheriffs, coroners, constables, gaolers, jury-men, and overseers of the poor: as also, the office of clerks of assize, and of the peace, &c. / compil. Woodbridge, in New-Jersey: Printed for and sold by Garrat Noel, near the merchant's coffee House, in New-York, MDCCLXIV [1764].

A Dissertation Upon Drunkenness. Shewing to what an Intolerable Pitch that Vice is Arriv'd at in this Kingdom. Together with the Astonishing Number of Taverns, Coffee-houses, Alehouses, Brandy-shops, &c. Now Extant in London ... London: Printed for T. Warner, 1727.

A sermon, in which the union of the colonies is considered and recommended : and the bad consequences of divisions are represented : delivered on the public thanksgiving : November sixteenth, 1775. New-York: Printed by John Holt, in Water-street, near the Coffee-house, 1776.

A Speech intended to have been spoken by the Bishop of St. Asaph, on the bill for altering the charters of the colony of Massachusetts Bay... Philadelphia: London, printed: Philadelphia, reprinted and Sold by Benjamin Towne, in Front-Street, near the Coffee-House, 1774.

Adams, John. *Elegant anecdotes, and bons-mots, of the greatest princes, politicians, philosophers, orators, and wits of modern times; Such as His present Majesty Prince of Wales Duke of Clarence Peter the Great King of Prussia Henry IV. Empress of Russia Charles XII. Lewis XIV. Sir Isaac Newton Lord Chesterfield Lord Mansfield Dr. Johnson Voltaire Sterne Garrick Savage Steele Mr. Hume Sheridan, &c. Calculated to inspire the minds of youth with noble, virtuous, generous, and liberal sentiments. By the Rev. John Adams, A.M. A new edition greatly enlarged.* London, MDCCXC. [1790]. Eighteenth Century Collections Online. Gale. CMU Libraries – library.cmich.edu.

Addison, Joseph. *The Guardian, with Notes, and a General Index ... Complete in One Volume.* Philadelphia, PA: J.J. Woodward, 1831.

Addison, Joseph. *The Works of Joseph Addison; complete in three volumes, embracing the whole of the 'Spectator', etc.*, volumes 1 and 2. New York: Harper, 1845.

Alpaugh, Micah. 'The British Origins of the French Jacobins: Radical Sociability and the Development of Political Club Networks, 1787–1793'. *European History Quarterly* 44, no. 4 (October 2014): 593–619, Accessed 7 September 2015. https://journals.sagepub.com/doi/abs/10.1177/0265691414546456.

Anburey, Thomas. *Travels through the Interior Parts of America; in a Series of Letters. By an Officer. A New Edition*, vol. 2. London, MDCCXCI. [1791]. Eighteenth Century Collections Online. Gale. CMU Libraries – library.cmich.edu.

Austen, Jane. *The Novels of Jane Austen, Persuasion.* Edinburgh: John Grant, 31 George IV. Bridge, 1905.

Bell, Robert. *The Annotated Edition of the English Poets.* London: John W. Parker and Son, West Strand, 1857.

Boswell, James. *Boswell's Life of Johnson, Abridged and Edited, with an Introduction by Charles Grosvenor Osgood.* New York: Charles Scribner's Sons, 1917.

Boswell, James. *Boswell's London Journal, 1762–1763.* New York: McGraw-Hill Book, 1950.

Burke, Edmund. *Selected Writings and Speeches.* Edited by. Peter J. Stanlis. Washington, DC: Regnery Gateway, 1963.

Burnaby, Andrew. *Travels through the middle settlements in North America, in the year 1759 and 1760; with observations upon the state of the colonies. By the Rev. Andrew Burnaby, D. D. Archdeacon of Leicester and Vicar of Greenwich. Edition the third;*

revised, corrected, and greatly enlarged, by the author. London, 1798. Eighteenth Century Collections Online. Gale. CMU Libraries – library.cmich.edu.

Bushe, Gervase Parker. *Case of Great-Britain and America*. London: Printed, Philadelphia, Re-Printed by William and Thomas Bradford, at the London Coffee-House, 1769.

By a Coffee Man (n.d.). *The Case Between the Proprietors of News-papers, and the Coffee-men of London and Westminster, Fairly Stated: Being Remarks on Their Case Lately Publish'd. Wherein the False Pretences, Wild Projects, and Groundless Complaints of that Insolent Set of Men are Duly Examin'd, Properly Expos'd, and Thoroughly Confuted; and Their Calumny of Abuses and Impositions Justly Retorted. With a Proposal for Remedying the Flagrant, Scandalous and Growing Impositions of the Coffee-men Upon the Publick. To which is Annex'd, I. Henley the Orator and the Butchers, Or the Butchers and Henley. II. A Whip for the Post-Boy, to Enable Him to Ride Out Every Day. III. An Inspection Into the Spectator and Other News-papers, Without News, Truth, Or Even Original Nonsense. IV. Polly Peachum's Child; Its Name, Father, &c. V. The Reigning Devil; Or, Hell Upon Earth: Giving an Account of the Women Mollies; and Whether the Clergy Pour More Prayers Than the Army Do Curses, Into the Ear of the Almighty. VI. The Cormorant Upon St. Paul's, a Surprising Omen. VII. A Solution and Farther Observation Not to be Nam'd But Understood by Those that are Masters of the Art of Thinking*. R. Walker at the White Hart, adjoyning to the Anodyne Necklace, without Temple Bar, 1729.

Byrd, William. In *The Secret Diary of William Byrd of Westover, 1709–1712*, edited by Louis B. Wright and Marion Tinling. Richmond: The Dietz Press, 1941, National Humanities Center, 2009. nationalhumanitiescenter.org/pds.

Catalogue Descriptive of the Various Curiosities to be seen at Don Saltero's Coffee House and Tavern, in Chelsea. to which is prefixed, a complete List of the Donors thereof. The forty-sixth edition. London, s.n., 1795.

'Change Alley Carricatur'd: Or, a Dream about Jonathan's Coffee-House'. In *The beauties of all the magazines selected. For the Year 1762. Including the several original comic pieces. To be continued the middle of every month. … Vol. 1*. London, Mcxxlii [1762]–4. Eighteenth Century Collections Online. Gale. CMU Libraries – library.cmich. edu: 436–7.

Coffee-houses Vindicated in Answer to the late Published Character of a Coffee-House Asserting From Reason, Experience, and good Authours, the Excellent Use, and Physical Vertues of that Liquor. With The grand Conveniency of such civil places of Resort and Ingenious Conversation. London: Printed by I. Lock for I. Clarke. 1675.

Colman, George. *The Connoisseur. By Mr. Town, Critic and Censor-General, Numb. 1, Thursday, January 31, 1754*. London: Printed for R. Baldwin, 1755–6.

Correspondence of Governor Sharpe, 1757–1761: volume 9, Pages 237–93. Copyright 31 October 2014. Archives of Maryland Online. Accessed 18 November 2021. https://msa.maryland.gov/megafile/msa/speccol/sc2900/sc2908/000001/000009/html/am9--237.html.

Cowan, Brian. *The Social Life of Coffee: The Emergence of the British Coffeehouse*. New Haven, CT: Yale University Press, 2005.

Curwen, Samuel. *Journal and Letters of the Late Samuel Curwen Judge of Admiralty, Etc., ed. George Atkinson Ward*. New York: C. S. Francis and Co., 1842.

Dalrymple, Sir. J. 'Historical and Biographical Anecdotes. [From the Second Volume of Sir J. Dalrymple's "Memoirs of Great Britain and Ireland", lately published.] Earl of Stair'. In *The aberdeen magazine, literary chronicle, and review; for The Year MDCCLXXXVIII. … Vol. 1. 1788–90* Aberdeen. Eighteenth Century Collections Online. Gale. CMU Libraries – library.cmich.edu: 309–11.

Dalton's The Country Justice, 1690, volume 153, Page 55, Archives of Maryland Online. Accessed 18 November 2021. http://aomol.msa.maryland.gov/000001/000153/html/am153--55.html.

Damrosch, Leo. *The Club: Johnson, Boswell, and the Friends Who Shaped an Age*. New Haven, CT: Yale University Press, 2019.

de Moncrif, M. 'Extract of a Letter from Moka; written to M. PAbbc Teffier, by M. de Moncrif, Agent des Affairs for the King of France, in that City'. In *The aberdeen magazine, literary chronicle, and review; for The Year MDCCLXXXVIII*. ... vol. 1. 1788–90 Aberdeen. Eighteenth Century Collections Online. Gale. CMU Libraries – library.cmich.edu: 491–2.

Dickinson, John. *Address to the Committee of correspondance in Barbados*. Philadelphia: Printed and sold by William Bradford, at his bookstore in Market street, adjoining the London coffee-house, 1766.

Directions for the Gulph and River of St. Lawrence, with some remarks. Philadelphia: Printed by William and Thomas Bradford, at the London Coffee-house, 1774.

Doctrine of absolute predestination stated and asserted: with a preliminary discourse on the divine attributes; A sermon, in which the union of the colonies is considered and recommended: and the bad consequences of divisions are represented: delivered on the public thanksgiving: November sixteenth, 1775 / translated, in great measure, from the Latin of Jerom Zanchius by Augustus Toplady, A.B., Vicar of Broad Hembury, Devon and Chaplain to the R...
New-York: Printed by Hodge and Shober, for Samuel Loudon, on Hunter's Key, 1773.

Fielding, Henry. *The Coffee-House Politician: or, the Justice caught in His Own Trap. A Comedy. As it is Acted at the Theatre-Royal in Lincoln's-Inn Fields Written by Mr. Fielding*. London: Printed for J. Watts, 1730. Ann Arbor: University of Michigan Library, January 2007. http://name.umdl.umich.edu/004770944.0001.000.

Fothergill, John. *The Works of John Fothergill, M.D.* ... vol. 2, edited by John Cookley Lettsom. London: Printed for Charles Dilly, in the Poultry, 1783.

Gipson, Lawrence Henry. 'Criminal Codes of Pennsylvania'. *Journal of Criminal Law and Criminology*, vol. 6, no. 3, Article 2 (1915): 323–44.

Johnson, Samuel. *The Works of Samuel Johnson, LL.D.: A New Edition, with an Essay On His Life and Genius, by Arthur Murphy, ESQ. in two volumes*. London: Henry G. Bohn, York Street, Convent Garden, 1850.

Johnson, Samuel. *The Yale Edition of the Works of Samuel Johnson, Volume II: The Idler and The Adventurer*. New Haven, CT: Yale University Press, 1963.

Johnson, Samuel. *The Yale Edition of the Works of Samuel Johnson, Volume X: Political Writings*. New Haven, CT: Yale University Press, 1977.

Hancock, John. *An Oration, 6, Monticello Digital Classroom*. Accessed 1 September 2018. https://classroom.monticello.org/media-item/john-hancocks-boston-massacre-oration/.

Hickes, William. *Coffee-House Jests. By the Author of the Oxford-Jests. This may be printed. March 30. 1677. Roger L'Estrange*. London: Printed for Benj. Thrale at the Bible in the Poultrey near Cheapside, 1677.

Irving, Washington. *The Sketch-Book of Geoffrey Crayon, Gent*. New York: G. P. Putnam's Sons, 1882.

Mather, Cotton. *Everlasting gospel. The gospel of justification by the righteousness of God; as 'tis held and preached in the churches of New England: expressed in a brief discourse on that important article; made at Boston in the year, 1699. By Cotton Mather. And, asser.*

Boston: Printed by B. Green, and J. Allen, for Nicholas Buttolph, and sold at the corner of Gutteridges coffee-house, 1700.

Mather, Increase. *An Arrow Against Profane and Promiscuous Dancing, Drawn Out of the Quiver of the Scriptures*. Boston, 1684.

Murther Upon Murther: Being a Full and True Relation of a Horrid and Bloody Murther, Committed Upon the Bodies of Mrs. Sarah Hodges, Wife of Mr. Thamas Hodges, Mrs. Elizabeth Smith and Hannah Williams, the Loyal Coffee-House near Well-Gose at the end of East-Smith-field, on Saturday the 17th. of this Instant January 1691. London: Printed by G. Croom, at the Blue Ball in Thames-street, 1691.

New York (Colony) General assembly, 1773. New-York: Printed by John Holt, near the Coffee house. 1773.

'No. 291. Sir John Cope trode the north right far'. In *James C. Dick, The Songs of Robert Burns: Now first printed with the Melodies for which they were written …*, 274–5. New York: Henry Frowde, London, Edinburgh, Glasgow, and New York, 1903.

Nonentity, Nich. 'To the Author of The Trifler, Feb. 29. 1788'. In *The aberdeen magazine, literary chronicle, and review; for The Year MDCCLXXXVIII. …* Vol. 1. 1788–1790 Aberdeen. Eighteenth Century Collections Online. Gale. CMU Libraries – library. cmich.edu: 163–4.

Ogilvie, John. *Providence, an allegorical poem*. Boston: Printed for and sold by J. Mein, at the London Book-store, second Door above the British Coffee-house, North-side of Kingstreet, 1766.

Philadelphia, Nov. 10th, 1790: Sir, the wish of many respectable citizens … proposals for opening a coffee-house, corner of Market and Water Streets. 1790.

Phillips, John. *Horse-Flesh for The Observator: Being a Comment upon Gusman, ch. 4. v. 5. Held forth at Sam's Coffee-House / / by T.D.B.D. chaplain to the Inferiour clergies guide.* London: Printed for R. Read, 1682.

Proceedings and Acts of the General Assembly, 1766–1768, Volume 61, Page 481. Maryland State Archives. Copyright 31 October 2014. Accessed 18 November 2021. http://msa.maryland.gov/megafile/msa/ speccol/sc2900/sc2908/000001/000061/html/am61--481.html.

Proceedings and Acts of the General Assembly, 1771 to June-July, 1773. Volume 63, Page 86. Maryland State Archives. Copyright 31 October 2014. Accessed 18 November 2021. http://aomol.msa.maryland.gov/000001/000063/html/am63--76.html.

Proceedings and Acts of the General Assembly, September, 1704–April, 1706. Volume 26, Page 582. Copyright 31 October 2014. Accessed 18 November 2021. Archives of Maryland Online. http://aomol.msa.maryland.gov/000001/000026/html/am26--582.html.

Proceedings of the Convention for the province of Pennsylania, held at Philadelphia, January 23, 1775. Philadelphia: Printed by William and Thomas Bradford, at the London coffee-house, 1775.

'R. Charlton's Coffeehouse'. *Colonial Williamsburg*. Accessed 18 October 2014. http://www.history.org/almanack/places/hb/hbcoffee.cfm.

Rivington, James. *A catalogue of books, sold by Rivington and Brown, booksellers and stationers from London, at their stores, over against the Golden Key, in Hanover-square, New-York: and over against the London coffee-house, in Philadelphia …* Philadelphia: Heinrich Miller, 1762.

Shakespeare, William. *The Tragedy of Macbeth*. New York: American Book, 1895.

Smith, Anna Marion. *Mother Goose and What Happened Next*. New York: E. P. Dutton, 1909.

Society of the Cincinnati, Circular letter: addressed to the state societies of the Cincinnati, by the general meeting, convened at Philadelphia, May 3, 1784. Together with the institution, as altered and amended / Society of the Cincinnati. Philadelphia: Printed by E. Oswald and D. Humphreys, at the Coffee-house, 1784.

St Serfe, Thomas. *Tarugo's Wiles: or, the Coffee-House. A Comedy: as it was acted at His Highness's the Duke of York's Theater / written by Tho. St Serfe, Gent.* London: Printed for Henry Herringman, 1668.

Strictures on a pamphlet, entitled, a 'Friendly address to all reasonable Americans, on the subject of our political confusions.' Philadelphia: Printed and sold by William and Thomas Bradford, at the London coffee-house, 1774.

Swift, Jonathan. 'Modern History Sourcebook: Jonathan Swift (1667–1745): Hints Towards An Essay On Conversation, 1713.' *Internet Modern History Sourcebook*, Paul Halsall, Aug. 1998. Harvard Classics series, 1909. Accessed 13 January 2021. https://sourcebooks.fordham.edu/mod/1713swift-conversation.asp.

'The Adventures of a Speculist, in his Journey through London'. In *The beauties of all the magazines selected. For the Year 1762. Including the several original comic pieces. To be continued the middle of every month. ... vol. 1*. London, Mcxxlii [1762]–4. Eighteenth Century Collections Online. Gale. CMU Libraries – library.cmich.edu: 294–6.

The character of a coffee-house wherein is contained a description of the persons usually frequenting it, with their discourse and humors, as also the admirable vertues of coffee / by an eye and ear witness. London: s.n., 1665, Ann Arbor, MI; Oxford (UK): Text Creation Partnership, 2006–2 (EEBO-TCP Phase 1). Accessed 28 August 2017. http://name.umdl.umich.edu/A31685.0001.001.

The Character of a Coffee-House, with the Symptoms of a Town-Wit. London: Printed for Jonathan Edwin, at the three Roses in Lud-Gate-Street, 1673.

'The Declaratory Act, March 18, 1766: An Act for the Better Securing the Dependency of His Majesty's Dominions in America upon the Crown and Parliament of Great Britain'. Constitution Society. Accessed 8 June 2018. http://www.constitution.org/bcp/decl_act.htm. Taken from 6 George III, c. 12.

The Gentleman's Magazine. London: Printed by F. Jeffries,etc., 1731–1907. Hathi Trust Digital Library. Accessed 19 September 2018. https://catalog.hathitrust.org/Record/000542092.

The Maidens Complaint Against Coffee. or, the Coffee-House Discovered, Besieged, Stormed, Taken, Untyled and laid Open to publick view, in a merry Conference between... Being Very pleasant and delightful for Old and Young, Lads and Lasses, Boys and Girles [Latin phrase] as the devout Ironmonger quotes it in his Annotations upon Toby and his Dog. Written by Merc. Democ. at his Chamber in the World in the Moon, for the benefit of all the mad-merry-conceited people under the Sun. J. Jones: Royal Exchange, London, 1663.

The process for extracting and refining salt-petre, according to the method practised at the Provincial Works in Philadelphia. Printed by William and Thomas Bradford, at the London Coffee House, 1776.

The Statutes at Large, edited by Danby Pickering, XXVII, 19–20. London, 1767.

The Vertues of coffee set forth in the works of [brace] the Lord Bacon his Natural hist., Mr. Parkinson his Herbal, Sir George Sandys his Travails, James Howel Esq. his Epistles / collected and published for the satisfaction of the drinkers thereof. London: Printed by W.G., 1663.

Voltaire. *The Portable Voltaire*, edited by Ben Ray Redman. New York: Penguin Books, 1981.

Wales, Samuel. 'The Dangers of our National Prosperity; and the Way to Avoid Them', Hartford, 1785. In *Political Sermons of the American Founding Era, 1730-1805*, vol. 1, 2nd edn, edited by Ellis Sandoz, 835-63. Indianapolis, IN: Liberty Fund, 1991.
Ward, Edward. *The School of Politicks: or, the Humours of a Coffee-House*. London, 1698.
Washington, George. 'Circular to the States'. *The Founders' Constitution*, vol. 1, Chapter 7, Document 5. University of Chicago Press, 1987, published 2000. Accessed 20 October 2017. http://press-pubs.uchicago.edu/founders/documents/v1ch7s5.html.
Washington, George. *The Diaries of George Washington*. Vol. 3, edited by Donald Jackson and Dorothy Twohig. The Papers of George Washington. Charlottesville: University Press of Virginia, 1978.
Washington, George. 'Washington's Farewell Address 1796'. *Lillian Goldman Law Library, The Avalon Project* (2008). Accessed 20 October 2017. http://avalon.law.yale.edu/18th_century/washing.asp.

Secondary sources

Adelman, Joseph M. *Revolutionary Networks: The Business and Politics of Printing the News, 1763-1789*. Baltimore, MD: Johns Hopkins University Press, 2019.
Albrecht, Peter. 'Coffee-Drinking as a Symbol of Social Change in Continental Europe in the Seventeenth and Eighteenth Centuries'. *Studies in Eighteenth-Century culture*, vol. 18 (1988): 91-103.
Anderson, Benedict. *Imagined Communities: Reflections on the Origin and Spread of Nationalism*. New York: Verso, 1995.
Anderson, Fred. *Crucible of War: The Seven Years' War and the Fate of Empire in British North America, 1754-1766*. New York: Alfred A. Knopf, 2000.
Anderson, Fred. *The War that Made America: A Short History of the French and Indian War*. New York: Viking, 2005.
Appleby, Joyce. *Liberalism and Republicanism in the Historical Imagination*. Cambridge, MA: Harvard University Press, 1992.
Arkle, A. H. 'The Early Coffee Houses of Liverpool'. *Transactions of the Historical Society of Lancashire and Cheshire*, vol. 64 (1912): 1-16.
Armitage, David. 'Three Concepts of Atlantic History'. In *The British Atlantic World, 1500—1800*, edited by David Artmitage and Michael J. Braddick, 11-27. Houndmills: Palgrave Macmillan, 2002.
Aubertin-Potter, Norma, and Alyx Bennett. *Oxford Coffee Houses, 1651-1800*. Kidlington: Hampden Press, 1987.
Bailyn, Bernard. *Atlantic History: Concept and Contours*. London: Harvard University Press, 2005.
Bailyn, Bernard. *The Ideological Origins of the American Revolution*, fiftieth anniversary edn. Cambridge, MA: Belknap Press of Harvard University Press, 1967, reprinted 2017.
Barker-Benfield, G. J. *The Culture of Sensibility: Sex and Society in Eighteenth-Century Britain*. Chicago: University of Chicago Press, 1992.
Barrell, John. 'Coffee-House Politicians'. *Journal of British Studies*, vol. 43, no. 2 (April 2004): 206-32. Accessed 7 March 2017. http://www.jstor.org/stable/10.1086/380950.
Baugh, Daniel. *The Global Seven Years War, 1754-1763: Britain and France in a Great Power Contest*. New York: Pearson, 2011.
Bayles, W. Harrison. *Old Taverns of New York*. New York: Frank Allaben Genealogical, 1915.

Benjamin, Thomas. *The Atlantic World: Europeans, Africans, Indians and Their Shared History, 1400–1900*. Cambridge: Cambridge University Press, 2009.

Bennett, G. V. *The Tory Crisis in Church and State 1688–1730: The Career of Francis Atterbury Bishop of Rochester*. Oxford: Clarendon Press, 1975.

Berry, Helen. 'Coffee Houses, Exoticism and the Evolution of Eighteenth-Century Culture'. Master's thesis, V&A, 20 November 2003. 1–22.

Berry, Helen. 'Polite Consumption: Shopping in Eighteenth-Century England'. *Transactions of the Royal Historical Society*, vol. 12 (2002): 375–94. Accessed 20 October 2016. http://www.jstor.org/stable/3679353.

Berry, Helen. 'Rethinking Politeness in Eighteenth-Century England: Moll King's Coffee House and the Significance of "Flash Talk": The Alexander Prize Lecture'. *Transactions of the Royal Historical Society*, vol. 11 (2001): 65–81. Accessed 20 October 2016. http://www.jstor.org/stable/3679414.

Bickham, Troy. '"A Conviction of the Reality of Things": Material Culture, North American Indians and Empire in Eighteenth-Century Britain'. *Eighteenth-Century Studies*, vol. 39, no. 1 (2005): 29–37.

Bickham, Troy. 'Eating the Empire: Intersections of Food, Cookery and Imperialism in Eighteenth-Century Britain'. *Past & Present*, vol. 198, no. 1(2008): 71–109.

Bowen, H. V. *Elites, Enterprise and the Making of the British Overseas Empire 1688–1775*. New York: St. Martin's Press, 1996.

Breen, T. H. 'An Empire of Goods: The Anglicization of Colonial America, 1690–1776'. *Journal of British Studies*, vol. 25, no. 4 (October 1986): 467–99. Accessed 18 October 2014. http://www.jstor.org/stable/175565.

Breen, T. H. *The Marketplace of Revolution: How Consumer Politics Shaped American Independence*. New York: Oxford University Press, 2005.

Breen, T. H. *Tobacco Culture: The Mentality of the Great Tidewater Planters on the Eve of Revolution*. Princeton, NJ: Princeton University Press, 1985.

Brumwell, Stephen. *Redcoats: The British Soldier and War in the Americas, 1755–1763*. New York: Cambridge University Press, 2002.

Bryant, Lillywhite. *London Coffee Houses: A Reference Book of Coffee Houses of the Seventeenth, Eighteenth, and Nineteenth Centuries*. London: G. Allen and Unwin, 1963.

Bucholz, Robert O., and Joseph R. Ward. *London: A Social and Cultural History, 1550–1750*. New York: Cambridge University Press, 2002.

Bushman, Richard L. *The Refinement of America: Persons, Houses, Cities*. New York: Vintage Books, 1992.

Bushnell, Amy Turner, and Jack P. Greene. 'Peripheries, Centers, and the Construction of Early Modern American Empires'. In *Negotiated Empires: Centers and Peripheries in the Americas, 1500–1820*, edited by Christine Daniels and Michael V. Kennedy, 1–14. New York: Rutledge, 2002.

Caldwell, Mark. *New York Night: The Mystique and Its History*. New York: Scribner, 2005.

Callow, Edward. *Old London Taverns: Historical, Descriptive and Reminiscent with some Account of the Coffee Houses, Clubs, Etc*. London: Downey & Co. Limited, 1899.

Carson, Cary, Ronal Hoffman and Peter J. Albert, ed. *Of Consuming Interests: The Style of Life in the Eighteenth Century*. Charlottesville: Published for the United States Capitol Historical Society by the University Press of Virginia, 1994.

Chaplin, Joyce E. 'The British Atlantic'. In *The Oxford Handbook of The Atlantic World c. 1450 – c. 1850*, edited by Nicholas Canny and Philip Morgan. New York: Oxford University Press, 2011.

Clark, Peter. *British Clubs and Societies, 1580–1800: The Origins of an Associational World.* Oxford: Clarendon Press, 2000.

Claydon, Tony. *Europe and the Making of England, 1660–1760.* New York: Cambridge University Press, 2007.

Copley, Stephen. 'Commerce, Conversation and Politeness in the Early Eighteenth-Century Periodical'. *British Journal for Eighteenth-Century Studies*, vol. 18, no. 1 (Spring 1995): 63–77.

Cowan, Brian. 'Mr. Spectator and the Coffeehouse Public Sphere'. *Eighteenth-Century Studies*, vol. 37, no. 3 (Spring, 2004): 345–66. Accessed 20 October 2016. http://www.jstor.org/stable/25098064.

Cowan, Brian. 'The Rise of the Coffeehouse Reconsidered'. *Historical Journal*, vol. 47, no. 1 (March 2004): 21–46. Accessed 29 October 2013. http://www.jstor.org/stable/4091544.

Cowan, Brian. *The Social Life of Coffee: The Emergence of the British Coffeehouse.* New Haven, CT: Yale University Press, 2005.

Cowan, Brian. 'What Was Masculine about the Public Sphere? Gender and the Coffeehouse Milieu in Post-Restoration England'. *History Workshop Journal*, vol. 51, no. 1 (Spring 2001): 127–57. Accessed 20 October 2016. http://www.jstor.org/stable/4289724.

Cox, Caroline. *A Proper Sense of Honor: Service and Sacrifice in George Washington's Army.* Chapel Hill: University of North Carolina Press, 2004.

Craveri, Benedetta. *The Age of Conversation.* Translated by Teresa Waugh. New York: New York Review Books.

Curits, Julia B. 'Chinese Export Porcelain in Eighteenth Century Tidewater Virginia'. *Studies in Eighteenth-Century Culture*, vol. 17 (1987): 119–44.

Damrosch, Leo. *The Club: Johnson, Boswell, and the Friends Who Shaped an Age.* New Haven, CT: Yale University Press, 2019.

Daniels, Bruce C. 'Sober Mirth and Pleasant Poisons: Puritan Ambivalence Toward Leisure and Recreation in Colonial New England'. *American Studies*, vol. 34, no. 1 (Spring 1993): 121–37.

Darnton, Robert. *The Literary Underground of the Old Regime.* Cambridge, MA: Harvard University Press, 1982.

Davis, James M. 'The Colonial Coffeehouse'. *Early American Life*, vol. 9, no. 1 (1978): 26–9, 86.

Dayton, Cornelia Hughes. 'Excommunicating the Governor's Wife: Religious Dissent in the Puritan Colonies Before the Era of Rights Consciousness'. In *Religious Conscience, the State, and the Law: Historical Contexts and Contemporary Significance*, edited by John McLaren and Harold Coward, 29–45. Albany, NY: Suny University Press, 1999.

Dayton, Cornelia Hughes. 'Was there a Calvinist Type of Patriarchy? New Haven Colony Reconsidered in the Early Modern Context'. In *The Many Legalities of Early America*, edited by Christopher Tomlins and Bruce H. Mann, 337–56. Chapel Hill: University of North Carolina Press, 2001.

Dayton, Cornelia Hughes. *Women before the Bar: Gender, Law, and Society in Connecticut, 1638–1789.* Chapel Hill: University of North Carolina Press, 1995.

De Krey, Gary S. *A Fractured Society. The Politics of London in the First Age of Party 1688–1715.* New York: Oxford University Press, 1985.

Ditz, Toby L. 'Secret Selves, Credible Personas: The Problematics of Trust and Public Display in the Writing of Eighteenth-Century Philadelphia Merchants'. In *Possible Pasts: Becoming Colonial in Early America*, edited by Robert Blair St. George, 51–80. Ithaca, NY: Cornell University Press, 2000.

Ditz, Toby L. 'Shipwrecked; or, Masculinity Imperiled: Mercantile Representations of Failure and the Gendered Self in Eighteenth-Century Philadelphia'. *Journal of American History*, vol. 81, no. 1 (June 1994): 219–42.

Doerflinger, Thomas M. *A Vigorous Spirit of Enterprise: Merchants and Economic Development in Revolutionary Philadelphia*. Chapel Hill: University of North Carolina Press, 1986.

Ellis, Joseph J. *Founding Brothers: The Revolutionary Generation*. New York: Vintage Books, 2000.

Ellis, Markman, 'Coffee-Women, *The Spectator* and the Public Sphere in the Early Eighteenth Century'. In *Women, Writing and the Public Sphere, 1700–1830*, edited by Elizabeth Edgar, Charlotte Grant, Clíona Ó Gallchoir and Penny Warburton, 27–52. Cambridge: Cambridge University Press, 2001.

Ellis, Markman. 'Pasqua Rosee's Coffee-House, 1652–1666'. *London Journal*, vol. 29, no. 1 (2004): 1–24.

Ellis, Markman. *The Coffee House: A Cultural History*. London: Weidenfeld & Nicolson, 2004.

Engerman, Stanley L., and Robert E. Gallman, ed. *The Cambridge Economic History of the United States, Volume 1, The Colonial Era*. Cambridge: Cambridge University Press. doi:10.1017/CHOL9780521394420.006.

Epstein, James. '"Equality and No King": Sociability and Sedition: The Case of John Frost'. In *Romantic Sociability: Social Networks and Literary Culture in Britain, 1770–1840*, edited by Gillian Russell and Cara Tuite, 43–61. Cambridge: Cambridge University Press, 2002.

Essays in the History of Early American Law, edited by David H Flaherty. Chapel Hill: University of North Carolina Press, 1969.

Flaherty, David H. *Privacy in Colonial New England*. Charlottesville: University Press of Virginia, 1972.

Foster, Thomas A. *Sex and the Eighteenth-Century Man: Massachusetts and the History of Sexuality in America*. Boston, MA: Beacon Press, 2006.

George, M. Dorothy. *London Life in the 18th Century*. New York: Capricorn Books, 1965.

Goodman, Dena. *Becoming a Woman in the Age of Letters*. Ithaca, NY: Cornell University Press, 2009.

Goodman, Dena. *The Republic of Letters: A Cultural History of the French Enlightenment*. Ithaca, NY: Cornell University Press, 1994.

Greene, Jack P. 'The American Revolution'. *American Historical Review*, vol. 105, no. 1 (1 February 2000): 93–102. Accessed 9 June 2018. https://doi.org/10.1086/ahr/105.1.93.

Habermas, Jürgen. *The Structural Transformation of the Public Sphere*. Cambridge, MA: MIT Press, 1991.

Habermas, Jürgen. *The Theory of Communicative Action: Lifeworld and System: A Critique of Functionalist Reason*, vol. 2. Translated by Thomas McCarthy. Boston, MA: Beacon Press, 1987.

Hancock, David. *Oceans of Wine: Madeira and the Emergence of American Trade and Taste*. New Haven, CT: Yale University Press, 2009.

Harris, Jonathan. 'The Grecian Coffee House and Political Debate in London 1688–1714'. *London Journal A Review of Metropolitan Society Past and Present*, vol. 25, no. 1 (2000): 1–13.

Hertz, Deborah. *Jewish High Society in Old Regime Berlin*. Syracuse, NY: Syracuse University Press, 2005.

Hinderaker, Eric. *Boston's Massacre*. Cambridge, MA: Belknap Press of Harvard University Press, 2017.
Holmes, Geoffrey. 'Introduction: Post-Revolution Britain and the Historian'. In *Britain after the Glorious Revolution 1689-1714*, edited by Geoffrey Holmes, 1-37. New York: Macmillan St. Martin's Press, 1969.
Holton, Woody. *Forced Founders: Indians, Debtors, Slaves, and the Making of the American Revolution in Virginia*. Chapel Hill: University of North Carolina Press, published for the Omohundro Institute of Early American History and Culture, 1999.
Holton, Woody. *Unruly Americans and the Origins of the Constitution*. New York: Hill and Wang, 2007.
Hoppit, Julian. *A Land of Liberty? England 1689-1727*. Oxford: Clarendon Press, 2000.
Jasanoff, Maya. *Liberty's Exiles: American Loyalists in the Revolutionary World*. New York: Vintage Books, 2012.
Johnson, Christopher H. *Becoming Bourgeois: Love, Kinship, and Power in Provincial France, 1670-1880*. Ithaca, NY: Cornell University Press, 2015.
Ketcham, Michael G. *Transparent Designs: Reading, Performance and Form in the Spectator Papers*. Athens: University of Georgia, 1985.
Kirk, Russell. *The Conservative Mind: From Burke to Eliot*, 2nd edn. Washington, DC: Regnery, 1986, reprinted 2001.
Kirk, Russell. *The Roots of American Order*. Wilmington, Delaware: ISI Books, 1974, 2008.
Klancher, Jon. *The Making of English Reading Audiences 1790-1832*. Madison: University of Wisconsin Press, 1987.
Klein, Lawrence E. 'Coffeehouse Civility, 1660-1714: An Aspect of Post-Courtly Culture in England'. *Huntington Library Quarterly*, vol. 59, no. 1 (1996): 30-51. Published by: University of Pennsylvania Press. Accessed 20 October 2016. http://www.jstor.org/stable/3817904.
Klein, Lawrence E. 'Politeness and the Interpretation of the British Eighteenth Century'. *Historical Journal*, vol. 45, no. 4 (December 2002): 869-98. Accessed 29 October 2013. http://www.jstor.org/stable/3133532.
Klein, Lawrence E. *Shaftesbury and the Culture of Politeness: Moral discourse and Cultural Politics in Early Eighteenth-Century England*. New York: Cambridge University Press, 1994.
Konig, David Thomas. 'A Summary View of the Law of British America'. *William and Mary Quarterly*, vol. 50, no. 1 (January 1993): 42-50.
Konig, David Thomas. '"Dale's Laws" and the Non-Common Law Origins of Criminal Justice in Virginia'. *American Journal of Legal History*, vol. 26, no. 4 (October 1982): 354-75.
Konig, David Thomas. *Law and Society in Puritan Massachusetts: Essex County, 1626-1693*. Chapel Hill: University of North Carolina Press, 1979.
Kurlansky, Mark. *Salt: A World History*. New York: Penguin Books, 2003.
Lambert, John. 'From Travels through Canada, and the United States of North America in the Years 1806, 1807, 1808'. In *Empire City: New York through the Centuries*, edited by Kenneth Jackson and David Dunbar, 111-15. New York: Columbia University Press, 2002.
Landes, Joan B. *Women and the Public Sphere: In the Age of the French Revolution*. Ithaca, NY: Cornell University Press, 1998.
Langford, Paul. *A Polite and Commercial People: England, 1727-1783*. New York: Oxford University Press, 1994.

Lombard, Anne S. *Making Manhood: Growing up Male in Colonial New England*. Cambridge, MA: Harvard University Press, 2003.

Lyons, Clare A. *Sex Among the Rabble: An Intimate History of Gender and Power in the Age of Revolution, Philadelphia 1730–1830*. Chapel Hill: University of North Carolina Press, 2006.

Macaulay, Thomas Babington. *The History of England from the Accession of James II*, vol. 1. Project Gutenberg EBook, produced by Ken West and David Widger, 2013.

Marshall, P. J. *Making and Unmaking: of Empires: Britain, India, and America c.1750–1783*. New York: Oxford University Press, 2005.

Matthee, Rudi. 'Exotic Substances: The Introduction and Global Spread of Tobacco, Coffee, Cocoa, Tea, and Distilled Liquor, Sixteenth to Eighteenth Centuries'. In *Drugs and Narcotics in History*, edited by Roy Porter and Mikulas Teich, 24–51. Cambridge: Cambridge University Press, 1995.

McCusker, John J. 'The Business Press in England before 1775'. *Library Sixth Series*, vol. 8, no. 3 (September 1986): 205–31.

McCusker, John J. 'The Early History of "Lloyd's List"'. *Historical Research*, vol. 64, no. 155 (October 1991): 427–31.

Melton, James Von Horn. *The Rise of the Public in Enlightenment Europe*. New York: Cambridge University Press, 2001.

Middleton, Richard, and Anne Lombard. *Colonial America: A History to 1763*. 4th edn. Malden, MA: Wiley-Blackwell, 2011.

Middleton, Simon, and Smith, Billy G., ed. *Class Matters: Early North America and the Atlantic World*. Philadelphia: University of Pennsylvania Press, 2008.

Miller, Christopher L., and George R. Hamell. 'A New Perspective on Indian-White Contact: Cultural Symbols and Colonial Trade'. *Journal of American History*, vol. 73, no. 2 (September 1986): 311–28.

Miller, John. 'Crown, Parliament, and People'. In *Liberty Secured? Britain Before and After 1688*, edited by J. R. Jones, 53–87. Stanford, CA: Stanford University Press, 1992.

Mintz, Sidney W. *Sweetness and Power: The Place of Sugar in Modern History*. New York: Penguin Books, 1986.

Mokyr, Joel. *A Culture of Growth: The Origins of the Modern Economy*. Princeton, NJ: Princeton University Press, 2017.

Monod, Paul Kleber. *Jacobitism and the English People, 1688–1788*. New York: Cambridge University Press, 1993.

Morgan, Edmund S. and Helen M. Morgan, *The Stamp Act Crisis: Prologue to Revolution*. Chapel Hill: University of North Carolina Press, 1953.

Morton, Graeme. *Unionist Nationalism: Governing Urban Scotland, 1830–1860*. East Linton: Tuckwell Press, 1999.

Nagel, Paul C. *John Quincy Adams: A Public Life, a Private Life*. New York: Alfred A. Knopf, 1997.

Nash, Gary B. *The Unknown American Revolution: The Unruly Birth of Democracy and the Struggle to Create America*. New York: Viking, 2005.

Norton, Mary Beth. *Separated by Their Sex: Women in Public and Private in the Colonial Atlantic World*. Ithaca, NY: Cornell University Press, 2011.

Olson, Alison G. *Making the Empire Work: London and American Interest Groups, 1690–1790*. Cambridge, MA: Harvard University Press, 1992.

Olson, Alison G. 'The Board of Trade and London-American Interest Groups in the Eighteenth Century'. *Journal of Imperial and Commonwealth History*, vol. 8, no. 2 (1980): 33–50.

Oresko, Robert. 'The House of Savoy in Search for a Royal Crown in the Seventeenth Century'. In *Royal and Republican Sovereignty in Early Modern Europe: Essays in memory of Ragnhild Hatton*, edited by Robert Oresko, G. C. Gibbs and H. M. Scott, 272–350. New York: Cambridge University Press, 1997.

Palmer, R. R. *The Age of the Democratic Revolution: A Political History of Europe and America, 1760-1800, The Challenge*. Princeton, NJ: Princeton University Press, 1959.

Pares, Richard. 'The London Sugar Market, 1740–1769'. *Economic History Review*, vol. 9, no. 2 (December 1956): 254–70.

Pelzer, John, and Linda. 'The Coffee Houses of Augustan London'. *History Today*, vol. 32, no. 10 (October 1982): 40–7.

Pincus, Steve. *1688: The First Modern Revolution*. New Haven, CT: Yale University Press, 2009.

Plumb, J. H. *Origins of Political Stability: England 1675-1725*. Boston, MA: Houghton Mifflin, 1967.

Pobranski, Stephen B. ' "Where Men of Differing Judgements Croud": Milton and the Culture of the Coffee Houses'. *Seventeenth Century*, vol. 9, no. 1 (1994): 35–9.

Pocock, J. G. A. *The Machiavellian Moment: Florentine Political Thought and the Atlantic Republican Tradition*. Princeton, NJ: Princeton University Press, 1975.

Price, Martin. 'Manners, Morals, and Jane Austen'. *Nineteenth-Century Fiction*, vol. 30, no. 3 (December 1975): 261–80. Accessed 19 March 2016. http://www.jstor.org.cmich.idm.oclc.org/stable/2933070.

Quinan, Jack. 'The Boston Exchange Coffee Houses'. *Journal of the Society of Architectural Historians*, vol. 38, no. 3 (1979): 256–62.

Raymond, Joad. *Pamphlets and Pamphleteering in Early Modern Britain*. New York: Cambridge University Press, 2003.

Reinke-Williams, Tim. *Women, Work and Sociability in Early Modern London*. Basingstoke: Palgrave Macmillan, 2014.

Rogers, Nicholas. *Whigs and Cities: Popular Politics in the Age of Walpole and Pitt*. New York: Oxford University Press, 1989.

Rosenheim, James M. *The Emergence of a Ruling Order: English Landed Society, 1650-1750*. New York: Longman, 1998.

Russell, Gillian. *Women, Sociability and Theatre in Georgian London*. New York: Cambridge University Press, 2007.

Russell, Gillian, and Clara Tuite. 'Introducing Romantic Sociability'. In *Romantic Sociability: Social Networks and Literary Culture in Britain, 1770–1840*, edited by Gillian Russell and Cara Tuite, 1–23. Cambridge: Cambridge University Press, 2002.

Schmid, Susanne. *British Literary Salons of the Late Eighteenth and Earl Nineteenth Centuries*. New York: Palgrave Macmillan, 2013.

Schocket, Andrew M. 'Corporations and the Coalescence of an Elite Class in Philadelphia' and Goloboy, 'Business Friendships'. In *Class Matters: Early North America and the Atlantic World*, edited by Simon Middleton and Billy G. Smith, 111, 124–7. Philadelphia: University of Pennsylvania Press, 2008.

Schwoerer, Lois G. 'The right to resist: Whig resistance theory, 1688 to 1694'. In *Political Discourse in Early Modern Britain*, edited by Nicholas Phillipson and Quentin Skinner, 232–52. New York: Cambridge University Press, 1993.

Shannon, Timothy J. 'Dressing for Success on the Mohawk Frontier: Hendrick, William Johnson, and the Indian Fashion'. *William and Mary Quarterly*, vol. 53, no. 1 (January 1996): 13–42.

Shields, David S. *Civil Tongues and Polite Letters in British America*. Published for the Institute of Early American History and Culture, Williamsburg, Virginia by University of North Carolina Press: Chapel Hill, 1997.

Smith, Billy G. 'Death and Life in a Colonial Immigrant City: A Demographic Analysis of Philadelphia'. *Journal of Economic History*, vol. 37, no. 4 (December 1977): 863–89. Accessed 9 September 2017. http://www.jstor.org.cmich.idm.oclc.org/stable/2119346.

Smith, F. E. 'Land and ships Ere Sold over a Cup of Coffee'. *Lancashire Life*, vol. 5, no. 5 (May 1957): 35.

Smith, S. D. 'Accounting for Taste: British Coffee Consumption in Historical Perspective'. *Journal of Interdisciplinary History*, vol. 27, no. 2 (Autumn 1996): 183–214.

Smith, S. D. 'Sugar's Poor Relation: Coffee Planting in the British West Indies, 1720–1833'. *Slavery & Abolition: A Journal of Slave and Post-Slave Studies*, vol. 19, no. 3 (1998): 68–89.

Snyder, Terry L. *Brabbling Women: Disorderly Speech and the Law in Early Virginia*. Ithaca, NY: Cornell University Press, 2003.

Sommerville, C. John. 'Surfing the Coffeehouse'. *History Today*, vol. 47, no. 6 (June 1997): 8–10.

Steele, Ian K. *English Atlantic, 1675–1740: An Exploration of Communication and Community*. New York: Oxford University Press, 1986.

Stewart, Larry. 'Other Centres of Calculation, or, Where the Royal Society Didn't Count: Commerce, Coffee-Houses and Natural Philosophy in Early Modern London'. *British Journal for the History of Science*, vol. 32 (1999): 133–53.

Taylor, Alan. *American Revolutions: A Continental History, 1750–1804*. New York: W. W. Norton, 2016.

Topik, Stephen C. 'Coffee'. In *The Cambridge World History of Food*, vol. 1, edited by Kenneth F. Kiple and Kriemhild Conee Ornelas, 641–53. Cambridge: Cambridge University Press, 2000.

Ukers, William Harrison. *All about Coffee*. New York: New York The Tea and Coffee Trade Journal Company, 1922.

Van Horn, R. Lee. *Out of the Past: Prince Georgeans and Their Land*. Riverdale, MD: Prince George's County Historical Society, 1976.

Walsh, Lorena S. *Motives of Honor, Pleasure, and Profit: Plantation Management in the Colonial Chesapeake, 1607–1763*. Chapel Hill: University of North Carolina Press, 2010.

White, Richard. *The Middle Ground: Indians, Empires, and Republics in the Great Lakes Region, 1650–1815*. New York: Cambridge University Press, 1991.

Williams, Abigail. *The Social Life of Books: Reading Together in the Eighteenth-Century Home*. New Haven, CT: Yale University Press, 2017.

Wilson, Kathleen. *The Sense of the People: Politics, Culture and Imperialism in England, 1715–1785*. New York: Cambridge University Press, 1995.

Wilson, Jr, Samuel. 'Maspero's Exchange: Its Predecessors and Successors'. *Louisiana History*, vol. 30 (1989): 191–220.

Wood, Gordon. *The American Revolution: A History*. New York: Modern Library, 2003.

Wood, Gordon. *The Radicalism of the American Revolution*. New York: Vintage, 1993.

Index

A Botanical Description and the History of Coffee (1774) 159
A Defense of the Constitutions of Government of the United States of America (1787-8) 143
Aberdeen Magazine 15, 27, 55
Adams, John 82, 141-3, 170, 181
Adams, John Quincy 143-5
Adams, Samuel 82, 177
Addison, Joseph 5-8, 9, 20-1, 24, 44-9, 55, 73, 75, 88-9, 96, 108-11, 113, 132, 158, 170, 207 n.10, 212 n.6
Addisonian 6, 37-9, 45, 48-9, 89, 109-10, 113, 130-1, 142, 190-2
Aikin-Barbauld, Anna 186
Aitken, R. 114
Anglicization, 'empire of goods' 3, 8, 32, 74, 149, 172-3, 192-3
Articles of Confederation 9
Ashley-Cooper, Anthony, 3rd Earl of Shaftesbury 5, 7, 60
assembly/free association 1-4, 7-9, 37, 39, 52, 74-5, 93, 99-101, 111-12, 116, 119, 128, 130, 138, 146, 149, 159, 162, 168, 170, 184, 190
'associational world 22, 75, 100, 127, 130-1
Austen, Jane 18, 77, 94

balls, ballrooms 4, 8, 15, 17-18, 20, 22-3, 26, 31, 35, 39, 42, 48, 54-6, 78, 82, 85-6, 96, 138, 161, 168, 174, 179, 181
Bath, city of 4, 18, 22, 84
Baxter, Richard 114
Belcher, Jonathan, Governor of New Hampshire (1730-41) 136-7
Blackstone, William 44, 142
Board of Trade 7, 41, 117-20, 123-4, 129, 136, 193
Boswell, James 10, 20, 23-4

Boyle, Richard, 3rd Earl of Burlington 4
Boyle, Robert 83
Braddock, Edward (General) 120-1
broadside(s) 6, 26, 54, 107-8, 118
Burke, Edmund 21, 24, 93-4, 103, 135, 143
Butler, James, 1st Duke of Ormond 64-5
Button twisting 111, 207 n.10
Byrd, II, William 48, 137-8, 146
Byron, 'Lord' George Gordon 94

caffeine (molecule) 26
Calmady, John (naval captain) 66
Calvinism, Calvinist 35, 114
censor(s), censorship 77, 80, 105
Cherokee War (1759-61) 123
clubs, societies
    American Thursday dinner club (London) 137
    Beefsteak Society (London) 48, 75
    Brothers or Scribblers Club (London) 169
    Calves' Head Club (London) 169
    Cheshire Cheese Club (London) 48
    Hanover Club (London) 109
    Homony Club (Annapolis) 48
    Honorable Board of Loyal Brotherhood (London) 64
    King's Head Protestant Club (London) 169
    Kit-Cat Club (London) 48
    Liverpool Conversation Club 136, 158
    London Corresponding Society 185
    Loyal Society of Worsted Weavers (Norwich) 109
    Marine Society (Liverpool and London) 158
    Merchants Club (Boston) 141
    Mug House Club (London) 169
    Rota Club (London) 6, 19, 169
    Royal Society (London) 84, 144, 150-1

Society for Constitutional Information (London) 108, 140
Society for Promoting the Manumission of Slaves (New York) 35
Society of Revolutionary Republican Women (Paris) 92
Society of the Cincinnati (United States) 35, 86
Society of the Friends of Truth (Paris) 92
Tory Recorder's Club (London) 109
Ugly Face Club (Liverpool) 158
Whig Constitution Club (Norwich) 109, 182
Coffeehouse(s),
  Names of
    Abiongton's Coffeehouse (London) 106
    Admiralty Coffeehouse (London) 2, 51, 191
    American Coffeehouse (Norfolk, Virginia and Boston) 87, 178
    Anderson's Coffeehouse (London) 106
    Annapolis Coffeehouse 11, 23, 38–9, 48, 50, 85, 115, 138, 192
    Atlantic Garden House (New York) 35
    Baker's Coffeehouse (London) 106
    Bath Coffeehouse (Liverpool) 158
    Bedford's Coffeehouse (London) 23, 106, 111
    Bragg's Coffeehouse (Oxford) 154
    British Coffeehouse (London and Boston) 40, 50, 64, 114, 118, 141, 177–8, 181
    Burns Coffeehouse (New York) 36
    Burton's Coffeehouse (London) 64
    Button's Coffeehouse (London) 19, 20, 62, 89, 108, 111, 128, 153
    Chapter Coffeehouse (London) 60, 105
    Don Saltero's Coffeehouse (London) 155–6
    Elford's Coffeehouse 106
    English Coffeehouse (Paris) 17, 56
    Exchange Coffeehouse (Boston, New York, and New Orleans) 35–6, 40, 50, 118, 161, 177
    Garraway's Coffeehouse (London) 18, 67, 84, 87, 100, 103, 105–6
    Grecian Coffeehouse (London) 5, 150–1
    Gutteridge Coffeehouse (Boston) 40, 113
    Hamilton's Coffeehouse (London) 64
    Hyde's Tontine Coffeehouse (Philadelphia) 138–9
    Jamaican Coffeehouse (London) 11, 19
    James Coffeehouse (Philadelphia) 34
    Jerusalem Coffeehouse (London) 2, 19, 51, 102, 189, 191
    John's Coffeehouse (London) 106–7
    Jonathan's Coffeehouse (London) 18, 55, 68, 84, 103, 187
    Kent's Coffeehouse (London) 106
    King Street Coffeehouse (London) 56
    King's Arms Coffeehouse (Norfolk, Virginia) 86, 117
    Lane's Coffeehouse (London) 56
    Lloyd's of London 18–19, 41, 63, 67, 97–8, 100, 102, 106, 127, 159, 187
    London Coffeehouse (Philadelphia and Boston) 23, 32–4, 40, 50, 82, 114, 130, 132, 176
    Loyal Coffeehouse (London) 54, 57
    Man's Coffeehouse (London) 83
    Mary-le-Bone Gardens Coffeehouse (London) 17, 56, 85
    Merchants Coffeehouse (Philadelphia, New York, Liverpool) 34–6, 50, 84, 158
    Miles's Coffeehouse (London) 19
    Moll King's Coffee House (London) 7, 10, 73, 80–1
    Mrs. Leslie's Coffeehouse (London) 64
    Nando's Coffeehouse (London) 47, 135, 142, 150
    "Neptune" Coffeehouses (Liverpool) 158
    New Coffeehouse (New York) 35
    New England Coffeehouse (London) 132, 136–7, 191
    North-End coffeehouse (Boston) 40
    Ozinda's Coffeehouse (London) 64
    Parliament Street Coffeehouse (Westminster, London) 66

Pennsylvania Coffeehouse (London) 130-1, 182, 191
Pontacks Coffeehouse (Liverpool) 158
Richard Charlton's Coffeehouse 11, 39, 116-17, 166, 233 n.47
Robert's Coffeehouse (Philadelphia) 34
Robin's Coffeehouse (London) 106
Saint George's Coffeehouse (Liverpool) 136, 158
St. James's Coffeehouse 7, 19-21, 47, 56, 64, 68, 105, 107, 187
St. Paul's Coffeehouse 105, 134, 183
Somerset Coffeehouse (London) 23
Sword Blade Coffeehouse (London) 2, 51, 61, 191
Tennis Court Coffeehouse (London) 65
Tillyard's Coffeehouse (Oxford) 154
Tom's Coffeehouse (London) 19, 20, 21, 106-7, 125
Tontine Coffeehouse (New York) 36, 42, 97
Turke's Head Coffeehouse (London) 19, 169
Virginia and Baltick (London) 18
Virginia and Maryland Coffeehouse in Newman's Court, Cornhill (London) 19, 100, 130, 135, 191
Virginia Coffeehouse (London) 17-18, 62, 134
Wellingtons Coffeehouse (London) 114
White's Chocolate House (London) 19-21, 47
Will's Coffeehouse (London) 2, 7, 11, 19-20, 46, 51, 53, 56-7, 61, 63-8, 88, 106, 111, 191
'Ye Coffee House' (Philadelphia) 33
York Coffeehouse (London) 67
Young Man's Coffeehouse (London) 47
Licensure (of coffeehouses) 6, 8, 75, 77, 82, 86, 96, 107, 115, 155, 191
Lobbyists (from coffeehouses) 2, 8, 41, 50, 74, 99-100, 103, 117-20, 124, 127-9, 136, 146, 191

Murders and Crimes (in coffeehouses) 51-2, 54, 141, 177-8
  Highwayman, King Street, Goldsquare 54
  Hodges, Sarah 54
  Joyce, James, Mrs. 51-2, 54
Postal service and networks (in coffeehouses) 1-2, 8-9, 18-20, 23, 33-4, 50-3, 56, 59, 60-1, 66-9, 97, 107, 112, 118, 126, 129-34, 139, 145, 157, 168, 174, 176, 177, 189-92
Proprietors (of coffeehouses)
  Abington, George (Abiongton's Coffeehouse, London) 106
  Ashley, James (Kent's Coffee-house, London) 106
  Baker, Richard, "Master of Lloyd's" 19
  Ball, William (Bragg's Coffeehouse, Oxford) 154
  Bradford, William (London Coffeehouse, Philadelphia) 32-4, 82, 114, 132, 176, 203 n.13, 204 n.14
  Braithwaite, William (Robin's Coffeehouse, London) 106
  Button, Daniel (Button's Coffeehouse, London), 111, 128, 153, 201 n.19
  Charlton, Richard (Richard Charlton's Coffeehouse, Williamsburg) 39, 116-17
  Day, Dorothy (Tillyard's Coffee House, Oxford) 154
  Fielder, William (John's Coffeehouse, London) 106-7
  Gutteridge, Mary (Boston) 81
  Hall, James (Oxford) 154
  Harris, Timothy (London) 103
  Johnson, Thomas (Elford's Coffeehouse, London) 106
  Jones, Dorothy (Boston) 39, 81
  Julian, Mrs. (Fredericksburg, Virginia) 39
  Lloyd, David, "Master of Lloyd's" 67
  Lloyd, Edward (Lloyd's of London) 19
  Molins, Charles (Anderson's Coffeehouse, London) 106
  Morris, John (Garraway's Coffeehouse, London) 106
  Muse, Meredith (Fredericksburg, Virginia) 86

Newell, Mary (Maryland) 86
Page, Lawrence (Will's Coffeehouse, London) 106
Pearse, Teresa (Norfolk, Virginia) 86, 117
Saltero, Don (Saltero's Coffeehouse, London) 155
Taylor, Thomas "Master of Lloyd's" 63, 67, 98
Wiggan, Stephen (Baker's Coffeehouse, London) 106
Wills, Thomas (Tom's Coffeehouse, London) 106
Unnamed coffeehouses (by region)
  Fredericksburg, Virginia (coffeehouses) 39, 50, 85, 117, 160, 181
  Newcastle (coffeehouses) 22–3, 108–9, 182
  Norrkiöping (coffeehouse) 144
  Norwich (coffeehouses) 22–3, 108–9, 182
  Paris (coffeehouses) 17, 20, 39, 56, 142, 165, 182–4, 192
  Warehouse(s) (for coffee and tea supply) 2, 99–100, 102–3, 127, 153, 175, 178, 191
constitution, (US) 119, 142, 143, 167, 172, 174, 187, 221 n.90
'Conversible world', 'polite world' 4, 6
Coote, Richard, 1st Earl of Bellomont, Governor of New York (1698–1701) 35, 136
customs office 1–2, 8, 50, 55, 99, 101–3, 118, 126–7, 130–4, 145, 164, 167–8, 174–6, 190, 193

Douglas, George, 1st Earl of Dumbarton 51
Dryden, John 19, 24, 57, 113
Dudley, Joseph (Governor of Massachuetts) 136
duel, duels, dueling 8, 35, 50, 53, 56, 58, 108, 177, 185, 207 n.10

East India Company 2, 8–9, 32, 55, 100, 102–3, 127, 152–3, 170, 174, 176–7, 180, 191, 193

Eden, (Sir) Robert, 1st Baronet, of Maryland (Governor of Maryland, 1769–76) 11, 39, 48, 85, 138
Enlightenment 1, 9, 37, 39, 43–4, 75, 77, 81, 88, 90–2, 95, 100, 109–10, 177, 127, 130, 172, 186–7, 190
Exchange Alley, London 18–19, 80, 87
Exclusion Crisis (1679–81) 107, 170

Female Parliament 108
Fielding, Henry 24, 44, 81, 85
Fletcher, Benjamin (Governor of New York) 35
Flower, Henry (Postmaster) 33, 132
Forbes, John (General) 56, 122–3, 139
Founders, American Founding 9, 119, 127, 142–6, 172, 174, 187, 227 n.53
Fox, Charles James 67, 92
Franklin, Benjamin 1, 33, 48, 89, 90, 96, 113, 126, 130–5, 144–6, 161, 176, 182, 186, 192
Frost, John 140

Gage, Thomas (General) 167, 175, 180
Garrick, David 21, 202 n.39
Gibbon, Edward 127
Goldsmith, Oliver 20–1, 24, 44, 115
Gordon riots (1780) 109
Grenville, George (Prime Minister) 41, 66–7, 123
Grub Street writers 91–2

Halley, Edmond 150
Hamilton, (Dr.) Alexander 48
Hancock, John 52, 115, 167
Handel, George Frederick 20
Harrington, James 6, 19, 169
Hogarth, William 21, 28, 82
holiness 34, 77, 204 n.16
Hooke, Robert 10, 83
Horace 113
Hughes, John (stamp distributor) 1, 133
humane/polite letters 21, 44, 79, 81–2, 86, 89–91, 95, 109–10, 112, 116–17, 127, 131
Hunter, Robert (Governor of New York) 129, 136

imperial spaces 3, 173
Independence Hall, Philadelphia 174
insurance 2, 19, 33, 36, 41, 75, 81, 118, 129–30, 191–2
Iroquois 120–1, 123

Jacobin(s) 55, 92, 184–5
Jacobite(s) 54–5, 64–5, 156
James, Duke of York (II of Great Britain) 107, 170
Jefferson, Thomas 9, 143, 168, 172, 186, 192
Johnson, Samuel 20, 23–4, 26–7, 42, 45, 81, 93, 113, 157
Johnstone, David (naval captain) 62
Jones, Katherine, Viscountess 'Lady' Ranelagh 83
Joseph, Pierre, Céloron de Blainville (captain) 120

Ker[r], 'Lord' Mark (Army officer, b. 1676- d. 1752) 55–6, 59

Lafayette, Marquis de 119
Levant Company 153
Livy 91
Locke, John 44–5, 127, 172
luxury 17, 43, 49, 149–51, 154, 160, 175

Macaulay, 'Lord' Thomas Babington 5, 92, 94, 169
Madeira wine 32, 160, 167, 175
Masquerades (see balls, ballrooms)
'Man of pleasure' 27, 31, 45–7
Mather, Cotton 40, 48
Mather, Increase 136
Mein, J. (bookseller) 40, 113
Mercer, (Colonel) George 123, 178–9, 233 n.47
Milton, John 20, 57, 158, 169–70
Montesquieu 90, 93, 127

natural rights 7, 44, 93, 142–3, 149, 168, 170, 183
Navigation Acts 32, 41, 172
Newgate prison 54
newsfeeds 2, 7–8, 100, 108, 100, 128, 130, 145, 190
newspapers, magazines, journals, gazettes

Aberdeen Magazine 15, 27, 55
Athenian Mercury (London and Philadelphia) 110, 112, 219 n.48
Boston Chronicle 177
Boston Gazette 33, 49, 114, 177–8
Boston News-Letter 112
Craftsman (London) 20, 108
Farley's Bristol Journal 108
Freedholder's Journal (London) 18
Gazetteer and new daily advertiser (London) 176
Gentleman's Magazine (London) 11, 80, 108, 110
Gloucester Journal 108
Guardian (London) 3, 21, 89, 108, 110–11
Idler (London) 2, 110
London Evening Post 108
London Journal 18, 20
Lloyd's List (London) 19, 101
Lloyd's News (London) 19
Louisiana Courier 161
Louisiana Gazette 161
Maryland Gazette 48, 85, 113, 150, 160
Newcastle Chronical 109
Newcastle Courant 108–9
New England Courant (Boston) 110
New-London Gazette 173
New York Gazette 33, 45, 54
New-York Weekly Journal 110
Norwich Gazette 108
Pennsylvania Journal 33
Philadelphia American Weekly Mercury 33, 89
Philadelphia Gazette 113, 131
Poor Richard's Almanac 131
Public Occurrences 40
Rambler 2, 24, 44–5, 110, 220 n.48
Salisbury Journal 108
South Carolina Gazette 112
Spectator (London) 3, 5–6, 20–1, 37, 44, 46, 75, 80–1, 88, 108, 110, 157, 170, 212 n.6
Tatler (London) 2, 6, 20–1, 26–7, 37, 44, 46–7, 56, 69, 88, 110, 155
The Maidens Complaint (1663) 83
Virginia Gazette 11, 39, 45, 49, 87, 99, 113–17, 135–6, 150, 158, 160, 167, 176–8, 181, 230 n.46, 233, n.47

Weekly Post Boy (New York) 157
York Courant 108
Newton, (Sir) Isaac 150-1
Nicholson, Francis (Lieutenant Governor of Virginia, 1690-1692) 42
Northumberland House (London) 24

Otis, James 82, 141-2, 170-1, 177-8
Ovid 44, 91, 114

pageant(ry) 9, 82, 85, 95, 142, 155, 162, 165, 168, 174, 179-81, 187, 192
Paine, Thomas 9, 67, 93, 109, 140, 142-3, 168, 182-3, 185-7, 192, 227 n.53
  Rights of Man (1791) 93, 109, 142, 171, 183, 185
Palladian 4, 40
Parker, James (customs officer) 1, 131-4, 176
Penn, William 82
Pepys, Samuel 10, 19, 57, 59, 169
Pigot, John (Major) 66, 183
Pitt, William, 1st Earl of Chatham, 'the Elder' 121-2
Pitt, William, 'the younger' 7, 183
pleasure gardens and parks
  Hyde Park (London) 17
  Ranelagh Gardens (London and New York) 38, 85
  Vauxhall Gardens (London and New York) 17, 38, 50
Plutarch 113
politeness 4, 6, 7, 11, 16, 24, 36-7, 39, 42, 44, 46-7, 52-3, 57, 61, 68, 73-5, 77-81, 86-7, 90-3, 95, 104, 106, 109-12, 116, 119, 128, 140, 151, 161, 172, 185, 186, 190-1
Pontiac's War (1763-6) 123
Pope, Alexander 20, 24, 57, 111, 158, 169
'Print-capitalism' 109, 128, 130, 145, 191
printers
  Aitken, R. (Boston) 114
  Allen, J. (Boston) 40, 113, 205 n.29
  Buttolph, Nicholas (Boston) 40, 113-14
  Dixon, John (Williamsburg) 131
  Green, B. (Boston) 40, 113, 205 n.29
  Hall, David (Philadelphia) 113, 131-2
  Holt, John (New York) 113
    Humphreys, D. (Philadelphia) 114

Loudon, Samuel (New York) 113-14
Oswald, E. (Philadelphia) 114
Purdie, Alexander (Williamsburg) 131
'public sphere' 2-7, 9-10, 36, 39, 45, 49, 50, 53-4, 56-7, 63, 67-8, 73-7, 79, 86-8, 90, 93, 101, 104, 106-9, 111, 115, 119, 130, 135-7, 140, 143, 159, 163, 168-70, 174, 176-8, 182, 184-7, 190

Quaker(s) 34, 35, 77, 89, 118, 140
Quebec 2, 19, 121-3, 156, 191

Reconnaissances 124-6, 146
Regency 7, 77, 90, 92-4, 187
Reign of Terror 92
'remote neighborhoods' 7, 74, 100, 109, 130, 135, 145, 149, 162
'Republic of Letters' 4, 82, 86, 90-1, 107-8, 143
republican(ism) 5, 6, 49, 53, 82, 85, 92, 94, 106, 143, 165, 168-74, 179-81, 183, 186-7
Revere, Paul 82, 170, 177
Revolution of 1688/constitution 73, 143, 170, 183
Reynolds, (Sir) Joshua 20-1, 24
Rivington and Brown (booksellers) 114
Robinson, John 141, 177-8
Romantic(s) 7, 91, 94, 185-6
Ross, David (British army medical doctor) 139
Royal Exchange 2, 18, 19, 67, 80, 84, 99, 112, 118, 129, 151, 183, 187, 191
Royal Navy, naval officers 2, 4, 7, 8, 10, 11, 23, 32, 35, 50-4, 59-63, 65-9, 121-2, 129-30, 138, 154, 167, 175-7, 179, 190-1, 193

salon(s) 4, 20, 56, 75-6, 90-3, 95, 185-6
salonnières
  Éléonore de Lespinasse, Jeanne Julie 90
  Fox, Elizabeth, Baroness 'Lady' Holland 92-5, 186-7
  Geoffrin, Marie-Therese 90
  Levin, Rahel Varnhagen 91
  Mendelssohn-Schlegel, Brendel ('Dorothea') 91
  Necker, Suzanne 90

'Sappho' 88
Scott, (Sir) Walter 83, 94
Seven Years War, 'French and Indian War' (1754–63) 22, 120, 124, 126, 173
Shakespeare, William 20, 42, 88, 113, 117
Sharpe, Horatio (Governor of Maryland) 11
Shays' Rebellion (1786–7) 167
shops, shopping 3, 5, 8, 10, 15, 17, 24, 40, 76–80, 85, 87, 95, 101, 114–15, 117, 138, 152–5, 160, 170
slave(s), slavery 9, 18–19, 31, 35, 78, 136, 149–50, 152, 154, 156–63, 176, 184, 230 n.46
Sloane, (Sir) Hans 103, 150
sociability 2, 4–7, 11, 15–17, 21–2, 37–9, 42, 45, 47, 50–1, 53, 59–60, 63, 74–8, 81, 83–4, 87, 90–3, 95, 104, 107, 109, 112, 117, 127–8, 130, 135–6, 141–2, 145, 153, 159, 163, 168, 173–4, 185–7, 190–1, 213 n.11
Sons of Liberty 1, 82, 133–4, 141, 144, 167–8, 171, 173–4, 176–7, 180, 192
South Sea Company 2, 18, 87, 102–3
spy, spies 8, 54, 63–5, 107, 168, 182–3, 185
St John, Henry, 1st Viscount Bolingbroke 108
Stamp Act (1765) 1, 3, 41, 99, 123, 132–4, 168–9, 171–3, 175–80
Stanhope, Philip, 'Lord' 4th Earl of Chesterfield 44, 60
Steele, Richard 5–6, 9, 21, 24, 44, 46–9, 56–7, 69, 73, 75, 88–9, 108, 110–11, 155, 170, 207 n.10, 212 n.6
sugar 2, 9, 16, 21, 26, 44, 99, 101, 103, 123, 145, 159, 151–2, 154–5, 157, 158, 160–2, 172, 174–7
Sugar Act (1764) 41, 171–2
surgeons (Navy) 60–2, 131
Swift, Dean 169
Swift, Jonathan 20, 21, 44, 57, 64, 75, 83, 87–8, 96, 110, 219 n.47

Tarugo's Wiles: or, the Coffee-House (1668) 83, 159
taverns and inns
  Blue Anchor (Boston) 40
  Bunch of Grapes (Boston) 40, 170, 177, 179, 181
  Golden Key (New York) 114
  Green Dragon Inn (Boston) 40, 82, 170, 177
  Indian Queen (Boston) 40, 180
  King's Arms (New York, Williamsburg, London, Boston) 35–6, 99, 137, 179
  King's Head (London, Norwich, Boston) 22, 40, 180, 183
  Province Arms (New York) 42
  Ship Tavern (Boston) 40
tax crisis (1764–5) 9, 52, 116, 123, 133, 171–3, 178, 180, 186, 190, 193
Tea Act (1773) 172–3, 175
The School of Good Manners (1715) 44
The School of Politicks (1698) 57, 159
The Young Man's Companion 44
theatres
  Bigg Market theatre (Newcastle-Upon-Tyne) 22
  Chestnut Street Theatre of Philadelphia 43
  Covent Garden Theatre (London) 24
  King's Theater, Haymarket (London) 20
  New Theater (Philadelphia) 138–9
  Newcastle Theatre Royal (Newcastle-Upon-Tyne) 22
  Norwich Theatre Royal 22
  Southwark Theatre (Philadelphia) 43
  Theatre Royal, Drury Lane (London) 24, 158
tidewater elites 3, 19, 31, 48
Tory (party) 64, 83, 108–9, 111, 170–1, 179, 182
Towne, Benjamin (bookseller) 114
Townsend Acts (1767) 172
trifling, 'triflers' 2, 15, 17–18, 22–4, 27, 31, 34, 43, 45, 48, 53, 59, 75, 88, 105, 110, 113, 146, 219 n.48
Turk, 'Turk's Head' 19, 22, 150–1, 153–4, 156, 159, 162, 169
Twining, Thomas 21, 153, 201 n.19

Virgil 91, 113
Voltaire 90–1, 127

Walpole, (Sir) Robert 18, 99, 118, 169
Ward, Edward 57, 159

Washington, George 9, 42, 85–6, 119–21, 126–7, 138, 145, 165, 174, 176, 179, 181–3
Watson, Thomas 114
West Indies 2, 23, 33, 44, 65, 145, 150, 153–5, 157, 160, 162, 174–6, 191
Westminster Confession of Faith (1647) 114
Whig 4–7, 11, 18–19, 21, 44, 73, 75, 77, 83, 90, 92–5, 100, 107–11, 212 n.6

Whiskey Rebellion (1791–4) 167
Wilks, John 22, 65, 109, 181–2
Wolfe, James (General) 123
Wollstonecraft, Mary 94, 186
Wycherley, William 20

Youth's Behavior, or Decency in Conversation among Men 44

www.ingramcontent.com/pod-product-compliance
Lightning Source LLC
Chambersburg PA
CBHW062130300426
44115CB00012BA/1875